ORIGINS OF MODERNISM
VOL. 5

GERARD MANLEY HOPKINS AND HIS CONTEMPORARIES

GARLAND REFERENCE
LIBRARY OF THE HUMANITIES
VOL. 1476

ORIGINS OF MODERNISM:
GARLAND STUDIES IN BRITISH LITERATURE

TODD K. BENDER
Series Editor

GERARD MANLEY HOPKINS AND HIS CONTEMPORARIES

Liddon, Newman, Darwin, and Pater

Jude V. Nixon

GARLAND PUBLISHING, Inc.
New York & London / 1994

Library of Congress Cataloging-in-Publication Data

Nixon, Jude V., 1953–
    Gerard Manley Hopkins and his contemporaries,
Liddon, Newman, Darwin, and Pater / by Jude V.
Nixon.
        p.   cm. — (Garland reference library of the
humanities ; vol. 1476. Origins of modernism ; vol. 5)
        ISBN 0–8153–0386–6 (alk. paper)
        1. Hopkins, Gerard Manley, 1844–1889—Knowledge
and learning. 2. Hopkins, Gerard Manley, 1844–1889—
Contemporaries. 3. Great Britain—Intellectual life—
19th century. 4. Liddon, Henry Parry, 1829–1890—
Influence. 5. Newman, John Henry, 1801–1890—
Influence. 6. Darwin, Charles, 1809–1882—Influence.
7. Pater, Walter, 1839–1894—Influence. I. Title.
II. Series: Garland reference library of the humanities ;
vol. 1476. III. Series: Garland reference library of the
humanities. Origins of modernism ; vol. 5.
PR4803.H44Z7227   1994
821'.8—dc20   93–28007
                                                          CIP

Printed on acid-free, 250-year-life paper
Manufactured in the United States of America

To my mother

Contents

Acknowledgments

To cite the selfless involvement of numerous individuals in an enterprise such as this is a poor expression of deep and sincere appreciation. And as many go unrecognized as are here acknowledged. Lacking a more suitable representation, I resort to these lagging lines. This work would not have come to life were it not for the labor of many individuals. I wish to thank Don Rackin of Temple University and Jerry Bump of the University of Texas at Austin for initiating the idea for this book and, along with David Downes, for reading portions of it and suggesting ways it can be improved. I wish to thank Norman McKenzie, Norman White, Joe Feeney, and Cathy Phillips for their always cheerful replies to my queries, and my colleagues Jack Herring, Jay Losey, and Mike Beaty for their insights on Browning, Pater, and on the nineteenth-century philosophers, respectively. Many other colleagues, too numerous to mention, have been a source of constant encouragement and inspiration. I wish also to thank my research assistants for their work on this project, especially Susy Schultz whose timeless commitment to the manuscript improved its quality, and my copy editor Melanie McQuere, whose close scrutiny rescued the manuscript from egregious errors. The manuscript would not have seen its present aesthetic form had it not been for the painful efforts of Vicky Gerik and Baylor's computations department.

I am also indebted to numerous institutions and their staff. Baylor's University Sabbatical Committee and the Department of English granted me time away from teaching to work on this project, and the university's Research Committee and College of Arts and Sciences gave sustained financial support to it. Permission to quote from unpublished manuscripts in their holdings was granted by the Warden and Fellows of Keble College, Oxford, Balliol College, Campion Hall, the Bodleian Library, the Warden and the Governors of Liddon House, and the Trustees for Roman Catholic Purposes. I will be ever grateful to the staff at these libraries, Mrs. J.E. Robinson, librarian at Keble, Penelope Bulloch and Alan Tadiello, librarians at Balliol, Fr Brian Ferme of Campion Hall, Miss. C.H. Starks, Judith Priestman, and Colin Harris, librarians at the Bodleian, and Charles Brown, Governor of the Liddon House. I am also indebted to the librarians and staff at Baylor's Moody and Armstrong-Browning libraries for their unfaltering assistance; to *Renascence*, *Texas Studies in*

Literature and Language, and AMS Press for permission to cite, at times extensively, from earlier essays of mine.

I am grateful to the late John A. Huzzard who stirred in me an early passion for literary texts and scholarship, to my father, his wife, and my brother Clifford for a room of my own in their London home where I spent countless undisturbed hours writing and examining manuscripts. But most of all, I will be forever indebted to my wife, Jennifer, and children, Jackie, Jason, and Jeremy, who selflessly granted me the freedom to pursue this project. Their inspiration has been my constant stay. And to my mother, Bernadette, to whom I dedicate this book, I will be forever grateful for life, education, direction, and inspiration. To all of these who spent themselves in giving life to this book, these lagging lines, I trust, have caught my carol and their creation.

Introduction

When Walter Pater's celebrated collection of essays was first published (1873), he entitled it *Studies in the History of the Renaissance.* Four years later when the second edition came out, the title was changed to *The Renaissance: Studies in Art and Poetry* (1877). That change reflects, it seems to me, not only a response to the serious challenge directed to the historical accuracy of his assumptions but equally a recognition that he, like so many other Victorians, saw the Renaissance period suitable to a revisionary formulation of his own aesthetic historicism. The change, then, was to accommodate conscious recognition of that revisionary goal. No longer was the concern solely with the Renaissance as history but with the Renaissance as a model by which to study, in a dialectical way, all art and poetry, and especially that of the nineteenth century. Carolyn William states best Pater's revisionary strategy: "Pater's aesthetic historicism is established through the act of historicizing his own chief influences." He establishes his own place in the critical tradition by "taking a perspective on Ruskin and Arnold." By

> assuming this critical distance with respect to his own most powerful contemporary influences, he figuratively casts them further into the past. By subsuming their positions in his own and differentiating himself from them, he establishes his voice as more comprehensive, diversified, and therefore   modern. He asserts his own critical identity, then, by opening a space of difference that is at once aesthetic and historicist.[1]

Recognizing the intellectual symbiosis of the Italian Renaissance and the rise of the modern spirit in it, Pater believed the movement to be adaptable to the nineteenth century. His 1873 "Preface" to *The Renaissance* points to such cultural tendencies: "The various forms of intellectual activity which together make up the culture of an age, move for the most part from different starting–points, and by unconnected roads." While academic disciplines operate in "intellectual isolation" and are often oblivious to the things they share, as "products of the same generation they partake indeed of a common character, and unconsciously illustrate each other." Pater calls this "one complete type of general culture." In it, the keen minds of artists and philosophers "do not live in isolation, but breathe a common air, and catch light and heat from each other's thoughts." Also at work in that culture is a "spirit of general elevation and enlightenment in which all alike communicate."[2]

Pater's chapter on Winckelmann illustrates one such convergence. In Winckelmann, he locates a confluence of the Hellenic and Hebraic spirits, believing, and rightly so, that the "spiritual forces of the past" gave birth and shape to the "culture of a succeeding age" but remain alive "within that culture, but with an absorbed, underground life." Convinced that there are few, if any, cultural orphans, Pater calls the artist, the "type," a "child of his time," and asserts that "individual genius works ever under conditions of time and place: its products are coloured by the varying aspects of nature, and type of human form, and outward manners of life."[3] Establishing the intellectual agenda for what T.S. Eliot argued many years later in "Tradition and the Individual Talent," Pater points out that while the artist is part of an "intellectual tradition," catching light and heat from his generation, his greatness derives from an ability to create his own "sense of beauty." Put differently, "it is not enough," says Pater, "for a poet to have been the true child of his age, to have conformed to its aesthetic conditions." Rather, "it is necessary that there should be perceptible in his work something individual, inventive, unique, the impress there of the writer's own temper and personality."[4] Not surprisingly, then, Wolfgang Iser finds a revisionary principle at the heart of Pater's comments on Coleridge. "It is therefore no coincidence that a critical but entirely well–disposed study of Coleridge," says Iser, "led Pater to a concrete formulation of his own ideas. In this encounter with English Literature's last speculative systematist, Pater proclaims his own originality."[5]

Though all of the preceding remarks were made by and about Pater, they apply equally to Hopkins and characterize superbly the nature and scope of this study. Hopkins's poetry, poetics, and epistemology demonstrate that he did catch light and heat from his relationship with prominent contemporaries and their writings. Corresponding to Bridges on 25 September 1888 from Dublin, Hopkins responded to a letter in which Bridges, sensing some inadequacy, had urged him to expand his reading. Hopkins apparently agreed ("I *must* read something of Greek and Latin letters"), but felt that extensive reading would do little to influence his composition and even less his judgment. In Hopkins's thinking, studying masterpieces first creates admiration then displacement. That methodology, he believes, must be embraced by "every original artist to some degree"; by him, however, to a "marked degree." Thus, more reading, he felt, would only cause him to "*refine [his] singularity*," which is not what he believed Bridges wished. Extensive reading, Hopkins elaborated, either expands knowledge or refines the judgment; and the more learned the judgment the less singular it is.[6] What Hopkins pursued, then, was on the one hand originality and on the other hand a less singular judgment. And this "fine balance" between tradition ("popular judgment") and individual talent ("to make me admire and do otherwise") can be negotiated only if one overcomes the manneristic quality of the Parnassian impulse, whereby mechanical imitation (plain mimesis) rather than spontaneous creation (defamiliarization) presides.

Hopkins's task throughout his career was in part, if not to a large degree, revisionary; thus he can be seen subtly subverting his precursors as well as his contemporaries in an attempt at creation through correction. Using, then, the same language as did Pater, that "As you read a poet you are more and more raised to his level, you breathe his air," Hopkins felt that the "influence of great men has been . . . always overrated, —that is to say the individual influence; the collective influence, of wh. in one kind the higher literature is partly the channel, partly the effect." Hopkins pointed to Shakespeare who, to him, seems "the highest point in the range given to intellect, and his fame is, if not proportionally great, at least very great." Yet, says Hopkins, "his individual influence is, we may believe, compared with his greatness of mind, almost incredibly small." The "scientific way to look at great men," Hopkins concluded, "wd. be to discover their frequency and chances of development before saying that their real effect on history is inappreciable, however much we might think the latter to be near the truth."[7] Written as early as these comments were in his undergraduate days, Hopkins was even then attempting to sort out tradition and influence from individual talent.

What follows is an attempt to show Hopkins's relationship of indebtedness to four prominent literary figures of the nineteenth century, an attempt that says as much about Liddon, Newman, Darwin, and Pater as it says about Hopkins. Equally significant, the study also illustrates Hopkins's interaction with nineteenth–century discourse on religion, science, and aesthetics. Except for the treatments of Liddon and Newman, whose influence on Hopkins proceeds chronologically from his years at Oxford through his Jesuit career, the work for

the most part ignores rigorous chronology. Rather, it wrestles with critical
Victorian concerns and engages Victorian texts and documents hitherto slighted
or unexamined in order to illuminate in a new way the historical context in which
Hopkins lived and that helped to shape his writings.

Chapter 1 on Hopkins and Henry Parry Liddon first appeared in the journal
Renascence. Gone, however, is the sketch of that relationship and Hopkins's
notes on Liddon's Sunday evening lectures on Corinthians. The chapter follows
Liddon from Cuddesdon to Oxford, examining his Anglo–Catholic practices,
the genesis and topics of his Sunday evening lectures, and his Bampton lectures,
all in an attempt to demonstrate how Liddon's ideas on Christ shepherded
Hopkins's poeticizing of christology. Equally meaningful, the chapter illumi-
nates Liddon's intimacy with Oxford students, who confided almost everything
to him. Forming part of Liddon's circle of intimates was the impressionable
ascetic Hopkins who attended Liddon's lectures, confessed to him, and all in all
saw him as protection against the storms of Balliol's liberal climate. Citing
extensively from Liddon's unpublished diaries and other valuable documents,
I have sought to focus primarily on the religious milieu—for the most part
liberal—at Oxford in the 1860s. Following Newman's departure from Oxford—led he felt by the liberals ("Catholics did not make us Catholics," he once
remarked, "Oxford made us Catholics")—and Pusey's deteriorating health,
Liddon felt chiefly responsible for checking that liberalism and for leading the
religiously conservative efforts at Oxford. Hopkins's religious and poetic years
at Oxford, then, was shaped by no one more significant than by Liddon. Thus,
to estimate correctly the religious dimension of his poetry and its historicity, the
chapter shows the crucial role Liddon, and the arguments he raised, played in
shaping the life from which that poetry emerged.

When Liddon's influence "gave way," when his compromising religious
stance, again in Hopkins's words, could no longer "hold water," Hopkins turned
naturally to John Henry Newman. The move from Liddon's High Anglicanism
to Newman's Roman Catholicism was not a distant one. The chapter on Hopkins
and Newman first appeared in the journal *Texas Studies in Literature and
Language*. Then, I was more interested in the relationship between Hopkins and
Newman and less in epistemological and literary similarities and differences
between them. Manifesting that new direction, the chapter deals not only with
the spiritual and career guidance Newman provided Hopkins but also with
related echoes in their works, and the points at which their epistemological and
literary ideas converge. More is made, for example, of their emphasis on a
conversational style and their interest in formulating or adopting a Tractarian
poetics. To argue this, I examine extensively John Keble's Tractarian poetics as

understood and practiced by Hopkins following Wordsworth and Newman. Newman, we might recall, attributed the commencement of that movement to Keble's 14 July 1833 Assize Sermon on Apostolic succession. Also critical in Newman and Hopkins is the philosophical process by which one arrives at assent. Thus, the chapter examines Newman's *An Essay in Aid of a Grammar of Assent* (written when Hopkins was teaching at the Birmingham Oratory), Hopkins's repeated requests to do a commentary on it, and ways in which that appeal informed Hopkins's own religious assent. The governing trope of this chapter is that Hopkins's religious practice and poetry is the exercise of a religious assent not unlike Newman's.

Chapter 3 pursues Hopkins's relationship with Darwinism, a study that emerges from an earlier attempt at the epistemological relationship between these two seemingly dissimilar Victorians. That earlier study is part of a collection (forthcoming) entitled *Hopkins and Critical Discourse*. This new reading explores, more comprehensively, the discourse relationship between Hopkins and Darwin based on science. It traces, for example, Hopkins's subtle yet incontrovertible workings with and against the philosophical materialism of Darwin and John Tyndall. Hopkins was familiar with the writings of both men. He knew Tyndall personally, once, by chance, accompanying him on one of his famous treks through the Alps. Hopkins would later wish for Tyndall's conversion. The first attempt to explore Hopkins's relationship with Darwinism was Tom Zaniello's *Hopkins in the Age of Darwin*. While Zaniello's pioneering study provides invaluable information on the scientific milieu in which Hopkins lived and wrote and on his interest in science, by ignoring Hopkins's poetic discourse, the study fails to illuminate the more meaningful levels of Hopkins's engagement of Darwinism. This chapter, then, pursues such an approach. It illustrates the concealed ways Hopkins approached Darwinism. The study turns to such nineteenth–century religious figures as Liddon, Newman, and Pusey— people influential to Hopkins—to show how their discourse on science in general and Darwinism in particular related to and possibly influenced Hopkins's. The study also treats the status of science at Oxford during Hopkins's tenure there, the idea of "one culture" (that science and literature, emerging from related cultural assumptions, influence and are influenced by each other), and Hopkins's preference for special creation as opposed to evolution, a tendency shown in his preference for diatonicism rather than chromaticism. Additionally, the study explores Hopkins's philological speculations and praxis, argument for the distinctiveness of the self, and interest in the design argument and the origin of music in order to show that these all assume meaningful associations within a developmental or evolutionary epistemology. Adopting Wordsworth's claim, the chapter shows that not only are the poet and scientist one, but so also are the unified ways in which literature and science functioned in the nineteenth century.

In Chapter 4, I focus on Hopkins and Pater in an attempt to situate Hopkins's aesthetic theory and praxis. My endeavor here sketches the friendship—if it can be so characterized—Hopkins and Pater had for twelve years, beginning with Pater coaching Hopkins for Greats. The two were driven by aesthetic concerns, concerns Pater no doubt shared with Hopkins, however dissimilar at times were their approaches. For example, Hopkins's, more so than Pater's, is an aesthetic of renunciation that sees beauty more as a motivation to action and awe rather than passive contemplation. Art to Hopkins is neither a substitute for life nor for religion. Rather, it is a vital means to a meaningful life and an equally meaningful religion. Without art, both life and religion would be bankrupt. The ways Hopkins and Pater relate to a Victorian aesthetics, the chapter shows, more often than not represent a divergence with similarities.

Considered jointly, the chapters explore four notable Victorians whose views on religion, science, and aesthetics shaped significantly the discourse of nineteenth–century literature, informed the poetry of an equally notable Victorian, and opened up a wide range of perplexing questions on modern epistemological assumptions.

Abbreviations

Darwin	*Origin*	*The Origin of Species.* London: J.M. Dent & Sons, 1971.
Hopkins	*Journals*	*The Journal and Papers of Gerard Manley Hopkins.* Edited by Humphry House and Graham Storey. London: University Press, 1959.
	Letters 1	*The Letters of Gerard Manley Hopkins to Robert Bridges.* Edited by Claude Colleer Abbott. London: Oxford University Press, 1970.
	Letters 2	*The Correspondence of G.M. Hopkins and R.W. Dixon.* Edited by Claude Colleer Abbott. London: Oxford University Press, 1970.
	Letters 3	*Further Letters of Gerard Manley Hopkins.* Edited by Claude Colleer Abbott. 2nd ed. London: Oxford University Press, 1970.
	Poems	*The Poetical Works of Gerard Manley Hopkins.* Edited by Norman MacKenzie. Oxford: Clarendon Press, 1990.
	Sermons	*The Sermons and Devotional Writings of Gerard Manley Hopkins.* Edited by Christopher Devlin. London: Oxford University Press, 1959.
Liddon	*The Diaries of Liddon*	The Unpublished Diaries of Henry Parry Liddon. Housed at the Liddon House, London, and at the Bodleian Library, Oxford.
Newman	*Apologia*	*Apologia Pro Vita Sua.* Edited by Martin J. Svaglic. Oxford: Clarendon Press, 1967.
	Grammar	*An Essay in Aid of a Grammar of Assent.* Edited by I.T. Ker. London: Oxford University Press, 1985.
Pater	*Appreciations*	*Appreciations: With an Essay on Style.* London: Macmillan, 1915.

Gaston	*Gaston de Latour: An Unfinished Romance.* London: Macmillan, 1910.
Marius	*Marius the Epicurean: His Sensations and Ideas.* 2 vols. London: Macmillan, 1914.
Miscellaneous Studies	*Miscellaneous Studies: A Series of Essays.* London: Macmillan, 1913.
Plato	*Plato and Platonism: A Series of Lectures.* London: Macmillan, 1912.
Renaissance	*The Renaissance: Studies in Art and Poetry.* Edited by Donald L. Hill. Berkeley: University of California Press, 1980.
Uncollected Essays	*Uncollected Essays by Walter Pater.* NewYork: AMS Press, 1978.

Gerard Manley Hopkins and His Contemporaries

Chapter 1

Cold Limbo: Hopkins, Liddon, and Oxford Liberalism

The name Henry Parry Liddon evokes little recognition among nineteenth–century literary scholars and historians; and it remains just as obscure to Hopkins critics. Scholarly neglect has left unexplored a significant influence on nineteenth–century thought and just as formative an influence on the ritualism, asceticism, and Christology of Gerard Manley Hopkins.[1] This disregard occurs because Liddon's career was primarily religious, personal, and not literary, unlike, say, Newman's or even Keble's, whose writings advanced their reputation. Liddon certainly possessed the mental ability and discipline to have flourished in a literary career, should he have pursued one, and was, in fact, often rebuked by Pusey for his indolence in matters of scholarship in favor of teaching, pastoral care, and Church life, activities Liddon pursued in conformity with Saint Edmund of Abingdon, a just as obscure Oxford cleric of the thirteenth century. Consequently, Liddon left behind few written remains except for his valuable diaries, some sermons, his Bampton lectures, and his more familiar part in writing the biography of E.B. Pusey, notable because of Pusey's acclaimed reputation. Yet Liddon's influence on Oxford's religious life and on its undergraduates during the mid–nineteenth century remains unrivaled. And had he been successful in persuading Hopkins to remain Anglican during the wake of the Oxford Movement, as he had done to countless other undergraduates during its storm, Liddon would probably today be a conspicuous figure on the landscape of nineteenth–century religious thought and life.

Less than three weeks after becoming a Balliolite in Trinity Term 1863, Hopkins wrote to his mother half–apologizing for his juvenile affection for Oxford, a place for which his fondness, probably because he had not come from Eton or Rugby, was just as keen two years later when he boldly claimed it "my park, my pleasaunce."[2] He apprised her of his disbursements and of the many activities around Oxford. Two such notable events were the Bampton lectures, delivered by Archdeacon J. Hannah, and a Liddon lecture, "one of a series on the first epistle to the Corinthians" at St. Edmund Hall, which left a marked impression on Hopkins. He describes it in that 4 May 1863 letter:

> The lecture, I need scarcely say, was admirable. Liddon, perhaps you do not know, is Pusey's great "protege" and is immensely thought of. After lecture, tea and coffee, while Liddon goes around chatting. Gurney introduced me, and I shall now go every Sunday evening[3]

The occasion was Liddon's 3 May 1863 lecture at St. Edmund Hall. Liddon noted the event in his diary: "My lect. in evening very fully attended indeed. Much interesting talk afterwards. The Balliol element steadily increasing."[4] Although Hopkins was, conceivably, aware of Liddon's reputation, this was his first direct contact with Liddon, one that he would foster during his undergraduate years.

Liddon arrived at St. Edmund Hall, named after Edmund Rich of Abingdon, around Easter 1859. He had been forced by Samuel Wilberforce, the celebrated Bishop of Oxford known for his abhorrence of Romish doctrine and practice, to resign his position as vice–principal of Cuddesdon, a position he had held since this Anglican Theological College just outside of Oxford was founded in 1854. Cuddesdon was chartered for Anglican ordinands, for it was felt that the university was deficient in such preparation, a sentiment never openly expressed lest it injure Oxford pride; it was hoped that Cuddesdon would check the Germanizing influence at Oxford. During Liddon's tenure there, the college had drawn severe criticism of its Romish practices, in particular its attitude toward ornament and ritual; in fact, in 1857 the chapel had to be redecorated to appear less "gaudy," meaning less Catholic. A year later, on 13 February 1858, Wilberforce ordered the chapel whitewashed, all the painted murals of saints and apostles blotted out, and the reredos removed. The prayer book at Cuddesdon contained prayers other than those of the *Book of Common Prayer*. The expression "diocesan seminary" was whispered around Oxford as a description of Cuddesdon.

Liddon was accused too of, among other things, his adoration of the Eucharist. In an 11 November 1848 note described as *"Most strictly private"* and signed with the remark "I record this interview in case of its ever being quoted against me," Liddon disclosed his censuring by Wilberforce. Third on Liddon's recorded list of accusations Wilberforce leveled against him was "leaning to the Roman Church in my Theological Views: and especially for praying to S. Mary"; the fifth accusation was "for keeping a 'clique' of certain Theological

Views—and doing but little good to other men in College by my example—also being viewed by my authorities with distrust." Liddon confessed his great affection for the Church of England, did not disclaim reverence for Mary but denied papal supremacy, and felt that "Rome appeared to go too far."[5] Liddon was also charged with the defection of an inordinate number of Cuddesdon students to Rome, an accusation not entirely inaccurate. Liddon's belief in the Catholicity of the Church of England, and his attempts at such conformity and ambiguous religious stance did have a residual effect, for it made Rome appealing to more than a few of Cuddesdon's ordinands; and his attempts to stave off the flow often proved futile. But Liddon's high–church views, Wilberforce felt, had so prejudiced the students at Cuddesdon that the bishop's own authority was being undermined. Students leaving Cuddesdon had grown so accustomed to high–church forms of worship that they became critical of the bishop's neglect of certain ritualistic observances—not facing the altar, for example, and not observing the ceremony of washing the vessels.[6]

But however readily Liddon accepted Wilberforce's decision, leaving Cuddesdon was not painless. He received some forty–three letters from well–wishers, all expressing regret over his leaving and all noting the loss for Cuddesdon. Liddon knew or felt at the beginning of 1859 that his time at Cuddesdon was short. His diary of 1 January expresses such apprehension: "The year begins with the dreary prospects as to Cuddesdon." Four months later, on 21 April 1859, the day before Good Friday, he had received his instructions and "In the morning saw all the students individually. This is the last time I shall ever do so at Cuddesdon. How very very solemn." He spent Easter Monday packing, and on Wednesday, 27 April, "*Left Cuddesdon.*" Liddon departed noting on two occasions being "In low spirits about my work at S.E.H. and my future work there," an uncertainty that prompted him to seek guidance in the Syriac New Testament and Homer. On 5 May on his way to Oxford, he met W.C. Lake and Benjamin Jowett at Didcot train station. Lake, Liddon recalled, was "infinitely amused at my going to S. Edm. Hall."[7]

Liddon went into residence at St. Edmund Hall on Friday, 6 May 1859 with some apprehension. Still he looked forward to the relocation, for it promised him the opportunity for self–culture, the chance to study Oriental languages, and the means to assist Pusey on a Bible commentary that would help rectify current biblical controversies, a project he began enthusiastically on 12 June. W.M. Whitley tells us that "It was in opposition to the flood of Old Testament criticism that Liddon began his work at Oxford."[8] But as was the case with the academic profession in Oxford at this time, it was the "opportunity of working among undergraduates," as J.O. Johnston, Liddon's understudy, biographer, and principal of Cuddesdon, points out, that "chiefly attracted him to St. Edmund Hall."[9] To reach these undergraduates, many of whom viewed him as a prophet, Liddon instituted his Sunday soirees on 6 November 1859. Seven students, none from the Hall, attended his first series of lectures on the Epistle to the Hebrews. The numbers grew slowly but steadily, Liddon noting anxiously every slight decrease in numbers and every new face and college affiliation: 4 March 1860: "23 men at my Greek Testament Lecture. It seems to increase more and more"; 10 June 1860: "My Lecture reduced to 13—the smallest number this term"; 5 May 1861: "A smaller attendance at my lecture than for some time: only 15 & many new faces"; 9 February 1862: "A very good attendance at evening Lect. Addis present"; "No S.E.H. men"; "Mr. Cuthbert came for the first time"; "Webb of Corpus came"; "Ogle of Magd. who got the Ireland there"; "The Balliol element steadily increasing."[10]

A serious illness in the summer of 1862 caused Liddon to resign his official position at St. Edmund. He noted feeling unwell on Monday, 12 May 1862, the complaint an inflamed throat, the beginning, it seems, of some form of throat cancer. His health worsened for the next three months, and especially during the month of August when his illness was aggravated by his travel. On 19 August, while at Clifton, near Bristol, he tried unsuccessfully to see the physician Dr. Budd. He had his throat cauterized on 22 August, which did little to reduce the inflammation. His diary of 2 September 1862 notes: "The pain today more than yesterday. . . . But it really an inflammation set up by my journey." Two days later: "During the whole day in great pain. . . . Thought much of resigning my post at Saint Edmund Hall." The next day Liddon resigned. His diary listing the following day, 6 September, seems to suggest that his resignation was brought on not only by his illness, but more by his growing discomfort at the Hall (Thursday, 21 March 1861: "In low spirits abt. the Hall") and not having made any strides on the Pusey commentary: "Feel very thankful that the die is cast about St. Edmund Hall and that I am free to work at the Commentary."[11] But by 13 September Liddon felt better, recovered shortly thereafter, and had second thoughts about his impulsive resignation. He left the Hall for Christ Church College where, as a former student, he still held permanent rooms; but his Sunday evening lectures at St. Edmund continued unabated and were for the next year Liddon's most sustained activity. The lectures continued at St. Edmund until 19 March 1865, when, because of the increasing numbers of students in such cramped quarters, Liddon moved across Queen's Lane to a larger hall at neighboring Queen's College; at this time some 125 students attended regularly. Pointing to Liddon's three years at the Hall, Alfred Emden felt that it was there that he "laid the foundation of that influence within the

University, especially among undergraduates, which was to be one of the most fruitful features of his career."[12]

Critics of Liddon had felt that his Sunday evening soirees were used mainly for propagandistic purposes; and quite frankly they were, given the politically charged atmosphere, the religious factions, the vying for undergraduate loyalty at Oxford, and given too that Liddon encouraged his faithful undergraduates to report on the activities of certain professors within their college. In his diary of 5 November 1866, Liddon noted a furious attack on the high church movement in Oxford in one of the daily newspapers: "Among other things the writer [Liddon speculates G. Smith] thinks that my Lectures have been given with a view to organizing a party."[13] The same charge was made by one writer in the *Theological Review* who compared Liddon's reputation with that of Newman's. Liddon's 15 October 1867 rebuttal called the comparison "altogether misinformed as to the extent of my 'influence' among Oxford undergraduates." As to the success of his Sunday evening lectures, which the review mentioned, Liddon saw it "due simply to the fact that the lecture supplies a felt want in Oxford undergraduate life, and not to any intrinsic attractiveness"; and, Liddon continued, "if anything could make me at once resolve to give the lectures up, it would be the existence of an impression that I valued it as a means of gaining 'personal influence.'" As effective a need as the lectures met, they did consolidate his influence at Oxford and among undergraduates, which he was more unwilling to recognize than deny. For earlier in the letter he admitted regret that the "main currents of Oxford thought" were "slid[ing] now in a direction with which I have no sympathies, and are under the guidance of minds, in whose judgment my faith, as that of a thorough going English churchman would appear to be little else than a stupid superstition."[14] The accused here is obviously Jowett.

It was these lectures, then, that Hopkins, after only a month's residence in Oxford, attended and vowed never to miss. This was because Liddon understood, W.M. Whitley tells us, "the difficulties of the times" and the questions that "pressed hard on the faith of a young man."[15] Liddon developed a fondness for the Balliol gang, many of whom were gadflies bringing news to him about what Jowett felt, read, and taught. He was especially fond of Addis, Gurney, and Hopkins, in that order, breakfasting with them and inviting them often to his rooms. He was impressed by their seriousness of purpose and saw himself as a counter to Jowett's skeptical influence. Addis and Gurney began attending Liddon's lectures in early 1862. They took frequent walks with him, and Addis on several occasions confessed to him. Hopkins and these other Ritualists (Anglo–Catholics and sympathizers with the tenets of the Oxford Movement) were seeking an intellectual haven from the threatening liberalism at Oxford.

Addis, who confessed knowing more about Hopkins than did anyone else, recalled that Hopkins was "at first a little tinged with the liberalism prevalent among reading men," a sentiment that changed after Hopkins's "first confession to Liddon (that kindest and best of men)."[16] Hopkins admitted this penchant in a 1 June 1864 letter, telling E.H. Coleridge that he, Hopkins, once thought that he could *adopt an enlightened Christianity*," a sure sign, warned Hopkins, of "infidelity, if consistently and logically developed."[17]

Hopkins also felt that Anglicanism was powerless to counteract this liberal threat. In *A Son of Belial*, a witty satire of Balliol life during this period, Martin Geldart, alias Nitram Tradleg, correctly recalled the reaction of his "Ritualistic friend": "Gerontius Manley and I had many talks on religion. He was quite at one with me on the hollowness of Protestant orthodoxy, but he had a simple remedy—the authority of the Church. The right of private judgment must in the long run inevitably lead to Rationalism, as historically it has done, meaning by Rationalism . . . Neologian theories generally." Geldart agreed with Hopkins that the "Rome–ward movement" in his days at Oxford was "not a question between two rival authorities" but rather "a question between authority and private judgment."[18] This, in other words, is Hopkins's version of the *"enlightened Christianity"* he told E.H. Coleridge he once thought possible.[19] Other Liddon disciples felt similar rationalist threats. Addis, for one, in a 14 March 1864 walk with Liddon above Bagley wood, "thought that the Liberals in Oxford were much frightened at the prospect of a reaction." Another Balliol student and close friend of Hopkins, Coles, expressed similar feelings. During a walk with Coles, Liddon expressed sorrow at the "uneasiness about the Engl. Ch. among the younger men." E.A. Simcox, a Christ Church student, during a walk with Liddon also expressed dissatisfaction with the claims of Roman Catholicism. "The scepticism in wh. he has been breathing during the last 3 years has created," Liddon felt, "a desire for repose in the strongest most definite system of dogma that can be met with. I felt that I made but little impression."[20]

Students became part of Liddon's coterie partly because he was personable and because he saw himself and was seen as a shelter against the prevailing liberalism. He was remembered as being humorous and witty. T.B. Strong, a former Christ Church student and later Bishop of Oxford, recalled that "the charm of [Liddon's] humour depended much more upon the way in which he mixed in ordinary conversation, and gave it an unexpected turn." Strong contrasted him to C.L. Dodgson (Lewis Carroll), another common–room fellow: "In all this, he was an admirable foil to Dodgson, who loved to develop queer consequences from ordinary ideas." The two of them "depended mainly upon the conversation which happened to be going on: Dodgson was apt—like the Caterpillar and other great characters in *Alice*—to reveal the logical pitfalls that lie around ordinary talk."[21] About Liddon, says E.S. Talbot, "nothing was cold, nothing was dull, nothing was dry.... Warmth there was, colour there was, intensity there was"; and these were, says Talbot, in an analogy similar to Newman's idea of personality, "characteristics of his speech, because they were characteristic of himself."[22]

Liddon's Greek New Testament lectures brought together a cross section of undergraduates from various Oxford colleges and even some from Cambridge. Hopkins invited the "grey google eyes" Geldart to the lectures. "He induced me," Geldart recalled,

> to come with him to Canon Parry's tea–and–toast–and–testament. . . . Canon Parry was, I believe, his father–confessor, and the idol of the few Ritualists we had at Belial. About three hundred undergraduates used to assemble in the hall of Ann's to hear him expound the Greek New Testament on a Sunday evening.

Geldart described Liddon as a

> gaunt, cadaverous–looking man, with a face which Gerontius called "marred," in reference, I suppose, to the expression in the fifty–third of Isaiah; but which, certainly, was attractive. He had a sweet, somewhat sickly smile, especially when indulging in sarcasm at the cost of the Neologians. He was a popular University preacher, an exceedingly voluble rhetorician, crouching in his pulpit in a catlike attitude as though ready to spring on his adversary, which he did with a feline ferocity as opportunity occurred. Had it not been for some awkward tricks of pronunciation, such as "jest" for "just," he might have been called a polished preacher.

A cynical disciple, Geldart admitted that Liddon

> exercised a considerable influence over me for some time, and I never missed an opportunity of hearing him. I liked his style and manner, and enjoyed his hard hits at Pantheism, Atheism, German scholarship, and the like. But he "added nothing to me." No rhetoric of his could blind me to the

> fundamental flaw in the High Anglican position. It was, I
> pointed out to Gerontius, the principle of majorities, if it had
> any meaning at all. . . . Now, the principle of majorities, once
> candidly accepted, could only lead logically to Rome.[23]

This point Hopkins well remembered, later using it to charge Liddon with
maintaining an inconsistent religious stance. Geldart also gave a fairly authentic
depiction of the open and diverse political environment at Oxford:

> Never in all my life before or since was I among a company
> of men so young and ardent, yet so utterly devoted to plain
> living and high thinking. Never was I in an intellectual
> atmosphere so fearless and so free. I never knew what true
> tolerance without indifference was till I came to Bosphorus.
> It was a new experience to me altogether—to me, who had
> been brought up to regard Ritualism and Rationalism as the
> two right arms of the devil, to find myself suddenly launched
> among a lot of men who were some of them Ritualists of the
> deepest dye; some of them Rationalists, some of them Posi-
> tivists, some of them Materialists, all eager in advancing their
> respective views, and yet all ready to listen with courtesy to
> their respective opponents.[24]

Geldart's estimation of the climate at Oxford in the 1860s was by no means
exaggerated. John Addington Symonds, who came up to Balliol in the fall of
1858, was struck by the Ritualism he found there. He recalled the smell of
incense, the wearing of chasuble with gold border, and the ivory crucifix on an
ebony stand.[25] Though not an entirely secular place, Oxford of the 1860s was
advancing the liberal claims of the 1850s and was, as Geldart bore witness, rife
with all sorts of ideological zealots, including positivists, disciples of John
Stuart Mill, all vying for the allegiance of fickle Oxford undergraduates.

It was this overindulgent religious temper at Oxford that concerned Liddon,
for it fostered the growth and perpetuation of all sorts of spurious religious and
philosophical assumptions. From these Liddon, both in his lectures and his
extended casual contacts, sought to safeguard impressionable undergraduates.
When, for instance, on 4 January 1863 he was invited to remain at Salisbury until
Lent, he declined, feeling a sense of commitment to his Sunday evening lectures,
which, in his words, had a "prior claim." And when the number of students
dropped slightly, Liddon's wish and prayer were "that I could really suffer that

God would do good through such an one as I." It was for this reason too that Liddon held membership in a number of Anglo–Catholic groups and projects. Challis of Merton, in a 6 March 1865 walk with Liddon, expressed great anxiety over the spiritual state of things in Oxford. During their walk, Challis expressed an anxiousness "to form a publishing Essay club that should really act upon the thought of the University."[26]

The most notable of such organizations was the Hexameron, an essay society founded by Liddon in 1864, apparently on Hopkins's suggestion, as a foil for the liberal Old Mortality. According to Gerald Monsman, the Hexameron intended to counteract "'Germanism' promoted by the Old Mortality," a group whose membership boasted Pater and Swinburne.[27] During Hopkins's second walk with Liddon, on 7 March 1864, the Monday following one of Liddon's lectures, Hopkins told him of the substance of a Pater essay: "Walk with Hopkins of Balliol. He told me about Pater's paper on Fichte's Ideal Student at the Old Mortality Club, in wh. he denied the Immortality of the soul." Four days later in a walk with Arthur Towgood, Liddon had, in his words, "a *most* interesting talk about the state of things in Oxford." It was that same day that Hopkins mentioned to Liddon "the project of an Essay Club, of a Church character, as a set off against the Old Mortality."[28] The Hexameron's first secretary, S.R. Brooke, noted that the society was formed "to promote discussions upon subjects of interest so far as may be consistent with adherence to the doctrines of the Catholic Faith."[29] On 17 March 1864 Liddon briefed his spiritual father, the Bishop of Salisbury, on the character and purpose of the Hexameron and on Pater's essay:

> During the last fortnight I have been trying to organize an Essay Club among the abler undergraduates (some of them Jowett's own pupils) whom I happen to know. There are already two such clubs in existence, which are a great means of propagating sheer unbelief, e.g. one Paper which obtained great notoriety at the beginning of this Term was directed against the immortality of the soul. It was written by a junior Fellow of a College.[30]

The Hexameron Society, then, was Liddon's practical working out of Pusey's 5 August 1861 request that he serve as "a dam against all this wild speculation on Holy Scripture and the Faith" and as a voice resisting "Rationalism."[31] We know more from Liddon's diaries about the BHT (Brotherhood of the Holy Trinity), the more organized and radical Anglo–Catholic group, in which Liddon, but not Hopkins, held membership, than we do of the Hexameron. Liddon's diary refers to the Hexameron only once, this in an 8 November 1866 listing: "In the morning—an Hexameron breakfast party in the New Common–Room" at Christ Church. But however fragmentary the details on the Hexameron, we now know more about its conception, membership, and function than we formerly did. We know, for example, that on 10 September 1864 Hopkins was preparing an essay for the society "on some points of poetic criticism" with reference to Tennyson, the same essay he was "toiling through" five months later but never delivered.[32]

Liddon's Oxford sanctuary was a well–established concept. E.S. Talbot, Bishop of Winchester, who first met Liddon at one of his Sunday evening lectures and on one occasion carried his books, felt that "Liddon was always thinking of himself as a henchman, one whose duty it was to carry on a great tradition."[33] Rev. C. Kegan Paul also found this out. During numerous trips to Oxford, he had heard from dons and students alike that Liddon was "looked on as practically the great influence in the reaction against Liberalism which is so marked just now in Oxford." Liddon's enemies, the Liberals, agreed, considering him their "most dangerous opponent."[34] Canon Scott Holland described the crowd of undergraduates that flocked around Liddon:

> The Lent courses at S. Mary's, Oxford. Can we ever forget
> them? The swarms of undergraduates, herded in galleries, in
> deep rows, or crowded into every nook and corner on the floor
> . . . the mighty hush of expectation; and then the thrill of that
> vibrant voice, vehement, searching, appealing, pleading . . .
> we lived on the memory of it till next Lent came around, and
> then there we all were again; the same scene enacted itself, the
> same voice pleaded with us for our souls. So, from year to
> year in our weak, boyish hearts, the flickering flame of faith
> was saved from perishing under the gusty tumult of the
> perilous times.[35]

Liddon was always obsessed with the size of his audience. At his 25 October 1863 sermon at St. Mary's, he noticed the "undergraduate galleries crowded," and that same day mentioned the crowd attending his Sunday evening lecture at St. Edmund.[36]

The most profound mid–nineteenth–century threat came from the brazen but woefully assembled compilation, *Essays and Reviews*, called, among other disparaging names, "Septem contra Christum," an allusion to Aeschylus's "The

Seven against Thebes."[37] Appearing on 23 March 1860, and insignificant as it was in advancing current biblical criticism, *Essays and Reviews* was an important indicator that England had finally embraced German liberalism. The high churchman and rector at Hadleigh, Hugh Rose, was, Newman felt, the first in the late 1820s to warn "from the University Pulpit at Cambridge, of the perils to England which lay in the biblical and theological speculations of Germany."[38] In a 15 August 1830 letter to Simeon Pope, Newman predicted that the "tendency of the age is towards *liberalism*," whose "system of opinions" includes a "disregard of religion."[39] He considered, we might recall, his exile from Oxford as a triumph for the liberal cause, that "bottomless liberalism of thought," whose root cause is "subjecting to human judgment those revealed doctrines which are in their nature beyond and independent of it, and of claiming to determine on intrinsic grounds the truth and value of propositions which rest for their reception simply on the external authority of the Divine Word."[40] Basil Willey rightly sees *Essays and Reviews* as a "revival of the liberal spirit after its long eclipse after Newmanism."[41]

What Newman meant here can be seen from his remarks on *Essays and Reviews*, and especially from the distinction he drew between plenary inspiration, what he calls a "Protestant question," and the doctrine of tradition, the Catholic position arrived at from unanimous consent of the church fathers. He told Charles Crawley that he deplores *Essays and Reviews* because it attacks "inspiration, veracity or canonicity," issues relevant to Scriptural authority that were central to England's religion. This, says Newman, is "the reason of the consternation of serious members of the Church of England" at the book's appearance. But a Catholic holds to the inspiration of Scripture "thro' His Church. . . . Moreover, in matters of fact, there is nothing which binds the Catholic to belief in various portions of Genesis etc as popularly interpreted, to doubt which would simply shock, unsettle, break, the faith of most Protestants in the whole volume."[42] Responding to a letter from Malcolm MacColl expressing fear that "the intellect of Oxford was at the feet of Jowett" as a result of *Essays and Reviews*, Newman pointed out that one of his "severest trials" in leaving Oxford was "undoing my own work, and leaving the field open, or rather infallibly surrendering it to those who would break down and crumble to powder all religion whatever." He noted that the attack from the volume was one primarily aimed at the Old Testament, and reiterated that the historical or geological record as chronicled in Scripture presents no roadblock to the Catholic because the Church, not the Bible, is "the oracle and organ of Revelation."[43]

Essays and Reviews generated a plethora of intellectual and emotional reactions, almost all voicing disapproval. Bernard Reardon finds it the "most sensational theological event in England in the mid–nineteenth century"[44] that irreparably damaged the Victorian belief structure, and especially so for those nineteenth–century half–believers of their casual creeds. Describing Ernest Pontifex's return to Cambridge in 1858, Samuel Butler's *The Way of All Flesh* tells us that "Between 1844, when *Vestiges of Creation* appeared, and 1859 [actually 1860], when *Essays and Reviews* marked the commencement of that storm which raged until many years afterwards, there was not a single book published in England that caused serious commotion within the bosom of the Church." In fact, says Butler, "Ernest had hardly been ordained before three works in quick succession arrested the attention even of those who paid least heed to theological controversy. I mean *Essays and Reviews*, Charles Darwin's *Origin of Species*, and Bishop Colenso's *Criticisms on the Pentateuch*."[45] Because *Essays and Reviews* advocated a developmentalist or maturing epistemology—Temple's progress of mankind; William's progressive revelation; Goodwin's positivistic approach to revelation; and Jowett's scriptural development and the progress of the age as one from "childhood to manhood"—the document was by nature evolutionary. Progressive evolution was known to many observers as the "Law of Progress." Thus to situate the book in its cultural context, that is, to consider it in the same light as Darwin's *Origin of Species*, referred to in passing by both Powell and Jowett, is, Ieuan Ellis finds, "to see it as a religious counterpart of those historically–dominated studies . . . which proposed to explain society and its institutions by their historical origins, an evolutionary process from lower to higher, from simpler to more complex forms."[46] For this reason, many critics saw *Essays and Reviews* as a continuation of Darwinism, placing it, "perhaps alongside the *Origin of Species*," says Basil Willey, "as one of the blasts then troubling the stagnant waters of orthodoxy."[47] One *Guardian* reviewer observed that "two or three" of the essayists "unhesitatingly" embrace Darwin's "theory of the development of species."[48] Ellis finds again that the "Germanism" of the authors came through Hegel; and as a result of his and the "philosophical evolutionism" mediated by him and others, the essayists "accepted Darwin more easily."[49]

The most sustained poetic treatment of *Essays and Reviews* is Browning's poem "Gold Hair," subtitled "A Story of Pornic." But the poem has nothing really to do with Pornic, except that the tale it narrates allegedly took place in Pornic and came to Browning from Carou's *Histoire de Pornic*. The poem is meant to illustrate how best to handle new knowledge. A seraphic young girl with great locks of golden hair fell ill, and with her dying breath requested, though with a tinge of hidden guilt, that her hair not be disturbed when she dies and is buried. Her request granted, and before she died, she, unknown to anyone, carefully wove within her locks gold she had loved and hoarded. This girl, whom the entire citizenry thought inviolate, chose to bury her riches with her rather than bequeath it to some useful earthly cause. So virtuous was she considered that not only was she entombed near the church altar, a privilege usually accorded saints and benefactors, but in time she became a legend. Years later when the church needed repair, her grave was disturbed and the gold discovered. This finding generated a revised view of the girl. Human judgment, Browning intends to suggest, is fickle because it is incomplete and developmental. Her saintly character was now discredited; her gold became thirty pieces of silver and she a Judas. The sage priest of the church, however, soon grew weary of his parishioners' fickle opinions and offered a practical solution: that it is senseless crying over spilt milk; that the reputation even of great saints is as easily tarnished; and that the gold be used for the construction of a new altar.

Browning's remaining three stanzas in this structurally uneven allegory explain his reason for penning "this horrible verse," an admission of the poem's abstruseness. The poem, he tells us, is "As the text of a sermon" and the poet is the preacher. The mixture of good and evil in the human heart is both a mystery and a curse. Of late, Browning finds, it has become fashionable for the candid (i.e., the essayists) to proclaim Christianity false because of "our Essays and Reviews' debate," which "Begins to tell on the public mind." And even John Colenso's words, his liberal and unconventional approaches to Old and New Testament texts (*Critical Examination of the Pentateuch* and *Commentary on the Epistle to the Romans*), "have weight." Still Browning, for his part, continues to embrace Christianity, discovering in it convincing "reasons and reasons." Christianity, he concludes, is *the faith* that testifies to man's condition; it is "the faith" that "taught Original Sin, / The Corruption of Man's Heart." As such, it is the very faith that explains the immoral condition and action of the little Pornic girl. Browning's application of this faith to *Essays and Reviews* and Colenso's treatises suggests that such documents, rather than being hoarded away, might ultimately produce something useful; silencing them might indeed be the greater evil.

Browning's response to *Essays and Reviews* and other liberal documents expressed in "Gold Hair" must be interpreted contextually with "Development," a poem that defines his apologetics. In this supposedly autobiographical poem, Browning argues that being taught at age five that the *Iliad* is true is harmless to the developing mind which in time discovers "No actual Homer, no authentic text, / No warrant for the fiction I, as fact, / Had treasured in my heart and soul so long." But as myth, the *Iliad* is "as fact held still, still hold, / Spite of new knowledge." And that knowledge is no superficial and cerebral thing; it is lodged "in my heart of hearts / And soul of souls, fact's essence freed and fixed / From accidental fancy's guardian sheath." Browning refuses, then, to blame his father for suggesting he read Homer and for so perpetuating a myth, for he has grown to discover that much pleasure and experiences, even truth, reside in myths.[50]

As Browning and so many Victorians had observed, *Essays and Reviews* was a document on development. Among the controversial essays in the volume is the opening essay by Frederick Temple, "The Education of the World." Formerly delivered in a shortened version as a university sermon, the essay was thought by Temple to be relatively harmless. He told his sixth form boys at Rugby that the book contains "opinions which had long been lurking in corners; it was time they were dragged to light and faced."[51] In this loosely conceived, positivistic, study, Temple encourages mature Victorians to confront the recent theories in the historical and natural sciences. He holds, for example, that the "discoveries and inventions which characterize the different epochs of the world's history are [God's] works. The creeds and doctrines, the opinions and principles of the successive age, are his thoughts." But because physical science and historical criticism have "enlarged our philosophy beyond the limits which bounded that of the Church of the Fathers," and because Temple holds it "high treason" to safeguard a frail faith from scientific, philosophical, and historical investigation, he capitulates the historical literalness of the Bible to modern science:

> If geology proves to us that we must not interpret the first
> chapter of Genesis literally; if historical investigation shall
> show us, that inspiration, however it may protect the doctrine,
> yet was not empowered to protect the narrative of the inspired
> writers from occasional inaccuracy; if careful criticism shall
> prove that there have been occasional interpolations and
> forgeries in that book [the Bible], as in many others,—the
> results should be welcome.[52]

Temple views the education of the world as an analogy for growing up, the implication being that as an individual matures from childhood to adulthood, that individual sets aside, among other things, juvenile or arcane dogma.[53]

The second essay, Rowland Williams's "Bunsen's Biblical Researches," drew the most criticism and was, along with Henry Wilson's "Seances Historiques de Geneve—The National Church," used as evidence of heresy against the two authors. Although familiar to the British, Baron von Bunsen, the Prussian historian and career–diplomat, was the least recognized of the German critics of the Old Testament. He was championed only by Ewald, who regarded him the premier scholar.[54] Relying on progressive revelation, "the law of growth," Williams, through Bunsen, calls for the uncompromising pursuit of truth that will "revise some of the decisions provisionally given upon imperfect evidence." Failing to do so, we renounce all claims of truth and "our retreat will be either to Rome, as some of our lost ones have consistently seen, or to some form, equally evil, of darkness voluntary."[55] In his veneration of Bunsen's critical methods, and in his staunch support of Germanism, Williams remains equivocal on the point that Jesus is the fulfillment of the messianic prophesy given in Isaiah 52 and 53. Rather, he suggests that the man of grief, a shifting appellation throughout Jewish literature, is probably Jeremiah or some suffering prophet or remnant.[56] Regarding inspiration, Williams maintains that we should define it "consistently with the facts of Scripture, and of human nature. These would neither exclude the idea of fallibility among Israelites of old, nor teach us to quench the Spirit in true hearts for ever." Williams concludes that it is intellectually dishonest to maintain a "fabric of mingled faith and speculation, and in the same breath to violate the instinct which believed, and blindfold the mind which reasoned. It would be strange if God's work were preserved, by disparaging the instruments which His wisdom chose for it."[57] He ends his essay with a poem venerating Bunsen. The paean to Bunsen shows the "sons of Loyola" intimidated by Bunsen's discoveries ("would scare their startled fold"), which, in effect, confound Jesuit teachings and silence "all their garlands." Williams was apparently drawn to Bunsen because he saw him as a scholar in whom revelation and reason participated in similar discourse relationships. By embracing Bunsen, Williams is also endorsing a perfectible view of man, consonant with prevailing scientific attitudes.

Baden Powell's "On the Study of the Evidences of Christianity," from *Essays and Reviews*, solicits sympathy with the free play of ideas in matters of discourse. A philosophical treatise on how best to approach controversy, the essay is intentionally abstract. For example, Powell, Savilian Professor of Geometry at Oxford, does not specify the controversy nor identify the disputants. The essay, he claims, is "not intended to be of a controversial kind, it is purely contemplative and theoretical; it is rather directed to a calm and unprejudiced survey of the various opinions and arguments adduced."[58] Powell insists that to invoke argument is to solicit "perfect freedom of conviction." Such freedom means that one cannot be compelled to side with unconvincing claims;

and one should not be repudiated "as an unbeliever, because he is careful to find satisfactory grounds for his belief," or to be denounced a skeptic "because he is scrupulous to discriminate the truth." Powell separates "matters of *external fact*," should one find that such exist, from "moral or religious doctrine," urging that while external fact may appeal to "reason and intellect" alone, moral or religious doctrine appeals to "other and higher grounds of judgment and conviction."[59]

The fundamental argument, as Powell sees it, is between supporters of external and historical evidence and those who uphold faith and internal conviction as the only reliable bases of religion, without dismissing altogether the relevance of external facts. In this most positivistic of essays, Powell examines, even questions the survivability of, evidentiality or miracles, convinced that the "nature of the laws of all human belief, and the broader grounds of probability and credibility of events, have been too little investigated."[60] He dismisses accounts of miracles as unreliable, for "In nature and from nature, by science and by reason, we neither have nor can possibly have any evidence of a *Deity working miracles*; for that, we must go out of nature and beyond reason." Miracles, then, "become invested with the character of articles of faith."[61] Powell calls for a recognition of the "due claims of science to decide on points properly belonging to the world of *matter*, and the independence of such considerations which characterize the disclosure of *spiritual* truth." For even the most candid supporters of the evidential position, Luther, Huss, and Newman, among others, have admitted that "the appeal to miracles, however important in the early stages of the Gospel, has become less material in later times."[62] Powell draws a sharp distinction between knowledge and faith, overlooking the evidentialists' conviction that faith is rooted in knowledge, which, if suspect, causes faith to become capricious, as evident in Tennyson's *In Memoriam* and Arnold's "Dover Beach." But, says Powell:

> Matters of clear and positive fact, investigated on critical grounds and supported by exact evidence, are properly matters of knowledge, not of faith. It is rather in points of less definite character that any exercise of faith can take place; it is rather with matters of religious belief belonging to a higher and less conceivable class of truths, with the mysterious things of the unseen world, that faith owns a connection, and more readily associates itself with spiritual ideas, than with external evidence, or physical events: and it is generally admitted that many points of important religious instruction,

> even conveyed under the form of fictions (as in the insistence
> of doctrines inculcated through parables) are more congenial
> to the spirit of faith than any relations of historical events
> could be.[63]

Powell believes that as knowledge advances so Christianity, to remain a functional religion, must dissociate the spiritual from the physical. Like many of the other essayists, he too points to the discoveries of geology, the idea of "the development of species, and the rejection of the idea of 'creation,'" which to him were equally "new advances in the same direction."[64]

As shocking to the Victorians were the claims made by C.W. Goodwin's "On the Mosaic Cosmogony," which, with Powell's essay, identified a conflict between Christianity and the natural sciences. The only non–clerical contributor to *Essays and Reviews*, Goodwin, whose essay deals with the Book of Genesis in light of the geological records, attacks theological geologists and concludes that the creation story was a Hebrew myth that once satisfied the basis for theological instruction, the very point that the physicist John Tyndall would later make in his controversial "Belfast Address" when he calls Genesis "a poem, not a scientific treatise."[65] Goodwin reasons that if modern research shows the Genesis account untenable, our regard for it should not diminish; the narrative was instrumental to Providence in the process of educating man. In fact, says Goodwin, "if the value of the Bible as a book of religious instruction is to be maintained, it must be not by striving to prove it scientifically exact . . . but by frank recognition of the erroneous views of nature which it contains." He sees theology maintaining a "shivering existence, shouldered and jostled by the sturdy growths of modern thought, and bemoaning itself for the hostility which it encounters." And because Scripture was "not designed to teach us natural philosophy," it is "vain to attempt to make a cosmogony out of its statements."[66] A.O.J. Cockshut regards Goodwin's essay "perhaps the clearest contemporary account of the great dispute over Genesis,"[67] a narrative Samuel Butler again fictionalized in *The Way of all Flesh* (1903):

> It had never so much as crossed Theobald's mind to doubt the
> literal accuracy of any syllable in the Bible. He had never seen
> any book in which this was disputed, nor met with anyone
> who doubted it. True, there was just a little scare about
> geology, but there was nothing in it. If it was said that God
> made the world in six days, why He did make it in six days,
> neither in more nor less. . . . That was how it was done; there

was neither difficulty nor shadow of difficulty about the
matter. . . . This was the average attitude of fairly educated
young men and women towards the Mosaic cosmogony fifty,
forty, or even twenty years ago.[68]

The controversy over *Essays and Reviews* was in fact a hermeneutical one
and not technically a matter of belief. But interpretive paradigms, unconscious
as we are of them, always affect ideology and praxis, themselves founded on
certain hermeneutical strategies. All of the essayists urged the same hermeneutical
strategy that the Bible be treated like any other book. Temple, for example,
argues that a literalist approach to the Bible must recognize historical and
scientific claims that challenge literalist assumptions. Williams's argument is
also a hermeneutical one, for Isaiah's suffering savior, he insists, can be
interpreted as any number of Jewish afflicted individuals. Powell's approach
also courts interpretation, insisting that God is "entirely an inference from the
language of the Bible." Goodwin too adopts a similar hermeneutical model,
arguing that if the Bible is to be useful to religious instruction, we must refrain
from insisting on its scientific exactness. Patterson's and Jowett's essays argue
most convincingly for the privileging of hermeneutics.

Mark Pattison's "Tendencies of Religious Thought in England, 1688–
1750," also part of *Essays and Reviews*, was, according to Basil Willey, a
pioneering effort in the genre of "the history of ideas."[69] Pattison, a bibliophile,
was arguably the most conservative of the essayists and is remembered by
Newman as one of those intimate friends who visited him at Littlemore on the
eve of his departure from Oxford. Pattison even considered joining the Roman
church after Newman's defection.[70] In his essay, Pattison attempts to show that
the English divines of the eighteenth century differed from their counterparts in
the Middle Ages in their understanding of Scripture. The English divines
maintained that scriptural intention was not determined by the Church but
through reason. "The aids of history, the ordinary rules of grammar and logic,
were applied to find out what the sacred writers actually said. *That* was the
meaning of Scripture, the message supernaturally communicated."[71]   What
Pattison says next, what he in fact took from Whitelock in Johnson's *Life of
Selden*, was actually extracted by Hopkins when he read Pattison's essay on 27
January 1866.[72] Pattison's essay and Hopkins's extract read:

Where each text of Scripture has but one sense, that [Hopkins
has "the"] sense in which the writer penned it, it can only be
cited in that sense without doing it violence. This was the turn

by which Selden so discomfited the Puritan divines, who, like the Catholic mystics, made Scripture words the vehicle of their own feelings. 'Perhaps in your little pocket Bibles with gilt leaves [Hopkins has "edges"] the translation may be thus, but the Greek or Hebrew signifies otherwise.'[73]

From this most rational period of English religious thought, the eighteenth century, Pattison looks to the present and suggests that it would benefit modern man to turn to "Authority," "the Inward Light," "Reason," and "Scripture," either together or in combinations, as the instruments of revelation;[74] he also faulted the nineteenth century for not opening up the canonical books of Scripture for critical scrutiny. Pattison felt, as Duncan Nimmo appropriately points out, that "so far as Christianity is a historical phenomenon, it must be treated on the same terms as any other part of history." Nimmo traces Pattison's contribution to *Essays and Reviews* back to his 1857 article in the radical *Westminster* that reviewed the status of theology in Germany. Pattison praised what he called the "historico–critical" school of hermeneutics for its advances in historical criticism and examination of Christianity as a historical religion. Thus his contribution to *Essays and Reviews* was, as Nimmo again notes, "a realisation of the liberal programme he had outlined in 1857, namely the impartial and scientific investigation of 'so much of the Christian revelation as is matter of fact and record.'"[75]

Benjamin Jowett's "On the Interpretation of Scripture" is the last and most substantive contribution to *Essays and Reviews*. Five years earlier, he had collaborated with his friend, the Broad Churchman A.P. Stanley, on a liberal commentary on the *Epistles of St. Paul* (June 1855), the same year Jowett was elected Professor of Greek.[76] This work, which Jowett called their "Opus Magnum," not only departed from the *textus receptus*, the Greek text used for the Authorized Version of the Bible, but even more radically refrained from citing earlier and more traditionally accepted biblical criticism. One reviewer of *Essays and Reviews* saw it as "little more than the formal enunciation, illustration, and defence of principles of exegesis rendered familiar to the student by Professor Jowett's application of them in his work on certain of St. Paul's Epistles."[77] Both documents, along with Jowett's skeptical stance on the resurrection, firmed up his liberal reputation at Oxford, despite his evangelical beginnings and earlier attraction to Puseyism.[78] Located at the head of Oxford's Broad Street, Balliol was considered the seat of Oxford liberalism. Balliol was the birthplace of the radical Old Mortality. The former Balliol student Martin Geldart humorously recalled that at Oxford "Belial [Balliol] may be called the focus or center round which these currents and counter–currents formed a kind of vortex. The considerable man of the day was Professor Jewell [Jowett], Fellow of Belial, and Regius Professor of Greek. When I went to Bosphorus he was the hero of the hour."[79]

Jowett's controversial essay, which echoes remarks Stanley made fourteen years earlier in his sermons at St. Mary's, advocates reading the Bible as though it were any other literary or historical text and so subject to the same interpretative strategies:

> *Interpret the Scripture like any other book.* There are many
> respects in which Scripture is unlike any other book; these
> will appear in the results of such an interpretation. The first
> step is to know the meaning, and this can only be done in the
> same careful and impartial way that we ascertain the meaning
> of Sophocles or of Plato. The subordinate principles which
> flow out of this general one will also be gathered from the
> observation of Scripture.[80]

Any genuine doctrine of inspiration, Jowett maintains, "must conform to all well–ascertained facts of history or of science." For the "same fact cannot be true in religion when seen by the light of faith, and untrue in science when looked at through the medium of evidence or experiment."[81]   Thus he advocates separate examinations of the canonical books on grounds that the characteristics of each book or literary type are too dissimilar for the whole to be considered a consonant body of truth. "When interpreted like any other book, by the same rules of evidence and the same canons of criticism," says Jowett, "the Bible will still remain unlike any other book; its beauty will be freshly seen, as of a picture which is restored after many ages to its original state."[82] While not espousing unequivocally that the books are altogether inharmonious, Jowett believes that artificially imposing harmony on the biblical text obfuscates precise interpretation. The "time has come," he claims, "when it is no longer possible to ignore the results of criticism"; it is therefore important that Christianity be seen "in harmony with them."[83]

Hopkins read Jowett's *Epistles* and "On the Interpretation of Scripture" in February 1865 and might have responded to it the way Geldart did, however characteristically veiled was Geldart's response: "At last I determined to read with fear and trembling the 'Essay on the Interpretation of Scripture.' . . . I had always, it seemed, held the same, only without knowing. But at the end of the essay where was my orthodox faith? Overturned in irretrievable ruin, never to be rebuilt upon the old foundations."[84] During this time, Hopkins was still confessing to Liddon, much to Jowett's chagrin. Coles had told Liddon that "Jowett appears to be much horrified at the spread of confession in the Ch. of England: and especially in Oxford." Jowett, who was firmly against educators multiplying themselves among their undergraduates, still exercised a strong influence on Oxford undergraduates, an influence that together with Liddon's was often compared to Newman's.[85] But when Hopkins decided on Tuesday, 14 February 1865, to take a walk with Liddon rather than attend a Jowett lecture, he clearly signaled his philosophical and theological break with Jowett.[86]

Expectedly, Liddon was always critical of *Essays and Reviews*, and in particular Jowett's contribution to it. What Jowett has done, Liddon said, is to consider the "three first Gospels to be merely three forms of one tradition, but 'not three independent witnesses' to our Lord's sayings and acts." [87] In a 31 March 1860 letter, only one month after *Essays and Reviews* was published, Liddon launched what proved to be the earliest conservative attack. He told John Keble that the volume goes "further in the race of Rationalism than anything which I have yet seen. Between Jowett's and Wilson's essays, the Gospel history simply evaporates."[88] And "'How different,' sighed Liddon over Temple's essay in *Essays and Reviews*, 'from Newman's beautiful sermon *The Submission of the Reason and the Feelings to the Revealed Word*.'"[89] Liddon's most exhaustive comment on the volume came in a 6 January 1861 letter to William Bright, Canon of Christ Church, announcing a forthcoming critique of the volume in the *Times*:

> I imagine it will be hostile on the whole, yet making conces-
> sions. But "The Jupiter" must see that general opinion is not
> yet lips for wholesale approval of downright scepticism. I
> hope that unusually foolish and unwarrantable distinction in
> favor of Temple's essay will be eschewed. Although moder-
> ate his surface–expression, it is really just as "advanced" as
> Baden Powell or Wilson: it seems to me a simple profession
> of the creed of Positivism as applied to history with one or two
> very inconsistent reservations.

As to Williams's essay on Bunsen, and in particular the conclusion, Liddon called it a "real relic" and Williams's argument "very much in error: and the intermingled personalities and flippancies make the whole thing very distaste-ful. One cannot but mourn that it is so: he might do a great deal which needs doing in Oxford if he were less egotistical, and had something of the large &

generous sympathies of Catholicism."[90] One must also read some of Liddon's remarks in his 1869 lecture on the Epistle to Peter as attacks against the positions taken in *Essays and Reviews*. Commenting on 2 Peter 2:4–8, where the Apostle uses the antediluvian accounts of Noah, Lot, and the destruction of Sodom and Gomorrah to demonstrate the idea of a divinely chosen remnant, Liddon noted:

> These instances by which the Ap[ostle] supports his argu-
> ment are very remarkable, because in two of them the N.T.
> goes out of its way to confirm the truth of parts of the history
> of the O.T. which have always been more inclined to be
> questioned; viz. the flood & the destruction of the cities of the
> plain.

While Liddon concedes that the passage fails to argue decisively for the universality of the flood, an examination of Genesis would cause us, he believes, to

> scarcely doubt that a Universal Deluge is there meant. . . . The
> antiquity of the world may go back millions & millions of
> years before the creation of man; quite consistently with
> revelation. We are simply told that God created heaven &
> earth IN THE BEGINNING. The fossils that are now found
> produced & quoted to confute the truth of the O.T. narrative
> of of [sic] the Creation may perfectly well have belonged to
> some prehistoric age before the creation of man.[91]

Because of the feelings Liddon held toward *Essays and Reviews* and, indirectly, toward its subscribers, he wrote to Keble on 15 May 1861 explaining why he was uncharacteristically lukewarm to Pusey's proposal to increase the endowment of the Regius Professorship of Greek held by Jowett, a concern Pusey expressed in 1858 over all the Regius Professorships, not just Jowett's. Although one of the first English clergymen to show an interest in German theology, and to befriend the cantankerous but moderate German theologian Heinrich Ewald, Pusey, who held unequivocally to the divinity of Christ, regarded Jowett a heretic, once remarking that the only religious point on which he and Jowett agreed was the sonship of Jesus, a position he hastened to add also held by some non–Christian religions.[92] But while Pusey felt he would support any plan to prosecute Jowett, he respected Jowett's scholarly abilities and felt that as far as the professorship was concerned Jowett should be remunerated accordingly.[93] But ninety–one other committee members, still seething over Jowett's more recent heretical ideas in *Essays and Reviews*, could not be so objective. In this conspiratorial plot, Pusey's proposal of 7 May 1861 was defeated at convocation 91 to 70. One reason Liddon cited for the defeat was that Jowett's "whole influence in Oxford is thrown into the scale of negative and destructive thought."[94] And to increase the endowment at this time, Liddon felt, was to endorse Jowett's contribution to *Essays and Reviews*, the very thing Liddon pointed to a year later when on 25 January 1861 Mark Pattison was elected Rector of Lincoln College: "This is a strong measure after the 'Essays and Reviews.'"[95]

After the endowment question, now waged personally by Stanley, suffered a few more defeats, Pusey decided to turn his attention to challenging Jowett's orthodoxy, which, if resolved, would settle once and for all the endowment question. But Liddon's position had not yet changed by the end of that year. He still refused to separate the endowment issue from *Essays and Reviews* as Stanley and others had done. In a 24 November letter to the Bishop, Samuel Wilberforce, Liddon wrote that

> the Jowett question will come before Convocation, as Stanley has "stolen the hearts of the men of Israel" who ought to be on the side of Faith and Truth in Congregation. If this be so, we shall trust to your Lordship influence to save the University from giving that sanction to teaching of the Essays which those who hold with Prof. Stanley are naturally anxious to win for them.[96]

Liddon's position was clear, and was even able to educe agreement from his good friend Dodgson. In a 13 November 1862 diary entry, Liddon wrote: "In the aft. walked with Dodgson in the Wheatley Road. He thought legal proceedings agst Jowett perfectly defensible."

Two years later Jowett was exonerated, and at 2 p.m. on Tuesday, 8 March, the endowment again came up before convocation. At that "curious scene at the Theatre," Liddon, in a losing effort, now voted in favor of the endowment. He had rebuffed the conspiratorial solicitation of one of Jowett's detractors, the moderate churchman Montagu Burrows, who earlier had asked Liddon in a vituperous attack on Pusey to "come in this once & vote against" the endowment:

It is surely a most serious measure for Oxford. . . . Pusey's
letter [of support] is grievous. He had better have left his
blunder alone esp. after telling his friends he should not be
sorry if the measure were thrown out. I agree with _____ that
he is quite hopeless as a leader in University or any politics.
He is too retired & too much the victim of the first person who
gets his ear, & *then* too little straightforward. . . . You have
had the circulars we sent out of course—No one has dared to
answer them. The argument is all on our side, the names on
theirs.[97]

After six years, the endowment issue was finally settled on 21 February 1865,
and Jowett's stipend was raised to £500. In his usual sardonic manner, Geldart
captured the "fierce dispute" over whether Jowett should be paid £400 a year
"like the other Regius Professors" or whether he should continue to subsist on
the paltry £40 a year:

That our Professor was perhaps the hardest working and
hardest worked, not even his worst enemies disputed. But he
was a heretic and an apostate from the orthodox creed of
Bosphorus. He had, in addition to the questionable notes on
the Pauline Epistles, in these latter days contributed an essay
on the interpretation of Scripture to a volume by Broad
Church divines . . . which had set all England by the ears. I had
never read this essay, nor did I intend to do so, but, like many
others similarly qualified to judge, I believed it to be full of
soul–destroying errors . . . ; that, moreover, the University, by
endowing the professorship, was virtually endowing the
professor for the time being; and that since the professor for
the time being was a heretic, this would be the virtual
endowment of dangerous doctrine on the part of the University. . . . The controversy waxed loud and furious, and was
further complicated by the fact that a large number of the most
orthodox members of the University regarded the Professor
of Hebrew [Dr. Pusey], who was said to practise and encourage confession, as on the whole a rather worse heretic than the
Professor of Greek.[98]

But while Liddon finally supported the Jowett endowment, associating with Jowett was another matter. So averse was he to Jowett's views in *Essays and Reviews* that four years later he declined an invitation to share the pulpit at Westminster with Jowett, believing that to do so would imply acceptance of Jowett's doctrinal claims in the book.

The liberal or Germanizing causes at Oxford headed by Jowett and Balliol led Hopkins, then, to seek out a conservative haven in Liddon. But although he gravitated to Liddon in the midst of the religious and political turmoil at Oxford, how long Hopkins attended Liddon's Sunday evening lectures is unknown. Liddon's obsession with those who attended the lectures, noting repeatedly whether Hopkins's friends Addis or Challis attended, did not extend to Hopkins; not once did he note Hopkins's attendance, another sign of how little an impression Hopkins initially made on Liddon's circle. We do know that Hopkins first attended the lectures on 3 May 1863. He was probably also among the Balliol contingent who breakfasted with Liddon on 16 November, the morning following another Sunday evening lecture. On Monday, 8 February 1864, following a crowded lecture the evening before which Hopkins apparently attended, he took his first of several walks with Liddon: "Walk with Hopkins of Balliol, a long talk about eternal punishment." Two days later, Hopkins made his first of five confessions to Liddon: "Hopkins of Balliol cnf. at 7."[99] He would do so on four other occasions (26 November 1864, 25 March 1865, 6 February 1866, 17 May 1866), his last occurring a mere two months before he converted to Roman Catholicism.

In addition to these undergraduate contacts with Liddon, Hopkins on one other occasion, 11 o'clock in the morning of 28 March 1865, saw Liddon for an hour and a half. But more memorable were his walks with Liddon, two (possibly a third, 11 November) in 1864 (8 February and 7 March) and two in 1865 (14 February and 13 May). On the first they talked about eternal punishment, the second the Pater affair, and a possible third was the suggestion on the Hexameron. But perhaps the most notable was Liddon's last recorded walk with Hopkins: "Walked with Hopkins—Up the Happy Valley & round by Ferry Hinksey. The bluebells perfectly beautiful. The country just now is in its greatest beauty. O Lord lift my heart up to thee."[100] While this was penned by Liddon, the observation of nature and the language that captures it are obviously Hopkins's. Most of Hopkins's observations of bluebells took place in May, Mary's month, the same time it was when he drew Liddon's attention to them. He even detected that they grow often with primroses and make a good match; they also match with campion, though the three, bluebells, primroses, and campion, growing together forfeits the aesthetic charm that pairing or equipoise seems always to hold for Hopkins.[101]

Hopkins's most impressive observations of bluebells occurred in May 1870 and on 11 May 1871. In the latter, he was drawn to the beauty of the flower and was taken with how "The bluebells in your hand baffle you with their inscape, made to every sense." That account is both scientific and poetic in description; but whether a thing of poetry or a thing of science, the bluebells testify to God's better beauty. But the former account in this context is more relevant. Uncharacteristically, Hopkins did not precisely recall the day that entry was made, so often was his attraction to bluebells. But the account too closely parallels Liddon's to be ignored. Hopkins's synoptic account reads: "One day when the bluebells were in bloom I wrote the following. I do not think I have ever seen anything more beautiful than the bluebells I have been looking at. I know the beauty of our Lord by it."[102] With all his passion for walking, Liddon never had the slightest eye for nature. Other than its shared appreciation with Hopkins, there is only one documented occasion of nature ever capturing Liddon's attention. He had been at Taunton on 28 April 1862, and while there "Gathered cowslips in great beauty in a field near Thurlbeer. The day one of unclouded beauty—the finest this spring." But the exercise remained rather superficial and Liddon's aesthetic taste insufficiently formed. Liddon would on another occasion gather "a great many wild flowers" while he was alone near Enfield (16 March 1866) and would again fail altogether to appreciate the reverential value the meanest flower holds: "Walked in the afternoon with Redington to Horspath & home by Cowley. . . . Picked some daffodils in a field at Cowley: a man came out, & I paid him a shilling for them. Rather dear for a wild nosegay!"[103] Hopkins would never have so estimated nature; his value was consistently the aesthetic and religious, the beauty present and prayer, patience, alms, vows.

When Hopkins first attended Liddon's Sunday evening New Testament lectures, he was then treating 1 Corinthians 5 and undertaking, judging from Hopkins's copious notes and the extended length of Liddon's lectures on a given book, a chronological and exegetical study of Paul's letter. Hopkins's notes from the lectures were recorded at one end of a college copybook; at the other end were poems copied from Manley Hopkins and Dante Gabriel Rossetti. "When I first attended these lectures," Hopkins noted in his preface, "they had reached only the fifth chapter of the first epistle, but my notes are on the sixth chapter." He later recovered his notes on verses 9, 10, 11 of chapter 5; his incomplete notes on 1 Corinthians ended with chapter 8.[104] The notes from the lectures would seem to suggest that Hopkins lost interest in these particular lectures and so withdrew from them, for the lectures continued unabated during

Hopkins's Oxford years. His 1865 diary does note: "Liddon not coming up next Sunday," a possible reference to Liddon's unavailability to give his 22 January lecture.[105] He had left Oxford on 16 January for Bristol and Brislington, and from there on Saturday, 21 January, for a special Cathedral service at St. Paul's. On that Sunday he preached for one hour and fifteen minutes, afterwards using the typical Victorian metaphor for extreme exhaustion: "Much knocked up."[106] Pusey had earlier used the same expression to describe Liddon's long sermons, to which, according to Pusey, no one listened, and, worse yet, caused Liddon to neglect his part of the commentary.

Liddon began his Sunday–evening lectures on 6 November 1859 with the Epistle to the Hebrews and finished the eighth chapter on 18 March 1860. He ended Hebrews prematurely because of faltering attendance, and then undertook the pastoral Epistles on 21 October, finding the lecture dull and the students disinterested. On 20 October 1861 he was on 1 John, ending it on 9 March 1862, his last lecture for that term. When the lecture reconvened on 11 May, he took up the Epistle to the Galatians and continued on it until 1 February 1863, when he began the lectures on 1 Corinthians. Hopkins entered Balliol in April of that year and began attending the lectures on 4 May. The lectures on 1 Corinthians ended on 30 October 1864. What book Liddon then undertook, possibly 2 Corinthians, remains uncertain until, on 10 December 1865, he began 2 John. The lectures had by this time moved to Queen's College. On 4 February 1866, Liddon began with the Epistle to the Romans, ending it on 20 October 1867, returning on 27 October to the Epistle to the Hebrews, which, when he first began the lectures, had failed to interest the students.

But however sporadically Hopkins attended the Liddon lectures, especially the ones on Corinthians, they, in addition to his personal contacts with Liddon, had a profound influence on his belief, religious practice, and poetry. When Liddon treated 1 Corinthians 5:9, he elaborated on the point that the epistle to which Paul refers is this present one and not some other, one presumably lost. Liddon argues this in the face of convincing evidence that nowhere in this present epistle is the phrase "not to keep company with fornicators." Paul had written other non–canonical epistles from which the phrase originated, letters not incorporated in the biblical canon, but Liddon was reluctant to entertain any ambiguity on the sacredness of the canon. One has to conclude that given different circumstances, Liddon, whose mind normally did not embrace such flimsy evidence, would not have been so literarily belligerent. No doubt, prevailing questions on inerrancy and authorship generated by *Essays and Reviews* influenced his self–censure, and he did not wish to repeat Frederick Temple's guilt of misguiding young minds.

In 1 Corinthians 6, Liddon engages the controversy over the use of the body. The Pauline argument is that although one has the liberty to enjoy all things, such freedoms are not always expedient. The question is directed not only to the Epicureans in Paul's day but also to those rampant in Hopkins's, manifested in such an Epicurean work as Edward Fitzgerald's *The Rubaiyat of Omar Khayyam*, published in March 1859. While this work went virtually unnoticed for many years, it did capture early the temper of the times and did anticipate the materialistic philosophy of Darwin and Pater. Liddon also speaks to this philosophy in his last Bampton lecture, claiming that "Among the forces arrayed against Christianity at this hour, the most formidable, because the most consistent and the most sanguine, is that pure materialism, which has been intellectually organized in the somewhat pedantic form of Positivism"; and needed to withstand the "reiterated attacks, the subtle and penetrating misgivings, the manifold wear and tear of a protracted controversy with so brutal an antagonist" as Positivism is, says Liddon, a "living, energetic, robust faith."[107]

In his notes on 1 Corinthians 6:13, a passage pointing to the temporality of the body and meats, Hopkins felt that this, like other Pauline passages, does not imply that "the sensual faculties will be destroyed"; and on a general observation of 6:20 wrote: "We are Christ's; he has bought us." The Epicurean concern merely broached here will be explored more fully in Hopkins's response to Paterean and Darwinian aesthetics and epistemology: how, for example, to respond to pointlessness and of what benefit is there to the resurrection, questions addressed in "The Caged Skylark" and "That Nature Is a Heraclitean Fire and of the Comfort of the Resurrection." More relevant here, however, is how Epicureanism challenges Hopkins's asceticism; for the Pauline passages indicate how the senses ought to be employed, an issue critical to Hopkins's spiritual development and early Oxford poetry.

Hopkins's Oxford correspondence reveals a growing asceticism. In a March 1864 letter he told his college friend, Alexander Baillie, that his mother prohibits his fasting, "and says I in particular must never do it again, and in fact I believe I must not." He added humorously: "I feel like the Hindoos when the Suttee was abolished; but that is to me almost greater mortification of the spirit than fasting of the flesh." The context of this letter provides some interesting details on the change in Hopkins. He commented that he found the idea of homes quite uncivilized, for they seem never to possess the "ordinary luxuries or necessaries. If it were Pleasures or Palaces," said Hopkins, "it would be the same." The cause for all of this, trivial as it sounds, is Hopkins's complaint over not finding the proper pen with which to write Baillie, a fussiness about writing utensils he no doubt picked up from Jowett. Although Hopkins was a year before frequent at wines, he now rejected its lure altogether, along with the notion from one of his aunts that the frivolous behavior at chapels did not encourage devotions and that the meetings were hardly religious events. "I shall put up Plato's motto over my door," Hopkins vowed: "WHOSO IS ABOSPHERETE LET HIM (OR HER WHICH IS MORE LIKELY) NOT ENTER HERE."[108] Veiled within this revised adage is the onset of Hopkins's departure from the pleasurable to the religious and ascetic. Veiled too within the statement is perhaps the first clue to Hopkins's vow of celibacy: "LET HIM (OR HER WHICH IS MORE LIKELY) NOT ENTER HERE." The vow rejects two types of love. The "HIM" can be read as Hopkins's disavowal of homosexual attraction and the "HER," the "MORE LIKELY," a dismissal of any likelihood of a heterosexual relationship. A year later, and not yet having worked through his aesthetic philosophy of giving beauty back to God, Hopkins renounced all aesthetic urge: "On this day by God's grace I resolved to give up all beauty until I had His leave for it."[109] Hopkins's asceticism was still in effect on 23 January 1866:

> For Lent. No pudding on Sundays. No tea except if to keep me awake and then without sugar. Meat only once a day. No verses in Passion Week or on Fridays. No lunch or meat on Fridays. Not to sit in armchair except can work in no other way. Ash Wednesday and Good Friday bread and water.[110]

In a letter to Liddon, Gerard's father, Manley Hopkins, pointed to Gerard's "growing love for asceticism."[111]   Although Hopkins came from Highgate to Oxford with these ascetic promptings, they became refined in his years at Oxford and relationship with Liddon.[112]

The poems of Hopkins's early Oxford years reveal a marked departure from the Keatsean sensuousness of his juvenile verses. Throughout the "Escorial" (1860) can be found the kind of sensuous imagery indebted to Keats's "The Eve of St. Agnes" and "Ode on a Grecian Urn," imagery that persisted in the "Plump–purple" and "rosy–lipp'd" of "A Vision of the Mermaids" (1862). Hopkins might also have deliberately signaled the movement away from his early Keatsean sensuousness when in "Il Mystico" (1862), he, following a device Milton employed in "L'Allegro" and "Il Penseroso," rejects "sensual gross desires, / Right offspring of your grimy mother Earth!" Hopkins proclaims the birth of a new spirit whose gestation is unlike that of the senses and whose wings cannot be encumbered by the earthiness of the senses. What Hopkins welcomes, instead, as "balm to aching soul," is not radical dismissal of the senses but their spiritual rebirth that in turn enacts an ethereal vision and a spiritualized olfactory appreciation. Discovered in these early Oxford poems are the "Lenten lips" of "Easter Communion," the unhousing of the senses ("ear," "lips," "eyes," "Palate," "Nostrils," "feel") as a prelude to housing the Lord in "The Kind Betrothal," and the "Beauty now for ashes wear" in "Easter." Now "Penance shall clothe me to the bone," and the poet's former "passion–pastured thought" turns "To gentle manna and simple bread" ("A Voice from the World").

But in these early Oxford poems, it is "The Habit of Perfection" (1866), an earlier version of "The Kind Betrothal," that most fully expresses Hopkins's asceticism. In the word *habit*, both as the apparel of the priest and the regularity of practice, the poet desires to be clothed with perfection. His first request is for music that does not cater to the sensual ear, a request not unlike Keats's "ditties of no tone" in "Ode on a Grecian Urn." While the music Hopkins requests is silence, so too is "lovely–dumb" the most pursued expression of eloquence. The eyes should find joy not from the distractions and chaos of external things that serve only to titillate "simple sight," but from a turning within to discover the "uncreated light." Or, as Hopkins more forcefully puts it in the poem's later version, it is by shutting both eyes (insight) that one apprehends both Christ and true intuition, "uncreated light." No longer now is one distracted; instead, the beauty that results from clear vision vitalizes "simple sight." The palate, "hutch of tasty lust," should not desire to be "rinsed with wine" unless that wine is the communion drink, the blood of Christ, and the nostrils should spend their breath not to sustain a life whose only aspiration is the "keep of pride" but to inhale the sweet incense of sacrifice. Finally, the hands and feet should desire not the softness of sensuality but the sacrifice of temporary, earthly luxuries for heavenly, permanent ones. The fact that Hopkins's language in a poem that solicits the redemption of the senses is itself sensuous is an aesthetic question that the final chapter explores.

In 1 Corinthians 7, to return to the Liddon lectures Hopkins found intriguing, Liddon emphasized Paul's injunction to renounce sexual desires. "Is it good for a man to have sexual intercourse with woman at all? or perhaps Is it better or in itself commendable for him?" Liddon asked. He pointed out that "If possible, it is better not; but there is no sin in it." This idea either of renunciation or of control would again be articulated in a series of lectures Liddon gave from 14 June to 17 December 1869 on the Epistles to Peter. In 1 Peter 2:11, Liddon refers to the *apechesthai* (the command to abstain from fleshly lusts) as "the great characteristic mark of Christian ethics, opposed to the idea that Nature is not to be *restrained*, that whatever N. suggests must be meant to be developed." Liddon argues that this notion "ignores the fact that there has passed over human nature, since the fall, a change that has made it untrustworthy." Thus the "passive virtues of restraint & mortification are inculcated by Christian ethics." Liddon evaluates modernist reaction to such restraint:

> Some Moderns think that the repression of self, impulse, affections leads to a poor weak effiminate [sic] character. But in Ch[ristian] Ethics the repression inflicted on self is one direction in repressing false instincts, is more than compensated for by additional active energy in another direction. But the self repression must be voluntary.[113]

While Hopkins was more than likely unfamiliar with these lectures, the positions they articulate were the very ones he would have heard from Liddon; and they would have influenced both Hopkins's understanding of the self and decision to be celibate, to be, in his words, "a eunuch . . . for the kingdom of heaven's sake."[114]

It was also Liddon who introduced Saint Ignatius to Hopkins. In 1865 the first volume of Liddon's University Sermons was published. One of the sermons, which he had earlier preached in 1863, echoes Saint Ignatius, an indebtedness brought to light by Rev. C. Kegan Paul, who charged Liddon with plagiarism. Responding to the charge, Liddon noted that he was unaware that the sermon owed anything to Ignatius, but conceded that he had read and copied notes from a French version of Ignatius a decade earlier; and that possibly some of those same notes were used when he prepared the sermon. Liddon disavowed any claim of total originality, but maintained that he had not deliberately concealed evidence showing indebtedness.[115] Hopkins no doubt heard the sermon or read the volume.

Hopkins also attended Liddon's Bampton lectures of 1866.[116] On 17 March 1865, Liddon was encouraged by Bright, the second such request, to be a candidate for the Bamptons, a decision Pusey opposed on the grounds that Liddon had already neglected his work on the commentary.[117] After deliberating for one day, Liddon submitted his name, by which time the selection committee had had its first meeting, already limiting Liddon's chances. When the vote was taken, he and another candidate, Rev. A.W. Haddon, received an equal number; Dr. Lightfoot of Exeter cast the deciding vote in favor of Haddon. At dinner with the President of Magdalen on 31 May 1865, Liddon received word of his defeat from the vice–chancellor. He was also told that his chances next year were better, unless he compromised it by publishing something objectionable. The first week of November 1865, Haddon became ill and requested to be released from the engagement. On 7 November, Liddon was elected unanimously as Haddon's replacement. The many letters of commendation that followed all pointed to Liddon's rising status. But the lateness of his appointment, current ill health, and preoccupation with the concerns of undergraduates all served to exacerbate Liddon's characteristic nervousness about public performances. His diary is replete with admissions of apprehension: "A week has now elapsed since my election: yet I have done nothing to them"; "scarcely felt apt to write anything"; "Out of heart about my Bamptons"; "not much to my satisfaction"; "They want heart and enthusiasm"; "a very feeble production"; "wretched about B.L."; "In very low spirits about my lectures." To make matters worse, during all this time students were visiting Liddon and staying the entire day. On one occasion, after several people had called on him, and another had even written complaining of problems with his creditors, Liddon responded: "Consequently no work done today in B. L. matter. What can I do?" When he was able to achieve something, he felt relieved: "Wrote some B. L. Rewriting B. L. no. 1. More fertile today than heretofore. Deo gratias."[118] But Liddon's feelings of unpreparedness and disappointment with the delivery of his Bampton lectures were not shared by his audience. The lectures were an astounding success and served, as Darwell Stone claims, to demonstrate Liddon's "theological great-ness."[119]

Liddon's attempt in the Bamptons to identify "some of those assaults upon the doctrine of our Lord's Divinity" was no accident. The topic was also in keeping with Rev. John Bampton's wish that the lectures attempt "to confute all heretics and schismatics." The very subjects dealt with by Liddon suggest that his aim was to present an apology of the divinity of Christ. Liddon's eight lectures were entitled: "The Questions Before Us" (Matt. 16:13), "Anticipation of Christ's Divinity in the Old Testament" (Gal. 3:8), "Our Lord's Work in the World as Witness to His Divinity" (Matt. 13:54–56), "Our Lord's Divinity as Witnessed by His Consciousness" (John 10:33), "The Doctrine of Christ's Divinity in the Writings of St. John" (I John 1:1–3), "Our Lord's Divinity as Taught by St. James, St. Peter, and St. Paul" (Gal. 2:9), "The Homoousion" (Titus 1:9), and "Consequences of the Doctrine of Our Lord's Divinity" (Rom. 8:32). It is also not coincidental that in preparing the lectures, one of the first things Liddon did was read George Eliot's 1846 translation of Strauss's *Leben Jesus,* the work that fourteen years earlier sought, like *Essays and Reviews,* to liberate Christianity from its historical moorings by presenting a solely histori-cal Jesus. Liddon's diary of 14 November 1865 chronicles his response: "Read some of Strauss's new Life of Jesus & felt wretched. His cold infidelity chills one's soul to the very core."[120] Of grave concern to the times, Liddon felt, a concern spawned by the Germanism at Oxford and exacerbated by *Essays and Reviews*, were issues surrounding the identity of Christ. Thus all eight lectures sought to challenge the prevailing spirit of Rationalism and Liberalism by addressing christological issues and assaults: the divinity of Christ, Arianism, Gnosticism, and the inspiration of Scripture. For example, Liddon's diary entry of 21 January 1866, at which time he was working on the fourth Bampton, notes: "Thought much about St. Paul on the doctrine of our Saviour's Godhead."[121] While the Bamptons afforded Liddon the opportunity to treat these issues comprehensively, his sermon preached around this time and his Sunday-evening lectures on Corinthians broached similar doctrinal concerns.

For example, on 21 February 1863 Liddon preached on 1 Corinthians 2 at Newbury Parish Church and on 5 March preached from the same text at All Saints in Margaret Street. The focus of the latter sermon, "The Victim–God," the third in a series of Lenten sermons, is on the divinity of Christ, regarded by Liddon as pivotal to the Christian faith. "The Doctrine of Our B[lessed] Lord's Divinity," he urges in that sermon, "is the centr[al] point of the X [Christian] Rev[elation]. It is the keystone of the ark of Revealed Truth—Unmove it, and the edifice crumbles into a shapeless ruin."[122] All six Lenten sermons at All Saints dealt with the divinity of Christ. The fourth was on "The Prophet on the Cross," the fifth on "The Priest on the Cross," and the sixth on "The King on the Cross." During this time he also preached on the "Sinlessness of Jesus" at St. Mary's in Stafford, and immediately after the Lenten sermons preached two other related sermons: "Effect of Christ's Presence," and "The Cross a Necessity." Similar christological concerns were taken up in his lectures on Corinthians.

For example, in 1 Corinthians 8, where Paul treats the controversy over the eating of meat offered to idols, Liddon argues that while Paul condones this dietary practice on the grounds that idols are nothing, he nevertheless warns the Corinthians against "resting on this superior enlightenment"; that is, he warns them against Gnosticism, estimating their higher knowledge of greater value than the frail conscience of some Christians. In this context we find Hopkins's first reference to "gnosis"—the "superior enlightenment" claimed by the Corinthians. The point Hopkins draws from the Pauline passage is that the choicest meat offered to idols that was now served in the dining halls of the "idolatrous temple," and "even before the offerings had been distributed about the town," demonstrates the length to which the Corinthians went in "contempt of the scruples of other Christians."[123] Liddon points to the sixth verse as "one of the passages shewing the co–equal divinity of Christ; proving Him (when compared with Col. 1:14–16) the creator and end of all things." This stance opposes Arianism, which relegates Christ to a mere tool or instrument and thus "subordinate of the Father. If approached in an Arian state of mind these passages read like Arianism," says Liddon, "but to a Catholic they present no real difficulty";[124] for this is "one of the passages," writes Hopkins, showing the "co–equal divinity of Christ; proving Him . . . the creator and end of all things, against the Arians who reduced Him to the [organ] and subordinate of the Father."[125] Arianism maintains that Christ is the first of the created beings, from whom other created beings generated. He may be called God, but not in the full sense of the term; for Christ had a beginning, and before that time he was nonexistent.

As in the Corinthians lectures, Liddon would again in the Bamptons argue for the Son possessing the same essence with the Father. Addressing Arianism to a crowded attendance at his first Bampton, Liddon points out that the doctrine claims that "Christ existed before His Incarnation, that by Him, as by an instrument, the Supreme God made the worlds, and that, as being the most ancient and the highest of created beings, He is to be worshipped." Thus, Christ "cannot therefore be called God in the sense in which that term is applied by Theists to the Supreme Being."[126] His argument, like the one waged in his lectures on Corinthians, is that while Arianism accepts a pre–existent being who through the Incarnation became Jesus, the doctrine "parts company with the Catholic belief, by asserting that this being is himself a creature, and not the very Substance of the Supreme God."[127] Liddon concludes that Arianism is essentially the halfway house between Catholicism and Humanitarianism.[128] Opposing Arianism, then, Liddon maintains that "As the Son of Man, then, our Lord is the Messiah," so Christ is "truly and perfectly Man" and "Very and Eternal God," and His divinity is "not to be thus emptied of its most solemn significance."[129] As if speaking directly to the positions on the Christology assumed in *Essays and Reviews*, Liddon employs a most remarkable image of Christ's body as a sacred fount to petition honest doubters to "probe the wounds with which from age to age error has lacerated Christ's sacred form, and thus to draw from a nearer contact with the Divine Redeemer the springs of a fresh and deathless faith, that shall win and own in Him to all eternity the unclouded Presence of its Lord and God."[130]

The second Bampton, "on the testimony of the O.T. to the Doctrine of O. L's Divinity," to use Liddon's own description, addresses skeptics like Jowett who questioned inspiration and the unity of the canonical books. While Liddon concedes the point that Scripture exhibits great variety, he yet maintains that careful probing will reveal "such manifest unity of drift and purpose, both moral and intellectual, as to imply the continuous action of a Single Mind."[131] This belief in the "organic oneness of Scripture" is held by the patristic writers, all of whom, Liddon finds, avowed that Scripture is "an harmonious and integral body of Sacred Truth."[132]

The fourth and fifth Bamptons touch slightly on other significant themes of the Corinthians lectures: the Resurrection and Gnosticism.[133] In the lectures on Corinthians, Liddon notes that "our bodies shall be raised as surely as Christ's was; they are members of Christ."[134] But in the fourth Bampton, he additionally considers the Resurrection the "central fact up to which all leads, and from which all radiates";[135] thus to deny its literalness in relationship to Christ is "nothing less than an absolute and total rejection of Christianity."[136] As to Gnosticism, Liddon calls it "as much a mischievous intellectual method as a formal heresy." With their insatiable desire for superior enlightenment, their hubris over *epignosis* (full knowledge), the Gnostics, like other rationalists, value revealed truth "merely in light of an addition to the existing stock of materials ready to his hand for speculative discussion."[137]

Liddon's most comprehensive treatment of the Christology occurs in the sixth Bampton. It looks to 2 Peter and finds that the "prominence given to the Person of Christ" in the doctrine of the *epignosis* "leads us up to the truth of His real Divinity." Here the Apostle does not merely "proclaim the Divinity of Jesus in formal terms; he everywhere feels and implies it."[138] Most of this Bampton lecture, however, deals with Pauline Christology: to what degree in the writings of Paul is Christ dealt with as God and as man. Liddon discovers that Paul's emphasis on the manhood of Christ is done chiefly for incarnational purposes, to present him as the instrumental link between heaven and earth. "There is no room in St. Paul's thought," says Liddon, "for an imaginary being like the Arian Christ."[139]

No other epistle deals more comprehensively with the divinity of Christ than does Colossians. In it Christ's divinity is presented as the very icon or imprint of the invisible, meaning that not only is Christ "derived eternally from the Father" but that "He is of One Substance with the Father."[140] The icon, says Liddon, is "indeed originally God's unbroken, unending reflection of Himself in Himself"; it is also the "Organ [instrument] whereby God, in His Essence invisible, reveals Himself to His creatures." He is not, in an Arian sense, "merely an inferior workman [organ] creating for the glory of a higher Master, for a God superior to Himself." Rather, in Christ dwells the *pleroma*, the full attribute of God. Thus the *icon* in Paul's writings is equivalent in rank and function to the *logos* in John's: "Each exists prior to creation; each is the one Agent in creation; each is a Divine Person; each is equal with God and shares His essential Life; each is really none other than God." Yet, says Liddon, Christ is "both personally distinct from, and yet literally equal to, Him of Whose Essence He is the adequate imprint." This unique relationship Christ shares with God is described in what is probably the most exquisite analogy in Liddon's entire Bampton lectures: "He is One with God as having streamed forth eternally from the Father's Essence, like a ray of light from the parent fire with which it is unbrokenly joined."[141] Hopkins draws a stunningly similar analogy in the poem "Thee, God, I come from," where he too describes his relationship to God using joint elements of water and fire:

> Thee, God, I come from, to thee go,
> All day long I like fountain flow
> From thy Land out swayed about
> Mote–like in thy mighty glow.

Hopkins also uses a similar analogy to describe the *pneuma*: "as the breath is drawn from the boundless air into the lungs and from the lungs again is breathed out and melts into the boundless air so the Spirit of God was poured out from the infinite God upon Christ's human nature."[142] As elsewhere explained in the Bampton: "The Word made Flesh is God condescending to our finite capacity; and this condescension has issued in a clear, strong sense of the Being and Attributes of God."[143]

Hopkins was particularly impressed with the seventh Bampton, delivered on 13 May. It contained, he felt, "the most beautiful sentence I ever remember hearing of Liddon's."[144] While Hopkins did not identify that sentence, three sentences from this Bampton seem likely candidates. The first finds the symbol an invaluable literary convention that preserves and conveys ultimate truth—an understanding of the symbol best articulated by Coleridge and what Geoffrey Hartman calls in Hopkins his "unmediated vision."[145] The passage from Liddon reads:

> In the Homoousion [Christ having the very essence of the
> father], after such hesitation as found expression at Antioch,
> the Church felt that she had lighted upon a symbol which was
> practically adequate to an expression of the truth which she
> had from the first possessed, and capable of resisting the
> intellectual solvents which had seemed to threaten that truth
> with extinction.[146]

Another passage appears just as likely, and it too emphasizes the importance of language: "It [the Homoousion] clothed the doctrine in a vesture of language which rendered it intelligible to a new world of thought while preserving its strict unchanging identity."[147] This passage, like the first, articulates what Hopkins expects from language: that words convey refreshingly novel ideas yet preserve their etymological ancestry. Yet a third passage from this seventh Bampton surfaces: "Doubtless the language addressed to Him in the Gospels represents many postures of the human soul, ranging between that utter self–prostration which we owe to the Most High, and that trustful familiarity with which we pour our joys and sorrows, our hopes and fears into the ear of a human friend."[148] The sentence is particularly striking because it describes the reconciliatory role of the tall nun in *The Wreck* (stanza 19) who "rears herself to Divine / Ears."[149] Four days after he had attended this Bampton, Hopkins made what seems his last confession to Liddon, but skipped out on his New Testament lecture that next Sunday. He chose, instead, to attend a Pusey university sermon at St. Mary's in the afternoon and then a walk to the Cumnor area of Arnold's "Scholar Gypsy" to listen to the syncopated calls of cuckoos, returning home late in the evening.

But Hopkins had not yet broken free of Liddon. The next day he walked to the Binsey area with Addis, who then walked with Liddon the following day, confiding to Liddon that Jowett was reading his (Liddon's) sermons and that Wood of Balliol was about to seek ordination. Hopkins again missed Liddon's next Sunday evening lecture. Two friends, Wood and Urquhart, had accompanied him to the ordination of William Awdry, another Balliol student, which took place at Cuddesdon; they returned that evening along the scenic route. Hopkins was, however, in attendance on 3 June 1866 at Liddon's last Bampton, which, though shortened, still lasted nearly two hours. The lecture sought to delineate the use and abuse of inferential reasoning. "Within certain limits, and under due guidance," says Liddon, inference is "the life of theology. The primal records of revelation itself as we find them in Scripture are continually inferential; and it is at least the business of theology to observe and marshall these revealed inferences, to draw them out, and to make the most of them." Liddon contends that theology is nothing more than a "continuous series of observed and systematized inferences . . . drawn from premises which rest upon God's authority,"[150] and "a living faith is pretty certain to draw inferences"; for "implanted in the soil of thought and feeling," it "cannot but bear its proper flower and fruit in the moral and intellectual life of a thoughtful and earnest man." What inference does, Liddon suggests, is to resituate language from a "too servile literalism" to the symbolic and metaphoric, which in turn yields "pregnant and momentary truths" from incidents that on the surface seem trite.[151]

Liddon obviously read John Henry Newman, whose notion of inferential reasoning is the kind of logic that leads to assent, a point Newman two years earlier asserted in the *Apologia Pro Vita Sua*.[152] So when Hopkins finally turned from Liddon to Newman and proposed writing a commentary on Newman's *Essay in Aid of a Grammar of Assent*, the arguments he found in Newman were already familiar to him. Liddon concludes this last Bampton and his divinity lectures by turning again to the Corinthian letters. He warns against sacrilege to the human body, for it houses the divine, in which case not only is the divinity of Christ denied, but the very "language which asserts the true incorporation of an Almighty Saviour with our frail humanity is resolved into the fantastic drapery of an empty metaphor." Liddon also warns against a pride that conflicts with conscience, reminders of the Corinthians who, failing to recognize the intrinsic evil of pride, "indulged it without scruple."[153] As to the divinity of Christ, Liddon reasserts its significance, calling it the "very heart of our Christian faith" and so "cannot be denied without tearing out the vitals of a living Christianity."[154]

Both the Corinthians and Bampton lectures, then, helped to shape Hopkins's Christology, for he found in Liddon, in the words of James Finn Cotter, "his own distinctive expression for his Christian insight"; and nowhere is this expression more clearly at work than in the "eucharistic and penitential themes" in Hopkins's early Oxford poems, themes that "draw from traditional imagery to express his personal effort to make contact with Christ."[155] Consequently, these Oxford poems might well be referred to as Hopkins's "authentic cadence . . . discovered late" and the "dominant of my range and state" ("Let me be to Thee"). Many of these early Oxford poems deal with christological themes. The poem "Pilate," for instance, deals with the dilemma this governor confronted in handling charges against Christ. Half–reluctant to sentence Christ to death, and fearing the likelihood of not being "ransom'd" from a sort of quasi–purgatorial, quasi–infernal, state, Pilate admits that the worst form of punishment is not hell but chilling exile from Christ. In an interesting reversal, Hopkins allows Pilate to fashion a last idea with which to vicariously crucify himself: "Thus crucified as I did crucify."

Another poem, "Barnfloor and Winepress," is built on 2 Kings 6 in which an Israelite requests the King's son as food for the famished. Unable to provide for his citizens sustenance from the barnfloor and winepress, the King, Ben–Hadad, surrenders his son who is subsequently cooked and eaten. This account presents a true picture of Christ as the communion host, "Sheaved in cruel bands, bruised sore, / Scourged upon the threashing–floor." In the morning, he became the "heavenly Bread." As the fruit of the vine, Christ is "fenced" with the stigmata ("Five ways the precious branches torn") and "racked from the press," only to become the "sweet Vintage of our Lord." His Resurrection plants us as vines where we become one with him, "sheaved . . . in His sheaf" and "grafted on His wood." The crucifixion theme continues in "New Readings," though with slight variation. Hopkins incorporates the parable of the sower to show, metaphorically, that only Christ can bring to fruition what was sown on infertile soil: Out of this supposed "wastes of rock" Christ can cause to bear "food for five thousand"; and from his own thorny head "Shed / Grains," rather than succumb either to the temptation of turning stone to bread or of allowing himself to be borne to heaven by angels "upon easeful wings." Christ, according to Hopkins, chose suffering and death rather than the bliss of translation.[156]

Yet another early Oxford poem deals with Christology, and here too the imagery is one of harvesting and the theme one of spiritual aridity. "He hath abolished the old drouth" (1864) assures the poet of being "sheaved with one band / In harvest and in garnering" and of the spiritual change from aridity ("drouth") to fertility ("rivers"). "Easter Communion" focuses on Lenten practices, whose reward more than compensates for the sacrifice: "o'er–brim the measures you have spent / With oil of gladness, for sackcloth and frieze / And the ever–fretting shirt of punishment." Its companion, "Easter," is an even more powerful poem. Its lively, even reckless, cadence calls not for Lenten restraint but for the jubilant excesses that celebrate new life. New perfume should be extravagantly spilt, the choicest wine hoarded should now flow for heavenly mirth, and we should reclothe ourselves as the earth discards its wintry robes and reclothes itself for Easter and spring:

> Beauty now for ashes were,
> Perfumes for the garb of woe,
> Chaplets for disshevelled hair,
> Dances for sad footsteps slow.[157]

In "Myself unholy," the poet recoils into himself by yielding to the "sultry siege of melancholy," an expression echoing Milton's "hateful siege / Of contraries." He finds that while his friends are not altogether blameless, yet he, in contrast, seems to possess every spiritual flaw, and his only salvation is in anti–selfconsciousness, to turn from self to none other "Save Christ." This spiritual eclipse persists in "My prayer must meet a brazen heaven." Consistent with nineteenth–century notions of an indifferent God, the poet's pleas cannot reach a seemingly unresponsive God. But the locus of this impasse to Hopkins is not the skepticism of the age, a view held by many of his fellow Victorians, but his own spiritual condition: "I cannot buoy my heart above," "I cannot entrance win," because of "the long success of sin." It is his heaven that remains "brass" and his earth that remains "iron." And because these elements comprise the very materials of his body, "praying fails to do away." Even tears, "beauty's veriest vein" that later in "Felix Randal" would be so instrumental in effecting change, melting a hardened self, here become ineffectual; they are merely idle. His prayer becomes a literal battle with God, a spiritual warfare that persists in "Nondum" and reappears later in "Carrion Comfort" and the dark sonnets that plague Hopkins's later years.

The personal spiritual condition confessed in "My prayers must meet a brazen heaven" is replaced in "Nondum" with a characterization of the spiritual condition of the age. Earth and the heavens still proclaim his existence, though not his presence; God himself remains hidden, his creation cold and indifferent. The one who dares confront the dilemma risks spiritual nausea and emptiness. Man's only option, it seems, is, like the Israelites faced with an absent Moses, to fashion his own god in his own likeness, a "shadow in Thy seat." But God remains silent even in the face of religious contentions and wars fought in behalf of truth, becomes, in its tearful richness, a mere "moaning voice among the reeds." Like Tennyson's insomniac infant whose pre–verbal response is a whimper, so too the speaker attempts to calm his "desponding sob" while walking "along life's tomb–decked way." But Hopkins does not succumb to nothingness. With patience, he continues to insist on a personal God who will in his time, either through some sign or symbol, "One word," disclose himself.

These poems written during Hopkins's early Oxford years (1863–66) show his beginning attraction to Christology fostered by Liddon. Granted, these poems, with the exception of "The Kind Betrothal" and "Nondum," do not exhibit the mastery of Hopkins's later christological and "winter world" poems. They do not, for instance, show the heroic exploits of Christ richly displayed in *The Wreck* and "The Windhover," the instressing of God in the creation and the sustaining ministry of the Holy Ghost in "God's Grandeur" and "The Starlight Night"; nor do they show the *pleroma* of Christ playing in "ten thousand places, / Lovely in limbs and lovely in eyes not his / To the Father through the features of men's faces." But these early poems meaningfully presage *The Wreck* and the poems that follow in which Hopkins's christological range finds its true manifestation.

Hopkins's Oxford was still experiencing the aftershocks of the Tractarian Movement. Droves of young undergraduates continued to flee from what to them seemed a theologically compromising Anglicanism into the relatively safe carapace of Roman Catholic theology. Read allegorically, then, the storms of

Hopkins's "Heaven–Haven" from which the speaker desires escape is a fighting symbol of the liberal climate of the 1860s. The wish to be "where no storms come" and "out of the swing of the sea" might well be theological. But in spite of the influence of Liddon's Christology on Hopkins and the intimacy of their relationship, Liddon could not keep Hopkins. Like Newman's before him, Hopkins's own *via media* was beginning to collapse, and his extremism too would find any halfway house in Anglicanism unacceptable.[158] His decision to convert was made on 16 July 1866, two months after he made his last confession to Liddon and one month after he attended Liddon's Bampton lectures: "It was this night I believe but possibly the next that I saw clearly the impossibility of staying in the Church of England, but resolved to say nothing to anyone till three months are over."[159] However, a week later, during a walk with Comyn Macfarlane, Hopkins divulged his intention. Macfarlane noted in his diary: "Walked out with Hopkins and he confided to me his fixed intention of going over to Rome." Hopkins regretted his impulsiveness in this untimely disclosure, for on that same day he noted in his journal: "Spoke to Macfarlane, foolishly."[160]

Now convinced about converting, Hopkins wrote to Newman on 28 August 1866: "I am anxious to become a Catholic." In the meantime, Hopkins's stipulated three–month's silence had elapsed; on 21 September, he wrote to his close friend Urquhart: "I thought what I said led but to one result, but you perhaps were prevented fr. seeing by thinking of me as an unusually exacting Anglican, and not, what by the mercy of God I am, a penitent waiting for admission to the Catholic Church." He implored Urquhart not to disclose his conversion until he was received. However, three days later Hopkins informed Urquhart that Macfarlane and Garrett knew of his conversion; also, "one of my brothers knows it; he forced it from me by questions. Dr. Newman of course and one or two other Catholics know, but no one else: Addis does not." He then added in a postscript:

> although my actual conversion was two months ago yet the
> silent conviction that I was to become a Catholic has been
> present to me for a year perhaps, as strongly, in spite of my
> resistance to it when it formed itself into words, as if I had
> already determined it.[161]

The timing here is consistent with Hopkins's 16 July admission. Dating his ideological conversion to Catholicism one year earlier than the actual step further confirms Liddon's role in the decision. But although many close acquaintances knew of Hopkins's conversion and subsequent reception, Liddon was not informed: "Challis I have not told, nor Mr. Liddon," Hopkins wrote to Urquhart on 4 October. "That is a deeply painful thought. I got no letter from him at Challis' conversion."[162]

Liddon was at Bristol when Challis converted, and wrote to Bright on 29 August 1866: "I have heard that Challis of Merton has become a R.C.–though on second hand authority. . . . I fear that a certain margin of such like disloyalties is a normal condition of the position of the English Church."[163] Challis's conversion had not shocked Liddon, who had a premonition of it a year earlier: "Walk with Challis to Littlemore. Talk about the Roman question all the time."[164] Had Hopkins known of this response of Liddon's to the conversion of Challis, an early protégé too of Liddon, he would have been less anxious about Liddon's reaction to his own conversion. In other words, this would have been the green light Hopkins sought. But left unsupported, Hopkins made a bold move. Two weeks later, Liddon learned of Hopkins's conversion from Coles. Liddon noted in his diary of Wednesday, 17 October: "A most distressing letter from Coles. He says that Addis of Balliol, Garrett of Balliol, & Wood of Trinity have just joined the Ch. of Rome and that Hopkins of Balliol is on the brink of following. Wrote to Hopkins & to Coles." Though Liddon was about to lose to Rome all of his most cherished intimates, he had all along felt that Oxford liberalism and Anglican compromises would not long hold his most zealous undergraduates. But in this affair, like so many others throughout Liddon's career in which he seemed to have weathered well his losses, he was unwilling to part with Hopkins without a fight.

In a 16 October 1866 letter to his father, Hopkins mentioned that he had heard from Liddon, in a letter written that same day, imploring him to delay. Because Liddon was not at Oxford at the time and would not be returning for a few days, Hopkins decided to appease his father by seeing Pusey, who was expected back in Oxford the next day. As to Bishop Wilberforce, Hopkins felt that he was "too much engaged to listen to individual difficulties." Pusey never sought to prevent Hopkins, nor for that matter other undergraduates, from defecting. His only letter to Hopkins, in which he uses the pejorative "pervert" (to describe Roman Catholic converts accused of moral deterioration), warns him that any who gain from his action "will be the unbelievers." All told, the letter is curt, formal, and defensive.[165] But Liddon felt it his religious obligation to deter as many undergraduates as possible from converting. For in spite of the problems with Anglicanism, he still felt that turning Romewards remained unacceptable.

Liddon's reputation of thwarting the conversion of students began when he was at Cuddesdon. Rev. Alfred Pott, Cuddesdon's first Principal, admitted that

Liddon's intimacy with his students made his influence far greater than his; and more successful than Liddon's "direct theological teaching" were his "chapel addresses and his private intercourse with individuals." For example, while at Cuddesdon Liddon unapologetically advised a potential dissenter "to avoid as a matter of conscience all intercourse with Roman Catholics,"[166] the same advice he would later give Hopkins regarding Newman. Another student, I. Arthur Mande, writing to Liddon on 24 September about leaving Cuddesdon for Roman Catholicism, was asked to submit to him the names of other students tending to Roman Catholicism, a request to which Mande did not comply.[167] Yet another Cuddesdon student whom Liddon had earlier sought to steer away from Roman Catholicism charged him, along with Pusey, with preventing students from "doing what their conscience tells them is the right thing, viz. to join the Catholic Church." The student expressed the hope that Liddon, whom he was told was once near to the Church, would someday also join. In reply, Liddon pointed out that his prayer was that he might live and die a "true son of the Church of England," and that he had always "endeavoured to look the Roman arguments in the face."[168]

The mere change from Cuddesdon to Oxford failed to quell Liddon's extensive reputation and influence. Residents of Oxford, as Bishop Talbot pointed out, considered Liddon a "summit to which they looked up."[169] And "in the reaction which is undoubtedly taking place against Liberal opinions among the younger students at Oxford," wrote Rev. C. Kegan Paul in the *Theological Review*,

> Mr. Liddon stands out by the common consent of all as the man who has had the greatest sway. He exercises a personal open influence such as had not been known at Oxford since the days when the Heads of Houses were alarmed because the undergraduates flocked in troops to attend Mr. Newman's lectures at St. Mary's. . . . What Newman was to the men of his time in his University, that is Mr. Liddon to those of the present.[170]

Although Liddon bristled at the comparison, calling it a most "ridiculous position by directly comparing me with a man of Dr. Newman's genius," and charging Paul with being "altogether misinformed as to the extent of my 'influence' among Oxford undergraduates," Paul's comparison was indeed fitting.[171] Liddon did not so much wish to have his influence at Oxford be compared to what Newman's was as to have it so openly proclaimed. His

legendary reputation among Oxford undergraduates led many parents to solicit
his help in dissuading their sons from turning Romewards. Rev. E.F. Sampson,
a friend and fellow student at Christ Church, recalled Liddon's personal contact
with a large number of people; "fathers and guardians, indeed, all who knew
Liddon, and some, I think, who did not, would write and ask him to be kind to
a youth in whom they were interested. . . . Where he found he could be really
useful, there was no trouble he would not take."[172] In fact, in one year alone
(1868), Liddon received six solicitations requesting his involvement in deter-
ring others from becoming Roman Catholics, none of whom was from Christ
Church where Liddon was in residence. It was not unusual, then, for the
distraught Manley Hopkins to turn to him on 15 October 1866 for similar
assistance: "Among those who listened to your Lectures & who were affected
by your influence in Oxford was my eldest son." Manley Hopkins told of having
heard from Gerard about his determination to become a Roman Catholic,
characterizing it as a blow "so deadly & great that we have not yet recovered
from the first shock of it." The elder Hopkins recalled Gerard's "growing love
for asceticism and high ritual," and implored Liddon to exert

> whatever of influence you may still possess over his mind,
> and his immature judgment . . . I earnestly desire that you
> would bring your influence & your great arguments to work
> on Gerard. That you would seek him out, before he takes any
> irrevocable step. . . . That you would disabuse him of the usual
> arguments & threats of Roman teaching, & save him from
> throwing a pure life and a somewhat unusual intellect in the
> cold limbo which Rome assigns to her English converts. The
> deepness of our distress, the shattering of our hopes & the
> foreseen estrangement which must happen, are my excuse for
> writing to you so freely & so pressingly.[173]

Five days later Manley Hopkins, still distressed, wrote thanking Liddon for his
assistance and requesting that he maintain the force of his intellectual arguments
on Gerard in order "to make our Wanderer return," here depicting Gerard as both
a Cain and prodigal son.[174]

At the time of Gerard's religious crisis and Manley Hopkins's annoyance,
Liddon was in Bristol preparing his Bamptons for publication. From there he
dispatched four letters to Gerard, the first written on 16 October and then one
letter for each of the next three days. In the first he urged hesitation, regretted
not being able to return to Oxford immediately, and, in the meantime, pointed

to belief in papal supremacy as the decisive Roman claim. He appealed to Hopkins on the basis of their "intimate friendship with each other." In the second letter, Liddon questioned Hopkins's motive for converting, convinced that it was solely on the basis of his "love & sympathy for Addis," who had himself just converted.[175] Liddon reminded Hopkins that the gravity of such a decision demands not sympathy but personal conviction, which he felt Hopkins did not possess because he had not taken the time to examine the issues. "I cannot tell you how earnestly I trust that Our Lord will keep you from making a very serious mistake indeed."[176] Liddon had apparently heard from Hopkins before firing off his third letter; in it he indicated that consulting first with a member of the Church of England would have been more prudent, that Newman was the most inappropriate person to have consulted in this matter, that delay was a "moral duty," and that he had heard from Manley Hopkins and "wish[ed] I could have told him that I thought you would listen to what I have to urge." He also hoped that Gerard had not visited Newman at Birmingham.[177] Receiving Hopkins's second letter, Liddon mailed his last on the morning of 20 October 1866. In it he pointed out that the Church of Rome is not the only true Catholic Church, that loyalty to an interpreting body of truth, which requires resigning oneself to acquiring truth "by the same process as his uneducated brother man who sweeps a crossing," asserting here intellectual elitism, is a most unwise theological position, and that going to Newman for advice on whether to become a Catholic is like going to his brother, the agnostic Francis, for advice on becoming a Deist.[178]

Liddon was also implored by Bright to do something practical about these conversions and about Hopkins's in particular. In a 17 October letter he asked Liddon to get hold of Hopkins "even at this last moment. . . . It is very deplorable. I cannot (as I told Urquhart) believe that Hopkins, for instance, has made himself competent, in so grave & complex a question, to affirm the Roman position. . . . I wish you wd. think practically of saying a word or two to our junior brethren . . . on their duties to the English Church."[179] Unable to return to Oxford immediately, Liddon wrote to Bright from Bristol on 19 October:

> I have written 4 letters successively to Hopkins, and one to his Father. The latter is of course in the greatest possible distress, naturally enough. I do not suppose that H. will yield: he seems to have quite made up his mind. He told me in his letter that "more conversions would follow." I have been trying to think who could possibly be meant but (with one exception) in vain. I hope on Monday to find out from Coles.[180]

Believing, as he once told Wilberforce, that "It is very difficult to deal with so intricate a thing as a human soul by letter,"[181] Liddon returned to Oxford on Monday, 22 October. That same day he had "A long talk with Coles about the present danger in Oxford."[182] As expected, Liddon was held responsible for the conversions. The earlier Cuddesdon experiences had come back to haunt him. One Metcalfe of Lincoln told Liddon on 26 October of having heard that he "had sent 3 men over to the Church of Rome." Two day later Liddon again notes another charge: "The Balliol Secenians had been entirely set down to my account—I 'looked like' a R. C. and all that sort of thing—Well it does not matter, & will be all the same 100 years hence."[183]

In a letter written to his mother on 20 October, Hopkins acknowledged Liddon's efforts but felt that both Liddon and Pusey were "intellectually inconsistent" in not being Catholics,[184] a view Newman also shared regarding Pusey. It was primarily for this reason that Liddon failed to dissuade Hopkins, and obviously could not have done so had he himself converted. In other words, Hopkins's complaint was that either Liddon should have championed vigorously the High Anglican cause or else should have himself converted. Any *via media* position, Hopkins felt, was unthinkable, if not downright dishonest. Providing some rationale for Hopkins's decision, Keating suggests that had his "vision been less unclouded, or his purpose less sincere," Hopkins "might well have found in Liddon's advice a reasonable ground for holding back."[185] However, not discovering such grounds, Hopkins could not be deterred. The next day he went up to Birmingham and was received by Newman.

But Hopkins felt he had left many things unsaid in his haste toward Rome. Thus, on 7 November 1866, at which time he was a Catholic for some two weeks, Hopkins wrote his longest letter to Liddon. He thanked Liddon for his efforts to prevent his reception, albeit unsuccessful, admitting that he had already committed himself to the decision—the precise point, we might recall, Pusey had raised. Most of the letter argues that the Anglican Church is not part of the Church of Rome. Hopkins also defended himself against the charge of impulsiveness, claiming that since the hold that the Church of England had on him for twenty years involved only a few of its clergy, the claims of the Catholic Church, weightier by far, made any delay unnecessary. He reminded Liddon that his conversion was only sudden because at last he consented to "answer simple questions," to "say yes," as in *The Wreck*.[186] Hopkins's apologetics, his own discourse on assent, sound very much like Newman's.

Following this exchange, Liddon and Hopkins did not communicate for eight months. Their correspondence did not resume until early July 1867. The Bampton lectures were published, and Liddon proposed to Dodgson that they take a trip to Russia. On Wednesday, 10 July, he journeyed to Dover to await Dodgson who was late in arriving. The delay afforded Liddon time to write four letters, one of which was his last to Hopkins. Hopkins, then on a two–week tour of Paris, received Liddon's letter when he returned and also had news from Coles on the tragic death of Digby Dolben, a close friend of Hopkins's and cousin to Bridges. Hopkins did not reply to the Liddon letter until he presumed Liddon had returned from Russia. While awaiting a teaching position beginning 10 October at Newman's Oratory, Hopkins spent the ensuing months visiting relatives and friends and sightseeing at museums and exhibitions.

On 26 August 1867, when he did not receive an expected letter of invitation to join Walter Pater at Sidmouth, Hopkins took the opportunity to visit his friend Urquhart, who was at that time curate at a church in Bovey Trace. From there, on 3 September 1867, he replied to Liddon's letter, believing that by this time he would have returned from Russia. Hopkins expressed regret over not seeing Liddon the last time he, Hopkins, was at Oxford, presumably when he returned to Oxford in Trinity Term 1867 to take his degree; he promised that "I shall take the opportunity, if I may, the next time I am in Oxford."[187] Hopkins then left Bovey Trace for the Oratory, returning briefly to Oxford on 16 September "to fetch my things and back again."[188] It is not known whether Hopkins attempted to see Liddon, who in fact had returned from Russia two days earlier.

On 15 April 1868, Hopkins left the Oratory for a retreat at Roehampton where he would later enter his novitiate. He returned home from the retreat on 7 May, deciding then to join the Jesuits. Three weeks later he made a trip to Oxford to pick up his degree. While there he made several attempts, all unsuccessful, to see Liddon, who was at that time considering the headmastership of Keble College. In fact, Liddon was seldom at Oxford from mid–1868 to all of 1869, coming up only for meetings of the Hebdomadal Council of the university and for his Sunday evening lectures. For part of that time, too, he was with his sister in Europe, and quite often was either in Salisbury or Clifton caring for the ailing Bishop Hamilton, his "Father in Christ," and his own natural father. Hopkins wished he had informed Liddon earlier of his intended visit and regretted that he and Liddon may "never meet again." Thus he wrote: "I must now make my farewell by writing." Hopkins informed Liddon of a planned tour of Switzerland, following which he was to enter his novitiate. "I do not think there is another prospect so bright in the world," Hopkins wrote optimistically, and concluded: "With all the best wishes believe me, dear Mr. Liddon, ever affectionately yours."[189] Hopkins's conjecture proved accurate, for he never saw Liddon again. Thus, this 5 June 1868 letter, written when Liddon was in Salisbury and did not acknowledge receiving it, marked Hopkins's last contact with Liddon; the "national old Egyptian reed" finally "gave way" to the "cross–barred rod or rood."[190] On 3 July Hopkins left for Switzerland, accompanied by Edward Bond, returned home on 1 August, and set off on 7 September for his novitiate at Roehampton.

A decade later Hopkins returned to Oxford as priest at St. Aloysius, the unpretentious parish church on Woodstock Road where a font donated by his friends, the Paravicinis, memorializes him. During Hopkins's year there (from December 1878 to September 1879), Liddon was officially still at Oxford. However, most of his time was spent either at St. Paul's, Hatfield, or Longleat, coming to Oxford only for his Professorial Lectures. And when he was there, most of the time was taken up caring for the ailing Pusey. Neither he nor Hopkins sought each other out, and understandably so, for they had long severed all relational ties and were singularly preoccupied with their religious duties.

Yet Liddon's formative influence on Hopkins's religious life and poetry cannot be underestimated. His formal and informal lectures informed Hopkins's Christology, and he personally created the religious climate in which Hopkins's fledgling Catholicity took wing and flight. Liddon was the first to mount a formal attack on the Liberalism of the 1860s that Tractarianism had failed to eradicate, and the personal care he gave to Oxford undergraduates remains a testimony to the warmth and charm of his personality. Why so profound an influence on Hopkins, Oxford undergraduates, and nineteenth–century religious life has for so long gone unexplored is enigmatic. No doubt the chief contributing factor, at least regarding Hopkins, is the excessive attention to his Jesuit life, a preoccupation that often slights significant literary and religious precursors.

Chapter 2

The Comfortable Gloom: Hopkins, Newman, and the Shattering of the Via Media

The move from Liddon to Newman was to Hopkins one from obscurity to notoriety. However invaluable an influence Liddon had on Oxford undergraduates and on Hopkins in particular, it was Newman who most gave direction to that life and stirred in it the achievement of poetry. Critics have generally acknowledged Newman's reception of Hopkins and have credited him with initiating Hopkins's teaching career at the invitation to join the staff at the Birmingham Oratory. But the degree to which Newman influenced Hopkins is insufficiently chronicled. Little has been written, for example, on the legacy of Tractarianism in Hopkins's poetry, on the religious and temperamental affinities between Newman and Hopkins, and on Newman's role in guiding Hopkins's career.

First to have identified the extent and fecundity of that relationship was Joseph Keating. Citing the few letters available to him, Keating recognized, albeit cursorily, Newman's role in Hopkins's reception and the friendship that ensued. "What strikes one in Father Hopkins's dealings with Newman," Keating discovered, is the "spirit of sacrifice that could deliberately part fellowship with a man who must . . . have satisfied every exigency, intellectual and moral, of the young convert's being, to follow the obscure and humble career of a Jesuit."[1] By 1930, before Hopkins's letters were released but with access to them, G.F. Lahey also examined the relationship. He pointed to Newman's "refined sensibilities and exquisite delicacy" and felt he was Hopkins's "ablest guide." In his second contact with Bridges on 4 February 1929 regarding his (Lahey's) discovery of Newman's letters to Hopkins, Lahey pointed out that withholding these letters from publication "seems to me intolerable, and contrary to the principles of scrupulous and painstaking biography." Hopkins's next biographer, John Pick, armed with even more letters, provided then the most satisfactory assessment of the relationship with Newman and surveyed the religious milieu of 1860 Oxford.[2]

The most recent biographies, Robert Martin's *Gerard Manley Hopkins: A Very Private Life* (1991) and Norman White's *Hopkins: A Literary Biography* (1992), both acknowledge the Newman connection. Martin's calls Newman Hopkins's "model" and "arbiter" and feels that "time after time Hopkins seems to have been deliberately stepping like a dutiful child in Newman's tracks." While Jowett and Liddon were both "temporary father figures for him," it was Newman whose "influence persisted" and it was he on whom Hopkins finally settled on as a "surrogate father," sharing with him a "striking similarity in the paths they chose, of which Hopkins must have been aware."[3] But as usefully as Martin's biography advances the relationship, his is not a critical biography, and so ignores the meaningful literary relationships between Hopkins and Newman. In his review of Martin's biography for the *Washington Post*, Ian Ker remarks that Hopkins, like his religious mentor Newman, was a "quintessentially Victorian figure," though his poetry, like Newman's, "strikes a very contemporary chord. His life resembles Newman's, too, in that both became Catholic priests, both were happier humanly–speaking as Anglicans, and both were written off as failures in their Catholic lives." And that failure is poeticized by Hopkins when he so often echoes Newman.[4] For all that Ker claims here, he all but neglects Hopkins in his recent biography of Newman. He refers only to Newman's reception of Hopkins, Hopkins's informing Newman of his decision to join the Jesuits, Hopkins's request to do a commentary on the *Grammar of Assent*, and Newman's warning to Hopkins to liberalize his stance against Home Rule for Ireland.

Norman White's biography, while critical in approach, still points only obliquely to the relationship and indirectly to Newman as Hopkins's "mentor." Not entirely convinced of the relationship, White feels that Hopkins had achieved "a kind of friendship with Newman." Still White believes that "Hopkins, of course, had been exactly the type of convert Newman had hoped to catch." More to the point, White insists that Newman had "never been the naive imperialist that Hopkins was, nor an advocate of neo–Gothic," and that though sharing similar background in the professional classes and similar parental reaction to their conversions, both emerged dissimilarly out of their conversion: "Newman had a stubborn resistance to hard blows, while Hopkins was more cloistered in training, and less resilient."[5]

Another critic on the relationship, H.L. Weatherby, assumes an even more skeptical stance. He speculates that "one would have expected critics to have sought and found Newman's mark on the work of Hopkins," bearing in mind that the "search for, and discovery of, his influence on a modern Christian literature would seem a likely scholarly venture." But, Weatherby warns, mostly to argue his case for Newman's liberalism, that the fact that Newman shared so many of the liberal philosophical presuppositions of his contemporaries in turn isolated him from the poets following him whom he might have influenced and in whom can be found a medieval rather than a Victorian epistemology. Such is the case with Hopkins, says Weatherby. And while there is a certain sense in which "Hopkins could be said to owe both his religion and his poetry to Newman's influence," Hopkins, in fact, "learned his theology from Scotus, not from Newman"; furthermore, "both as theologian and as poet Hopkins embraced the Scholastic metaphysics of which Newman remained sceptical and surprisingly ignorant."[6]

These attempts to assess the relationship between Newman and Hopkins, although helpful in drawing our attention to its pertinence, have yet failed to present a clear picture of how profound an influence Newman had on Hopkins; "the life–long impression left on the younger man's mind and art by the books of Newman," Michael D. Moore observes, remains "a circumstance of literary history that deserves to be better known."[7] Though mere sketches, it was in fact the early biographies, not the most recent ones, that paid substantial attention to the Newman–Hopkins relationship. Still unfamiliar are the shaping effects of late Tractarianism on Hopkins's religious and poetic life; why it was that Hopkins relinquished the Anglo–Catholicism of Liddon and Pusey and the Broad Church leanings of Jowett for Newman's Roman Catholicism; Newman's direct and often recondite influence on Hopkins; their intimate and enduring friendship in spite of their infrequent communication (annually after 1868); and Newman's sustained influence on Hopkins's post–conversion religious, literary, and poetic development.

Hopkins matriculated at Oxford eighteen years after Newman's secession from Anglicanism. However, the aftershocks of Newmania were still being felt. Coming up from Harrow to Balliol in 1858, and graduating the term before Hopkins matriculated, John Addington Symonds was so struck by the ritualistic climate still at Oxford that he concluded sardonically: "I had thought the Tractarian humbug had died, and given way to philosophical cant of infidelity; but it seems that the very dregs and offscoring of Oxford youth still rock themselves upon this nonsense."[8] According to Raymond Chapman, "The fever did not abate until the century was nearly over."[9] Young Oxford undergraduates were still defecting to Roman Catholicism in as many numbers as during the Movement's heyday. Writing to Newman in 1866 about this exodus and of his planned reception, Hopkins confessed, "All our minds you see were ready to go at a touch," and "it cannot but be that the same is the case with many here." Later identifying the grounds for his conversion, Hopkins pointed, understandably, to his "increasing knowledge of the Catholic system (at first under the form of Tractarianism)."[10]

Eventually to be called the "Crashaw of the Oxford Movement" and the "Tractarian poet turned Jesuit,"[11] Hopkins perceived Anglicanism as powerless to counteract Oxford's religious skepticism, the same ineptness Newman earlier held accountable for so many conversions: "Catholics did not make us Catholics; Oxford made us Catholics."[12] Newman again urged this point in the *Apologia* when he claimed that he was driven out of Oxford by liberals. One former Balliol student and friend of Hopkins, the conspicuous Martin Geldart, recalled that religion was a topic on which he and Hopkins frequently conversed. "He was quite at one with me on the hollowness of Protestant orthodoxy, but he had a simple remedy—the authority of the Church. The right of private judgment must in the long–run inevitably lead to Rationalism."[13] Hopkins admitted as much to Liddon: "Now there is only one thing which can suspend the free use of reason . . . and that is the infallible authority of the Church."[14] These responses to rationalism parallel Newman's: "He gradually came to see in the Catholic church the one hope for withstanding a movement towards unbelief which threatened to be little less than a devastating flood," wrote Wilfrid Ward. Ward also felt that to Newman the Catholic Church was "a living power specially adapted to resist the excesses of Rationalism—the errors to which the human reason is liable if left to itself,"[15] as Newman was to express in *Certain Difficulties Felt by Anglicans*: "It is the Church's dogmatic use of History in which the Catholic believes; and she uses other informants also, Scripture, tradition, the ecclesiastical sense of [*phronema*, i.e. judgment, tied to the Illative Sense], and a subtle ratiocinative power, which in its origin is a divine gift."[16] Here Newman advocated not the sole exercise of reason but its synergetic partnership with other agents, notable among them Tradition, the position of Antiquity, which does not entertain diverse and contradictory opinions. He again wrote in an essay in *Certain Difficulties* on the matter of Church authority and private judgment:

> as Catholics consider that the truth is brought home to the
> soul supernaturally, so that the soul sees it and no longer
> depends on reason, so in some parallel way it was sup-
> posed, in the theology of the movement [Tractarian], that
> same truth, as contained in the Fathers, was a natural fact,
> recognised by the natural and ordinary intelligence of

mankind, as soon as that intelligence was directed towards
it.[17]

But although Hopkins inherited, mostly through Liddon, this sense of Tradition
and many other Tractarian legacies (ritualism, asceticism, fasting) championed
by Newman, he was yet to meet him.

Hopkins first referred to Newman a few days after he arrived at Oxford.
Reenacting a pilgrimage made earlier by Tractarian disciples of Newman,
Hopkins had visited Littlemore Church, the village (now officially a suburb) and
church three miles southeast of central Oxford, Newman's home after he
resigned the vicarage of St. Mary's and the site of his September 1843 Anglican
valedictory sermon, "The Parting of Friends." Hopkins was charmed by the
church's medieval features and atmosphere, which the Romantics and Scott had
earlier revived interest in and with which the Tractarians too became fond. The
medieval look was apparently not there during Newman's time, but was a
feature of later renovations, Norman White found. White was led to conclude,
a conclusion that on first blush appears reasonable, that "Whatever other
sympathies Hopkins had with Newman, they did not share aesthetic tastes."[18] "I
walked with Addis to Littlemore Church which Newman's mother built,"
Hopkins told his mother, "and where was Newman's last sermon before his
exodus."[19] Hopkins's information was not entirely correct. Although much
involved with Littlemore, Newman's mother did not in fact build the church.
Oriel donated the land, and Newman, assisted immeasurably by his mother and
sister Jemina, whose effort is memorialized on a plaque on the right wall,
solicited contributions from friends and acquaintances. A generous gift from the
Building Society of St. Clements Church saw the completion of the building.
Work on the church began on 15 July 1835, and Newman's mother, now living
at Rose Hill, on the outskirts of Oxford near Iffley, laid the first stone on
Tuesday, 21 July. Newman did seek his mother's advice in selecting the
appropriate corner of the building for a schoolroom.

Hopkins next referred to Newman on 10 September 1864. Detailing his
partial thoughts on an essay for the Hexameron, Hopkins drew a distinction
between extreme and moderate persons. He expressed an animus toward
religious extremism and regarded Newman "the extremest of the extreme, so
extreme that he went beyond the extremes of that standard and took a large
faction of his side with him"; but, in somewhat of a contradiction, Hopkins also
believed Newman a "MODERATE MAN."[20] Hopkins was apparently pointing
not so much to Newman's personality as to his controversialist reputation,
formed from the apologetic genre in which he seemed always to be working.

Newman's rhetorical and satirical brilliance, mixed, ironically, with a personality that courted approval and was sensitive to blame, has caused Ian Ker to call him a "consummate controversialist," and J. Cameron a "controversialist of superb gifts, perhaps the most remarkable in the history of English letters."[21]

Although Hopkins's correspondence provides no clues that he was then reading Newman, which would have explained his assessment, he was apparently becoming familiar with Newman through the *Apologia Pro Vita Sua*, published in 1864 and read extensively at Oxford. Somewhat surprisingly, nowhere in his correspondence and diary does Hopkins note this work. Newman's spiritual autobiography, the gradual process to and reasons for his conversion detailed in the *Apologia*, would certainly have intrigued Hopkins whose own conversion, sudden though it seemed, in fact underwent a similar lingering out sweet skill. But while he admitted fondness for Milton, Tennyson, Christina Rossetti, the Pre–Raphaelites, Keats, and Wordsworth, among others, Hopkins was relatively silent on Newman, admitting only some misgivings on Newman's prose style and admiration for the *Grammar of Assent*. Yet Newman's influence on Hopkins remains so pervasive that it is difficult to "exaggerate," as W.H. Gardner points out, "the influence exerted during these critical years by the example and published works of Dr. Newman."[22] Hopkins no doubt read Newman's *Lyra Apostolica* (1836) and *Loss and Gain: The Story of a Convert* (1848), discovering, quite possibly in Charles Reding a useful religious model of one who would "gain by becoming a Catholic"; and Hopkins must have been more than just casually acquainted with *Idea of a University* (1852), the compilation of lectures delivered to the faculty of the very university he would later join. Moreover, the many echoes of Newman's *The Dream of Gerontius* (1865) in Hopkins's poems, in particular the Dublin ones, corroborate his knowledge of that work. We know for certain that he read *Discourses Addressed to Mixed Congregations* (1849), *Certain Difficulties Felt by Anglicans* (1850), and *An Essay in Aid of a Grammar of Assent* (1870).

Hopkins's 1865 listing of Oxford poets does include Keble and Newman. But he withheld any reference to a work of Newman's until later that year, on 10 October, when he copied in full "Lead, Kindly Light," a poem in which Newman, like the wandering Israelites, sought guidance from the pillar of the cloud.[23] Two days earlier, on Sunday, Hopkins confessed being inattentive in church, laughing at the sermon, and "Repeated forecasting about the Ch[urch] of Rome. Talking about Dr. Newman at dinner etc in a foolish way likely to produce unhappiness and harm."[24] This is the first clue we have of the beginning of Hopkins's movement to Rome and of Newman's profound impact on that decision. Written at sea on 16 July 1833, "Lead, Kindly Light," like *The Dream of Gerontius* and so many other Newman poems, gestated from physical suffering. Consequently, the poem reflects what Ward calls "the sense of human frailty and sinfulness . . . accompanied by a self–abandoning trust in God."[25] About the time of Hopkins's transcription of this poem, he had himself written three related poems, all speaking to his current poetic and religious stance. One, "Trees by their yield," expresses the same spiritual aridity ("My sap is sealed, / My root is dry") and self–worthlessness ("I none can shew") that generated "Lead, Kindly Light," feelings that would later reappear in Hopkins's Dublin sonnets. Hopkins ended the poem, if indeed he ended it, with an inconclusiveness that marks his current half–way religious posture:

> Will no one show
> I argued ill?
> Because, although
> Self-sentenced, still
> I keep my trust.
> If He would prove
> And search me through
> Would He not find
> (What yet there must
> Be hid behind

> [. . . .]

After copying "Lead, Kindly Light," Hopkins composed the sonnet "Let me be to Thee as the circling bird." Both poems employ the bird motif. Hopkins's "the circling bird" recalls Newman's "encircling gloom," and both poems (especially Newman's) echo Keats's "Ode to a Nightingale": in the time of day (Hopkins's "half–light," Newman's "The night is dark" and the inability to "see my path"); in the desired imaginative escape from the fretful world (Hopkins's "departing rings," Newman's "O'er moor and fen, o'er crag and torrent"); and in the context of irretrievable time (Hopkins's "authentic cadence . . . discovered late," Newman's "remember not past years"). Additional similarities between Hopkins and Newman can be found in "To. F.W.N.," Newman's birthday poem to his brother Francis. The lines "Must buckle on thy sword; / A high employ, nor lightly given, / To serve as messengers of heaven!" clearly anticipate Hopkins's "Buckle" and images of "minion" and chivalry in "The Windhover."

That Hopkins was currently undergoing intensive spiritual inventory, even contemplating secession from Anglicanism, is evident in these early poems and in a diary notation on Provost Fortescue: "If ever I should leave the English Church the fact of Provost Fortescue . . . is to be got over," he reminded himself.[26] Like Provost Fortescue, Hopkins apparently felt that it was conceivable to remain within the Church of England (as both Liddon and Pusey advised him) while still worshiping as a Catholic. This temporary religious halfway house is masked in certain lines from "Let me be to Thee":

> And every praised sequence of sweet strings,
> And know infallibly which I preferred.
> The authentic cadence was discovered late
> Which ends those only strains that I approve
> And other science all gone out of date.

Following this poem Hopkins wrote "The Half–way House." The poem again admits Hopkins's religious ambivalence between Anglicanism and Roman Catholicism and reveals the continuing influence of Newman on his religious and poetic development. Taken, it would appear, from the *Apologia*, the poem's title addresses Newman's two alternatives: Romism or Atheism. Newman saw Anglicanism as the halfway house to Romism and Liberalism the halfway house to Atheism.[27] Hopkins's Anglicanism, his own "Half–way House" to Rome, camouflaged as his "national old Egyptian reed," eventually "gave way" to Roman Catholicism, his "cross–barred rod or rood." A year later he told his father of having seen the "Tractarian ground . . . broken to pieces under my feet."[28]

"A soliloquy of one of the spies left in the wilderness" (1864), a poem on spiritual indecision, was the earliest poetic clue to Hopkins's exodus from Anglicanism and so should be read autobiographically. The poem opens with expression of abhorrence for conditions in the wilderness, for the bland diet of manna and quails, and for the glare and dust from the sun and sand. The speaker's mind returns to the opulence of Egypt, symbolic of both Anglicanism and Oxford, "the valley of our pleasaunce." Both Anglicanism and Oxford offered Hopkins an epicurean garden, ideologically distinct from the seclusion requested in the poem "Heaven–Haven."[29] Here in the "comfortable gloom," a relative paradise of Lower Egypt where "Goshen is green and fair" and where the "Wasteful wide huge–girthed Nile / Shall cool our shoulders and unbake our flesh. / Unbakes my pores, and streams, and makes all fresh," the speaker, like Ulysses, is able to "gather points of lote–flower from an isle / Of leaves of greenest flesh," and, in a sensuousness akin to Keats's, to languish "In beds, in gardens, in thick plots . . . / Handle the fig, suck the full–sapp'd vine–shoot." Here in Egypt, the speaker can binge on the epicurean comforts of food, music, and mirth, where all thoughts of the resurrection ("waking trumpet") and the temporariness of the Christian's earthly pilgrimage are easily disremembered. The expression "Here are sweet messes without price or worth" echoes the price–less and worth–less (intended obviously as a pun) sensuousness of Christina Rossetti's "Goblin Market." Hopkins obviously intends a double–entendre. To the sensuous mind these pleasures are invaluable; but to the ascetic they are valueless. Not only did Hopkins see himself in this soliloquy as the spy, supposedly for Liddon on Jowett, but he expressed reluctance to leave the familiar Anglicanism with its narcotic and lethargic sensuousness for the ascesis that Canaan or Roman Catholicism offers: "Go then: I am contented here to lie . . . / Sure, this is Nile: I sicken, I know not why, / And faint as tho' to die."

The reference to Provost Fortescue in Hopkins's diary anticipated two poems written sometime in December 1865. The short lyric, "Moonless dark-ness stands between," is a Yuletide poem. Between Hopkins's past and future is the darkness of some spiritual eclipse, one not unlike that of his persona in *The Wreck* who finds "The frown of his face / Before me, the hurtle of hell / Behind." Seeking safe haven, Hopkins's heart, like the windhover, fled to the "heart of the Host." But the line "Past, the Past, no more be seen" of "Moonless darkness" appears an adieu not simply to the old year but also to the old faith; and the request to be led by the light to "the sight of Him who freed me / From the self that I have been" prefigures some sort of religious conversion and again echoes Newman's "Lead, Kindly Light." The expression also points to *The Wreck* where the poet's own conversion is again poeticized in images of light: "To flash from the flame [presumably of hell] to the flame" (presumably of the Holy Ghost). "The earth and heaven, so little known," companion to "Moonless darkness," and consistent with the late nineteenth–century sensitivity to change ("The unchanging register of change") and flux ("Nor permanence in the solid world"), ends on a note altogether religious: "O lovely ease in change of place! / I have desired, desired to pass." To the poet, the move from a high church Anglicanism to Anglo Catholicism seemed not all drastic.

But although he was about to adopt Newman's injunction in "Lead, Kindly Light"—"remember not past years"—thus rejecting an earlier reluctance to change expressed in "A soliloquy of one of the spies left in the wilderness," Hopkins had not yet passed. The poem "Nondum" ("Not yet") masks that imminent conversion. The darkness in the poem, analogous to the experience of the prophet Isaiah, recalls a similar darkness in "Lead, Kindly Light." But while

Newman's poem affirms God's presence, Hopkins's entertains his transcendence, even his imperceptibility. "Nondum" also echoes the existentialism found in the *Apologia*.[30] Embracing a sacramental vision of the world—"that material phenomena are both the types and the instruments of real things unseen," that "the exterior world, physical and historical, was but the manifestation to our senses of realities greater than itself," and that the Holy Church is "but a symbol of those heavenly facts which fill eternity" and her mysteries "expressions in human language of truths to which the human mind is unequal"—Newman is disheartened when he turns from himself to find in the world of nature some analogue of the sublime, something there far more deeply interfused.[31] To his consternation he encounters a universe unable to appreciate "that great truth of which my being is so full." Like Augustine, who seeks God in the creation, only to be rebuffed, and must then turn to a higher creation, the self, so Newman too must turn existentially to himself for that authentication of the divine: "If I looked into a mirror, and did not see my face, I should have the sort of feeling which actually comes upon me, when I look into this living busy world, and see no reflection of its Creator." He proceeds with a long list of man's achievements and slippages, concluding that "all this is a vision to dizzy and appal." This proves, Newman reasoned, that "either there is no Creator, or this living society of men is in a true sense discarded from his presence."[32] Newman's idea of an absent or imperceptible Creator, presented contrariwise in his poem "Desolation" ("O, SAY not thou art left of God, / Because His tokens in the sky / Thou canst not read"), is appropriated in the first two stanzas of "Nondum." The desperate pleas of Hopkins's diligent searcher are met with deafening silence and a cool reception: "No answering voice comes from the skies," "no forgiving voice replies," and "Vacant creation's lamps appal." Hopkins's "As kingfishers catch fire," however, bridges the fissure between God and the creation. The variegated creation first "speaks and spells" itself: kingfishers self-ignite, dragonflies attract flame, stones ring, and every tucked string or bow gives out a distinctive sound. But to the degree that the creation declaims its true self, what Hopkins called its own "tankard," as, for instance, when it "Acts in God's eye what in God's eye [it] is" or the architect "Who built these walls made known / The music of his mind," it illustrates Christ. In other words, the creation chimes christologically when it chimes univocally.

By February 1866, Hopkins was on the threshold of a conversion bearing some similarities to Newman's, crossing it on 17 July and keeping it undisclosed for a time. On 20 June 1866 (not 1865 as Addis or Lahey alleged), Hopkins and Addis walked to the Benedictine Monastery at Belmont. There the two met Canon Raynal, the first Catholic priest with whom Hopkins ever spoke, according to Addis. So moved were they by Raynal that Addis marked that event as the "time our faith in Anglicanism was really gone."[33] Because Hopkins felt it hypocritical to worship and observe the Sacraments in a church in which he no longer believed, the only place open to him was the little chapel of St. Ignatius where Newman himself on two critical occasions, immediately after he seceded to Roman Catholicism and just before he left Oxford for good, attended Mass. In visiting the chapel after his own secession, Hopkins was indicating, according to Robert Martin, just "how closely he followed in the footsteps of Newman."[34] The pressure on Hopkins to join the Catholic Church mounted, although Liddon, Pusey, and Manley Hopkins all tried to diffuse it, when Addis and Henry Challis converted.[35] Two other close friends, Alfred Garrett and Alexander Wood, had also joined the Church before Hopkins did, although their conversion, Hopkins was quick to remind his father, was later than his. Newman himself had earlier gone through a similar experience, one bordering, he felt, on timidity. He had planned to write *Essay on the Development of Christian Doctrine*, the "theological counterpart of the *Origin of Species*,"[36] because of its extensive use of biblical analogy with biological evolution, and had decided to wait until its publication before taking that inevitable step. But Newman decided against waiting, claiming too that "the departure of others [Dalgairns, Stanton, St. John, and Christie] had something to do with it, for when they went, it was as if I were losing my bowels."[37] Jowett noted Hopkins's conversion in an October 1866 letter to Florence Nightingale: "You may have seen in the newspapers, perhaps, that three foolish fellows [presumably Hopkins, Addis, and Garrett] at our College & three at other Colleges have gone over to Rome."[38]

When Hopkins did reveal his conversion, he wrote his first of some thirty letters to Newman confessing his anxiety to become a Catholic.[39] Newman was then on a one–month holiday in Switzerland (from 30 July to 6 September) with Ambrose St. John, and did not reply to Hopkins's letter until 14 September. He regretted the delay and expressed a desire to accommodate Hopkins: "I will gladly see you as you propose, if you will fix a day." How often the two communicated between 14 September and 15 October remains unknown. That Hopkins met Newman for the first time on 21 September is certain, for in a letter to William Urquhart he told of having "today seen Dr. Newman, whose advice I wanted about my immediate duty," and the following day described Newman to Bridges as "most kind . . . genial and almost, so to speak, unserious."[40]

Newman's amiable temperament is well documented. The historian James Froude remembered him having "a most attaching gentleness, sweetness, singleness of heart and purpose. . . . I had then never seen so impressive a person."[41] R.W. Church recalled that Newman "was accessible; he allowed his friends to bring their friends to him, and met them more than *half–way* [italics mine]. . . . He was very patient with those whom he believed to sympathise with what was nearest his heart."[42] Converts turning Romeward stirred Newman's heart. Not surprising, then, Hopkins felt a special kinship to him; and the attraction he no longer found in Liddon and Pusey he rediscovered in Newman.[43] What Hopkins saw in Newman, writes James Cotter, was a man possessing the "kind of sanctity and scholarship he emulated," and one in whom "nature and grace, culture and discipline, suffering and peace fused in a personal, intimate union with Christ."[44]

Hopkins paid a clandestine visit to the Oratory on 27 September 1866 to make final preparations for his reception. The visit was important enough to Newman to record in his diary: "Mr. Hopkins called about this time."[45] To make his conversion less painful to his family, Hopkins wrote to Newman on 15 October requesting an immediate reception. Three days later Newman replied, agreeing with Hopkins's decision. On 20 October, when all efforts from Liddon and his parents failed to dissuade him, Hopkins informed his mother of his intent to be received the next day. The following day he was received at the Birmingham Oratory: "Mr. Hopkins came from Oxford and was received," Newman noted in his diary.[46]

Hopkins had always felt that to remain loyal to a church in which he no longer believed was duplicitous. In explaining to his father the grounds for his conversion, Hopkins felt that he must "obey the Church by ceasing to attend any service of the Church of England." And if he is to wait, as his father suggested, then he must be "altogether without services and sacraments, which you will of course know is impossible, or else I must attend the services of the Church—still being unreceived."[47] The story of the young Agellius, from Newman's historical romance novel *Callista* (1855), who seeks to practice his religion without the Sacraments, could have been a warning to the young Hopkins. Thus he immediately dismissed any sense of duty whatever to the Church of England and any sentiments to a Branch Church on the premise that neither was a lawful church. Hopkins must also have been aware of Newman's own claim gradually attained, that "the Anglican Church was formally in the wrong" and "the Church of Rome was formally in the right." That conclusion, once reached, gave Newman no valid reason for "continuing in the Anglican, and again that no valid objections could be taken to joining the Roman."[48] Hopkins's decision not to delay and rejection of a Branch Church position was a repudiation of all *via media* positions, described dramatically as having been "broken to pieces under my feet."[49] This radical stance reveals Hopkins's keen understanding of Newman's argument in his lecture "The Providential Course of the Movement of 1833 Not in the Direction of a Branch Church": "We are inquiring," Newman posited, "whether the National Church [Church of England] can obtain the grace of Christ, necessary for our salvation, at its hands?" Newman denied that availability on the grounds that the National Church is a Branch Church, and as such an "Erastian [heretical] body." Thus he warned potential converts like Hopkins: "If you must . . . leave the existing Establishment, yet, on the other, not seek or form a Branch Church instead of it." Branch Churches "may differ in accidents certainly; but, after all, a branch is a branch, and no branch is a tree." Thus he advised all Branch Church sympathizers to "cease to be an Anglican by becoming a Catholic"; for "the Catholic Church, and she alone . . . is proof against Erastianism."[50]

Hopkins and Newman resumed contact on 21 November 1866. Newman was, against the wishes of Rome, active with plans for an Oratory in Oxford to acquaint Catholic students with the tough questions asked in institutions of high academic learning. After encouraging Hopkins to return to Oxford and get the best degree possible, displaying the liberal opinion on education for which Newman is so recognized and that so often angered Rome, Newman requested from him "a line or two . . . to say how you were getting on—& whether your difficulties were arranging themselves." Hopkins reassured him that his conversion had not severely strained the relationship with his family. The friendship with Newman grew closer when he invited Hopkins to spend Christmas at the Oratory. However, Hopkins thought it more prudent to spend the holidays with his family, a decision Newman supported. But Newman's growing interest in the young convert and in his spiritual nurture soon prompted another invitation, this time for February; his reason: "to see you for the pleasure of seeing you," and because it is "good that a recent convert should pass some time in a religious house, to get into Catholic ways."[51] Newman's diary of Thursday, 17 January 1867, confirmed Hopkins's arrival at the Oratory; one week later, on Friday, 25 January, his diary noted: "Hopkins went."[52]

Hopkins returned to Oxford to prepare for his final examinations. The next letter he received from Newman, stamped "Private," was in reply to a letter Hopkins had written earlier that had enclosed a note from Digby Dolben, a former Newman devotee who felt that "his faith was gone or going" and so wished to see Newman.[53] In June, Hopkins sat for his degree, left in early July for Paris accompanied by Basil Poutiatine, and returned to London on 17 July, where a letter awaited him on Dolben's death. So pained was Hopkins by this incident that in his journal entry for that day he cross–referenced an earlier day, 28 June (that entry has not survived), which presumably contrasted Hopkins's activities with Dolben's disaster.[54] Hopkins was to do the same in *The Wreck* when he contrasted his own peaceful location at St. Beuno's, a "pastoral forehead of Wales," to the nuns' disaster, "And they the prey of the gales." He immediately informed Newman of Dolben's tragic death. "He had not given up the idea of being a Catholic," Newman wrote of Dolben, "but he thought he had lived on excitement, and felt he must give himself time before he could know whether he was in earnest or not." Regretfully, Newman confessed, "I never saw him."[55] In one of only three extant letters from Bridges to Hopkins, Bridges acknowledged Newman's compliments of Dolben, but felt that the remark on Dolben living in excitement had not "at all measured Dolben"; however, he added, "I should not dare to criticize what *he* said." Bridges then told of having had a "curious dream the other night in which your Dr. Newman, Dolben, and a strange Roman Catholic priest [obviously Hopkins] and myself had the most wonderful discussion possible."[56]

The invitation to become a master at the Birmingham Oratory, founded by Newman in 1848, was extended to Hopkins on 22 February 1867. Although Hopkins admitted to Newman his dislike for schooling, Newman was convinced that he would fit in and be well liked. A week later Newman again wrote to Hopkins concerning the offer: "You will not find your work hard here—the terms would be those which Mr. Darnell offered you. . . . I am glad we shall have you."[57] Replacing John Walford, Hopkins was to be paid £10 a month. But although fond of the students, Hopkins despised the Oratory. He was given the fifth form and "a kind of super–sixth form, consisting of two boys [Sparrow and Bellasis] who are staying to coach."[58] Ignorant of the demands of the academic profession, Hopkins had felt that the work would not be strenuous and so planned ambitiously to read "almost every thing that has ever been written."[59] This was on 15 September. A short two weeks later, however, his idealism shattered:

> With reading the class books and looking over exercises
> (which takes a long time) I find my time occupied. . . . I
> wonder if there is anything I cd. do, though the income
> were less, wh. wd. give me more time, for I feel the want
> of that most of all.[60]

On 5 November, Hopkins noted in his journal: "I did a great deal of work, clinched with the exam. papers, and am much tired."[61]

Hopkins was assisted when his Oxford friend, Henry Challis, joined the Oratory on 11 November. Still, by 12 February 1868, his frustration with life at the Oratory had so peaked that he confided to Baillie an anxiousness to "get away from this place"; he felt he had grown "very weak in health and do not seem to recover myself here or likely to do so."[62] The letter continues: "Teaching is very burdensome, especially when you have much of it: I have. I have not much time and almost no energy—for I am always tired—to do anything on my own account. I put aside that one sees and hears nothing and nobody here." Life at the Oratory also affected Hopkins's mental state and overall attitude:

> . . . I am perfectly reckless about things that I shd. other-
> wise care about, uncertain as I am whether in a few months
> I may not be shut up in a cloister, and this state of mind,
> though it is painful coming when reached gives a great and
> real sense of freedom.[63]

Ironically, this was the very anxiety of the nun about to take her veil and the "heart in hiding," if one were to read both "Heaven–Haven" and "The Windhover" autobiographically. For while the poet wishes to be out of the swing of the sea, he still desires his free fells, no prison.

Responsible in the main for Hopkins's disaffection with life at the Oratory was the camaraderie he anticipated but did not find. In fact, despite their intellectual intimacy prior to Hopkins's joining the Oratory, he and Newman saw little of each other. When Hopkins's Highgate friend Coleridge wrote requesting a visit to the Oratory to see Newman and hear him preach, Hopkins replied sardonically: "At the Oratory one never seems to know anything of that sort. . . . I will try and find when Dr. Newman will preach, but I am not sure that asking will find it. I cannot tell you now about the life here."[64]

During Hopkins's tenure at the Oratory, Newman was embroiled in controversy with Rome over the Oxford Oratory and the alternative in a new Jewish school near Windsor. His superiors did not endorse such a school in Oxford, for they were sensitive about mixed education and feared that a school there would attract Catholics to go on to the university, an institution still ideologically hostile to Catholics. In October, plans for the school were finally scrapped and Newman, comparing himself to Job, felt that his trials were over. But he was still preoccupied with the *Grammar*, the one non–occasional work that had been on his mind for twenty–two years.[65] Yet he was sufficiently in touch with Hopkins to sense his increasing uneasiness. On 30 December 1867, Newman advised him or, rather, supported his decision to enter into "retreat at Easter, & bring the matter before the Priest. . . . If you think that this is waiting too long," wrote Newman, "I must think of some other plan." Hopkins returned to the Oratory on 21 January 1868. On 7 February, Newman encouraged him not to hasten his return to his teaching duties following the retreat, for "we shall be able to manage matters whether you stay, or we have the mishap to lose you."[66] Hopkins went into retreat on Palm Sunday, 5 April 1868, at the Oratory with Father Henry Coleridge, who would seven years later, as editor of *The Month*, refuse to publish *The Wreck*. The retreat ended four days later, and on Wednesday, 15 April, Hopkins left for home. Speculating that Hopkins would not return to the Oratory, Newman noted in his diary that day: "Hopkins went for good."[67]

Following an unrequired retreat on 27 April at Roehampton, Hopkins resolved to enter into the priesthood, "still doubtful," however, "between St. Benedict and St. Ignatius."[68] Within a few days he opted for the Jesuits, that most self–denying of clerical orders. Apparently the first person notified was Newman. Hopkins's particular devotion to Newman, according to Martin, "was that he felt a shared identity with him because they had passed through many of the same crises."[69] Newman confessed both surprise and pleasure at Hopkins's decision, but dismissed any notion that he felt Hopkins had a vocation at the Oratory. So conspicuously out of place was Hopkins that Newman sensed it the day of Hopkins's arrival: "This I clearly saw you had *not*, from the moment you came to us." As to the Jesuits, an order Newman saw as "modern" and "Practical," he informed Hopkins not to call "*the Jesuit discipline hard*, it will bring you to heaven. The Benedictines would not have suited you."[70] Newman was an eyewitness to the very life on which he was now advising Hopkins. While attending the College of Propaganda in Rome in the spring of 1846, Newman had observed the rigid discipline of the Jesuits and in particular the Jesuit Rector, Padre Bresciani. Newman remarked: "What a self denying life theirs is, as regards their enjoyment of this world! They have no enjoyment of life . . . ; nothing is there to support him but the thought of the next world."[71] This earlier observation influenced Newman's reminder to Hopkins on the rewards of the afterlife. Newman's share in assisting Hopkins toward his goal is clearly important, writes Thomas; "what could be more natural than to discuss the question of your vocation with the priest who received you into the Church."[72]

Hopkins disclosed his decision to Urquhart and, as part of his continuing effort to see Urquhart converted, raised Newman's argument. An Anglican priest, Urquhart apparently felt that he could profit from the efforts of Tractarianism without ever having to convert to Catholicism. With "the interest of a catholicwards movement to support you," Hopkins told Urquhart,

> it is most natural to say *all things continue as they were*
> and most hard to realise the silence and severity of God, as
> Dr. Newman very eloquently and persuasively had said in

> a passage of Anglican Difficulties; but this plea or way of
> thinking—all things continuing as they were—is the very
> character of infidelity.[73]

While Hopkins confessed here a perceptive understanding of Newman's lectures on *Certain Difficulties Felt by Anglicans*, he did not identify the passage.
Apparently the lecture he had in mind is the one entitled "On the Relation of the
National Church to the Nation." In addressing the benefits Tractarianism
brought to England and the national church, the very point Hopkins was urging
on Urquhart, Newman pointed out that because of the Movement, "Opinions
which, twenty years ago, were not held by any but Catholics, or at most only in
fragmentary portions by isolated persons, are now the profession of thousands";
the reason: "The Fathers have catholicised the Protestant Church at home pretty
much as the Bible has evangelised the Mahometan or Hindoo religions abroad."[74]

In that same lecture from *Certain Difficulties*, Newman used a series of
nautical metaphors to characterize the Catholic Church as "the one ark of
salvation to bring you to land from off your wreck." He pictured Anglican
England as floundering passengers thrown adrift "upon the waves" or "clinging" to the rigging of the doomed ship, or "sitting in heaviness and despair upon
its sides." The English church, he concluded, is "a mere wreck." As a result,
the "great ocean has suddenly swelled and heaved, and majestically yet
masterfully snaps the cables of the small craft which be upon its bosom and
strands them upon the beach. . . . One vessel alone can ride those waves; it is the
boat of Peter, the ark of God."[75] Newman employed similar nautical metaphors
in the *Apologia* to describe his religious activities and the process to his
conversion: his essay on the Council of Nicea was a way "to launch myself on
an ocean with currents innumerable"; his involvement with the tracts was like
being "on board a vessel, which first gets under weigh, and then the deck is
cleared out, and the luggage and live stock stowed away into their proper
receptacles"; left to him the Movement would have remained "but a floating
opinion"; he felt that "in some sense or other I was on a journey," and going over
to Rome was like having "arrived at the end of my journey," my "ultimate
destination," and gave the feeling like one "coming into port after a rough sea."[76]

Hopkins no doubt chimed with these particular metaphors. Both *The Wreck*
and *The Loss of the Eurydice*, although written to commemorate actual ship-
wrecks, used similar nautical metaphors, much of it deriving from a family
business in shipping disasters. Consistent with the dual purposes of elegies, the
metaphors also intended to present Roman Catholicism as the only refuge for a
spiritually shipwrecked nation and Church. The closing stanza of *The Wreck*

presents the nun as intercessor for those "Unchrist"; her role is to restore Roman
Catholicism as England's legitimate religion. In *The Loss of the Eurydice*, the
poet expresses his dismay over England's spiritual plight—"Day and night I
deplore / My people and born own nation, / Fast foundering own generation.../
The riving off that race / So at home, time was to his truth and grace." These lines
ring with Hopkins's typical nationalistic fervor. The poem ends with an appeal
to Christ as "Hero" to those shipwrecked lives; the poet hopes that his prayers,
like the tall nun's "one fetch," will equally "fetch" even those "souls sunk" in
the abyss of hell.

Sometime between Hopkins's July 1868 Alps expedition with John Tyndall
and his leaving for his novitiate in September, Hopkins saw his Balliol friend
Richard Nettleship, to whom he disclosed his intention to join the Jesuits.
Writing to another Balliol undergraduate, Henry Scott Holland, who was with
Nettleship during Hopkins's visit, T.H. Green noted the event and tied it to
Newman. In that 29 December letter, Green, Hopkins's former philosophy tutor
at Balliol, was delighted that Nettleship and Holland had seen Hopkins. "A step
such as he has taken, tho' I can't quite admit it to be heroic," said Green,

> must needs be painful, and its pain should not be aggra-
> vated—as it is pretty sure to be—by separation from old
> friends. I never had his intimacy, but always liked him
> very much. I imagine him—perhaps uncharitably—to be
> one of those, like his ideal J.H. Newman, who instead of
> simply opening themselves to the revelation of God in the
> reasonable world, are fain to put themselves into an
> attitude—saintly, it is true, but still an attitude.[77]

On 7 September Hopkins went into his novitiate at Roehampton. The significance of that event is tea–tabled in rather relaxed language: "In the evening when
I had said goodbye at home I found my train did not go for three quarters of an
hour, so I walked to Victoria Road in the meantime and Aunt Annie came back
with me to the train.— Then to the Novitiate, Roehampton."[78] One might hazard
the notion that Hopkins recalled the memorable train motif connected with
Newman's dramatic departure from Littlemore and Oxford, and that the
stabilizing presence of Hopkins's Aunt Annie was a sort of intertextual exchange for Newman's snapdragon.

Earlier Hopkins had informed Bridges that he "cannot promise to correspond, for in that way the novices are restricted."[79] The first letter to his mother,
written only three days after he arrived at Roehampton, noted the same

restriction: "Just now I cannot write any more because of the post and disposition of our times and I thought you wd. rather have a short letter than none."[80] During these two years of a strict disciplined life, Hopkins wrote only six letters to his mother, two to Bridges (the second a terse six lines), and none to his close friends Urquhart and Baillie. In addition, his journal entries during these two years at Roehampton occupy a mere eleven pages, compared to twelve pages of entries made during the previous year (1867) alone.[81] The new novices spent the first few weeks of a probationary period separated from the more advanced novices. The next thirty days were then given exclusively to prayer and meditation, and except for a break the novices received for three days, silence was to be maintained. "The usual practice during the Long Retreat is that letters are neither written nor received, thereby enabling the retreatant to cut himself off as far as possible from all secular interests."[82] These restrictions help explain the lapse in Hopkins's correspondence. Thus, the reason Lahey cites for the decrease in letters between Hopkins and Newman—that "firmly established in his vocation" Hopkins "no longer needed the advice of his great friend"—is not altogether accurate. While as Hopkins matured in his vocation he relied less on Newman's advice, he never outgrew the need for Newman's approbation. More to the point is Lahey's comment that "their mutual esteem and affection never lessened."[83]

Hopkins and Newman resumed correspondence on 26 September 1870.[84] Hopkins reinitiated the contact to inform Newman that he had completed his novitiate, taken his Jesuit vows, and relocated to Stonyhurst for his reading in philosophy and mathematics. Newman offered his congratulation—"so solemn and so joyful to you," he wrote. "I will say Mass please God, for your intention upon it."[85] Hopkins again read and wrote little while at Stonyhurst. Preparing to leave there, he went to Roehampton on 21 January 1873 to consult with Father Fincham. Three weeks later he wrote Newman, possibly to inform him of that meeting. Hopkins also extended birthday greetings to Newman. "I feel it especially kind when friends recollect my birthday," Newman replied, "for they can't well think of my beginning without thinking also of my end."[86] This letter marks the first of Hopkins's several birthday letters to Newman, letters as spots of time that bound for the remainder of his life this young man to his religious and literary mentor.

On 2 August 1873 Hopkins received orders to teach rhetoric at Roehampton; the following day he left Stonyhurst. He spent Christmas week at home and then traveled to Roehampton from where he again sent remembrances of Newman's birthday. Now seventy–three, Newman replied on 23 February 1874, confident that Hopkins had committed his aging to the Lord. He expressed surprise that

Hopkins, who was obviously aware of the defection of their mutual friend, Henry Challis, from Catholicism, had chosen not to mention it. Apparently, Hopkins wished to suppress a painful issue on such a joyous occasion. Newman picked up on that reticence: "You speak as if you did not know what a sad state of mind Challis is in—but perhaps you do know, though you don't speak of it."[87] On 28 August 1874 Hopkins left for St. Beuno's, where he read in recreation Newman's highly successful, though controversial, *A Letter to the Duke of Norfolk*, a work in response to Gladstone's criticism of the Decrees of the First Vatican Council in 1870. Newman's treatise addresses the nature and workings of the conscience, which Newman felt was the essential factor in Catholics being loyal British citizens. The letter addresses too papal infallibility, which, together with Roman Catholic loyalty, Gladstone felt, made a slave of conscience. Newman's was an attempt to defend Catholics against Gladstone's denouncements that, among other things, Catholics compromise their loyalty to Britain because they are ecclesiastically bound to Rome.[88] In that same letter to Newman, Hopkins remembered his birthday even though the "close pressure of my theological studies leaves me time for hardly anything."[89] Newman's 21 February 1875 response recalled the "great honour" the pamphlet brought him.

During August 1875, Hopkins wrote "The Silver Jubilee," published along with a sermon (not his), in anticipation of the visit by Bishop James Brown to St. Beuno's to commemorate the twenty–fifth anniversary of his bishopric at Shrewsbury and the area around St. Beuno's. The poem, more appropriately a song that "looks nicer in print," acknowledges the general disregard for the anniversary: "Though no high–hung bells or din / Of braggart bugles cry it in." The silence was even more disappointing because the occasion was named after the very horn used to proclaim it. However, Hopkins's Christian Romanticism redeems the event by rejecting artificial sound for that from nature; "Nature's round" is summoned to commemorate the occasion; and still feeling disappointed that the "velvet vales" of the Welsh landscape, ordinarily the muse of Hopkins's poetry, "Should have pealed with welcome," the poet offers his own song ("chime of a rhyme") as a celebratory substitute for the otherwise silent bugles and bells.

The expression "Nature's round," one critic observes, "serves as a reminder of Newman's famous sermon of 1852 in which he had described the return of the hierarchy as a "Second Spring."[90] Newman preached this sermon at Oscott on 13 July 1852. Images of transitoriness appear in the sermon's opening:

WE HAVE FAMILIAR EXPERIENCE of the order, the constancy, the perpetual renovation of the material world

> which surrounds us. Frail and transitory as is every part of
> it, restless and migratory as are its elements, never–ceasing
> as are its changes, still it abides. It is bound together by a
> law of permanence, it is set up in unity; and, though it is
> ever dying, it is ever coming to life again.

The sermon continues:

> We mourn over the blossoms of May, because they are to
> wither; but we know, withal, that May is one day to have
> its revenge upon November, by the revolution of that
> solemn circle which never stops. . . . We look at the bloom
> of youth with interest, yet with pity; and the more graceful
> and sweet it is, with pity so much the more; for whatever
> be its excellence and its glory, soon it . . . grows into
> exhaustion and collapse.[91]

Hopkins's "Spring" sonnet shares notable parallels with the sermon. Images of
fragile newness and innocence inform the octave of the poem: the "Thrush's
eggs," "glassy peartree," and exuberant "racing lambs" connote strained reminders of a prelapsarian innocence "in the beginning / In Eden garden."
Images of seasonal change are likewise camouflaged in the "blooms" and in the
urgent appeal to "Have, get, before it cloy, / Before it cloud."

The two versions of spring share additional parallels: both refer to the
blooms in spring; Hopkins's Christ as "Mayday in girl and boy" parallels
Newman's "perpetual May"; and his "cloy" is a disguised substitute for
Newman's "grows into exhaustion." Furthermore, Hopkins's concealed appeal
to Mary ("maid's child") for a second spring, found also in *The Wreck* and in
"The Blessed Virgin compared to the Air we Breathe," can be discovered in
Newman's sermon: "O Mary . . . fulfil to us the promise of this Spring. A second
temple rises on the ruins of the old."[92] Both works seek for rebirth not in a season
but in a person. Although built on seasonal metaphors and their related images,
both texts reject the natural for the supernatural. Hopkins's poem particularly
reveals the energy and vitality representative of new life and exhibits a
movement away from things evanescent to things permanent, from season to
Christ. However, the supernatural does not obviate the natural; rather, the two
become transubstantiated into a divine union of signifier and signified, exem-
plifying a familiar analogical technique at work in many of Hopkins's quasi-
nature poems.

Newman had earlier talked of spring in ways similar to his sermon. In a 16 April 1833 letter to Walter Trower written from Naples, Newman referred to the season as "the most elevating and instructive time of the year—somehow it whispers of the good that is to come, when our bodies are to rise—and it throws the thoughts back upon Eden we have lost, and makes the heart contrite by the contrast between what is and what might be."[93] Hopkins's spring sonnet echoes similar Wordsworthian intimations of immortality and deals too, obviously coincidental to the Newman passage, with seasonal and, by analogy, spiritual consequences of a lost Eden. He considers the resplendent images of spring residual of what Eden, "in the beginning," was and signified; but to reclaim the true *quidditas* of Eden is to find Christ who is both the symbol and the quintessence of spring.

Hopkins's "Penmaen Pool," an advertisement for this resort frequented by St. Beuno's students, also reads like another Newman work, "My Lady Nature and Her Daughters." Both poems present nature's restorative powers, providing for the wealthy and powerful rest, freedom, and pleasure.[94] Another poem, "The Sea and the Skylark," also demonstrates Newman's influence. In the *Apologia*, Newman talked of the "many races of man . . . their aimless courses, their random achievements and acquirements . . . the blind evolution of what turn out to be great powers or truth . . . the dreary hopeless irreligion, that condition of the whole race, so fearfully yet exactly described in the Apostles's words, 'having no hope and without God in the world.'"[95] Hopkins too augured the disintegration of man himself and even his accomplishments. Once "life's pride and cared-for-crown," nature's "bonniest, dearest to her, her clearest-selved spark," as Hopkins would again say in another context, man has forfeited that "cheer and charm of earth's past prime"; consequently, "Our make and making break, are breaking, down / To man's last dust, drain fast towards man's first slime."

Written in close proximity to "The Sea and the Skylark" was "The Windhover." Its dedication "to Christ our Lord" forges a symbolic nexus between the falcon and Christ. The bird's "mastery," "Brute beauty," and "valour" all "Buckle" in Christ, and its graceful and dangerous plunge becomes a metaphorical "fire" that, though retold as a story ("breaks from thee") "a billion / Times," fails to lose its original splendor.[96] Norman MacKenzie associates these christological characteristics of the windhover to a remark Newman once made: "any approach to a holy and all-powerful God demanded the combination of love and fear which we call Christian Reverence."[97] Nowhere does this awful attribute of God abound as in the numerous Blakean contraries found in *The Wreck*: "what with dread / Thy doing"; "Thy terror, O

Christ, O God"; "Glow, glory in thunder"; "with fire in him forge thy will"; "to breathe in his all–fire glances"; "Thou art lightning and love"; "winter and warm"; "Deutschland, double a desperate name"; "Gertrude, lily, and Luther, are two of a town"; "Abel is Cain's brother and breasts they have sucked the same."

Hopkins left St. Beuno's in late 1877 for Mount St. Mary's College in Chesterfield. From there he informed Newman of the completion of his theological studies and the termination of his formal Jesuit training. Newman replied on 13 November, apologizing for his short letter—"as my hand is rather weak." His postscript congratulated Hopkins on attaining the priesthood and promised to consider prayerfully Hopkins's "requests," probably regarding new directions. Newman informed Hopkins of his 26 February 1878 return trip to Trinity College, Oxford, to be honored as an honorary fellow: "I have not been there for 32 years. . . . It is very kind of the Trinity men, but it is a trial."[98] Hopkins's former spiritual leader, Liddon, gave a not too favorable impression of Newman's visit in a 9 March 1978 letter to Henry Lewis Thompson: "Dr. Newman came to Oxford last week, and I met him at dinner at Waytes." He sat next to Mark Patterson "who looked all that is implacable and remorseless in criticism. . . . He was, I think, greatly pleased at the occasion of his return to Oxford; —I had seen him in August last year, & was struck by the absence of a stern—pathetic element—which then as before unimpressed me. The other day he purred all over."[99]

Hopkins was soon to leave Chesterfield to coach students at Stonyhurst for their London University degree. He was then to take up assignment at Mount Street, London. While at Stonyhurst, Hopkins wrote three polyglot poems dedicated to the Virgin Mary: "Ad Mariam," "Rosa Mystica," and "The May Magnificat," the few liturgical poems in his canon. His fondness of Eucharistic poems ("The Bugler's First Communion," "Barnfloor and Winepress," "Easter Communion," and "Easter") and acclaimed recognition of *The Wreck* and *Eurydice* show that he, like Newman, worked best in the genre of the literature of occasions.[100] "The May Magnificat," a poem dedicated to the month assigned to Mary, is related to two of Newman's May pieces, "The Month of Mary" (really a song) and "The Queen of Seasons," all of which were published in *The Stonyhurst Magazine*. The seasonal images in "The May Magnificat" resemble those in Newman's "The Month of Mary." However, Hopkins's poem has closer affinity to "The Queen of Seasons," especially in its designation of May to Mary. Both poems conclude rather similarly; Newman's ends attributing all seasons to Mary ("O Mary, all months and all days are thine own"), while Hopkins concludes in unusually prosaic lines that blend a romantic view of nature with Hopkins's own Catholicism: "This ecstasy all through mothering earth / Tells Mary her mirth till Christ's birth."[101]

Hopkins left Stonyhurst on 1 July 1878 for Mount Street. By 3 November he was in his yearly retreat at Beaumont Lodge, Windsor, and on 9 December was assigned to St. Aloysius Church in Oxford. From there he wrote Newman to commemorate his birthday and to recognize the honor of the cardinalate conferred on him. Newman replied on 8 March: "Among letters which have touched me very much have been those from St Beuno."[102] While at Oxford, Hopkins penned "Andromeda" ("ruler of men"), a religious poem based on an Ovidian myth. Because Hopkins is using the myth as religious typology, albeit gendered, his interpretation remains allegorical. This myth, as Adrienne Munich points out, is employed by "men rather than women" (George Eliot the sole exception) for "creative" purposes, rendering a "gendered aspect of Victorian culture."[103] The beautiful maiden Andromeda is, by nature of her persecution, a figure of the Catholic Church, and, in fact, an earlier autography of the poem bore the title "The Catholic Church Andromeda."

Her beauty matched only by her intense suffering, Andromeda is impaled on a rock. Her virginal "flower," which the ascetic devalues as "her piece of being," is "doomed dragon food," a relegation that implies suppressed sexual desire. In former times, Andromeda was assaulted by "many blows and banes," but now she hears the roar of a new and more lethal enemy, "A wilder beast from the West / . . . more lawless and more lewd." While it denotes evil, the term "lewd" connotes sexual violation, especially so in the context of Andromeda's "flower." Her violators are, analogically, the forces of liberalism and skepticism, all contemporary threats to Christianity. Munich thus correctly reads Hopkins's allegory as "the plight of the contemporary Church" and perceptively associates lewd, unnatural sexual appetite or actual cohabitation, to doctrinal heresy, as in *Paradise Lost* and *The Fairie Queene*.[104] This conflation of sexuality and heresy occurs as well in "Andromeda." Like the mythic Andromeda, the Church needs to be rescued by the chivalric Perseus, here Christ. Discussing Hopkins's treatment of the myth in the context of what she ironically calls "Manly Allegories," Adrienne Munich connects what Hopkins is doing to Alexander Ross's *Mystagogus Poeticus*. Here Perseus is depicted as a type of Christ who

> hath subdued all our spiritual *Gorgons*, and hath delivered
> the Church his fair Spouse, from the Devil, that great
> monster, who was ready to devour her; at last having
> conquered all his enemies, he hath ascended into glory,

and there hath prepared a place for his *Andromeda*, the
Church.[105]

But Perseus suspends all salvific actions, a suspension that Munich nicely
associates to his riding of the air before his buckle ("Pillowy air he treads a time
and hangs"), analogous to the windhover and thus Christ. Andromeda is
temporarily left, "to her extremes . . . forsaken." Meanwhile, her patience
"morselled into pangs" gradually accumulates and "Mounts." Only in Perseus's
slaying of the monster is the Church preserved and kept unadulterated (free from
Erastianism) for her true bridegroom. Thus the poem fittingly ends with the
monster's defeat at the hands of Perseus, who still carries with him the spoils of
an earlier victory, Medusa's head ("barebill / throngs and fangs").

Hopkins's poem resonates with echoes of Newman's heroine Callista, a
sculptor of pagan gods ("a maker of images") who renounced her trade after she
converted to Christianity. The novel ends with her torture on a rack. Also
informing the Hopkins poem is Newman's famous public speech delivered in
Rome on the reception of his cardinalate: "For thirty, forty, fifty years I have
resisted, to the best of my powers, the spirit of Liberalism in religion," he
proclaimed. Tracing the Andromeda narrative and attempting to read it as a male
myth, Munich fails to locate evidence of it in Newman, in whom Hopkins more
than likely discovered its analogical value. Newman also seemed to have had the
Andromeda myth in mind when he composed his sermon "Profession without
Ostentation." In the sermon, he talked of the Church "hated and calumniated by
the world." But while Christians are, by profession, a persecuted people, they
should not court persecution nor devise illegal means to defend themselves
against it. The image that follows is the one in which Andromeda most fully
participates, although Newman does not spell out the association: "*The Church
will witness on to the last for the Truth, chained indeed to this world*, its evil
partner, but ever foretelling its ruin, though not believed, and in the end
promised a far different recompense" (my italics).[106] Newman's instancing the
Andromeda myth shows how sometimes subtle and pervasive its employment
by Victorians, and especially, as Munich cogently shows, by Victorian men.
Hopkins's "Andromeda" could also have been drawn from Newman's allegorical poem "The Pilgrim Queen." In the tradition of Blake's Orchean myth,
Newman's "Lady" is circumscribed ("circled her round") by the "Rays of the
morning";[107] despite her royal lineage, she has been desecrated: "Robbers have
rifled my garden and store, / Foes they have stolen my heir from my bower."
Clearly Marie represents Mary and her "heir" the Church and its converts.

Hopkins left Oxford during October 1879 to substitute briefly at a church in Bedford Leigh, Lancashire, before going on to Liverpool. In a 2 March 1880 letter to his mother, he instanced having written to Newman:

> I wrote, as I do every year, to Cardinal Newman on his
> birthday the 21st of last month. I got by return of post a
> pretty little card of a spray of dogwood leaves, one green,
> two red and withered, symbolical perhaps of age, run
> through a card or piece of paper on which was written
> "Many, many thanks. Pardon so brief an answer."[108]

Again Newman's correspondence discloses no record of even so personal a letter. Hopkins's next known letter to Newman was to commemorate his birthday of 1881. The letter, it appears, enumerated his unpleasant experiences at Leigh and Liverpool, for Newman remarked on Hopkins's "self–denying life" that must be "heaping up merit." Hopkins had also asked Newman for his opinion on Carlyle and Eliot. Admitting that he had read "little of Carlisle's [sic] and less of George Eliot," Newman found Eliot "over–rated" and felt that "one page of C. goes for many of G.E."[109]

Hopkins again wrote to Newman in February 1884 from Dublin. His appointment to Ireland was sudden and fraught with political maneuvering. Fortune's football had received another kick. Hopkins was now corresponding regularly with Bridges, Dixon, Patmore, Baillie, and less frequently with his parents; but Newman was the first to be informed of his appointment as a fellow in the department of classics at University College, Dublin, founded by Newman in 1851 to see "if Oxford [can be] imported into Ireland."[110] Hopkins was drawn to the university, according to Martin, because most importantly "he would be following in the tracks of his beloved John Henry Newman, just as he had done ever since he was an undergraduate."[111] In one of only three extant letters to Newman, Hopkins also brought up the unsanitary conditions at the college, "like living at a temporary Junction," he once described it. "These buildings since you knew them have fallen into a deep dilapidation."[112] Newman responded appropriately on 29 February: "I hope you find at Dublin an opening for work such as you desire and which suits you. I am sorry you can speak of dilapidation."[113]

The move to Ireland made Hopkins "seem the stranger," and especially so to this patriot, one might argue nationalist, for whom not loving England most means the unraveling of his very being, the loss of self–scape. His strenuous teaching, more accurately tedious examination, responsibilities, increasing distemper, and mounting frustration with political and religious squabblings in Ireland made him feel "a third / Remove." In a not entirely uncharacteristic response to relocation, Hopkins calls Dublin a "joyless place."[114] But that very despair, so often the germ of poetry, sired Hopkins's celebrated terrible sonnets, the seven or so poems detailing his despair and melancholia in Ireland. Of those, "No worse, there is none" describes the poet beyond the "pitch of grief," that vacuous state characterized by the most extreme form of suffering. The poet cries out to the Holy Ghost and Mary for comfort and relief, acknowledging that his persistent cries coalesce and seemingly fail to penetrate; they only glance off and echo as though one were striking "an age–old anvil." The poet acknowledges that the mind is still able to mount, but ironically it is that unthinkable height that makes its "fall / Frightful, sheer" more dreadful, a tragedy "no–man–fathomed"; for humans are unable to "deal with that steep or deep." The poet's only solace—if solace there be—is that "Life death does end and each day dies with sleep." This condition is similar to the one Newman's protagonist experiences in *The Dream of Gerontius.* Hopkins's speaker, like Newman's Gerontius, experiences a similar intellectual fall into the abyss of despair far worse than physical suffering. Both are in a state "worse than pain" and both look down from a "sheer infinite descent." And Hopkins's soul that creeps about awaiting only sleep or preferably death assumes the same passive role preferred by Gerontius.

Another of those sonnets, "Carrion Comfort," the so–called bloody poem, portrays the poet this time moving from a passive acceptance of his fate to actively fighting despair with a determination not to yield. Such spiritual warfare, he reasons, is a winnowing that eventually yields, in the words of another poem, an "immortal diamond." Brian Vickers was the first to recognize the poem's indebtedness to *The Dream of Gerontius.* The octave of "Carrion Comfort" makes full use of Gerontius's despair, negations, collapse of self, and taunting gestures of the adversary, despair:

> I can no more; for now it comes again,
> That sense of ruin, which is worse than pain,
> That masterful negation and collapse
> Of all that makes me man; as though I bent
> Over the dizzy brink
> Of some sheer infinite descent;
> Or worse, as though
> Down, down for ever I was falling through
> The solid framework of created things,

> And needs must sink and sink
> Into the vast abyss. And, crueller still,
> A fierce and restless fright begins to fill
> The mansion of my soul . . .
> Tainting the hallow'd air, and laughs, and flaps
> Its hideous wings,
> And makes me wild with horror and dismay.

The experience of a "strange innermost abandonment," Gerontius realizes, is as though "my very being has given way, / As though I was no more a substance now," but a mere shade confronting "utter nothingness." Gerontius thus rouses his "fainting" soul to "play the man."

Like *Gerontius*, "Carrion Comfort" concerns the despondency that once yielded to results in the fated disintegration of the self, the dreaded disentangling of "these last strands of man / In me." The poet admits a related threat in *The Wreck*. He recognizes that, like his progenitor Adam, he too confronts a similar uncreation of his being, but embraces the doctrinal certitude that he is instressed with God's grace, that God "hast bound bones and veins in me, fastened me flesh." Gerontius admits similar connectedness:

> That each particular organ holds its place
> As heretofore, combining with the rest
> Into one symmetry, that wraps me round,
> And makes me man.

But the responses from both Gerontius and Hopkins's speaker are dissimilar, a difference Vickers notes: "Hopkins seems to be repudiating Newman's presentation of the passive nature of the soul's collapse and urging a more intense heroic state, where the soul lies 'wrestling with (my God!) my God.'"[115] By italicizing the expression "*I can no more*," Hopkins also admits its importation, only to be repudiated with "I can."[116]

There appears to be yet more echoes from Newman. In his sermon, "Mental Suffering of Our Lord in His Passion," Newman remarks: "You cry out perhaps that you cannot bear more"; and in "Neglect of Divine Calls and Warnings," he refers to the agonized Demas as the "poor soul [who] struggles and wrestles in the grasp of the mighty demon which has hold of it, and whose every touch is torment. 'O, atrocious! it shrieks in agony, and in anger too, as if the very keenness of the infliction were a proof of its injustice"; Demas cries out: "'A second! and a third! I can bear no more! stop, horrible fiend, give over; I am a man, and not such as thou! I am not food for thee, or sport for thee!'"[117] Hopkins was quite familiar with this sermon. In evaluating Patmore's "Tristitia," Hopkins called the teaching of degrees of condemnation based on degrees of knowledge an "intolerable doctrine." This doctrine is familiar, Hopkins told Patmore, and "even Newman in his well known sermon about Demas [has] countenanced it."[118]

Newman's *Gerontius* poem, in particular the return of "That sense of ruin, which is worse than pain," raises yet another intriguing point of similarity between him and Hopkins—their joint advocacy of intellectual pain, far more traumatic than actual physical suffering. Newman posited this idea in his sermon "Mental Sufferings of Our Lord in His Passion" (1849), which Hopkins read on 9 April 1872 during his philosophate at Stonyhurst. Christ's agony, Newman reasoned, "a pain of the soul, not of the body," was the initial act of his great sacrifice. "It was not the body that suffered, but the soul in the body"; and the greater the consciousness, the more intense the pain. Consequently, Christ's passion was most intense because his soul was "so fully directed *upon* the pain, so utterly surrendered, so simply subjected to the suffering." Absence of pain, on the other hand, is evident when there is "no kind of inward sensibility or spirit to be the seat of it." Following this line of reasoning, Newman concluded that brute animals experience less pain than humans because they possess no "power of reflection or of consciousness." And though they have memory, it is not that of an intelligent being. A non–human, organic being experiences no pain because it possesses "no mind or sensible principle within it"; for "it is the intellectual comprehension of pain as a whole diffused through successive moments, which gives it its special power and keenness, and it is the soul only, which a brute has not, which is capable of that comprehension."[119]

Gerontius, then, calls his suffering "something too of sternness and of pain," and the Angel informs him that "the face of the Incarnate God / Shall smite thee with that keen and subtle pain . . . / And yet withal it will the wound provoke, / And aggravate and widen it the more." He experiences the negation and slackening of the very thing that should preserve his inscape, the stress that "makes me man." He envisions himself like Byron's Manfred, as on some precipitous cliff looking down, or worse plunging from it into unbounded emptiness. But far worse is the fear that takes hold of the inner recesses of the soul by assuming wings only to mock the soul's descent.

Hopkins's spiritual writings reveal just how acquainted he was with Newman's intellectual pain. "The keener the consciousness the greater the pain," he wrote in his meditations; and "the greater the stress of being the greater the pain . . . the higher the nature the greater the penalty. One sees that God could relieve this pain by diminishing consciousness."[120] While Hopkins took some eleven years to admit openly his knowledge of Newman's concept of intellectual pain, his poems illustrate that he was all along exploiting the idea. For example, the tall nun's suffering in the poem *The Wreck* is more mental than physical: more attuned to Christ in her heightened consciousness, spirituality, and obedience, she experiences his passion more acutely and thus more vicariously. While "Other, I gather, in measure her mind's / Burden," it is still she who cried out the "keener to come at the comfort for feeling the combating keen."

Newman's concept of intellectual pain is also manifested in "Binsey Poplars" and evident in young Margaret's developing ego–structure in the "little lyric," "Spring and Fall." The poet feels mentally and shares personally the agony of the demise of the aspens; and as vital to him as the fracturing of the ecology is the tarnishing of the landscape whereby "After–comers" cannot surmise "the beauty been." Early in "Spring and Fall" and in Margaret's life, her "fresh thoughts" of suffering are significantly limited; thus she superficially grieves over the yellow falling leaves that signify the end of the frolicsome summer, an object momentarily detached from her; here subject and object are distant, and not until she looks hard at the fall does it look hard at her. The word "unleaving" rhymes with "grieving" to establish a syntactical relationship in which Margaret's emotional outburst is presented as a thing distinct from her, yet rhythmically belonging to her. However, the very next phrase—"Leaves, like the things of man"—makes immediate that inexorable connection between Margaret's "fresh thoughts" and "older" heart, and in so doing anticipates the crass reality pronounced in the poem's last line: "It is Margaret you mourn for." That the demise of the leaves—its "unleaving"— is in fact synonymous and analogous to Margaret's own demise is seen in the object of her mourning. When "the heart grows older," the poet warns her, when the object of Margaret's grief will no longer be a trivial thing, then she will experience the greatest pain. Simply put, she will discover that there are more important things to grieve over. The onset of aging will call up an uncontestable outpouring of tears generated, not from something external to Margaret herself, but from something that is very much a part of her, her increased knowledge: she "*will* weep and know why."

The fact that Margaret's increasing knowledge will be commensurate to her suffering has an affinity to Keats's analogy of the Mansion of Many Apartments and the Chamber of Maiden–Thought. The theory compares human life to a roomed mansion. We occupy the first room, the infant or thoughtless chamber, "as long as we do not think." But when the "thinking principle" becomes operational, we are then thrust into the "Chamber of Maiden–Thought," where we see that "the world is full of Misery and Heartbreak, Pain, Sickness and oppression." This notion is probably what generated Keats's familiar request: "O for a Life of Sensations rather than of Thoughts," for he envisions the thinking principle as the seat of human suffering.[121]

The connection between cognition and suffering is further illustrated in three of Keats's great odes: "Ode to a Nightingale," "Ode on a Grecian Urn," and "To Autumn." In the first, the poet desires an imaginative oneness with the nightingale, a union that would allow him to "forget" the misery and suffering that, he presumes, the bird "among the leaves hast never known." Ruled apparently by instinct and not by memory or history, the nightingale is immune to suffering tied to intellectual pain, a fate reserved only for humans, for whom "to think is to be full of sorrow / And leaden–eyed despairs." In "Ode on a Grecian Urn," the frozen state of life historicized on the urn is, because it evokes thoughts of eternity, mentally perplexing: "Thou, silent form, dost tease us out of thought / As doth eternity." Somewhat similar thought processes operate in "To Autumn." The prolonged summer has generated a new harvest of flowers for the bees, deceiving them into thinking that "warm days will never cease." The personified autumn shares not so much in the deception but, rather, employs knowledge as a means to escape suffering and death. Knowing that winter offers death and that spring promises renewal, the poem's persona wishes to avoid winter altogether, calling instead for the rhythmical return of spring. But the poet disallows any circumvention of the natural cycle, offering, instead, the curtailment of the thinking principle, aware that the real pain is intellectual: "think not of them." But this solution is suspect, for the benefit of forgetting is seldom available to humans. Memory is both an anodyne and a blight.

Newman's intellectual pain, like Keats's thinking principle, influenced many of Hopkins's poems. The idea, as we have seen, is evident in "No worst, there is none," "Carrion Comfort," "Binsey Poplars," and "Spring and Fall." It can also be found in "My own heart" and "Spelt from Sibyl's Leaves." In the former, the poet wallows in self–pity and is determined to continue a life, if it can be so characterized, of sorrow. Trapped within the self, the poet can love only in a homoerotic way. This he hopes will give him some relief from his "tormented mind," a mental state similar to that found in "Spelt from Sibyl's Leaves." Like a luckless fisherman, the poet casts about for comfort. Echoes of Tennyson's persona in *In Memoriam* and of Coleridge's Mariner abound in the language of the poet's desperate search, for neither can he find faith in the dark world nor spiritual rejuvenation for his arid condition. But this condition—the rule rather than the exception in Hopkins's poems—seems more personal than universal, for he acknowledges a spiritual flood outside himself ("a world of wet"). In order once more to participate in that flood, the poet opts for intellectual inanition and patience, convinced that they make conducive a response from God. He beckons his soul to "call off thoughts awhile" in order to give "comfort" space to sprout, "root–room"; this temporary relaxation also provides joy an opportunity to grasp for some untimely and unknown object, presumably God's smile that is "not wrung" and that "lights a lovely mile." The mental abatement the poet desires in order to grant his hope–renewed life recalls Dido's request in the *Aeneid*. In a fit of insanity caused by Aeneas's refusal to accept her plea to reside in Libyan Carthage, Dido responded: "Time is all I beg, / Mere time, a respite and a breathing space / For madness to subside in."[122]

In "Spelt from Sibyl's Leaves," the disintegration of earth's being and loss of dappleness prefigure a similar human fate: the individual is "selfwrung, selfstrung, sheath–shelterless." Here too the poet struggles with psychic disintegration. Not only is the self threatened, but so too are the poet's "thoughts" engaged in a war "against thoughts in groans grind." In this context human fate is inextricably linked to the material and natural world, a fact evident also in "God's Grandeur," "Binsey Poplars," and "Heraclitean Fire." Man's deliberate and even unwitting violation of earth's dappleness has serious personal consequence, for it is tantamount to his own self–destruction. These poems all show that Hopkins exhibited as great a concern as did Newman with the psychology of mental suffering.

The influence of Newman's writings on Hopkins's post–conversion poetry is not unexpected, however much the connection has been overlooked. Hopkins was on friendly terms with Newman and well acquainted with his works. But what appears extraordinary is the degree of that influence on Hopkins's pre–conversion poems. For example, the spiritual discipline of the senses requested in "The Habit of Perfection," now called "The Kind Betrothal," approximates two poems of Newman's, "Prime" and "Terce." Hopkins's "uncreated Light" is taken directly from Newman's "Prime," and the poem's expressed asceticism, calling for the spiritual employment of the senses (lips that are "lovely–dumb," "shelled, eyes," "palate" that "Wish now no tasty rinse of wine") is strikingly similar to Newman's poem:

> O Christ, securely fence
> Our gates, beleaguer'd by the foe,–
> The gate of every sense.
> . . . lest the flesh in its excess
> Should lord it o'er the soul,

> Let taming abstinence repress
> The rebel, and control.

The poem "Terce" solicits the same spiritual use of the senses: "Let flesh, and heart, and lips, and mind, / Sound forth our witness to mankind." Yet a third Newman poem, "Flowers without Fruit," requests harnessing the excesses of words and thoughts ("Prune thou thy words, the thoughts control") as also the senses:

> But he who lets his feelings run
> In soft luxurious flow,
> Shrinks when hard service must be done,
> And faints at every woe.

Hopkins's astute analysis of Newman's style in his 1864 undergraduate essay "On the Signs of Health and Decay in the Arts" discloses, too, an acute familiarity with Newman. Hopkins differentiates between a chromatic and a diatonic literary style, and determines that Newman's style is chromatic while Carlyle's is diatonic. The "chromatic beauty" of Newman's style reveals, says Hopkins, such features as "emphasis" and "expression." Hopkins was using chromatic and diatonic metaphorically and idiosyncratically, and acknowledges a preference for the diatonic, the more imaginative.[123] The marked or abrupt kind of parallelism of the diatonic, in contrast to the chromatic or transitional type, exhibits features characteristic of his own poetry: metaphor, simile, parallelism, contrasts, antithesis, and the like. But Newman's chromatic style reveals expressive, dramatic, and oratorical features bearing the hallmarks of intensity, climax, and emphasis; in other words, Newman's is a combative or polemic style akin to that of speech, conversation, even argument.[124] Hopkins, as far as I can tell, was the first to have commented on Newman's oratorical style, what Newman himself in the *Grammar* calls "talk in prose."[125] Hopkins notes that the style reflects thinking aloud, as if with "pen to paper." He concedes certain advantages, but estimates that overall the style is flawed; it is marked by an absence of "proper eloquence" and a stylistic disruption that fractures the "continuity, the *contentio*, the strain of address." While he was presumably commenting on the *Apologia*, Hopkins remarked similarly on the *Grammar*, a treatise far less personal than the autobiographical *Apologia*: "What dissatisfies me (in point of style)," he told Edward Bond, "is a narrow circle of instance and quotation," which creates "a real want of brilliancy."[126] Newman's style lacks what to Hopkins was inscape, that "individually–distinctive beauty of style"

best represented in the diatonic. But despite this censure, Hopkins somehow felt
the need to compromise, describing Newman's style as in the tradition of the
"cultured, the most highly educated conversation."[127]

In his assessment of Newman's style, Walter Houghton relies on Hopkins's
perceptive analysis. Houghton finds in the style a desire simply to sketch "the
inner pattern and movement" of Newman's thoughts, Hopkins's thinking with
"pen to paper." Newman's "conversational idiom, in diction and rhythm," is
meant, says Houghton, to "translate the clash of ideas back into their original
human context." Gates, too, calls Newman's prose a "friendly discourse" and
"the familiar talk of a man of the world with his fellows."[128] Newman's heart–
to–heart style endeavors, then, to resituate literature within the arena of speech.
In effect, Hopkins was complaining about Newman's unaffectatious style,
which to Newman was a way of not allowing the style either to misrepresent or
supplant the genuine personality of the writer, to Newman the most persuasive
of factors.

Newman believed that the best style is conversational, spontaneous, and the
genuine reflection of an individual's self, emotions, and thoughts. "Persons
influence us," he writes in his Tamworth essay, "voices melt us, looks subdue
us."[129] He himself envisioned this an important criterion for a writer: "does he
image forth, to all does he give utterance, in a corresponding language, which
is as multiform as this inward mental action itself and analogous to it, the faithful
expression of his intense personality."[130] He consequently warned against unreal
words, the attention to words and language for their own sake whereby one is
led to speak, feel, and think right without any change in moral action. In fact, this
penchant even makes us disingenuous. "For to be ever attending to fitness and
propriety of our words, is (or at least there is a risk of its being) a kind of acting;
and knowing what can be said on both sides of a subject, is a main step towards
thinking the one side as good as the other." Thus Newman discredited the art
of composition as indispensable to poetry, for "attention to the language, for its
own sake, evidences not the true poet, but the mere artist."[131] Although he was
a frantic reviser of his own prose, Newman remained mindful that a sense of
artificiality and disingenuousness accompanies literary exercise, a point no
doubt of great disagreement between Newman and Hopkins. Despite the
conversational style of some of Hopkins's own poetry and its importance to
sprung rhythm, he felt that the business of words and language is the quintessence of poetry. Hopkins did concede an artificial quality to poetry but insisted
that a poem, somewhat oxymoronically, bears the marks of both a thing
spontaneous and a crafted work of art, the artificial, if it is to depict the

commonplace in a fresh light. Yet that "exquisite artifice" does not in fact "belong to artificial but to simple expression."[132]

The concept of a speech–based poetics is essentially Romantic. Newman, Hopkins, and the Romantics felt that the subtle and enigmatic ways of the mind required a new poetic medium, a conversational one. For example, central to the poetics of Wordsworth's *Preface to the Lyrical Ballads* was the attempt to choose situations from common life, to convey them in "the very language of men," and "to keep the Reader in the company of flesh and blood"; for true poetry, Wordsworth felt, is dialogic, "a man speaking to men."[133] Thus *The Prelude* was the baring of truth "As if to thee [Coleridge] alone in private talk"[134]; and on Coleridge reading the text: "With heart how full / Will he peruse these lines, this page—perhaps / A blank to other men."[135] In so personal an exchange, Wordsworth's readers become mere spectators or eavesdroppers.

Like the Romantics, then, Newman adopted this relaxed, conversational style he felt most convincing, and employed it even in the work meant to vindicate his maligned reputation. He self–consciously admits having a "loung-ing, free–and–easy way of carrying things on," evident in such homely expres-sions as "I came out of my shell; I remained out of it till 1841," speaking here of his emergence as a public figure; and before proceeding to flesh out the controversy between Rome and the Anglican Church warns the reader: "This will involve some dry discussion." Regarding his apology, Newman asks: "What then shall be the special imputation, against which I shall throw myself in these pages," a phrase he again uses to describe his peculiar reason for writing Tract 15: its subject came from a friend who "did not wish to be mixed up with the publication," and so "He gave it me, that I might throw it into shape."[136] This personableness in Newman's prose, what Hopkins described as a "charm of unaffected and personal sincerity,"[137] is advanced by the friendliness of his conversational idiom. But the *Apologia* is both a private and a public discourse, both Newman's "own testimony" and "pleading my cause before the world."[138] This apologetic posture, however, forced Newman to bridge all aesthetic distance between himself and the British public if he were to successfully exonerate himself in their eyes, if, that is, he were to reclothe himself as a living man and not as a scarecrow and to rescue his true voice from the phantom that now gibbers. To effect all this, Newman appeals directly to his English readers, here to their British sense of fairness: "Whatever judgment my readers may eventually form of me from these pages, I am confident they will believe me."[139] This joint private and public narratological stance is what distinguishes Newman from his Victorian contemporaries, many of whom in addressing a private cause often subsumed it to larger public mandates. Thus while at the outset the

Apologia could not presume a relationship with an audience, the goal was to forge that relationship as the narrative progresses and author and reader search for greater intimacy with each other.

Although critical of Newman's style, Hopkins singled out his conversational diction as a feature to be emulated. He felt that the best style is conversational. Throughout his essay, "Poetry and Verse," he characterized poetry as speech: "speech framed for the contemplation of the mind," "speech framed to be heard," "speech only employed to carry the inscape of speech," or "speech couched in a repeating figure."[140] Hopkins's prosodic theory of sprung rhythm, the rhythm of speech, is built on this idea of a conversational idiom. He employed sprung rhythm, he told Bridges, because it is "the nearest to the rhythm of prose, that is the native and natural rhythm of speech"; and again to Bridges: "My verse is less to be read than heard, as I have told you before; it is oratorical."[141] That desire to simulate conversation in poetry can often be found in the casual, friendly, and colloquial expressions present in Hopkins's poetry, qualities that made it attractive to modern poetics: "and few know this"; "Ah well! it is all a purchase"; "Fetched fresh, as I suppose"; "Why, it seemed of course; seemed of right it should"; "I might let bygones be"; "Felix Randal the farrier, O is he dead then"; "Ah well, God rest him all road ever he offended"; "Hand to mouth he lives"; "who knows how"; and, "Must you be gorged with proof?" Walter Ong is correct when he concludes that Hopkins's theology "lives where his poetry lives, in intimate contact with today's human lifeworld"; and this is so because "its roots were sunk directly and deeply into living vernacular English."[142] But while Hopkins held to the conversational idiom of poetry, he insisted that the diction of poetry is quite different from that of prose. Poetry does participate in the rhythm and, to a lesser extent, the diction of speech, but poetic form requires greater rigidity and stronger expression than one normally finds in speech or writing. Consequently, "The diction of poetry could not then be the same with that of prose," and the diction of prose "ought not to be that of poetry."[143]

Hopkins's distinction of the difference in the diction of poetry and prose was an obvious admission of a Romantic (a word he did not like) poetics, which he shared with Newman. While Newman and his fellow Tractarians were involved in writing religious tracts, they were as involved in the writing of poetry, especially poetry of a Romantic kind, a genre conducive to their religious cause and to the church. G.B. Tennyson's *Victorian Devotional Poetry*, a study of the literature written either by the Tractarians or poets whose writings evidence the survival of Tractarian aesthetics, finds that though a minor genre, Tractarian poetry was "the poetry of the early phase of the Movement . . . out of which the later poetry grew," and that that poetry and its aesthetics help clarify "the Victorian experience."[144] But Tractarian poetry was not limited to the Movement. While historians generally agree that the Movement began and ended with Newman, there are as many who argue that it did not end until the century was over. Thus later disciples of Newman, like Hopkins, would have participated in Tractarian poetics. The focus, then, on Tractarian poetry should not end with an examination of the poetry that pre–dates 1845, which gave greater access to the Movement otherwise confined to an exclusive handful of churchmen.

So closely related, even indebted, was Tractarian poetry to nineteenth–century Romanticism, especially to the particular epistemology advanced by Wordsworth and Coleridge, that Stephen Prickett calls Tractarianism "the tradition of Coleridge and Wordsworth in the Victorian Church."[145] The Tractarians, for instance, approached nature in a religious way and made much of the religious nature of poetry. Several of them admitted fondness of the Romantics and were aware that they were working with related aesthetics. But, not surprisingly, the Tractarians did not regard themselves Romantics. Hopkins, as far as I can tell, was the first critic familiar with the Tractarians to so tag them, and this was on the basis of their poetry and the particular epistemology on which the tracts were founded: the importance of the commonplace, the primitive church, and the sacramental imagination.

In a 1 December 1881 letter from Roehampton, Hopkins describes schools and their attributes. The Lake poets, he felt, employed an impure form of medievalism and a "sort of colourless classical keepings" in their descriptions. He called them realists and great observers of nature ("faithful but not rich") and saw their style and diction as "the mean or standard of English." Hopkins recognized in Keble, Faber, and Newman, the three most celebrated Tractarian poets, the expiration of the Lake School.[146] Hopkins was right about the Tractarians, for the accepted accusation against them had been that although they were concerned with nature, that concern did not always translate into a keen observation of and an emotional attachment to nature. Nature for its own sake was seldom contemplated; rather, it was used more often than not for analogical or typological purposes. But to apply that accusation to Wordsworth and Coleridge is hardly convincing. Hopkins was falsely reading the Romantics through Dixon and the Tractarians, who, although influenced by the Romantics, cannot be entirely claimed as their true representations. The same, to an extent, can be said of Hopkins. Many of his pre–Jesuit poems, like "A Vision of the Mermaids," are very much Romantic. But those typological poems, the Herbertian ones like "Easter," are, because of their analogical use of nature, more Tractarian than Romantic. His Jesuit poems where nature is the subject are even more Romantic. Nature has its own value, its own "sweet especial scene," and, far more than its referentialness, nature's very energy is a divine one; in nature is something far more deeply interfused; in it "lives the dearest freshness deep down things." Even in the more sophisticated religious poems, nature becomes sacramental, transubstantial.

Newman, for one, saw poetry as the religious expression or image of the emotion, what, in Romantic terms, he calls the "spontaneous overpouring of thought."[147] But it was Keble's *Lectures on Poetry,* dedicated to Wordsworth, that "champion" of the "poor and simple" and "chief minister" of "high and sacred truth," that more fully articulated the idea of poetry as a religious expression.[148] The forty lectures, known officially as the *Praelectiones*, were part of Keble's official responsibility to the Professorship of Poetry at Oxford, a position to which he was elected in 1831. In them, Keble notioned that the true essence of poetry is found not in the profundity of thought and expressions but in the "depths of the heart and the most sacred feelings of the men who write." Poets, said Keble, are of the two kinds—those who compose in order to seek relief by providing an outlet for "some disturbing emotion" or those who simply imitate other poets who are moved by such incitements. He claimed that the greater the degree of influence feelings exert on our affections, and the more permanent they are, the closer they become related to poetry. In turn, he associated these emotive characteristics of poetry to religion, seeing them as guides to nature and God. In this symbiotic exchange between poetry and religion, poetry "lends religion her wealth of symbols and similes: Religion restores these again to Poetry, clothed with so splendid a radiance that they appear to be no longer merely symbols, but to partake . . . of the nature of sacraments"; in fact, the very exercise of poetry, Keble held, "will be found to possess . . . the power of guiding and composing the mind to worship and prayer."[149] Clearly Keble's dedication to Wordsworth, as G.B. Tennyson points out, was not "merely a respectful nod from the younger poet to the Laureate, but the assertion of a close kinship in poetic practice and outlook between the two."[150]

Wordsworth had earlier envisioned poetry and religion serving what Thomas Vargish calls a "common psychic need, the need to represent and perceive spiritual realities in material forms."[151] Wordsworth talked of poetry in a religiously therapeutic sense, of poetry being most itself when it "administers the comforts and breathes the spirit of religion":

> The commerce between Man and his Maker cannot be
> carried on but by a process where much is represented in
> little, and the Infinite Being accommodates himself to a
> finite capacity. In all this may be perceived the affinity
> between religion and poetry; between religion—making up
> the deficiencies of reason by faith; and poetry—passionate
> for the instruction of reason; between religion—whose
> element is infinitude, and whose ultimate trust is the
> supreme of things, submitting herself to circumscription,
> and reconciled to substitutions; and poetry—ethereal and
> transcendent, yet incapable to sustain her existence without
> sensuous incarnation.[152]

The sacramental relationship religion and poetry share in forging a link between
man and God as between the material and the immaterial espoused here by
Wordsworth was readily accepted by Keble and Newman, both of whom were
seeking a poetics for spiritual and emotional revivification within the Church.
To them, as to Hopkins, poetry did not replace religion but served it.

When Newman turned to Keble, then, he saw his effectiveness as one whose
poetry heals and revitalizes religion. Keble, Newman claimed,

> found the Anglican system all but destitute of this divine
> element . . .—a ritual dashed upon the ground, trodden on,
> and broken piecemeal;—prayers, clipped, pieced, torn,
> shuffled about at pleasure, until the meaning of the
> composition perished, and offices which had been poetry
> were no longer even good prose. . . . Scripture lessons
> turned into chapters;—heaviness, feebleness,
> unwieldingness, where the Catholic rites had had the
> lightness and airiness of a spirit;—vestments chucked off,
> lights quenched, jewels stolen, the pomp and circum-
> stances of worship annihilated.

Thus Keble's poems, Newman insisted,

> became a sort of comment upon its formularies and
> ordinances, and almost elevated them into the dignity of a
> religious system. It kindled hearts towards his Church; it
> gave something for the gentle and forlorn to cling to; and it

> raised up advocates for it among those, who otherwise, if
> God and their good Angel had suffered it, might have
> wandered away into some sort of philosophy, and ac-
> knowledged no Church at all." [153]

This spiritual impoverishment of Anglicanism that Newman saw Keble addressing was in fact stated by Keble himself: "prayers in our churches are few
and far between; as for sacramental symbols . . . there is not the least thought of
such now . . . . Consequently, men gladly betake themselves to rural charms and
pastoral poetry and find in them a very real satisfaction."[154] Newman's point is
clear then: were it not for Keble's poetry, the Anglican Church would have
remained desecrated, prosaic, inert, and banal, and its people directionless. For,
as M.H. Abrams puts it, theological ideas, and one might add religious
observances, once lifeless can become "alive and drastically innovative when
transferred . . . into the alien soil of aesthetics."[155] Benjamin Jowett felt similarly
about Newman's ideas. While he voiced disagreement with many of Newman's
principles, he, nevertheless, could not help thinking that "they will have on the
whole a salutary influence on the Protestant Church in bringing back men's
minds to a class of duties which have been too much neglected."[156]

But to the Tractarians the relationship between religion and aesthetics was
not alien; rather both shared a harmonious and reciprocal relationship. *The
Christian Year*, wrote C.P.S. Clarke, "brought religious poetry in touch with the
Romantic Movement of the day, and paved the way for a revolt in religion, as
in poetry, against the formalism, coldness, and utilitarianism, which was then
fashionable."[157] Newman said much the same thing: "When the general tone of
religious literature was so nerveless and impotent, as it was at that time [1827],
Keble struck an original note and woke up in the hearts of thousands a new
music, the music of a school, long unknown in England." The historian, Owen
Chadwick, makes similar claims:

> Probably it is this element of feeling, the desire to use
> poetry as vehicle of religious language, the sense of awe
> and mystery in religion, the profundity of reverence, the
> concern with the conscience not only by way of duty, but
> by growth towards holiness, which marks the vague
> distinction between the old–fashioned high churchmen and
> the Oxford men.[158]

The religious became even more meaningful to the Tractarians than it was to the Romantics, so much so that one can argue, as G.B. Tennyson does, that it is "an almost irresistible temptation to say that the fundamental principle of Tractarian poetics is the subordination of art to religion."[159] Thus, believing that "Revealed Religion should be especially poetical" (Keble himself had claimed that "poetry was providentially destined to prepare the way for Revealed Truth itself"), Newman felt that Keble did for Anglicanism what "none but a poet could do: he made it poetical"; and because poetry, especially the Romantic kind, embraces the imagistic, emotive, and mysterious, it became a subterfuge for Tractarians who

> have not the Catholic Church to flee to and repose upon,
> for the Church herself is the most sacred and august of
> poets. . . . She is the poet of her children; full of music to
> soothe the sad and control the wayward,—wonderful in
> story for the imagination of the romantic; rich in symbol
> and imagery, so that gentle and delicate feelings, which
> will not bear words, may in silence intimate their presence
> or commune with themselves. Her very being is poetry.
> Such poets as are born under her shadow, she takes into
> service; she sets them to write hymns, or to compose
> chants, or to embellish shrines, or to determine ceremo-
> nies, or to marshall processions.[160]

The implication here is that Keble, Newman felt, had taken fundamental religious beliefs and given them vital poetic expressions, an alliance instrumental to the Movement. The poetic strand was "not an appendix to the Movement at its best, a tiara of jewels worn to sparkle but not needed for the hair," writes Chadwick. Rather, it was "as natural and integral to the Movement as the desire to make the churches numinous, to transform them from bare houses of preaching into temples evocative of prayer," for it became one with "that symbolic and sacramental consciousness which formed the deepest link, perhaps the only true and valid link, between Romanticism and Catholicism."[161]

The religious nature of poetry, then, was crucial to the Tractarians. A poetry such as Hopkins's that proclaims that God's "mystery must be instressed, stressed," that declares a world "charged with the grandeur of God," and seeks to inscape the numinous in nature, Christ's self playing in "ten thousand places," participates unequivocally in a Tractarian aesthetics. In fact, Keble's biographer, Georgina Battiscombe, ties Hopkins to Keble when she locates a relatedness between Keble's hymn for the "Fourth Sunday after Trinity" and Hopkins's "God's Grandeur." But, says Battiscombe, Keble's poem "lacks the immediacy" of Hopkins's.[162] In their revising of Coleridge, Newman and Keble have shown that poetry and religion converge because poetic language, in itself a reality that becomes transubstantiated into a higher reality, although not necessarily truer, at once takes on the convention of a sacrament. A related sacramental or incarnational poetics can be traced almost anywhere in Hopkins's most serious poetry, in which "Heaven and earth are word of, worded by," Christ. In Hopkins, "The divine manifests itself in concrete things through sacraments," writes Margaret Ellsberg; "poetry through such devices as symbolism and metaphor condenses an unseen reality into words"; and for Hopkins whose poetry seeks to discover God, poetic words share "the responsibility and power of sacramental words."[163]

In Hopkins's pre–conversion poetry, things from nature, it could be argued, are employed for typological purposes. For example, the bread and grapes of "Barnfloor and Winepress," as things in nature, are without vitality as natural things; they exist solely to illustrate Christ, operating then as types not symbols. The barnfloor and winepress represent the agony Christ experienced in order to become our sacrament. However, in the post–conversion poems for which Hopkins is best known, things from nature now operate symbolically though still sacramentally; the daylight falcon, the starlight night, and the season spring do not function in the same way the grapes do. These poems employ the natural not just as a picture of the supernatural but to invoke the supernatural. Through an Ignatian sort of contemplation, the ordinariness of the natural is soon transformed into the miraculous presence of the supernatural. In these poems the world is "charged with the grandeur of God," and the Holy Ghost can be inscaped brooding regeneratively "over the bent / World." The "May–mess," "March–bloom" stars that, when contemplated, become quite a "purchase" and a "prize" envelop the spiritual: Christ, Mary, and the saints. The spiritual ligature connecting heaven and earth is implicit in the "Thrush's eggs" that resemble "little low heavens," a connectedness even more subtly hinted in the "descending blue," the "lightnings," and in the "glassy peartree," the latter an image of paradisial innocence. Here too the locus of true spring is not in the natural season but in its transubstantiated form in Christ. The poet inscapes Christ ("glean our Saviour") in the skyscape and landscape, the very contours of which do not simply represent but actually are his "world–wielding shoulder." Finally, the falcon's supreme control, beauty, and chivalry all buckle in the person of Christ, whose own heroic acts and self–sacrifice become the things celebrated. Wendell Johnson is correct when he says that the images in Hopkins's rich verse are "real things in nature which in and *by* their reality have sacramental meaning . . . , seeing a windhover is glimpsing Christ incarnate."[164]

Poetry, to return to Keble and Newman, also served an invaluable therapeutic role, an indirect method known and exploited by poets. In his *Lectures on Poetry*, which argues repeatedly for reserve, Keble made the rather bold claim that God, or rather a sort of Shelleyan "Almighty Power," had "furnished amplest comfort for sufferers . . . in the gift of Poetry." For poetry exhibits great "efficacy in soothing men's emotions and steadying the balance of their mind." This happens when in lingering over "language and rhythm," our minds become occupied and diverted from "cares and troubles." Keble concluded then: "Let us therefore deem the glorious art of Poetry a kind of medicine divinely bestowed upon man: which gives healing relief to secret mental emotion."[165] The lectures show Keble's distrust of lyrical poetry because it allows the too–free rein of the emotions. But Keble insisted that the medicinal role of poetry does not fracture conventional reserve nor stifle enthusiasm. Rather, it orders and regulates the emotions.

Commenting on Keble's poetry and reserve, Newman described the method as one that provides relief for the "over–burned mind" and a "channel through which emotion finds expression, and that a safe, regulated expression. Now what is the Catholic Church, viewed in her human aspects, but a discipline of the affections and passions? What are her ordinances and practices but the regulated expression of keen, or deep, or turbid feeling, and thus a 'cleansing,' as Aristotle would word it, of the sick soul?"[166] Keble saw the cathartic quality as the *sine qua non* of poetry, an idea not entirely similar to Wordsworth's notion that in our increasingly modern society poetry will become indispensable to consolation and the completing agent to science and religion: "In middle and declining age, a scattered number of serious persons resort to poetry, as to religion, for a protection against the pressure of trivial employments, and as a consolation for the afflictions of life."[167] But Newman, following Wordsworth, did envision the turning to religious poetry as a modern substitute for conventional religion: "the taste for poetry of a religious kind has in modern times," he claimed, replaced "the deep contemplative spirit of the early Church." It may be said, he concluded, that "Poetry then is our mysticism," for it plummets the surface of things to transport the individual from "the material to the invisible world."[168]

Keble's immensely successful *The Christian Year*, published in 1827, a year in which he was emotionally exhausted, best exemplifies the medicinal role of poetry. This anonymously published collection of occasional poems, in which Keble, like Hopkins, felt he was unable to breed one work that wakes, reveals a melancholic disposition masked in Keble's ordinarily controlled, even buoyant, personality. Newman recognized this integrative quality in *The Christian Year*, calling it "the most soothing, tranquillizing, subduing work of the day; if poems can be found to enliven in dejection, and to comfort in anxiety; to cool the over–sanguine, to refresh the weary, and to awe the worldly; to instill resignation into the impatient, and calmness into the fearful and agitated—they are these."[169] In a 1 February 1828 letter of appreciation for a copy of *The Christian Year* Keble had sent him Newman noted the comfort the work gave his sister Mary, who died lisping some of the poems she had memorized from what to many was the Tractarian Bible. "No one can fully enter into their meaning but those who have been in deep affliction," he wrote Keble. Months later in that memorable ride to Cuddesdon in which Newman envisioned the dead Mary as part of the very landscape of that little village skirting Oxford ("Dear Mary seemed embodied in every tree and hid behind every hill"), he found himself quoting from Keble's *The Christian Year*: "Chanting with a *solemn* voice, mind us of our *better choice*." So personal was the line to Newman that he felt: "I could hardly believe the lines were not my own and Keble had not taken them from me. I wish it were possible for words to put down those indefinite vague and withal subtle feelings which quite pierce the soul and make it sick," echoing here again intellectual pain.[170]

Keble's poems in the volume certainly do attempt to express verbally the mystery of what, in a familiar Hopkins phrase, the "heart heard of, ghost guessed." In the dedicatory poem, for example, the poet, in the midst of a world too much with him and feeling out of tune with spiritual things, opts for tranquillity and prayer to reconnect with the heavenly and spiritual. He invokes the spirit of Harmony to once more provide the order it did at the creation while he, the poet, awaits spiritual direction. Both the order and direction the poet seeks involve the very task of writing, granting *The Christian Year* the aura of an epic. He admits unfitness for the task, before ending the poem with the metaphor of poetry as music. The poet holds little hope that his poetry will so rehabilitate him as did David's harp when it freed Saul's troubled spirit, but he continues listening to the music, i.e., writing the poems, convicted that the repetition will create a tranquilizing effect, similar to what Coleridge seeks when he attends to and interprets the witchery of sounds from the aeolian harp. The poems, and especially the writing of them, are the balm for those soul-piercing pangs. So vital to the Victorians was the devotional and cathartic purpose of *The Christian Year* that not only were ninety–two editions of the book published in Keble's lifetime (Mrs. Hopkins owned a copy of the forty-third edition, 1853, a gift presumably given to her by Manley), but even George Eliot's Maggie Tulliver initially turned to it in her despair. After soon putting it down, on the false premise that it was a hymnbook, Maggie turned instead to Thomas á Kempis's *Imitation of Christ*. But upon discovering that *The Christian Year* was not a hymnbook (a false assertion obviously), Maggie returned to it, along with the Bible and the *Imitation of Christ*, for emotional and spiritual resuscitation. A similar claim can be made for Newman's hymns, especially his familiar "Lead, Kindly Light." After Bathsheba Troy, nee Everdene, in Hardy's *Far From the Madding Crowd* (1874), had erected a tombstone on the grave of her husband Francis, she heard the church choir practicing a new hymn and was "stirred by emotions [religious no doubt] which latterly she had assumed to be altogether dead within her." On hearing the voices of the children, "all the impassioned scenes of her brief experience seemed to revive with added emotion at that moment, and those scenes which had been without emotion during enactment had emotion then." That hymn was Newman's "Lead, Kindly Light." The lines

> I loved the garish day, and spite of fears,
> Pride ruled my will: remember not past years

recalled to her mind Gabriel's true perception of her, and the line "Which I have loved long since, and lost awhile" her relationship to Gabriel.

Newman held out the same cathartic goal for poetry, suggesting in his essay on Aristotle that poetry provides a "solace for the mind broken by the disappointments and sufferings of actual life," that it is "the utterance of the inward emotions of a right moral feeling," and that it adopts "metaphorical language" as the only means available to communicate "intense feelings."[171] Wordsworth's "Ode: Intimations of Immortality" had a related effect on Hopkins. Attempting to impress Dixon with the healing power, perhaps the most important quality, in Wordsworth's poetry, Hopkins regarded the ode the best thing Wordsworth wrote; from it "human nature got another of those shocks, and the tremble from it is spreading. . . . I am, ever since I knew the ode, in that tremble." While Wordsworth's insight determines the value of each poem of his, in this ode "his insight was at its very deepest, and hence to my mind the extreme value of the poem." Commenting more specifically on the poem, Hopkins praised its subject, the execution, the "musically interlaced" rhymes, "the rhythms . . . (surely it is a magical change 'O joy that in our embers'), the diction throughout so charged and steeped in beauty and yearning (what a stroke 'The moon doth with delight'!)."[172]

The joint devotional and cathartic function of poetry is frequently admitted in Hopkins's correspondence. He reminded Dixon that "the only just judge, the only just literary critic, is Christ, who prizes, is proud of, and admires, more than any other man . . . the gifts of his own making." He again told Dixon: "If you value what I write, if I do myself, much more does our Lord," who "chooses to avail himself of what I leave at his disposal."[173] The gradual release of Hopkins's poems by Robert Bridges in such anthologies as *Lyra Sacra: A Book of Religious Verse* (1895), *Prayer from the Poets: A Calendar of Devotion* (1898), *A Little Book of Life and Death* (1902), and *The Spirit of Man: An Anthology in English & French from the Philosophers & Poets* (1916) shows that Bridges recognized, though seldom endorsed, the devotional mode of Hopkins's poetry.

In the preface to *The Spirit of Man*, an anthology of poems written to console those who lost loved ones during the War, the editor, Bridges, felt that "From the consequent miseries, the insensate and interminable slaughter, the hate and filth, we can turn to seek comfort only in the quiet confidence of our souls," proposing here a sort of Romantic retreat within the self, akin to Coleridge's "I may not hope from outward forms to win / The passion and the life, whose fountains are within." Thus we must "look instinctively to the seers and poets of mankind, whose sayings are the oracles and prophesies of loveliness and lovingkindness . . . ; and it is in their abundant testimony to the good and beautiful that we find support for our faith."[174] The six poems by Hopkins included in this anthology, which features mostly Romantic poets and offers verses for various moods (*The Christian Year* offered verses on various occasions), are classified under such categories as sorrows, worship, conscience, and self–renunciation. In a 1973 edition of *The Spirit of Man* for Longman, W.H. Auden suggested that Bridges's organizational strategy was more aesthetic and ethical than literary, "to offer consolation to hearts in suffering and distress and to strengthen the wills of the dejected." To have included Hopkins was to certify that his poems, like those of the Romantics and Tractarians, afford a search for "purity and a truth" denied by the world, and that they evoke in us a "natural sympathy with everything great and splendid in the physical and moral world."[175]

Hand in hand with the Romantics, the Tractarians envisioned poetry as lyrical, as religious, and as a return to the primitive and commonplace. They readily appropriated the lyre, the preeminent symbol of Romantic poetry. A series of Keble's poems were entitled *Lyra Innocentium*, the poems in *The Christian Year* were all called hymns, and he corroborated with Newman and others on *Lyra Apostolica*, titles admittedly Romantic. Newman's collection of poems in *Lyra Apostolica*, what R.W. Church describes as "sermons which arrested the hearers by their keenness and pathetic undertones,"[176] was inspired by "historical sites and beautiful scenes,"[177] and was thus a joint Romantic and apostolic lyric. "The very title of the work," writes G.B. Tennyson, "tells the story of its Tractarian blend of religious and romantic sensibilities." However, missing in it are the waywardness and unpredictability endemic to Romantic inspirational poetry. "For the Tractarians, inspiration is not an errant breeze, or even whisperings of the muse, but rather the breath of the divine."[178] But Newman does assert the familiar Romantic lyric, the inception of which derives from nature. As the soul in *Gerontius* prepares for purgatory, it hears a hymn sung by the Second Choirs of Angelicals. Echoing both Coleridge's "The Eolian Harp" and Shelley's "Ode to the West Wind," the song simulates the Romantic's intellectual breeze playing upon the lyre:

> The sound is like the rushing of the wind—
> The summer wind—among the lofty pines;
> Swelling and dying, echoing round about,
> Now here, now distant, wild and beautiful;
> While, scatter'd from the branches it has stirr'd,
> Descend ecstatic odours.

Another poem, "My Lady Nature and Her Daughters," discovers too the inception of poetry in "Nature's earth, and sea, and sky," where "Fervid thoughts inspire." Newman is mindful here of his own comment that "It is the charm of the descriptive poetry of a religious mind, that nature is viewed in a moral connection."[179]

Several of Hopkins's poems flirt with this idea that nature animates the human spirit, inspires poetry and might even be divine. His love letter to nature, "Binsey Poplars," elegizes aspens unwittingly felled on an otherwise graceless landscape in Godstow. The poem's ideological double, "Duns Scotus's Oxford," protests the destruction of the city's natural beauty—more specifically against the fracturing of the equipoise that "country and town did / Once encounter in." The "cordial air" of the "Valley of the Elewy" "made those kind people" (the Watsons of Shooter's Hill) "a hood / All over, as a bevy of eggs the mothering wing." And it was in their house "where all were good / To me, God knows, deserving no such thing: / Comforting smell breathed at very entering, / Fetched fresh, as I suppose, off some sweet wood." In "Ribblesdale," the "sweet Earth, sweet landscape, with leaves throng / And louched low grass," though without mouth and heart, yet cries out to heaven against man's wanton destruction of nature:

> Thy plea with him who dealt, nay does now deal,
> Thy lovely dale down thus and this bids reel
> Thy river, and o'er gives all to rack or wrong.

"Inversnaid," celebrating Loch Lomond and the neighbouring landscape, asks "What would the world be, once bereft / Of wet and of wildness?" And "Ashboughs" opens with the very idea that nature sires poetry:

> Not of all my eyes see, wandering on the world,
> Is anything a milk to the mind so, so sighs deep
> Poetry to it, as a tree whose boughs break in the sky.

The titles of these poems all come directly from nature, naming either trees or places. To Wordsworth, Keble, Newman, and Hopkins, nature gives impulse to poetry and is that metaphorical book that instresses and stresses a divine presence.

The connections between nature, music, and poetic composition represented in the lyre were as critical to Newman and Hopkins as they were to the Romantics. The collection of poems entitled *Lyra Apostolica* appeared monthly in the *British Magazine*, founded and edited by Hugh James Rose, Rector of Hadleigh and a Tractarian sympathizer. These poems show that Newman was convinced that poetry, like the tracts and university sermons, can also be an apt vehicle for propaganda. That the work was veiled in anonymity meant that Newman envisioned it as partly religious and partly political, describing it himself as a "quasi–political engine." And in fact the very motto for the volume that describes Achilles's return to battle suggests the work's propagandistic intentions. Writing to Frederick Rose about the work's political intention, Newman noted: "Do not stirring times bring out poets? Do they not give opportunity for the rhetoric of poetry, and the persuasion?"[180] The Tractarian Isaac Williams recalled a conversation he and Newman had about *Lyra Apostolica* during a walk in the gardens at Trinity College: "He said in his manner, 'Isaac, we must make a row in the world. Why should we not? Only consider what the Peculiars, i.e. the Evangelicals have done with a few half truths to work upon! And with our principles, if we set resolutely to work, we can do the same.'" Newman told Samuel Rickards much the same thing about *Lyra*: "I trust the stimulus we have been able to give to Churchmen has been like the application of volatile salts to a person fainting, pungent but restorative."[181]

The lyrical nature of Tractarian poetry lends itself, not easily however, to musical settings, and in fact the writing of hymns was felt by Newman to be essential to Tractarians who were outside the pale of the Catholic Church: "Such poets as are born under her shadow, she takes into service; she sets them to write hymns, or to compose chants, or to embellish shrines, or to determine ceremonies, or to marshall processions."[182] Thus, quite a number of Tractarian poems ultimately occupied, however painfully at first, a natural place in Anglican hymnody. According to Owen Chadwick, "In 1827 nearly all high churchmen still refused to allow hymns in their churches." So taciturn were they, says Chadwick, that they were later called "the high and dry, for their sobriety consisted of a rational fear of emotional riots which they believed themselves able to discern among dissenters and English evangelicals."[183] But the Evangelicals, or "Peculiars" as they were pejoratively called, had taught the High Church that vitality in worship can be achieved without any threat to conventional reserve—a restrained emotionalism that refuses to bare the emotions in public. Evangelical hymns taught English Christianity "the worth of poetry as a kindling and satisfaction of devotional aspiration."[184] But opposed early by the High Church because of its "enthusiasm" and ties to Methodistical evangelicalism, hymn singing was by 1860 accepted in almost every Anglican church as a vital part of worship. Such popularity is evident in Isaac Williams's *Hymn on the Catechism* (1842), Keble's *Hymns for Emigrants* (1854), and William Henry Monk's *Hymns Ancient and Modern* (1861). Monk's 1882 version was used in some twenty–one cathedrals and in most London churches. Frederick William Faber, a close friend of Wordsworth and a Tractarian turned Catholic, also left what Wordsworth thought was successful poetry to writing hymns. His most celebrated and still popular is "Faith of Our Fathers," which, while patristic in intention, found immediate acceptance in almost every congregation.

Of Newman's poems in *Lyra Apostolica*, nine were meant to be sung and three were designated hymns. Still the most familiar is "Lead, Kindly Light." Two hymns, "Firmly I Believe and Truly" and "Praise to the Holiest in the Height," were taken from *The Dream of Gerontius*, hymns that Owen Chadwick judged the "best Victorian credal hymns."[185] So acclaimed was "Praise to the Holiest in the Height," taken from the fifth choir of Angelicals, that it was played at the funerals of Gladstone and R.W. Church. On Newman's proposal, the famed Sir Edward Elgar produced a famous oratorio from *Gerontius*. In addition, several revised editions of the *Birmingham Oratory Hymn Book* (1854, 1862, 1888) contain hymns written by Newman.[186] So close a nexus did hymns and Tractarian ideas form that, according to Louis Benson, "it is doubtful if anything short of Tractarian principles, or any urgency less than the Oxford upheaval, would have had the force to overcome the deep prejudices and deliberate ignorance that had kept the old church hymns outside the pale of Protestant sympathy."[187] Even the religious skeptic Robert Bridges was not exempt from the literary and historical, if not religious, interest in hymns. He himself arranged a hymnbook of congregational songs, *The Yattendon Hymnal* (1899), which contained forty–four hymns written by Bridges himself. Thirteen other hymns by Bridges, celebrated mostly for their poetic quality, were later included in *The English Hymnal* (1906).[188]

Hopkins falls squarely in this hymnal tradition. He did not generally consider his poetry hymns, that is, meant for communal worship, the one exception being the "Silver Jubilee," which was "set effectively by a very musical and very noisy member of the community and was sung as a glee by the choir."[189] But the joint musical and devotional nature of his poetry means that they could be so considered, for hymns are in effect, as G.B. Tennyson points out, "the closest of the subdivisions of religious poetry to . . . devotional poetry."[190] Indeed, English devotional poetry is one with hymnody. Hopkins emphasized repeatedly that his poetry should be read, "loud, leisurely, poetical (not rhetorical) recitation." He called "Morning, Midday, and Evening Sacrifice" a song and "Spring and Fall," a "little lyric" that has "some plainsong music to it"; the "long sonnet" (presumably "The Starlight Night") "shd. be almost sung"; and "The Leaden Echo and Golden Echo" has in Hopkins's canon no musical competitor.[191]

The poem "Who shaped these walls" associates a piece of architecture beautifully built with musical composition, linking both arts under the same aesthetic rubric:

> Who shaped these walls has shewn
> The music of his mind,
> Made known, though thick through stone,
> What beauty beat behind.

Hopkins especially liked the music of Henry Purcell, the celebrated seventeenth–century British composer. He most revered in Purcell, in addition to his expressing in music the "moods of man's mind," the ability to render musical utterances to the very being of man, to the "rehearsal / Of own, of abrupt self." In "The Kind Betrothal," "Silence sing[s] . . . The Music that I care to hear"; amid the cacophonous "rabble" and "babble" on board the wrecked *Deutschland*, a "virginal tongue" rang out to the foundering passengers; and the reverberating song of the spring thrush "strikes like lightnings to hear him sing." Hopkins's sister Kate "specially remember[ed]" his homecoming during his priestly years when he would repeat Bridges's "the Skylark to us beating with his hand to mark the measure. At other times he was full of musical composition."[192] The Hopkins family owned a copy of Benjamin Webb's and Canon W. Cooke's *The Hymnary: A Book of Church Songs* (1870, 1872), generally known as "Barnby's Hymnary," after its musical editor, Sir Joseph Barnby. The collection, according to Benson, is thought to be the most complete manual of High–Church hymnody, making provisions for hours, days, seasons, and occasions.[193] So important was music to the Hopkins family that Madeline House called it "another household activity," and stated that not only was there in the house music written by family members (mostly by Manley and Grace) but the family owned much public music.[194] At times the very writing of poetry, because of its ties to music, redeemed for Hopkins his uninspirational winter worlds:

> Every impulse and spring of art seems to have died in me,
> except for music, and that I pursue under almost an
> impossibility of getting on. Nevertheless I still put down
> my pieces, for the airs seem worth it; they seem to me to
> have something in them which other modern music has not
> got.[195]

This idea relates to Keble's claim that lingering over the language and rhythm of poetry actually liberates the mind from cares.

A final profound parallel between Hopkins and Newman relates to their understanding of the relationship between reason and belief. Faith, as Newman describes it, is "assenting to a doctrine as true, which we do not see, which we cannot prove."[196] This kind of reasoning is most exhaustively argued in Newman's *An Essay in Aid of a Grammar of Assent*, a work to which Hopkins was most attracted. When in February 1883 Hopkins wrote from Stonyhurst on the occasion of Newman's eighty–second birthday, he requested publishing a sixth edition of the *Grammar* with a commentary. Newman, however, rejected the idea, enumerating an impressive list of the book's remarkable current successes to establish the inexpediency of a new edition. In fact, when the book was published in 1870 it was sold out on the first day, and two additional editions were published in that year alone. Newman also felt that any commentary, "however brilliant," will serve only as a kind of life–support devise for the book, a project, says Newman, that "has no charms for me. Therefore, sensible as I am of your kindness, I will not accept it." But Hopkins was not to be so easily dismissed. Two months later he repeated the request, this time denying that his motive was gratuitous. "I must still say," Newman responded, "that you paid me a very kind compliment."[197]

Hopkins began reading the *Grammar* in August 1873 while on vacation on the Isle of Man. "It is perhaps heavy reading," he told his friend Edward Bond. Mindful of his earlier remarks on Newman's sincere and conversational style, he again commented that "The justice and candour and gravity and rightness of mind is what is so beautiful in all he writes."[198] He was attracted to the *Grammar* because of the veracity of its argument against the sole exercise of reason ("notional assent") in matters of faith and the premise that it is not only possible, but credible, to assent without total knowledge. Newman in fact felt that "there is an assent which is not a virtual certitude, and is lost in the attempt to make it certitude."[199] Not that reason is feeble in itself, but it must cooperate with the senses and the imagination to attain certitude, a form of assent but ancillary to it. This process from "conditional inference to unconditional assent" becomes in the *Grammar* Newman's theory of cognition, "assent," the mental assertion and totally unconditional acceptance of a proposition; or, to use his precise words, "the mental assertion of an intelligible proposition, as an act of intellect direct, absolute, complete in itself, unconditional, arbitrary, yet not incompatible with the appeal to argument, and at least in many cases exercised unconsciously."[200] Newman believed that to insist always on proof is to invite paralysis; and advocating as he always does the active rather than the passive life of the religious, intellectual and spiritual warfare rather than spineless surrender, he insisted that to act one must "assume, and that assumption is faith."[201] His letter to William Brownlow on the *Grammar* is one example of how assent operates: "I believe in design because I believe in God; not in a God because I see design."[202] This psychology of belief engages the intellect and the imagination in an ineffable union, "creating a certitude of its truths by arguments too various for direct enumeration, too personal and deep for words, too powerful and concurrent for refutation."[203]

Rather than embrace design or other philosophical arguments, Newman proposed "real assent," which he subdivided into "simple assent" (belief exercised unconsciously) and "complex or reflex assents" (belief exercised consciously and deliberately). He called the two modes of apprehension (assent)—the process from images to notions—the notional and the real. Real assent, also "imaginative," is more effective than notional because it vitalizes "the affections and passions" and values memory and the imagination. The imagination is tied to the principle of action, for assent to a "real proposition" is, in fact, "assent to imagination," which in turn supplies objects to our "emotional and moral nature." Thus Christ becomes accessible to us notionally through the sacraments; but he is also accessible in a real way, for he "lives, to our imaginations, by His visible symbols, as if He were on earth."[204] Real assent, then, synonymous with "Belief," results when the imagination stimulates "those powers of the mind from which action proceeds." Assent by itself does not spur action; what does is the "power of the concrete upon the affections and passions." But there is no clear predictor, according to Newman, of how the mind receives data, which it can use either for pleasure or for certitude. In fact, what influences most our certitude are the pleasurable ways information is impressed on the mind. The "acquisition of new images, and those images striking, great, various, unexpected, beautiful" is "highly pleasurable" and "quite independently of the question whether there is any truth in them."[205]

Newman's entire discourse on the psychology of belief, from the *Apologia* to the *Grammar*, can strike even the most liberal ecclesiastical minds as heresy, and more so those arch–conservatists who wished him silent on such dangerous truths. He avowed, for example, that "real assent" is premised on the same dubiety as disbelief or skepticism, for "absolute certitude" on matters of natural theology and revelation "was the result of an *assemblage* of concurring and converging possibilities." He called certitude a "habit of the mind," a "quality of propositions," and maintained that even "probabilities which did not reach to logical certainty, might suffice for a mental certitude." Newman believed that mental certitude "might equal in measure and strength the certitude which was created by the strictest scientific demonstration." So confident was he of this theory of assent that he grounded his own belief in God, in Christianity, and in Catholicism on probability and on a "certitude which rises higher than the logical force of our conclusion." Such beliefs demand "one and the same in nature of proof, as being probabilities—probabilities of a special kind, a cumulative, a transcendent probability but still probability." And as we arrive at certitude in mathematics "by rigid demonstrations," so in religious inquiry we arrive at certitude on the grounds of "accumulated probabilities,"[206] or, as the *Grammar* prefers it, "multiplicity of premises." To achieve certitude on such tenuous grounds, Newman turned to the "Illative sense" (the "power of judging and concluding, when in its perfection"), in which the imagination is exercised and becomes joined with "plain duty"[207]: "It is a duty to accept the arguments commonly urged for its truth as sufficient, and a duty in consequence to believe heartily in Scripture and the Church."[208] Hopkins's entire argument for his conversion, waged most persuasively to his father, and dutiful priestly career show that he clearly understood, as David Downes concludes, "the workings of Newman's illative imagination." And Hopkins's close reading of Newman, according to Norman MacKenzie, can "readily be gauged" from a lecture Hopkins wrote on the subject of duty.[209]

On Hopkins's first visit with Newman at the Oratory, Newman immediately picked up on his Oxford "Intellectualism," an inclination Archbishop Tait characterized as "a great danger" at Oxford in the 1860s: "Students in our Universities, wearied of the dogmatism which ruled unchecked there some years ago, are very apt now to regard every maxim of theology or philosophy as an open question."[210] Hopkins early admitted this very leaning to his friend Coleridge and warned him against it: "Beware of doing what I once thought I could do, adopt an enlightened Christianity."[211] Newman's warning to Hopkins, then, was that the most enlightened have the greatest excuse for claiming "invincible ignorance,"[212] the very point Newman makes in *Certain Difficulties*: "He who believes the dogmas of the Church only because he has reasoned them out of History, is scarcely a Catholic."[213] Hopkins's acquaintance with the Hexameron and Old Mortality societies, both of which assumed a rationalistic approach to contemporary theological and ethical issues, caused him to envision "Catholic intellectualism"—a possible explanation for his attraction to the Jesuits—as, according to Downes, a religious answer to his Platonic impulses.[214] Thus, although not wanting his conversion "rationalized," so as to "empty it of any influence," Hopkins still could not acquiesce to the conviction that "anyone ever became a Catholic because two and two make four more fully than I have."[215]

Hopkins illustrated his knowledge of the kind of reasoning reflected in the *Grammar* when in enumerating the grounds of his conversion he cited both "simple and strictly drawn arguments" and "common sense,"[216] the very qualities that comprise assent. The *Grammar*, then, afforded Hopkins a means to resolve his own intellectual anxiety between faith and reason and thus to realize his own real assent. Only months before he offered to do the Newman commentary Hopkins was wrestling with this tension. Quibbling with Bridges on the "ecstasy of interest" in the Incarnation, a doctrine that may be believed even by such skeptics as Bridges, Hopkins called it "an incomprehensible certainty" and not, as Bridges would have it, "an interesting uncertainty," whereby interest becomes heightened the more profound the formulation of the doctrine. But, according to Hopkins, the Incarnation does not require having one's "curiosity satisfied." "If the Trinity is to be explained by grammar and tropes," Hopkins insisted, mindful of that same argument urged by Francis Newman, the Cardinal's younger brother, "where wd. be the mystery? the true mystery, the incomprehensible one."[217]

To some, then, the Trinity is a doctrinal equation to be explained through some theologically mathematical process; but to others, like Hopkins, such a doctrine, "poised, but on a quiver," remains perfectly unexplainable without any hint of "doubt on the subject." So too is the Incarnation. Like the doctrine of the Trinity, it remains a mystery, however "less incomprehensible," and the right response to it is in "the locked and inseparable combination, or rather it is in the person in whom the combination has its place." Therefore, one can assent to the oxymoronic, but fundamental, belief that the "child in the manger" is one and the same person with "the culprit on the gallows"; both is God.[218] Hopkins argued similarly, again to Bridges, on Corpus Christi, the feast of Real Presence. "Naturally the Blessed Sacrament is carried in procession.... But the procession has more meaning and mystery than this: it represents the process of the Incarnation and the world's redemption. As Christ went forth from the bosom of the Father as the Lamb of God and eucharistic victim to die upon the altar of the cross for the world's ransom ... so in the ceremony his body *en statu victimali* [in a sacrificial state] is carried to the Altar of Repose."[219]

Although Newman indicated expediency as the basis for his rejection of Hopkins's two requests, philosophical disagreements seem likelier, differences concealed in Newman's remark that "a comment is but one aspect of translation."[220] And wanting the *Grammar* to be his final literary work, Newman did not desire any controversy that would necessitate further polemics. Newman seemed aware too of differences with Hopkins, possibly expressed during his tenure at the Oratory when Newman was working on the *Grammar.* Earlier in his Tamworth essay, and repeated in the *Grammar*, Newman observed that the heart is "commonly reached, not through the reason, but through the imagination, by means of direct impressions, by the testimony of facts and events." He repeated the claim, adding that "man is *not* a reasoning animal; he is a seeing, feeling, contemplating, acting animal."[221] In a 6 May 1881 letter to Coventry Patmore, Hopkins expressed disfavor with Patmore's use of the reasoning animal passage from the *Grammar.* Extracted from their immediate context, the claims should not imply the devaluation of reason in the process to religious assent. Hopkins believed that Newman's remarks should be taken more as rhetorical devices than as actual epistemological admissions. Newman's exaggerated claim, what Ian Ker calls "rhetorical hyperbole,"[222] was meant to indicate the fallacy of man's reasoning, especially in following the argument from natural theology. "I always felt," Hopkins wrote, "that Newman made too much of that text; it is still worse that you should build upon it."[223] Patmore, Hopkins felt, was making too much of Newman's anti–rationalist stance.

Hopkins was keenly aware of Newman's corpus, especially the *Grammar*, in which human reasoning plays a vital role in assent.

Hopkins's last correspondence to Newman was from Ireland. All five birthday letters complained about Irish religion and politics. In an 1885 reply, Newman admitted his increasing frailty—"I fear the weakness is permanent"— and added: "I grieve to find you corroborat[e] from your own experience what other friends tell me about the state of Ireland."[224] By this time Newman's writing was barely legible; he complained often of how unreliable his penmanship was; "a single letter must have taken him hours at that time," writes his biographer Wilfrid Ward.[225] One year later, in reply to Hopkins's 1886 letter, Newman referred to its "sad part," an obvious reference to Hopkins's growing uneasiness with Irish life and politics. Now eighty–five, Newman felt that his birthday was "more clouded in prospect of the future to me than my doctor will allow on his own part." He requested Hopkins's "good prayers," adding, "I am sure I shall have them in my necessity."[226]

On 17 February 1887, Hopkins informed Bridges of having spent "three years in Ireland, three hard wearying wasting years." The letter ended with a tirade against the Irish and details Hopkins's position on Home Rule: "I shd. be glad to see Ireland happy, even though it involved the fall of England. . . . But Ireland will not be happy: a people without principle of allegiance cannot be." Completing the letter the next day, he predicted a shipwrecked Ireland and, still imperialistic, wished that when it does occur he would be "cast up on the English coast."[227] In this frame of mind Hopkins again remembered Newman's birthday. Newman's dictated reply of 3 March called Hopkins's letter "an appalling one—but not on that account untrustworthy." But Newman, who knew more of Irish history and culture, was more sympathetic than Hopkins with their plight. From this former supporter of the established order who fifty years earlier avoided the tricolour flag on a French vessel, Newman urged a moderate, if not radical, stance on Irish nationalism and schooled Hopkins on the Irish question. He reminded Hopkins that because the Irish reject English rule, they never see themselves "under her law and have never been rebels." Assuming an even more adversarial position, and one that no doubt would have troubled Hopkins, Newman added: "If I were an Irishman, I should be (in heart) a rebel."[228] From Dublin Hopkins wrote to Baillie, coming around slightly to Newman's position and adopting a more learned position: "Home Rule of itself is a blow for England and will do no good to Ireland. But it is better than worse things. You would understand that if you lived in Ireland. My position is not at all a favourable one for observing the country, still it is much better than people in England can have." Hopkins finally came around, albeit moderately, to Newman's view: "Be assured of this, that the mass of the Irish people own no allegiance to any existing law or government. And yet they are not a worthless people; they have many true and winning virtues."[229]

Hopkins sent his last letter to Newman in February 1888. With an almost unreadable hand, Newman replied on 24 February: "You are one of those friends and well wishers, who have so kindly addressed to me letters of congratulations on my birthday, —letters which have touched me much, and for your share in which I hereby offer you my sincere thanks."[230] This literary hand that guided Hopkins's religious and literary career for twenty–two years, whereby over again he felt Newman's finger and found him, had penned its last words to his devoted protégé, a "no common character," writes Keating of Hopkins, that could "win and retain for so long the regard of so great a man" like Newman.[231]

As ailing as Newman was becoming, he was to outlive Hopkins by one year. Hopkins was hardly sleeping at night, was complaining endlessly about the weather, and often escaped south to Monasterevin; he felt even more sickened by the political weather. On 1 May 1889 he complained to his mother of having what he thought was rheumatic fever. A week later his condition was diagnosed as a mild form of typhoid, contracted apparently from the poor drainage system underneath the college. He rallied for six weeks before succumbing to his infliction on 8 June. Considering Hopkins's close ties to the Birmingham Oratory, one would assume that the authorities there were notified of his death. But nowhere in Newman's few dictated letters after 1889 is there even a hint that he knew of the death. The inconceivable silence leads one to speculate that news of it was deliberately withheld from Newman, fearing its effect on his already feeble condition. But one has to weigh this with the fact that the death of Father Hecker (the Newman of America because of how successfully he advanced the Catholic cause) was disclosed to Newman in February of that same year. Hopkins was buried in an unmarked grave at Glasnevin. On the morning of 11 August 1890, Newman lapsed into a coma; that evening he died, never having regained consciousness in this life. The infrequent but extended letters exchanged between Newman and Hopkins reveal how profound a spiritual and literary mentor he was to Hopkins whose own life in numerous ways paralleled Newman's.

Chapter 3

Continuity without Fixed Points: Hopkins and Darwinism

At the Thursday 1 July 1858 meeting of the Linnean Society, Charles Darwin's and Alfred Russell Wallace's collaborated paper on the theory of evolution, entitled, "On the Tendency of Species to Form Varieties; and on the Perpetuation of Varieties and Species by Natural Means of Selection," was read in their absence. The paper was published one month later on 20 August and attracted, as Darwin correctly estimated, little attention. Its real impact, however, was to soften up Victorians for the blow that was to be launched on 24 November 1859, the publication of Darwin's *On the Origin of Species by Means of Natural Selection, or the Preservation of Favoured Races in the Struggle for Life*. This was Darwin's long–delayed assemblage of what in a Dickensian sense he was fond of calling "facts." While the work failed to generate as much press and create quite the stir as *Essays and Reviews*, the damage that it inflicted was felt to be just as severe and far more lasting. Leo Henkin felt that the *Origin* hit the theological world "like a plough into an ant–hill," and effected, says Lionel Stevenson, a "complete revaluation of all mental equipment," changing the way man viewed the universe. Cyril Bibby expressed a similar opinion. He observed that the book not only "catalysed a complete rearrangement of ideological patterns over a wide range of human thought," but appeared even to the "average believer" to be "not simply promulgating a new scientific theory, but destroying the foundations of belief." As early as 1863 Charles Kingsley presciently remarked to F.D. Maurice: "Darwin is conquering everywhere and rushing in like a flood, by the mere force of truth and fact."[1] Put simply: "The most dramatic confrontation between religion and science occurred in the nineteenth century, and the Christian community remains uneasy about the problem of 'man's place in nature' which became acute in the Darwinian debate."[2]

But while Victorian society was ripe for an evolutionary theory because of the legacy of Romanticism, it was, Alvar Ellegard felt, ill prepared for "the sort of evolutionary theory that Darwin actually propounded."[3] What was unique about Darwin's brand of evolution was the assertion of the mechanistic process called natural selection. "I soon perceived," Darwin wrote in July 1837 when he opened his notebook on transmutation, "that selection was the keystone of man's success in making useful races of animals and plants"; and a year later from reading Malthus's *Essay on Population* came to appreciate the "struggle for existence which everywhere goes on" and that "under these circumstances favourable ones would tend to be preserved, and unfavourable ones destroyed. The result of this would be the formation of new species."[4] By natural selection, then, Darwin meant that nature, not the Divine, selects what survives and what perishes, however uneasy he remained with the connotation and would have preferred "Natural Preservation." The theory rendered redundant supernatural causes as an explanation of origin. Natural selection, then, is in Darwin's theory privileged over the Divine, an accusation actually made by Charles Lyell and J.D. Hooker who felt that Darwin made "too much of a Deus of Natural Selection."[5] By placing that act at the hands of an impersonal process, Darwin believed that his theory let God off the hook, as it were, for it explained the cause of suffering and thus deflected all attributions of suffering away from an otherwise beneficent First Cause. Darwin arrived at the conclusion that species were not independently created but were marked instead by "strongly defined varieties" formulated almost wholly by "the selection of what may be incorrectly called *chance* variations or variability."[6] This theory, as Darwin's son and editor, Francis Darwin, saw it, not only led Darwin to transform biological science, but elevated him as the "chief of the moderns" who wrote and worked in "so essentially a non–modern spirit and manner."[7]

Both the *Origin* and *Essays and Reviews*, coming one year apart, urged positivistic approaches—one to the origin of life and the other to interpretation. But the two enterprises were essentially one and the same, for both were driven by the same hermeneutic of suspicion that called into question the ensconced privileged status of the Bible. Literary reactions to *Essays and Reviews*, like Rev. Gilbert Rorison's "The Creative Week," invoked evolution and the efficacy of special creation. Of the writers of *Essays and Reviews*, only two, more attuned to science and to the shared discourse between it and religion, immediately acknowledged Darwin. Baden Powell saw Darwin's theory of natural selection and its rejection of the creation account as an advance in the direction to which current theology was inclined; he believed that Darwin's theory would soon inaugurate an ideological revolution espousing the theory of designless powers in nature.[8] Religion, not science, held greater interest to Victorians. Sales of both the *Origin* and *Essays and Reviews* were remarkable.

Though a thick book, the *Origin* sold its 1,250 copies on the first day, and another 1,250 were printed three months later. However, *Essays and Reviews* outsold the *Origin*. Some 13,000 copies were sold in the book's first year alone. Not surprisingly, then, Liddon did not once refer to the *Origin* in his diary, nor did he take up the issue in any of his Sunday evening lectures; he did not even discuss the book with any of the notable Church leaders. In fact, I cannot recall Liddon, whom Darwell Stone felt "made it his business to know what was going on in the world of thought,"[9] ever mentioning the book in any of his letters, even in the ones to Samuel Wilberforce ("Soapy Sam"), who in 1860 engaged Thomas Huxley in a celebrated debate on evolution. The *Origin* slipped by almost unnoticed because of the controversy over *Essays and Reviews* and the debate on the Jowett endowment. But although not immediate, reaction to the book from the general public, especially from the lesser–educated segment, was that its ideas assailed religious orthodoxy and disrupted the tenuous link that had long existed between science and religion.

The impact that the *Origin* had upon the culture of the last one hundred years remains complex. This is especially so, says Gillian Beer, because evolutionary ideas prove "more influential when they become assumptions embedded in the culture than while they are the subject of controversy."[10] Morse Peckham also observed that tracing Darwinian influences and assumptions throughout literature creates a fog in one's mind, through which one is able only to discern "twinkles of what may or may not be bits of genuine Darwinism." Or, as George Levine puts it, "Coming nonfictionally," Darwinism "enters into the dubious representational realms of narrative and fiction; the boundaries between the two kinds of narrative, the two kinds of representation, blur."[11] Yet there have been successful attempts to chart that relationship in the literature of the Victorian period, attempts showing not only that Darwin was Victorian, but that his ideas paralleled movements in theology, geology, and linguistics, even narratology. In other words, Darwinism is, as Gillian Beer describes it, "multivalent." For the issues, according to Robert M. Young, are "all related to changing notions of humanity and society, and that the points at which the distinctions of issue, discipline, or level are made are themselves of socioeconomic and ideological interest."[12] Consequently, any scientific theory, because it seeks to explain culture, however particular, must engage the concerns of religion, language, nature, and ecology. In other words, "scientific theories," writes Paul Feyerabend, "are ways of looking at the world and their adoption affects our general beliefs and expectations, and thereby also our experiences and our conception of reality."[13]

In her book *Darwin's Plots*, Gillian Beer looks to such conventions as the rejection of providentiality in narrative voice and plot, the loss of omniscient narration, teleological order, or purpose, the preoccupation with materiality, the broad assemblage of familial interconnections that effect plotting, and the shifting values assigned to certain metaphors, all in an attempt to locate the Darwinian impulse in Victorian literature. "What is remarkable about the mid and late nineteenth century," as Gillian Beer shows, is that rather than "ignoring or rebutting attempts to set scientific writing and literature side by side, as is sometimes the case in our time, both novelists and scientists were very much aware of the potentialities released by the congruities of their methods and ends."[14] Nineteenth–century writers were aware that, in the words of Paul Feyerabend, "science can and does profit from an admixture of unscientific ingredients."[15] Equally seminal in charting Victorian responses to Darwinism is George Levine's *Darwin and the Novelists*. Levine holds that scientific ideas pass most readily and spontaneously into works of authors unaware of science, for these ideas are part of the shared cultural discourse. Thus he examines writers whose works do not deliberately employ any scientifically intertextual hermeneutic. Believing that "What Darwin said was part of a much broader sweep of historical change," Levine turns to such figures as Austen, Dickens, and Trollope to locate places where, in his words, "Darwin's vision, his great myth of origins," was "shaping the limits of the Victorian imagination."[16]

When the *Origin* appeared, Gerard Manley Hopkins was in his fifth year at Sir Roger Chomley's Highgate School. Highgate's slight science curriculum, not unusual for public schools at the time, which focused mostly on Greek and Latin, meant that the book was probably inaccessible to Hopkins; but the controversy over the Darwin–Wallace paper on natural selection would no doubt have attracted this most precocious of schoolboys to the many reviews on the *Origin* and some time later to the book itself. But even if Hopkins did not read the book, its arguments were sufficiently chronicled, reviewed, and discussed in all of the major literary organs. In fact, it was there that the real debate over Darwinism took place. All of the major reviews, according to a survey conducted by Ellegard, dealt with the book and took positions consistent with the views of their readership. We know that Hopkins regularly perused the pages of *Fraser's*, *The Nineteenth Century*, *Athenaeum*, *Cornhill*, and *Contemporary Review*, among others. He would have had to in order to be conversant on contemporary issues, for the curriculum at Oxford was still weighted heavily on the classics. And, as one writer points out, while study of natural science had been "progressing rapidly in other universities and colleges" during the latter half of the nineteenth century, at Oxford it had progressed "very slowly indeed."[17] However, efforts were being made to remedy that. And to observe that change is also to witness how a precocious nineteenth–century undergraduate compensated for formal curricular shortcomings in natural science.

In the 1860s at Oxford, a new and expensive science museum was built, the laboratories were handsomely equipped, and the Radcliffe Science Library housed an enviable collection of scientific books, all designed to attract students to Oxford to pursue studies in science. In a 1 February 1867 report for the Hebdomadal Council, the university's governing body, John Phillips, Keeper of the Museum, laid out on behalf of the professors floor plans and costs for making the museum more effective for science education; the plans also included one from Professor Clinton of Experimental Philosophy to extend the south front of the building for experiments on lights and the safe preservation of instruments used for delicate research. Phillips reported that without "space and suitable arrangements, effectual teaching cannot be given to practical classes in some of the most important parts of Experimental Physics." Consequently, "candidates of ability who aspire to the highest honours in Physical Science . . . must seek instruction in the advanced parts of modern research in Light, Heat, Electricity, and Magnetism, in the more fully appointed Laboratories—such as that of Heidelberg—which are now growing up on the Continent . . . for the same reasons as those which are causing the construction of similar well–arranged institutions in England."

To argue the case more convincingly, Professor Clinton, in the Phillips report, gave the rationale for the study of natural science. Demonstrating an apparent familiarity with the arguments on the benefits of the study of abstract science advanced in John Herschel's *A Preliminary Discourse on the Study of Natural Philosophy* (1830), Clinton pointed out that "The great advantage of the study of Physical Science, as an aid to Education, is avowedly the exercise which it gives to the faculty of reasoning, combined with that of observation . . . . The development of the powers of observation, which may be commenced by attendance upon experimental lectures, can only be fully produced by engaging the student himself in experimental work."[18] Charles Darwin expressed a similar opinion. As early as 1852 when he was considering sending his eldest son William to Rugby, one of the leading feeder schools for Oxford and Cambridge, Darwin remarked that "No one can more truly despise the old stereotyped stupid classical education than I do; but yet I have not had courage to break through its trammels." He would liked to have seen "more diversity in education" instead of "the enormous proportion of time spent over classics." This lapse tolerated "no exercising of the observing or reasoning faculties, no general knowledge acquired—I must think it a wretched system."[19] But many Oxford tutors who were themselves products of a classical education and had a vested interest in its survival were not easily convinced. They were suspicious of the claims of science and did not readily welcome curricular innovations. Even Jowett, whose own scientific approach to the Bible urged greater openness in the pursuit of knowledge, was not so forthcoming when the threat was to his own academic turf. In a 31 August 1865 letter to Florence Nightingale, he voiced resentment toward curricular changes in the prestigious public schools and even at Oxford. "When I was an undergraduate," he reminisced, "we fed upon Bp. Butler & Aristotle's 'Ethics' & almost all teaching leant to the support of doctrine and authority. Now there are new subjects, Modern History & Physical Science.... See how impossible this makes a return to the old doctrines of authority."[20] Claims of authority and tradition sound strange coming from Jowett.

Other opponents of science were of the same mind. They believed, as A.J. Engel notes, that it was useless to support the study of science, and so encouraged "the more intelligent students to choose the greater rigour and intellectual discipline offered by classical studies rather than to accept the mere useful information provided by 'stinks.'" And because most tutors were classicists who encouraged the best students to read their own subjects, these students, even with generous financial support, did poorly in science. Scientists blamed the failure of science at Oxford on the Greek required of undergraduates at responsions, the matriculating examination given to students at the end of their first year.[21] One author felt that Oxford fostered "the exclusive study of classics in the public schools" and did its best to "shut its gates" against those who received what other schools called a *modern education*, an education that does not cater exclusively to the classics. "It was largely due to the Greek," which, by the way, was not given to women who then could not qualify for the bachelor of arts, "that the members of the science school at Oxford are kept in check." The most capable students were encouraged to sit for the classics, the less for law or history, and the least prepared for possibly political economy. "Neither honour men nor pass men hear of science unless they make particular inquiries about it; and if they do, they are as often or not told that it will not give them the breadth of education necessary for their future careers."[22] George Eliot's agronomic metaphor best describes education at Oxford: "the classics and geometry constituted that culture of the mind which prepared it for the reception of any subsequent crop."[23] Thus, responsible in the main for the poor status of science in Oxford were "the absence of any test of scientific acquirements in responsions and in most college entrance examinations, the severity of the Greek test, and the exiguous number of science tutors in colleges."[24]

But although the "existence of scholarships and fellowships reserved for scientists did not always call forth an adequate supply of qualified candidates," and, as a result, "well–paid professors often lectured to virtually empty lecture halls,"[25] the 1860s saw a steady increase of interest in natural science. J.P. Earwaker, in an article on "Natural Science at Oxford," noted that the University College Science Lectures increased in proportion to the number of students attending them, which in turn caused the School of Natural Science to become "recognised as on a par with the other three great schools of Philosophy, Mathematics, and Law and Modern History." Several scholarships and exhibitions for natural science were awarded to students by some colleges, and more lucrative fellowships were now available and, unlike the policy at Cambridge, open to all students at the university regardless of their college affiliation.[26] Thus by 1895, 43 of the 153 students enrolled in Literare Humaniores were in natural science and only 37 in theology. Yet the percentage of scholarships for natural science was significantly less. The blame was placed squarely on the paucity of matriculating students qualified in science, in comparison to students qualified in the classics; special criticism was reserved for the pedagogical training these students received in science during their secondary education. Cambridge solved this dilemma by making scholarships available to already matriculated students who, after their first year at the university, would then have been prepared to meet the appropriate qualifications. Consequently, Cambridge always had more than its optimum of qualified students in natural science, a point not lost on Darwin's educational choice.[27] And, as one W.E. Pusey pointed out in response to "The Position of Science at Oxford," the greater prestige attached to science at Cambridge hindered the status of science at Oxford.[28] A noteworthy aside must here be interjected. The colleges most accommodating to science, Keble and Christ Church, were religious, a factor not lost in the argument that science education endangers the religious nature of institutions.

This was, in effect, the scientific environment at Oxford during Hopkins's years there. He lacked formal training or instruction in science, but compensated for it through his avid interest in nature. That obsession attracted Hopkins to two series of lectures in April 1865 delivered by Charles G.B. Daubeny, professor of botany, on "The Trees and Shrubs of the Ancients." Five years earlier before the British Association, Daubeny had strongly supported Darwin's cause with an essay entitled "Remarks on the Final Causes of Sexuality of Plants, with Particular Reference to Mr. Darwin's Work, *On the Origin of Species by Natural Selection.*" But in spite of his exposure to Darwin, Hopkins made no explicit comments on Darwin until he had been a Catholic for some eight years. Yet his poetry and poetics, even his pre–Jesuit writings, sufficiently engage Darwinian

EXANIMATION AND EXAMINATION.

"Ah! then—poor fellow, he'll be wana beneath when luory flows from. One plunge and it's all over, my boy, forgoes, take courage!"

Hopkins's caricature of the "Dread of Classical Education."
Courtesy of the Bodleian Library.

ideas. But to understand how Hopkins negotiated his scientific interest in general and Darwinian concerns in particular involves a sense of how Victorian Catholics sought to contend with science and its positivistic assumptions. In many respects Hopkins's handling of the dilemma science posed to religion and literature must be read within the context of how both Catholic and Victorian contemporary ideas addressed this pressing issue. No Catholic Victorian offers as fitting a paradigm as Newman, whose mind worked in ways similar to Hopkins's. Charles Sarolea sees him as "the first to accustom Catholic thought to a new conception, so different from the conception of immutability, and to apply to theology the methods of biology."[29] We receive the first clue to Newman's position on the relationship between religion and science in a 13 April 1858 letter to Pusey. Pusey had consulted him on the subject of geology and the biblical record. Newman expressed no particular knowledge of the subject, but felt that "in the scientific world men seem going ahead most recklessly with their usurpations on the domain of religion." He wished that "divine and human science might each be suffered in peace to take its own line, the one not interfering with the other. Their circles scarcely intersect each other."[30] This was the same line Newman assumed in his three essays on the subject.

In all three essays by Newman on the relationship between religion and science, he expressed the belief that both religion and science are antithetical, and that distance should be preserved. Newman's ninth Discourse, "Duties of the Church towards Knowledge" (1852), which he felt caused him the greatest anxiety, shows his powers of foresight predating both the *Origin* and *Essays and Reviews*. This discourse addresses how the church should respond to "new" knowledge, and especially how that knowledge relates to received knowledge, a matter different from belief. Most significant about this discourse is not that Newman envisions no tension, "no real collision," between science and religion, for "Nature and Grace, Reason and Revelation, come from the same Divine Author, whose works cannot contradict each other," but that he sees no tension precisely because he sought to separate the warring forces of science and religion. The two coexist peacefully in so far as they ignore each other's existence, a sort of coexistence by exclusion. What Newman calls for, then, is not harmony or unity but a truce. The point comes across most clearly when, with Bacon in mind, he writes that "from religious investigations, as such, physics must be excluded, and from physical, as such, religion; and if we mix them we shall spoil both." Newman, for instance, acknowledges a restraint when the theologian is concerned with the laws of nature and simultaneously with God's omnipotence and when the scientist is concerned jointly with natural phenomena and the subject of God's omnipotence:

> If the Theologian, in tracing the ways of providence, were stopped with objections grounded on the impossibility of physical miracles, he would justly protest against the interruption; and were the philosopher, who was determining the motion of the heavenly bodies, to be questioned about their Final or their First Cause, he too would suffer an illogical interruption. The latter asks the cause of volcanoes, and is impatient at being told it is "the divine vengeance"; the former asks the cause of the overthrow of the guilty cities, and is preposterously referred to the volcanic action still visible in their neighbourhood. The inquiry into final causes for the moment passes over the existence of established laws; the inquiry into physical, passes over for the moment the existence of God.

Put frankly, "physical science is in a certain sense atheistic, for the very reason it is not theology."[31] This is not the place to offer an extended commentary on Newman's approach to science, still a void in Newman scholarship. My only concern is merely to sketch the conflict and to show that while on the one hand Hopkins's geniality with Darwinism derived in large part from his Roman Catholicism, on the other hand he was, because of his naturalist penchant, not as prone as was Newman to keep science at a distance and so to exclude it from his epistemology and poetics.

In a second essay, "Christianity and Physical Science" (1855), Newman again takes up the issue of science and religion, arguing the separateness of the two areas of discourse: "the two worlds and the two kinds of knowledge respectively are separated off from each other"; and because they are separate, they "cannot on the whole contradict each other." In being separate, then, both theology, "the philosophy of the supernatural world," and science, "the philosophy of the natural," cannot collide, and therefore need "never to be reconciled." While theology seeks to address questions about "the Author of nature" as the "Cause and Source of all things," science, on the other hand, is concerned with observable phenomena and the finite:

> The Physicist treats of efficient causes; the Theologian of final. The Physicist tells us of laws; the Theologian of the

> Author, Maintainer, and Controller of them; of their scope, of
> their suspension . . . of their beginning and their end. This is
> how the two schools stand related to each other, at that point
> where they approach the nearest; but for the most part they are
> absolutely divergent.

Newman's theory, then, is that kept so detached, the fields of scientific and
theological discourse do not in fact address each other and so have no grounds
for agreement or controversy, jealousy or sympathy. His analogy: "As well may
musical truths be said to interfere with the doctrines of architectural science."[32]
But while Newman here argues such separateness, Hopkins's aesthetics, like
Darwin's, Gurney's, and Pater's, asserts a oneness in theory and practice among
the arts and sciences. His poem "How all is one way wrought" weds both music
and architecture: "Who built these walls made known / The music of his mind."

In "Christianity and Scientific Investigation" (1855), a lecture presumably
never delivered, Newman again takes up the controversy between religion and
science. He calls for a truce when he asks practitioners in each discipline to "go
on quietly, and in a neighbourly way" in their separate investigations, aware that
truth is not singular; and while there may be brief skirmishes and dissension,
their combined results will ultimately be uniform. While Newman's indetermi-
nate stance is soon compromised (requiring the investigator, for example, to be
mindful of Church dogma and the caprice of the popular mind), his rhetoric of
equivocation becomes more lucid when he reminds the investigator to be clear
in his focus and to be mindful of the reality that scientific discovery now valid
may, because of more recent findings, just as quickly be regarded erroneous.[33]

But when Newman leaves formal considerations of science for discourse
not directly engaging science, he becomes trapped in the very scientific rhetoric
he in practice disavows and in which he urges separation. For instance, Victorian
concern with change and continuity pervades Newman's *Apologia Pro Vita Sua*
and his *Essay on the Development of Christian Doctrine*. Central to the former
is not Newman's veracity but his conversion, his change. Not to have changed
or grown (along with "living" the most predominant metaphor in the *Apologia*),
constitutes, Newman believes, a deception. But the change he advocates is
gradual rather than abrupt, the type of change consistent with, even modeled
after, Darwinian gradualism. Newman so embraces the "lingering–out sweet
skill" (Hopkins's term) of Augustine's conversion, patterning his own conversion to Roman Catholicism after it, that in one of his sermons, "Sudden
Conversion," he distorts Paul's "crash" (again Hopkins's term) to read as the
culmination of a long and gradual process, all this to dramatize his own

conversion by way of a deviant misreading of Scripture. Naturally, then, metaphors of vitality and growth pervade the *Apologia*. Seeing the text as a product of himself, Newman calls it "the birth of my own mind," a metaphor related to the "gestation and childbirth" he associates with the composition of a book;[34] he wishes to be known as "a living man" and is anxious that the evolution of his opinions be recognized. He even employs atomistic language to describe that process: "how they developed from within, how they grew, were modified, were combined, were in collision with each other, and were changed." (A similar atomistic passage is used to describe individuals who comprise Catholic Christendom: people not "buried alive, but . . . brought together as if into some moral factory, for the melting, refining, and moulding, by an incessant, noisy process, of the raw material of human nature, so excellent, so dangerous, so capable of divine purposes."[35]) His chapter titles, employing signifiers of change ("to," "from," and "since"), show that he was indeed concerned with the "growth of time."

Newman's *Essay on the Development of Christian Doctrine*, first published in 1845 and revised extensively in the 1878 edition (the *Apologia* underwent similar evolutionary processes), reveals similar organic metaphors. *Development* speaks of the "growth of doctrine," that for ideas to take root in the mind it "may be said to have life," that the various Sacraments are connected by "cross relations . . . and grow together while they grow from one," and that modern Catholicism is "the natural and necessary development, of the doctrine of the early church," the latter point made in the section of *Development* (Part II) most Darwinian in language and epistemology. The work's very structure and *raison d'être*, then, is evolutionary, albeit pre–Darwinian. Newman's "idea of history, with change and development implicit in it," writes Brian Martin, no doubt with the *Apologia* in mind, "enabled him to comprehend Darwin's claims, which shocked so many well–educated men whose minds were dominated by a static view of history. . . . Newman's view of history was dynamic and he found no difficulty in reconciling his views to Darwin's." Speaking specifically to *Development*, Martin observes that "Newman's intellect proved there was no inconsistency between the theory of evolution" hinted by Lyell and developed by Darwin. "A theory which was shaking the faith of some, was accepted easily by Newman." Similar to Darwin, says Charles Frederick Harrold, "Newman was not the inventor of a hypothesis, but a bold and illuminating applier of the general nineteenth–century idea of 'growth' and 'development.'" But because Newman's "growth" ideas in *Development* antedate Darwin's by some fifteen years, to claim, says Charles Sorolea, "that Newman has been the Darwin of theology would therefore be as historically true as to assert that Darwin is contained in Heraclitus and Lucretius."[36]

Newman's failure manifested in the *Apologia* and *Development* demonstrates the inseparability of the two modes of discourse in the nineteenth century; both science and literature inform each other, and one should not be privileged above the other. In fact, it is inconceivable—if not impossible—to come to terms with Victorian literature unless we attend to the significant intersecting points of both disciplines, the point at which, as George Eliot found in Lydgate, science and art discovers its most true and direct alliance and interchange, blending intellectual conquest with social good, or the rational with the emotional. Pater also anticipated the shared discourse. In his essay on "Style," he asserts that "The literary artist, therefore, will be well aware of physical science; science also attaining, in its turn, its true literary ideal."[37] For science and literature, as Katherine Hayles claims, "are cultural products, at once expressing and helping to form the cultural matrix from which they emerge."[38] As a physicist taught to regard the two fields as polar, Thomas Kuhn vividly remembers discovering "the close and persistent parallels between the two enterprises." Kuhn also observes that the scientific writings that defend separateness still feel some obligation to insist "that art can readily be distinguished from science by application of the classic dichotomies between, for example, the world of value and the world of fact, the subjective and the objective, or the intuitive and the inductive."[39] Paul Feyerabend argues similarly: one suspects, he writes, that the methods of inquiry that enable the scientist "to form a coherent picture out of apparent chaos are much more closely related to the spirit of poetry than one would be inclined to think." One is left with the suspicion, says Feyerabend, that "the only difference between poets and scientists is that the latter, having lost their sense of style, now try to comfort themselves with the pleasant fiction that they are following rules of a quite different kind which produce a much grander and much more important result, namely, the Truth." Or, as Feyerabend comments elsewhere, "science is much closer to myth than a scientific philosophy is prepared to admit."[40]

George Levine's idea of "One Culture" presupposes this nexus; science and literature, he believes, share in the same cultural discourse; and that the two, although dissimilar, "should be studied as deriving from common cultural sources." Joint consideration of them matters, says Levine, because "the conjunction of the two sometimes radically separated worlds of discourse helps illuminate each, helps demystify each. . . . And it forces us to address issues of ultimate importance to the way our culture and our societies are currently shaping each other."[41] In addressing the status of science at Oxford at the turn of the century, John Perry, Professor of Engineering at the University of London, makes a similar point. "It is a curious kind of culture," he observed, "which scorns the lessons of history, the study of man in relation to nature, the study of the enormous new forces which are now affecting the relations of nations to one another."[42]

While assimilation of the theory of evolution, then, "appears as one of the chief currents of poetic thought during the Victorian era,"[43] how it relates to Hopkins has escaped critical attention. The five partial portraits of him, including the two most recent biographies, Robert Martin's *Gerard Manley Hopkins: A Very Private Life* (1991) and Norman White's *Hopkins: A Literary Biography* (1992), fail to explore the relationship to Darwin, and only in one is Darwin even mentioned.[44] Granted, Hopkins's was not yet a full–fledged Darwinian world; but when in 1888 he told Bridges that "everything is Darwinism," the entire culture had then become such. The least painstaking way to approach the relationship between Hopkins and science, and more particularly Hopkins and Darwin, is to ferret out explicit comments on the subject in his writings. But these admissions, especially ones to Darwin, are disappointingly few; and if, as I shall argue, his letters and diary mask Darwinian ideas and presumptions, his poetry makes that task even more arduous. Hopkins made too few pronouncements to allow us to show precisely what he thought about Darwinism, a fact not inconsistent with what Morse Peckham meant by the remark that "the locus of cultural history" is in fact "covert behavior."

As a result of Hopkins's relative silence on the subject, critics have not bothered to trace either the Darwinian influence on Hopkins or ways in which, knowingly or culturally, a Darwinian epistemology manifests itself in Hopkins's and by extension Victorian discourse. In the case of Hopkins this is even most fruitful, for he presents approaches to the period that are peculiar. No other Victorian is as committed uniformly to religion, nature and the poetic process. But even W.H. Gardner and Walter Ong have failed to locate describable relations between Hopkins and Darwin. Gardner intimates some probable connections, but his only meaningful contribution to the dialogue is that "in spite of Darwin, the *Book of Genesis* retained for [Hopkins] . . . its absolute theological value as the embodiment of abiding metaphysical truth." Ong assumes an even more distant stance; his sole comment is that "Hopkins refers to Darwin in passing . . . and appears everywhere singularly free of hostility or even uneasiness regarding Darwin's or other new discoveries that were shaping the cosmic scenario."[45] Ong is doubtlessly correct on Hopkins's relaxed stance on science; but not locating precisely the "everywhere" in Hopkins leaves the matter still murky. These oversights perhaps derive from the impression that

Hopkins and Darwin seem unlikely ideological bedfellows. However, Hopkins's admitted interest in science, ecology, and natural events, along with an obsessive scrutiny of nature, all should have prompted critics to explore possible Darwinian connections; and to offer any reading of Hopkins's nature poems all written at a time in which the received ontological positions on nature were being called into question and repudiated is to ignore the cultural context of these nature poems. Granted, Hopkins's reading of nature at times reverts to a Romantic conception: nature as benign and sacramental. But in the face of the challenges of Darwinism, that very view might be reemployed to check Darwinian encroachments. Yet there are poems of Hopkins that seem to address, at times even accept, Darwinism. And precisely how these strategies are employed by Hopkins remain critical to our understanding of him, Darwinism, and the period.

The major hindrance derives, it seems, not from any disagreement on Darwin's pervasive influence on the Victorians, including Hopkins, but from Hopkins's relative silence on Darwin, which has so far been misread as a sign of unfamiliarity rather than of oblique confrontation. Only in Tom Zaniello's *Hopkins in the Age of Darwin* (1988) has the connection between Darwin and Hopkins been afforded the attention it deserves. But as successfully as Zaniello acquaints us with the many levels of discourse in which Hopkins engaged Darwin, his study skirts the precise ways in which Hopkins's poetics relate to a Darwinian epistemology; it purports instead to explore the scientific milieu in which Hopkins lived and wrote.[46] This essay, then, attempts to trace both the conscious and coincidental discourse relationships and practices between Hopkins and Darwin. It shows precisely where Hopkins's poetics reveal a consciousness of Darwinism and where his poetry responds to, if not answers, epistemic and ontological issues Darwinism generated. Such an enterprise advances our understanding of Hopkins; it also, as A. Dwight Culler observes, "opens out into large and fruitful considerations which have important consequences for human life"; or as Gillian Beer just as meaningfully puts it, "The power of Darwin's writing in his culture is best understood when it is seen not as a single origin or 'source,' but in its shifting relations to other areas of study."[47] Hopkins so resonates with issues we have come to associate with Darwinism that Zaniello rightly characterizes him as "a key witness to the Age of Darwinism."[48]

Hopkins referred explicitly to Darwinism on only three occasions: a 20 September 1874 letter to his mother on John Tyndall, a 4 January 1883 letter to Bridges on Vernon Lee (actually Violet Paget), and an 18 August 1883 letter to Bridges on instinct and Darwin's hive bees. The first remark to his mother on

John Tyndall dealt with his controversial presidential address, called "The Belfast Address," delivered to the British Association on 19 August 1874.[49] The address was published the next day in *Nature*, but Hopkins read it in the 22 August issue of *The Academy*.[50] In tracing the history of the atomistic "doctrine" from Democritus through Epicurus and finally through Lucretius, the address acknowledges Greece as the birthplace of the sciences and credits the lapse in scientific investigation, especially during the Middle Ages, to the antagonism of established religion. Tyndall identifies Bacon, Descartes, Locke, and Newton as modern practitioners, fully or in part, of atomism, and especially cites Darwin, whose theory of the survival of the fittest, Tyndall maintains, goes back 2000 years to Lucretius, but is given contemporaneity by Tennyson.[51] Hopkins found this most engaging account of atomistic philosophy "interesting and eloquent," and was probably just as captivated by Tyndall's style, which uses such natural and apt biblical phrases as "there was heard the voice of one impatiently crying in the wilderness," and "to enable them [the intellect and emotions, and by analogy science and literature] in coming times to dwell together, in unity of spirit and in the bond of peace," phrases used to acknowledge Nature as that new voice supplanting religious and traditional authority, and to praise Goethe for reconciling the intellect and emotions.[52] In seeking to determine the origin of the universe, the intellectual minds, says Tyndall, turned from the super–sensible to the "sub–sensible," Lucretius's "First Beginnings," in atoms and molecules.

Atomism insists that all living things owe their existence to the random combination and separation of innumerable insensate atoms colliding together and aggregating not by any manipulation of an intelligent design but by adapting according to number, size, and variety. The fit atoms survive while the unfit ones perish. But while the Epicureans' main contribution was in dispelling the fear of death and superstition, says Tyndall, they still acknowledged the need for belief in a supernatural being, however distant it remains from the "creation." Such belief is necessary for ethical harmony here on earth, a point Carlyle urged on Tyndall. Man, Tyndall claims, will never be "satisfied with the operations and products of the Understanding alone; hence physical science cannot cover all the demands of his nature."[53]

Although not acknowledging it, Hopkins would surely have endorsed Tyndall's skillful handling of the conversation between a fictitious Lucretian and a fictionalized Bishop Butler in his address, a discourse resembling the Professor–Hanbury dialogue in Hopkins's undergraduate essay "On the Origin of Beauty." Hopkins would have been equally impressed with Tyndall's point that death, to Epicurus, was not to be feared for it is merely a state in which sensation is denied us. Later in "That Nature is a Heraclitean Fire and of the Comfort of the Resurrection" (1888), Hopkins would use this atomistic premise to argue the Christian belief in the soul's immortality and the redemption, through transformation, of the body.

The middle part of "The Belfast Address" is Tyndall's paean of unparalleled praise for Darwin's *Origin.* He commends its industriousness, summarizes its numerous arguments, and points to its illustrious examples of natural selection at work. Like Hopkins, Tyndall is particularly fond of Darwin's account of the cell–making instinct of bees. The address claims the dominance of science: "The impregnable domain of science may be described in a few words. We claim, and we shall wrest from theology, the entire domain of cosmological theory." But should critics assume that science in replacing theology renunciates all moral agendas, Tyndall, in a brief passage on science and literature, argues that, on the contrary, "Science desires not isolation, but freely combines with every effort toward the bettering of man's estate."[54]

However, the address fails to account for two crucial factors: the origin of consciousness and the nature of a First Cause.[55] The first problem Tyndall faced was the process from the organic to the inorganic, from matter to consciousness, or, in the words of his fictionalized Bishop Butler, from "molecular processes" to the "phenomena of consciousness." While Tyndall concedes that materialism has never satisfactorily unraveled the enigma of consciousness, he partially explains this scientific impasse with the notion that Matter is the First Cause. Tyndall expresses uncertainty as to how Darwin's one "primordial form" first came about: did the Deity create few original forms from which others evolve? But this theory, Tyndall believes, would show Darwin assuming the very anthropomorphism his theory assails. Tyndall, instead, argues for the vitality of Matter, which exercises spontaneous control. Seeking to redefine Matter, and to elevate it from its base associations, he calls it "not the mere naked, empty *capacity* which philosophers have pictured her to be, but," and here he employs a maternal metaphor to invoke both Eve and the Virgin Mary, "the universal mother, who brings forth all things as the fruit of her own womb." For, as he would again claim, "Divorced from matter, where is life? Whatever our *faith* may say, our *knowledge* shows them to be indissolubly joined. Every meal we eat, and every cup we drink, illustrates the mysterious control of Mind *by* Matter." Tyndall is able to "discern in that Matter . . . the promise and potency of all terrestrial Life" (the last italics is mine).[56]

The last third of the address concerns adaptation, instinct, and learning that ensure the survival of species. To show that science and literature need not be adversarial, that the mechanic need not be at war with the organic, that modern

materialism need not demystify the Mysterious, the address ends on a moral note
that attempts to reconcile Newton with Shakespeare, Darwin with Carlyle.
Tyndall maintains that in the doctrine of materialism man finds his most creative
potential. But confessing the untimeliness to pursue so compelling a topic, he
concludes by looking both ways simultaneously— to a time when we become
one with the elements from where we first evolved: "when you and I, like streaks
of morning cloud, shall have melted into the infinite azure of the past."[57]

Hopkins bristled at that decisive comment. Tyndall's modern materialism
left him "*most mad*," for it suggests, Hopkins felt, that not only has man "an
obscure origin" but even worse "an obscure future—to be lost *in the infinite
azure of the past*." But however unsettling, the expression also appealed to
Hopkins, and might have informed his 1877 "azurous hung hills." However,
he rejected the assertion, for he felt that Tyndall's allegation supplanted
Darwinism. "I do not think," he told his mother, "that Darwinism implies
necessarily that man is descended from any ape or ascidian or maggot, and so
on: these common ancestors, if lower animals, need not have been repulsive
animals. What Darwin himself says about this I do not know."[58] Darwin had
indeed painfully avoided man and the social implications of natural selection in
the *Origin*, believing that these topics were too controversial to be taken up in
this his first work on the theory of origins. However, these issues were addressed
in *The Descent of Man* (1871), which Hopkins, just emerging from a three–
year's rigorous study in philosophy at Stonyhurst, obviously did not read. Thus,
the very point on which he was excusing Darwin—that man descended from
some primordial form—was, though never broached in the *Origin*, detailed in
The Descent.

Hopkins was more resistant to materialism, and especially its revival in
Darwinism, than his former mentor Liddon, who knew little of science and cared
even less for nature. However, both men championed not the annihilation of the
senses but its proper use in spiritual worship. Hopkins's "The Kind Betrothal"
speaks most appropriately to that notion when it urges lips, eyes, tongue,
nostrils, and hands be put to spiritual service. This he probably picked up from
Liddon, whose notion of how useful the senses are to God and worship was the
subject of his Sunday, 23 April 1882, sermon, "The Place of the Senses in
Religion," preached at St. Paul's three days after Darwin's death, and called
"The star attraction that Sunday afternoon."[59] The sermon, containing a tribute
to Darwin, merits partial examination, for it not only illustrates the sorts of
accommodation to Darwinism made by even the most conservative of high
churchmen but also provides us with added evidence of how other Victorians
were reading Darwin. When the sermon was published three days later, Liddon

revised its title, now calling it "The Recovery of St. Thomas, with a Prefatory Note on the Late Mr. Darwin." The sermon reflects not so much a rousing endorsement of Darwinism, but a certain unpreparedness by Liddon and other Anglican clergymen to deal with Modernism within the Church. What results, then, is not a clearly defined epistemology but an uncomfortable and unconvincing compromise. Indeed, as Desmond and Moore conclude, Liddon's sermon "masked a deep anxiety."[60]

In the preface to the sermon, more an apology, Liddon points out that Darwin's death "naturally invited some allusions in the pulpit," however incidental and unplanned the allusions; and that such remarks were "ill adapted to do duty for 'a statement of the religious aspects of Darwinianism.'" He feels that Darwin's books show him to be "a believer in Almighty God." *The Descent of Man*, responsible perhaps for generating the greatest anxiety, shows Darwin twice speaking of "belief in God, as 'ennobling.' No serious writer would so speak of any belief, much less of the tremendous 'belief in the existence of an Omnipotent God,' unless," says Liddon, "he himself held it to be a true belief." Liddon felt that it need not be argued that the origin of species by natural selection does not oppose faith in God's relationship as Maker, Upholder, and Ruler of the material universe. "Mr Darwin has taught many readers how to think of God working in nature during long periods of time, not how to think of nature as excluding God." Liddon believes, however, that Darwin has invited "a modification of this judgment" when in *The Descent of Man* he writes of not regretting to have given natural selection great power, for such, Darwin believes, is "good service in aiding to overthrow the dogma of separate creations." Liddon concedes that the general theory has led Darwin to "deprecate what he calls 'separate creations,'" and as such to maintain "an impoverished idea of God, which he had probably derived, whether directly or unconsciously, from the older Deism. He sometimes writes as if natural laws, although enacted by God, had an independent existence apart from Him, and were not merely, as they are, observed forms of Divine activity." Liddon contends that "Darwin's objection to 'separate creations' is determined not by any anti–theological motive, but a too–exclusive devotion to a particular scientific object." Darwin's preoccupation as a naturalist "has led him to write, from time to time, as if God had really created once for all the machine of the universe, and then had left it to work by itself."

Addressing specifically *The Descent of Man*, Liddon finds that "objection to a theory of descent from 'a hairy quadruped' is not a wholly religious objection; it may spring from a feeling which is the counterpart in the race to the pride of birth in its individual families. After all," says Liddon, "our birth as individuals is due, under God, to physical causes which differ in no respect from those which determine the birth of lower animals around us; and the only serious question is the question of fact. Man's true dignity depends not upon the history of his physical frame, but upon the nature of the immaterial principle within him and above all upon the unspeakable honour conferred upon both parts of his being when they were united to the External Person of God the Son, in the Divine Incarnation." In an even more accommodating gesture, and especially from one who years earlier opposed Frederick Temple on precisely the same grounds, Liddon notes that should the Church "hereafter teach that this 'formation' was not a momentary act, but a process of development continued through a long series of ages, she would not vary the traditional interpretation so seriously. . . . Nor would the earlier description of the creation of man in the Sacred Record present any great difficulty. It is very far from clear," says Liddon, "that the Darwinian hypothesis has so established itself as to make such a modified interpretation necessary; only let it be considered that here, as elsewhere, the language of the Bible is wider than to be necessarily tied down to the terms of a particular account of man's natural history." If we were to accept the theory that humans derived from "more than one natural parent," Liddon argues, the "great antithesis of the First and the Second Adam" that espouses the salvific analogy between Adam and Christ "would disappear from our faith." Liddon concludes his preface on a reconciliatory note, urging that "No Christian who believes in the essential harmony of all truth will be other than anxious to reconcile the statements of men of science with the truths of Divine Revelation. . . . But God's word in Revelation will never pass away," although "theories respecting God's working in nature are, as we know, changing almost from year to year." Darwin deserves our respect for his "life–long diligence as a reverent observer and student of the works of God."[61]

The sermon itself addresses modern materialism through the exchanges the skeptical Apostle Thomas had with the resurrected Christ. There are certain truths, says Liddon, that the senses alone can ascertain and must be trusted. "It is a false spiritualism which would cast discredit on the senses, acting within their own province; it is false to the constitution of nature, and to the interests of truth. For if the bodily senses are untrustworthy, how can we assume the trustworthiness of the spiritual senses?" To doubt the trustworthiness of the senses is to enhance "the preciousness of the supersensuous and of our methods of reaching it. . . . Religion does touch the material world at certain points, and the reality of its contact is to be decided, like other material facts, by the experiment of sense." Verification of the Lord's resurrection was submitted to the senses; "and our Lord therefore submitted Himself to the exacting terms which St. Thomas laid down [i.e., the senses] as conditions of faith." When Christ said "This is My Body; This is My Blood," serious Christians will not take liberties with His language, by resolving it into metaphor and rejecting its strictly literal force. But then how are we," says Liddon, "to reconcile the two; the report of the senses on the one hand and the plain meaning of the words of Christ on the other?" Our difficulty with this, Liddon believes, is similar to the confusion over free will and divine sovereignty. The true function of the senses is that they "cannot test the reality of anything which lies properly beyond their ken," for the believer's life is one of faith not of sight. The senses, then, "have to do with matter: they cannot touch spirit"; thus to infer beyond this "limited capacity" of the senses to their use in the vast nonmaterial world of "spiritual existences" is "a worthless inference."

> Here is the great mistake of Materialism. Materialism is on
> strong ground, from which it cannot be dislodged, so long as
> it insists that the senses, so far as they reach, are trustworthy
> reporters of truth. Its mistake lies in saying that they are the
> only reporters of truth, and that nothing is to be held for truth
> which they cannot verify; that the whole world of mental and
> spiritual facts, with which the senses have no relation what-
> ever, is therefore an imaginary and non–existent world; that,
> in short, matter, in whatever shape, is alone real.

But to correct this abuse of the senses should not involve an attempt to discredit the proper use of the senses. To do so invites "the ravages of a scepticism which is even wider than that of the Materialists; since it denies the reality of matter as well as that of spirit, while it is clearly opposed to that high sanction which our Lord gave to the evidence of the sense when He bade Thomas,—'Reach hither thy finger, and behold My Hands; and reach hither thy hand, and thrust it into My Side: and be not faithless, but believing.'"[62]

Liddon proceeds in the sermon to venerate Darwin as that "eminent man" who "has been the author of nothing less than a revolution in the modern way of treating a large district of thought, while his works have shed high distinction upon English science." He reminds his congregation that when Darwin's two great works first appeared a decade or so earlier, "they were largely regarded by religious men as containing a theory necessarily hostile to the fundamental truths of religion." But Liddon now sees no such contradiction:

A closer study has generally modified any such impression.
If the theory of "natural selection" has given a powerful
impulse to the general doctrine of evolution, it is seen that
whether the creative activity of God is manifested through
catastrophes, so to call them, or by a way of progressive
evolution, it is still His creative activity, and that the really
great questions beyond remain untouched.[63]

Turning to the origin of evolution, and more specifically to the origin of matter,
Liddon speculated that the "evolutionary process, supposing it to exist, must
have had a beginning: who began it? It must have had material to work with: who
furnished this material?" These questions, Liddon believes, cannot be answered
by physical science now or even when Moses wrote. There remains, then, "three
important gaps in the evolutionary sequence":

There is the great gap between the highest animal instinct, and
the reflective, self–measuring, self–analyzing mind of man.
There is the greater gap between life, and the most highly
organized matter. There is the greatest gap of all between
matter and nothing. At these three points . . . the Creative Will
must have intervened otherwise than by way of evolution out
of existing material,—to create mind,—to create life,—to
create matter.[64]

Darwin's greatness, according to Liddon, lies primarily in his keen observation
and registering of single facts, then assembled into "groups of facts." But facts
are one thing, and theories and hypotheses, like evolution, which seek to account
for facts, another. These theories are not necessarily true; "science knows no
finality, and while theories pass and are forgotten, facts—like God's revelation
of Himself in Christ—remains." Like so many of his contemporaries, Liddon
points to his age as one of doubt and admits a skepticism pervading all discourse.
"In private intercourse, in general society, in clubs and in workshops, among
men of letters, and among artisans, truths are freely called in question which
were received unhesitatingly by our fathers" and for which they would have
given their lives. But, Liddon concludes reassuringly, "doubt is not the only
characteristic of our age; side by side with doubt there is faith,—strong,
penetrating, intelligent, definite,—and in its growth and strength lies the best
hope of the future."[65]

Liddon again addressed Darwinism in another sermon at St. Paul's, entitled "The Creation," the text of which was Genesis 1:1: "In the beginning God created the heaven and the earth." This text, Liddon holds, does not "merely tell us that God is the Author, both of our planet, and also of that vast system of worlds in which our planet is little more than a large aerolite. It does not merely assert that God created the immaterial as well as the material heavens and earth: that He created those vast multitudes of intelligences who have no bodily form, but who are wiser far and mightier than man." Rather, the passage makes implicitly clear that the process whereby these created things came into existence "was itself unique—an act strictly proper to God—an act impossible to a creature." As to the meaning of the word "created," Liddon writes: "It must mean that the Universe originally owes both its form and its substance to the creative fiat of God."[66]

Addressing materialism, and with the German materialistic philosopher Ludwig Feuerbach in mind, Liddon points out that it tells us that the universe is "eternal and self–existent," thus omitting God altogether from the process; "it holds Him to have no real existence. He is pronounced to be a creature of the human imagination, the product of the human mind at a particular stage of its development." Liddon finds that the most elaborate form of materialism "proposes to substitute two self–existent factors for the God of Heaven, two blind, all–powerful agencies—matter and force." Liddon then quotes Feuerbach:

> "No hand holds the earth in its course; no prayer can arrest the
> sun or lull the fury of the storm; no voice can raise the dead
> from their eternal sleep; no angel can deliver the captive; no
> hand stretched forth from the clouds can feed the hungry; no
> sign from heaven can tell us that we know anything beyond
> Nature. Beyond Nature there is nothing. . . . Nature has no
> answer that she can make to the griefs or the prayers of man;
> she drives him back inexorably upon himself."

"This," Liddon concludes, "is the sentence of Materialism and Atheism."[67]

Pusey did not care much for the position Liddon took on Darwin, especially in his 1882 tribute. Earlier in an 1878 university sermon, Pusey had addressed the relationship between religion and science. The sermon, "Un–Science, Not Science, Adverse to Faith," a treatise too long for the ailing Pusey to deliver, was presented by Liddon. While other divines of the nineteenth century seemed to have capitulated to Darwinism, Pusey held pertinaciously to his orthodox position, a dogged determinism indicative more of Pusey's personality than of his static ideas. He, like Newman, argues for a separation between science and religion. "The basis of a lasting peace and alliance between physical science and Theology is, that neither should intrude into the province of the other. For science is *certain* knowledge based on *certain* facts. The facts on which Theology rests are spiritual facts; those of physical science are material." Concerning the formation of the earth, theology, says Pusey, "would equally admit of Lucretius' combination of atoms floating in space, and drawn together by mutual attraction, provided only that He who gave them those impulses, and placed each individual at the distances, when that attraction would act, was— not chance, but God." To theology the workings of things in nature are the workings of God, and nature, though ascribed with wisdom and power, is "but a name for an effect, whose Cause is God." But the notable progress of natural science has caused it to look beyond its purview, especially in regard to the creation, when it argues the "unthinkable" proposition that being can emerge from matter. Darwinism, Pusey reasons, though not atheistic in itself unless it insists on the eternity of matter and spontaneous generation, is at odds with "belief in a Creator Who is to be eliminated from all interference with the works which He has made." Any "First Cause" introduced to us as a "'Deus ex machina,' to save us from the conception of the eternity of matter," who remains content to look disinterestedly on his creation, "would be an Epicurean god, whose being would be inconsistent not only with God's revelation of Himself, but with any conceptions of an intelligent Theism."[68] Newman, Liddon, and Pusey all addressed Darwinism and the discourse relationship between science and religion, and came away arguing at best for an annulment between science and religion and at worse for a compromise. But as one drawn more to science, Hopkins sought a closer symbiotic relationship between the two fields of discourse, science and religion.

In that 20 September 1874 letter to his mother on Tyndall's "Belfast Address," Hopkins drew her attention to St. George Mivart's *On the Genesis of Species* (1870). Hopkins was pleased that this Catholic biologist, although an "Evolutionist," still "combats downright Darwinism and is very orthodox."[69] Mivart, a close friend and admirer of Darwin who embraced evolution though not natural selection, was attempting to reconcile evolution with the Church Fathers. Concerned with the damaging effects of Darwin's assumptions on belief in God, the soul's immortality, and future rewards or punishments, in other words with things metaphysical, Mivart sought to reassure Hopkins and other Victorians that evolution "need alarm no one, for it is, without any doubt, perfectly consistent with strictest and most orthodox Christian theology."[70] Mivart had been the brunt of Darwin's humor (at one point Huxley described

Mivart as rabid), and Darwin had singled him out for being most critical of his views. So formidable was Mivart's challenge that Darwin accused him of an "accursed religious bigotry," and recruited Huxley and the American Chauncey Wright in his defense.[71] Mivart's work, according to Peter Bowler, was "the kingpin of a protracted effort to demonstrate the insufficiency of natural selection as an explanation of evolution."[72] Hopkins was sufficiently curious about Darwinism to assume Mivart's premise: it is theoretically possible to be an evolutionist and to remain religiously orthodox.

Hopkins next referred to Darwinism in a 4 January 1883 letter to Bridges on Vernon Lee's "Impersonality and Evolution in Music," an essay that appeared in the December 1882 issue of *Contemporary Review.* Lee's essay was based on Edmund Gurney's *The Power of Sound* (1880). Hopkins liked Gurney's ideas. They relied on but remained critical of some of Herbert Spencer's notions on the origin of music, ideas later modified by Darwin. However, Gurney more closely aligned himself with Darwin's assumptions on the origin of music. To know what Hopkins liked in Gurney, telling Bridges, for instance, that Gurney "appears to write very well on music,"[73] and disliked in Lee, one needs some acquaintance with the arguments and controversy. Spencer's essay, "The Origin and Function of Music," first appeared in the October 1857 issue of *Fraser's Magazine.* Based on the principle that music is the natural language of passion, the essay argues that pleasurable and painful sensations manifest themselves in sounds, and that the quality and pitch of those sounds are proportionally linked to the intensity of the sensations. Thus "each inflection or modulation is the natural outcome of some passing emotion or sensation."[74] How one feels then has everything to do with alterations in one's voice or the sounds one makes, which are then in consort with bodily movements. Departure and return from middle notes in any direction are connected to heightened and decreased emotions. For a song "employs and exaggerates the natural language of the emotions"; and in fact "what we regard as the distinctive traits of song, are simply the traits of emotional speech intensified and systematized."[75] Tying together a physiological and an emotive explanation of vocal sounds and the origin of music, Spencer attempts to account for loudness, quality or timbre, pitch intervals, and rate of variation.

Spencer sent Darwin copies of his essays. In a 25 November 1858 letter, Darwin thanked him for them, especially the one on music which "interested me much, for I had often thought on the subject, and had come to nearly the same conclusion with you, though unable to support the notion in any detail.... I must entirely agree with you that all expression has some biological meaning."[76] While it is conceivable that Darwin arrived at his ideas on the origin of music independent of Spencer, his subsequent denial of "not [being] conscious of having profited in my own work by Spencer's writings" fails to silence the unmistakable biological affiliation that both his and Spencer's theories share.[77] Darwin's speculations on the origin of music in *The Descent of Man* not only show a keen understanding of what Spencer argued fourteen years earlier, and in fact quote Spencer, but also exploit some of Spencer's own findings, biases (music and race, for instance), and hypotheses. Like Spencer, Darwin sought a physiological basis for vocal sounds. But unlike Spencer, who posits general, emotive causes for sounds and ties the function of music to the development of emotional speech, Darwin insisted that the sounds—and by extension music— evolved out of amatory feelings. On the one hand Darwin held that music is pre– speech, and so outlived its usefulness after speech evolved; yet on the other hand he insisted that music and dance were integral to courtship and sexual selection. "Although the sounds emitted by animals and all kinds serve many purposes," Darwin urged in *The Descent of Man*, "a strong case can be made out, that the vocal organs were primarily used and perfected in relation to the propagation of the species." The rhythmical repetition of certain notes in lower animals and the vocal sounds from mammals, made almost exclusively by males and during courtship, show that the "chief and, in some cases, exclusive purpose appears to be either to call or charm the opposite sex."[78]

Later when Gurney wrote "On Some Disputed Points in Music" for the *Fortnightly Review* (1876) and his two essays "On Music and Musical Criticism" for *The Nineteenth Century* (1878–79), all three of which evolved into *The Power of Sound*, he gave them the Darwinian materialistic spin (accentuating the desire for pleasure) and relied almost exclusively on Darwin's assertion (quoting in *The Power of Sound* a long passage from *The Descent of Man* on sexual selection and taking Spencer to task on movement excited by the emotions) that vocal and musical sounds derived from courtship rituals. In the *Fortnightly* essay, Gurney noted that music was first not appreciative but functional, used to excite the strongest passions during courtship; in time these evolved into an array of emotional meanings all related to the job of survival. Gurney was arguably the first formalist to assert that the definiteness of form and matter makes music, rather than poetry, more immediately accessible to our sensual apprehension. Rhythm, he pointed out, "gives the framework for the most effective applications of the other elements of proportion and form, which without it tend to sink into incoherence"; or, as he later stated, "Music, though dealing wholly with abstract proportions, is an art preeminent for the precision, individuality, and organic quality of its forms."[79] In the two essays "On Music and Musical Criticism," Gurney embraced, as he would again in *The Power of*

Sound, the Spencerean analogy between the presentational and representational arts: poetry, sculpture, and painting are arts of representation, while music and architecture are arts of presentation. But music is different from architecture because it is more complex and more mentally taxing. Gurney also argued for the organic wholeness of art, believing that the true artist must strive after organic unity. As this organic principle in music increases from moment to moment, so too does pleasure.[80]

Vernon Lee's "Impersonality and Evolution in Music," then, celebrates Gurney's *The Power of Sound* for dispersing with "all the old myths of personality and romanticism" and for elevating music as "an art of ideal form."[81] The essay is a ringing endorsement of Gurney's theory: that of all the arts music relies most on abstract form and caters least to personal emotion. Lee's second thesis argues her own theory that of all the arts music has developed most from the pressures inherent in artistic form and least from the personal influence of the artist. A self-proclaimed disciple of Gurney, and even more of a formalist, Lee asserts that music is the most patterned of the arts, and it is that quality to which we most respond with pleasure or aversion. Form is primary and the emotions that give rise to it ancillary: "the identity, the real existence of the composition, is entirely in the form; that what the composer creates is not an emotional suggestion . . . but the form." Thus it is that one particular emotion can generate hundreds of musical pieces, each uniquely different in form. And that form, that quintessential element of art, valuable in itself, which quickens the aesthetic judgment and continues to exist with the same intensity and clarity of identity even when all momentary impressions have long since departed, is not "invented by any particular man, but is evolved" spontaneously from other existing forms without manifesting any of the distinguishing marks of those forms. The "life of forms" in this "transmutation of musical forms," this "purely musical evolution of musical forms," is characterized as a "perfectly unbroken stream of change."[82] Hopkins's disagreement with Lee's assertion and endorsement of Gurney's, when in fact both theories argue much the same principle, show that he had not fully grasped, or else misread, Gurney's claims. His comment on Lee, then, revises his earlier acceptance of the theory. Now he sarcastically responded that the multiplicity of program annotations proves that music has evolved from the mating call of apes: "we enjoy music because our apist ancestors serenaded their Juliet–apes of the period in rudimentary recitative and our emotions are the survival." This "swing," he concluded, is "from pap to poison."[83] Given Hopkins's knowledge of Darwin, Gurney, and Lee, and fascination with philology and music, one could only wish that he had commented more fully on the controversy he saw fit only to adumbrate.

Hopkins's cursory remarks on Gurney's musical essays share, however, a contextual relationship to his two poems on music, "Henry Purcell" and "Who shaped these walls," the latter familiar to us as "On a Piece of Music." "Henry Purcell" is a tribute to the famed seventeenth–century English composer who, in addition to expressing in music the "moods of man's mind," has rendered musical utterance to the very being of man, the "rehearsal / Of own, of abrupt self." "Who shaped these walls" admires architecture, which it likens to musical composition, and insists that the work of art culls out the artist's very self: "Who shaped these walls has shewn / The music of his mind." Hopkins's analogy is consistent with Gurney's arts of presentation, which combine music and architecture. Both, said Gurney, are used to serve religion, and both have the potential to overload the senses. Gurney's essay, "Some disputed Points in Music," is also telling. It too uses an architectural analogy to explain music and argues that our various pleasurable responses to music of all kinds can be traced back to our semi–human progenitors. Darwin agreed, theorizing that "the fact that different people belonging to the same civilized nation are very differently affected by the same music" show, in a way, that "these diversities of taste and pleasure have been acquired during their individual lives." Darwin also applauded Gurney's simile of architecture, the appreciation of which, he felt, must also be individual; and, extending the analogy to an unusual degree in order to use natural selection to account for every natural phenomenon, Darwin hypothesized that the fear elicited from the sublimity of grand cathedrals might have some relation to the vague fears and terrors experienced by our ancestors who trek through great caverns and gloomy forests.[84]

Hopkins's most substantive comment on Darwinism was not made until 18 August 1888, when he observed to Bridges that "everything is Darwinism." He was commenting on the eighth chapter of the *Origin* where Darwin outlines his conclusions on the efficiently and economically designed structure of the honeycomb: bees are able to construct a hive that holds the greatest possible honey while using the least possible wax. Darwin contends that natural selection, utilizing the bees' highly evolved instincts, determines the cell–making ability of the humble bees to shape simple and irregularly rounded cells and of the hive bee to construct complex and perfect hexagonal cells. "The hive–bee has acquired, through natural selection," modified instincts that give her "immutable architectural powers." Her most unique instincts, Darwin maintains, "can be explained by natural selection having taken advantage of numerous, successive, slight modifications of simpler instincts."[85]

Probably because Darwin in the *Origin* and later in *The Descent* deliberately blurs whatever distinction that might otherwise exist between instinct and reason, Hopkins found it convenient to agree with him, holding that the cell's shape was determined not by mechanics but by instincts, the very controversy, he observed, that divided scholars. He pointed to Darwin's discovery that "the cell can only be symmetrical, with a true hexagonal section" and with the bees "stationed at equal distances, working equally"; in fact, he argued, "there is a considerable table of 'caetera paria' [other things being equal]. But this implies something more than mechanical to begin with"; for with mechanics the hexagonal shape will only be approached, "the type 'tended to' only," but seldom if ever achieved; thus the honeycomb will be "like the irregular figures of bubbles in the froth of beer or in soapsuds." Although wild bees do construct such irregular cells, Hopkins conceded, one has to "grant in the honey bees some principle of symmetry and uniformity"; what results, consequently, is something "beyond mechanical necessity . . . some special instinct determined to that shape of cell after all and which has at the present stage of the bee's condition, nothing to do with mechanics, but is like the specific songs of cuckoo and thrush," an avian analogy Darwin also used to advocate rationally instinctive abilities in animals. Hopkins made his position on mechanics and something beyond mechanics even clearer in an 1874 entry on waves receding after striking a sea wall. He observed that they "return in nearly the same order and shape in which they came." This, Hopkins felt, is "mechanical reflection . . . indeed all nature is mechanical, but then it is not seen that mechanics contain that which is beyond mechanics."[86]

Darwin's "instincts" and Hopkins's "special instincts" are therefore dissimilar. Special instinct suggests, as Zaniello points out, some "controlling force inherent in nature" and thus resembles the concept of instress.[87] It denotes too distinctiveness, as in the unique, almost undifferentiated, sounds of the cuckoo Hopkins registered in a 20 May 1866 journal entry: "Cuckoos calling and answering to each other, and the calls being not equally timed they overlapped, making the triple *cuckoo*, and crossed." A similar entry was made in his journal three years later: "The cuckoo 'has' changed his tune: the two notes can scarcely be told apart, that is their pitch is almost the same." Ten days later he called that sound "very timeless and wild,"[88] resembling the "rash–fresh re–winded new–skeined score" of the skylark. The cuckoo's arbitrary pitch intervals—whether "thrice and four times and again" or a pattern of "Five notes or seven—late and few"—derives from a "sweet–potential skill" ("A Voice from the World"), and as such is determined not by mechanics, which establishes regularity, but by special instinct. And it is that specially endowed force that induces the cuckoo to repeat a "delightfully sweet," "new–skeined score" whereby the "whole landscape flushes on a sudden at a sound" ("Repeat that, repeat"), the magic of which "Caps, clears, and clinches all" ("The May Magnificat").[89] In the case of the cuckoo, each new variation in sound produces a new song. An important nineteenth–century concern, the primacy of sound was addressed by such eminent scientists as Helmholtz and Tyndall. Sound resonates throughout Hopkins's poetry and versification. In fact, he defined poetry as spoken sound and speech possessing in whole or in part the same repetitive figure of sound. Present in the poems, then, are memorable sounds: "the echoing timber," "it strikes like lightnings to hear him sing," "the tide that ramps against the shore; / With a flood or a fall, low lull–off roar," "His rash–fresh re–winded new-skeined score / In crisp of curl off wild winch whirl," "Hack and rack the growing green," and "As tumbled over rim in roundy wells / Stones ring."

Such keen registering of nature's sounds certifies Hopkins as a naturalist. Like Darwin, he exhibited an abiding concern, even a tentative reverence, for the particulars of nature, an empirical scrupulousness Darwin saw necessary to the naturalist.[90] Poems such as "God's Grandeur," "Duns Scotus's Oxford," and "Binsey Poplars" register concern for the destruction of nature, whether for ecological or aesthetic reasons, and whether from industrialism or through human ignorance. "The Sea and the Skylark," "Spelt from Sibyl's Leaves," and "Heraclitean Fire" present an even more frightening apocalyptic picture of nature's loss of instress, its unfastening, the demise of its "once skeined stained veined variety." Additionally, Hopkins's journal reveals an obsession with cloud formation, topography, the uniqueness within species of floral life, the call, color, and behavior of birds, the pattern of waves, the source and variety of lightning, and the marvels of the constellation. Art, Hopkins felt, was the best way to represent and preserve natural phenomena: "What I noticed was the great richness of the membering of the green in the elms, never however to be expressed but by drawing after study."[91] G.F. Lahey, Hopkins's first biographer, recalled that his experience at age eight of "probing into the mysteries of nature" in the Hainault Forest "strengthened and improved his life–long delight in, and faithful recording of, what he saw in natural phenomena."[92] A novice colleague remembered Hopkins having "a keen eye for peculiarities in 'nature'"; and a fellow seminarian provided this memorable anecdote: "After a shower, he would run and crouch down to gaze at the crushed quartz glittering as the sun came out again. 'Ay, a strange youngman,' said the old brother, 'crouching down that gate to stare at some wet sand. A fair natural 'e seemed to us, that Mr. 'opkins.'"[93]

Floral life also intrigued Hopkins. He was particularly fond of elms, to him the national tree, once describing England as "elmy" ("St. Winefred's Well") and recognizing, "wherever an elm arches, / Shivelights and shadowtackle in long lashes" ("Heraclitean Fire"). "The run of the trees and their rich and handsome leafage charmed and held me," he confessed, noting also "the web of springing green with long curls moulds off the skeleton of the branches." His lenticular curiosity (Ruskin's term) caught "Fields pinned with daisies," and represented "buds of apple blossoms . . . like nails of blood," an analogy that, while religious, resonates with echoes of Tennyson's "Nature, red in tooth and claw." Hopkins even pondered the effects of climate and topography on the design of sycamores that "grew on the slopes of the valley, scantly leaved, sharply quained and accidented by perhaps the valley winds."[94] But his empirical method, as the botanist J.S. Gilmour detected, was often more poetic than scientific: "GMH looked at plants with the eye of an artist rather than of a botanist. He possessed remarkable powers of observation from his own very personal angle. . . . A botanist cannot help wishing that he had more botanical knowledge as a background to his genius for minute analysis of shapes and patterns." Hopkins's 6 July 1866 journal entry best fits the point Gilmour makes. He had been observing a variety of things in nature (beeches and carnations in particular), and turned his attention to roses, noticing particularly that their "richness" and "variety" "always make them necessary to the poets."[95]

Approximately one–third of Hopkins's poetic corpus is devoted to nature and especially the poet's response to it. In Ignatian fashion, the falcon "caught" his attention as a prelude to capturing his heart; however, in succumbing poetically to the otherwise clinical experience, he felt the pain that the vicarious all too often stirs; he was "possessed by" "A NOISE of falls," entranced by the "heavenfallen freshness" of the "Marble river, boisterously beautiful, between / Roots and rocks," disheartened by the senseless felling of aspens and beech, as he was also by the "neighbour–nature . . . grey beauty" now "grounded," and was delighted with Oxford's "Smells that are sweeter–memoried than the rose, / And pressed violets in the folds." He declared in "Ashboughs": "Not of all my eyes see, wandering on the world, / Is anything a milk to the mind so, so sighs deep / Poetry to it, as a tree whose boughs break in the sky," wondered "What would the world be, once bereft / Of wet and of wildness," beckoned his readers to observe the stars, and "caught" the majestic free fells of the falcon. But unlike Darwin, Hopkins's concern with nature was never to doubt its beneficence, never to determine its origin, so confident was he of nature's "ground of being, and granite of it." To him, the "busy working of nature" was always "a new witness to God"; flowering bluebells displayed "the beauty of the Lord," and the stars prevoked veneration to God, "to and in whom all beauty comes home."[96]

Hopkins's meticulous attention to nature also extended to poetic language, which, like nature, according to James Milroy, has its "laws, patterns and

Hopkins's sketch of Richard Garnett's "Humming Bird."
Garnett was a nineteenth-century poet and ornithologist.
Courtesy of the Bodleian Library.

inscapes" that "can be discovered and observed like natural phenomena." One of the very first areas the theory of evolution by natural selection challenged was language, long held to be the specific *differance* between humans and animals.[97] The arsenal of the Victorian sage is "philology, his instrument etymology. He is the prophet of words."[98] This remark by Hans Aarsleff describes not only Carlyle but Hopkins, the arch–especial Victorian sage. More than other Victorians, he was so obsessed with words that for readers to ignore them, says Milroy, is to forfeit all understanding of his "linguistic attitudes and poetic practice."[99] His lexical range manifests a taxonomy in which cognate forms of words are employed because of their patterns and variants. Hopkins was, as one of his Jesuit contemporaries recalled, "intimately versed in the whole range of scientific expression, and showed a preference for such terms as were most recondite and but seldom used."[100] Based on the linguistic principle that "All words mean either things or relations of things," Hopkins assumed that the genus of the word "grind" can be determined deductively: "Grind, gride, gird, groat, grate, greet. . . . Original meaning to 'strike, rub,' particularly 'together.' . . . 'Grief' possibly connected. 'Gruff,' with a sound of two things rubbing together."[101] Darwin would call this "metaphor of etymology" (Gillian Beer's term) a "long and only partially broken chain of affinities," or the "inextricable web of the affinities between the members of any one class." Darwin's theory differentiates between "real [or "true"] affinities," which deal with descent, and "analogical resemblances," which result from adaptation.[102] Hopkins draws a similar distinction in his linguistic theory. He speculates that although words display phonetic differences (each word in a phonetic chain differs from the preceding one in only one sound and each new vowel slides upward as on a musical scale),[103] they nevertheless exhibit phonological affinities because they all stem from a similar phonetic root. Consequently, pursuit of semantic similarities often led Hopkins to phonological affinities, many of which can be found in his poems: "The flange and the rail; flame, / Fang, or flood"; "The keener to come at the comfort for feeling the combating keen";[104] "daylight's dauphin, dapple–dawn–drawn" ("The Windhover"); "swift, slow; sweet, sour" ("Pied Beauty"); "selfwrung, selfstrung, sheathe– and shelterless" ("Spelt from Sibyl's Leaves").

Hopkins's onomatopoetic theory, in which words similar in sound, though morphologically dissimilar, share an affinity to each other, derives from the notion that words derive from a single genus or, according to Cary Plotkin, are "enforced by a shared semantic nucleus."[105] This "arch and original Breath," to Hopkins, is Logocentric, for he sees words connected to a fixed referent, a signified, in the incarnate Logos, which anchors language from its natural tendency to dissipate. Thus, "All words whatsoever, all permutations of all the letters of the alphabet," Hopkins assumes, "have a common source in the Word."[106] The Incarnation, wherein the Word becomes a word, to reside with us, holds both theological and linguistic relevance. "Heaven and earth," Hopkins tells us, are "word of" (incarnational) and "worded by" (creational) Christ (*The Wreck*); or, as he states elsewhere, "God's utterance of himself in himself is God the Word, outside himself in this world," which makes the world both God–spell and gospel, "word, expression, news of God."[107] "So close is the identification in Hopkins' mind among world, word, and the utterance," Edward Said observes, that the three converge as in a "moment of performance."[108] As God's "utterance," his instressing of himself, his own prepossession, Christ is linguistically perceived; for the "parallelism between the structure of language and the structure of the creation," as Miller notes, emerges from their "relation to the creator." Therefore, "the structure of nature in its relation to God" is to Hopkins one with "the structure of language in relation to the Logos, the divine Word." For Christ is the "Logos of nature, as of words."[109] But while to Darwin language is "anthropocentric," placing man "at the center of signification,"[110] for in his evolutionary development he increasingly grants words their conceptual meaning and relevance, to Hopkins, however, language is Logocentric, for words derive their signification and significance only from the Word.

Hopkins's approach to species of language shares, then, some affinity to Darwin's. Both cladistic methods involve tracing similarities and differences within and across species to determine origin, and both are based on the assumption that, in the words of John Tyndall, "all living powers are cognate" and "all living forms are fundamentally of one character."[111] And because nature and language are composed of individual parts, parts often illustrated as a tree of ancestry—Darwin's favorite metaphor employed to explain the verticalness of descent—the two fields are not dissimilar. Fond as he was of conceiving species as an "*irregularly branched*" tree, Darwin also referred to the association as the "simile of tree and classification,"[112] an analogy that came to him from observing the vital force in matter when cuttings were taken from a parent Chiloé apple tree or from branching corals. Darwin's classification model for evolution—the history of roots—was based on genealogy, on the historical relationship across species. The "tree," says S. S. Schweber, "embodied the evolution of species."[113] Darwin's friends, Lyell and Gray, felt too that language might be an effective illustration of the derivation of species. "Classification of organic forms," the English mental evolutionist George John Romanes cogently argues, in language characteristically analogic, "strongly resembles the classification of languages." Languages, like species, demonstrate strongly marked "genetic affinities," making possible the construction of "a Language–tree, the branches of which shall indicate, in a diagrammatic form, the progressive divergence of a large group of languages from a common stock." For example, Romanes supposes, "Latin may be regarded as a fossil language, which has given rise to a group of living languages—Italian, Spanish, French, and, to a large extent, English."[114] So popular was the theory of classification that one anonymous writer in the April, 1860, issue of *The Cornhill Magazine* made the same association:

> The development of numerous specific forms, widely distin-
> guished from each other, out of one common stock, is not a
> whit more improbable than the development of numerous
> distinct languages out of a common parent language, which
> modern philologists have proved to be indubitably the case.
> Indeed, there is a very remarkable analogy between philology
> and zoology in this respect: just as the comparative anatomist
> traces the existence of similar organs, and similar connec-
> tions of these organs, throughout the various animals classed
> under one type, so does the comparative philologist detect the
> family likeness in the various languages.[115]

Hopkins's logocentric curiosity, then, naturally derived from his interest in scientific etymology, debated aggressively in the nineteenth century. The catalysts in all of this were the writings of the famous comparative philologist, Friedrich Max Müller, who was primarily responsible for laying the foundation for the consideration of philology as a natural science. Hopkins discovered Müller apparently simultaneously in the pages of Manley Hopkins's *Hawaii* (1862) and in Müller's *Science of Language*, the product of two series of popular lectures (1861, 1863) delivered to teeming crowds at the Royal Institution of Great Britain. Hopkins might also have attended Müller's lectures at Oxford during his tenure there (1854–68) as Taylorian Professor of modern European languages and would have been familiar too with his lectures published in *Nature* and *Fraser's Magazine*, journals Hopkins frequently perused. In Müller, Hopkins found a philologist who corroborated his every notion: language has a rational base, and words are meaningful because they are the incarnation of thoughts and of the Logos. Müller maintained that words do not "spring into life by an act of spontaneous generation," for classification properly conducted shows that "nothing exists in nature by accident; that each individual belongs to a species, each species to a genus";[116] and so it is with human language.

Holding to what Hans Aarsleff calls "linguistic finalism," Müller, the self–proclaimed "Darwinian before Darwin,"[117] became engaged in serious literary exchanges with Charles Darwin and later William Dwight Whitney of Yale. Müller held unswervingly to the theory that phonetic types, like species, are fixed or stable and derived from an act of divine fiat and not, contrary to Darwin and other philological materialists, from natural selection.[118] But in embracing fixity rather than continuity, Müller was a most unlikely Darwinian. In fact, the "unsettling science" he sought to check, says Elizabeth Knoll, "was Darwinism."[119] As far as Müller was concerned, "Natural selection . . . is invariably rational selection," for what survives in species as well as in language is what comes "nearest to the original intention of its creator."[120] He elaborated further in an essay in *Nature*:

> A much more striking analogy, therefore, than the struggle
> for life among separate languages, is the struggle for life
> among words and grammatical forms which is constantly
> going on in each language. . . . Here, if anywhere, we can learn
> that what is called the process of natural selection, is at the
> same time, from a higher point of view, a process of rational
> elimination.[121]

Contrary to Darwin and other evolutionary philologists like Romanes and Whitney, Müller held pertinaciously to the view that "*Language*," because of its mental complexity, is the "specific difference" between the animal kingdom and man. "Man speaks, and no brute has ever uttered a word. Language is our Rubicon, and no brute will dare to cross it. . . . It admits no cavilling, and no process of natural selection will ever distill significant words out of the notes of birds or the cries of beasts."[122] This new alliance between language and science forged by Müller helped to sustain, as Aarsleff indicates, "the argument for final causes and for assurance of the Creator's presence in Creation."[123]

Darwin obviously did not share Müller's views on the origin of language. He read *Science of Language* in October of 1862 and found it "extremely interesting," except for the section on the first origin of language, which he found "the least satisfactory." Believing too that the book contained "covert sneers" directed at him,[124] Darwin took on Müller in *The Descent of Man*. He acknowledged the priority Müller granted language, but insisted that animals use vocal sounds and related gestures—more expressive, in fact, than words—to convey a range of emotions and requests. He further insisted that language, like species, evolved through natural selection, and that as far as the mental faculty is concerned, man's exhibited no greater complexity than that of higher mammals. What distinguishes man from the lower animals, said Darwin, is not his ability to understand articulate sounds nor to associate particular sounds to particular ideas. The real difference is man's greater ability, because of his more highly developed mental powers, to associate broader range and more diversified sounds to particular ideas. The process of sounds made by birds, Darwin felt, is the nearest we can come to understanding the development of language, for a young bird's effort to sing and its finally learning the song are processes analogous to an infant's babble that soon develops, because of parental instruction, into articulate language. Darwin extended the association further to speculate that musical cadences were used by some early progenitor of man to initiate sexual selection and courtship. He further speculated that the imitation of musical cries led to language expressive of intense and complex emotions. Through continued use, language assumed greater sophistication and the brain, to catch up, became more developed.[125]

Darwin proceeded to show how language, like species, goes through the process of natural selection. Language has a birthplace, it can be classified according to descent, it struggles to survive through a certain inherent ability to adapt, and once extinct it cannot reappear. "The formation of different languages and of distinct species, and the proofs that both have been developed through a gradual process," he posited, "are curiously parallel," and the "survival or preservation of certain favored words in the struggle for existence is natural selection." Darwin concluded that no proof exists to show that language owes anything to a special creative act, nor can one convincingly use the idea of language to challenge the theory that man developed from some lower form.[126] Responding to these claims before the Royal Institution on 29 March 1873, Müller reiterated his earlier opinion that language sets man apart from animals, and so dismisses all arguments in favor of evolutionary continuity. "By no effort of the understanding, by no stretch of the imagination," he insisted, "can I explain to myself how language could have grown out of anything which animals possess, even if we granted them millions of years for that purpose."[127]

As an amateur philologist concerned with roots and, Roman Jakobson believes, "an outstanding searcher in the science of poetic language,"[128] Hopkins would undoubtedly have been drawn to Müller's Aryan theory that all words must "in the last instance, be traced back, by means of definite phonetic laws, to those definite primary forms which we are accustomed to call roots."[129] The Müller connection can be detected in a number of places in Hopkins's poetry. Maintaining that words assume different forms in different languages, Müller used the example of the Latin "ipse."[130] Similarly, and in a rare instance of employing foreign words in his poetry, Hopkins uses "Ipse" ("the only one, Christ, King, Head") in the pivotal stanza (28) of *The Wreck* where the tall nun comes face to face, as it were, with the incarnate Word. Further evidence of Müller can be located in *The Wreck*. Distinguishing between "radical" and "poetical" metaphors in his second series of lectures, Müller cites this example of "poetical" metaphor (by which he means "when a noun or verb, ready made and assigned to one definite object or action, is transferred poetically to another object or action"): "the clouds are called mountains, the rain–clouds are spoken of as cows with heavy udders."[131] Hopkins apparently picked up on this unusual poetic metaphor and used it in a sermon at Farm Street Church, no doubt to the hilarity and embarrassment of the parishioners. In that sermon, according to John Pick, Hopkins compared the transmission of grace from the visible Church to "a cow with full udders, wandering through the pastures of the world, ready to nourish any one who came to milk it."[132] The analogy of grace to milk was familiar to the Roman Church of the third century, where, as part of Holy Communion, neophytes were made to drink milk and honey, symbols of new birth and signs of the Promised Land and to keep intact the idea of the communion as a meal. This ritual continued through the Middle Ages even up to the fourteenth century.[133] Hopkins again used the metaphor to address the need to venerate Christ, calling him "the body suckled at the Blessed Virgin's breasts."[134] A corresponding image also appears in *The Wreck*:

> For how to the heart's cheering
> The down–dugged ground–hugged grey
> Hovers off, the jay–blue heavens appearing
> Of pied and peeled May![135]

Hopkins's remark six years later on an image in Dixon's "Ode on the Death of Dickens" is likewise telling. Dixon wrote:

> The white precipitate clouds, that seem made
> More slowly to wander the sky, like a herd
> Of deep–uddered cows hotly bayed
> By a fierce dog beyond their own pace.

Commenting on these lines from the poem, Hopkins, in language reminiscent of Müller's analogy, found the "Aryan image of the cloud cows and the dog particularly striking," but punned that the anapests are "heavily loaded."[136]

Additionally, Müller's predicateness of being appears often in Hopkins's poetry. Müller asserts that "every word is originally a predicate," and that any word traced historically back to its primitive form "contains a predicative root and that in this predicative root rests the connotative power of the word."[137] Hopkins's kingfisher poem best corroborates this idea. The poem places great stress on the verbalness of being, that doing constitutes being: "kingfishers catch fire, dragonflies draw flame"; "each tucked string tells, each hung bell's / Bow swung finds tongue to fling out broad its name"; "'What I do is me: for that I came'"; "the just man justices"; and "Acts in God's eye what in God's eye he is." In every case each thing speaks and spells itself, and those verbal signifiers comprise a language of action. The idea of each thing ringing also echoes Müller. "There is a law," he claimed, that "runs through nearly the whole of nature": everything "struck rings. Each substance has its peculiar ring .... Gold rings differently from tin, wood rings differently from stone; and different sounds are produced according to the nature of each percussion." Man, the "most highly organized of nature's works," exhibits a similar chiming, possessing

> the faculty of giving more articulate expression to the rational conceptions of his mind. That faculty was not of his own making. It was an instinct, an instinct of the mind as irresistible as any other instinct. So far as language is the production of that instinct, it belongs to the realm of nature.[138]

In another series of Royal Institution lectures given in 1873, Müller theorized his predicateness of roots: "Why is a 'stable' called a 'stable'? Because it stands."[139] Hopkins could have been aware of this etymological affinity when he employed the "stallion stalwart" image to forge a connection between nature and Christ in "Hurrahing in Harvest." The *Oxford English Dictionary* traces "Stallion" from the Latin "stallum," meaning a stable, and "stalwart" from the Old English "staelwierthe," meaning a thing strongly or stoutly built, sturdy or robust. In the poem the two words describe the physical robustness of the hills as they stand silhouetted against the descending blue.

Another fertile connection between Hopkins and Müller that cannot be fully explored here is their shared concern with the dialectical nature of language. Müller believed that the nature and origin of roots are connected to "the mysteries of human speech."[140] In his essay in *Nature*, he further noted that the "natural state of language," like the principle that governs the origin of species, "consists in unlimited dialectical variety, out of which . . . more and more definite forms of languages are selected." New languages, conceptual from the outset, "do not spring from classical parents, but draw their life and vigour from the spoken rustic and vulgar dialects." He discovers in Darwin's writings an "analogous process"—though not to be exaggerated—that "pervades the growth of a new species of language and of new species of animals and vegetable life."[141] Hopkins's speech–based poetics, based on the notion that poetry must employ current but elevated language, is an endorsement of Müller's idea. Hopkins theorized that poetry is "speech wholly or partially repeating the same figure of sound" and is, in fact, "speech employed to carry the inscape of spoken sound."[142] His own poetic rhythm that frequently mimes the "natural rhythm of speech" is not only central to his theory of sprung rhythm but also stirred his interest in dialects, however infrequently poeticized. Müller's philological speculations—much of them scientifically discredited at the end of his career through such efforts as Romanes's *Mental Evolution in Man* (1888)— appealed, then, to Hopkins, who sought seemingly plausible theoretical challenges to philological Darwinism.[143]

Hopkins's response to Darwinism can also be traced through his metaphoric and idiosyncratic use of the musical terms "chromatic" and "diatonic," terms he apparently picked up from Gurney. The association between science and music, as we witnessed earlier in Spencer, Darwin, Gurney, Lee, and Hopkins, and as we will see in Pater, was not at all uncommon to writers of the nineteenth century, especially those writers who engaged atomism. For example, musical metaphors pervade Tyndall's writings, and are so used to describe the living and vital processes in nature. These writers of science, as Cosslett observes, "continually use music as a metaphor for the interplay of physical forces, the ordered movement that pervades the universe."[144] Similarly in Hopkins's nature poems is the rhythmic play of nature; rhythm is atomistic, but in Hopkins the music of the particular chimes both the individual and Christ. The song of the spring thrush becomes the very life of the forest, and in turn a metaphor for seasonal rebirth in the octave and for spiritual rebirth in the sestet;[145] the skylark with its "rash–fresh re–winded new–skeined score . . . pour / And pelt music," while man rings out his "sordid turbid time," both antiphonal of man's fall from grace. Kingfishers, dragonflies, and even stones ring out in language of speech and silence (when they cannot speak they spell),[146] justicing their uniqueness and proclaiming their logocentricity: "All things therefore are charged with love, are charged with God and if we know how to touch them give off sparks and take fire, yield drops and flow, ring and tell of him."[147] When, language itself fails, or when it resorts to a "babble," either nature or music takes over: "The sun on falling waters writes the text" or a "virginal tongue told."

Chromaticism, to Hopkins, denotes flux, instability, and change, hence evolution; diatonicism fixity. Chromaticism is "gradual" and "transitional," as "in the passing from one colour into another," and so reveals indistinctness. Diatonicism, by contrast, is "clearly marked," "intervallary," and "abrupt."[148] Preferring diatonicism to chromaticism, fixity to flux, Hopkins linked chromaticism to evolution, for both privilege the idea of continuity. In his 1867 undergraduate essay, "The Probable Future of Metaphysics," Hopkins recognized already the presence of the evolutionary idea at work in the Victorian period. He noted that Positivism predicted, much to the trepidation of people, that the end of all metaphysics is near and will be replaced by materialism. But such fear is unwarranted, for materialism must first resolve force and matter before it attempts to explain mind and thought. Hopkins's real fear is that metaphysics will be pushed to the outer limits of science, and that the new psychology will replace it. But such a prospect, he countered will not be the case. Science will remain atomistic, and without metaphysics will be loose and incomprehensible, "scopeless." Only metaphysics gives "meaning to laws and sequences and causes developments." Hopkins predicted "Historical Development," characterized by continuity, individuality, and detachment, as the "philosophy of the immediate future." But the current scientific trend is one of "continuity or flux" whereby "nature is a string all the differences in which are really chromatic." Although he maintained that species are accidentally "fixed only at definite distances in the string," which might seem to suggest that he intended to embrace the contradictory position of evolution with interruption, Hopkins reasoned that the philosophical status quo is "continuity without fixed points, not to say 'saltus' or breaks, of development in one chain or necessity, of species having no absolute types." Hopkins does not predict an altogether eradication of metaphysics; the new metaphysics, he believed, will more than likely encounter "atomism of personality," but it will bear "some shape of the Platonic Ideas."[149]

But in this prevailing diatonic state, drabness and uniformity reign, and all beings, forfeiting their dappleness, their God–emanated piedness, become "seared," "bleared," and "smeared" ("God's Grandeur"), and "self in self" becomes "steeped and pashed" ("Spelt from Sibyl's Leaves). Conceivably, the most "disquieting aspects of Darwinian theory," says Gillian Beer, is that it "muddied descent, and brought into question the privileged 'purity' of the 'great family."[150] The philosophy of flux Hopkins describes is essentially Darwinian. To Darwin, species are constantly changing, imperfect, and tend to evolve into new variations as mutations interact with an ever unstable environment. Thus, Hopkins associates chromaticism with the absence of absolute and fixed types

within species in perpetual flux. Because to him, as Hillis Miller rightly
concludes, chromaticism is consistent with the Darwinian idea that variety in
nature "has developed spontaneously from the shapeless slime."[151]

What appeals to Hopkins is not Darwin's "philosophy of flux," but the
Platonic idea of a First Cause, from whom fixed species emanate, an idea that
in–forms "Pied Beauty" and other poems. Hopkins forecast the imminent return
of this philosophy that espouses a force patterning itself on things external to
itself, including species of language as well as species in nature. This patterning
affects even the Godhead through what Hopkins called "the Great Sacrifice,"
whereby "God's utterance of himself in himself is God the Word, outside
himself is this world." Through this incarnation, then, God's particularized self
is the person of "Christ [playing] in ten thousand places": "in the elements giving
them being; in the plants giving them growth; in the animals giving them
sensations; in men giving them understanding; and so in me giving me being."[152]
This ontological stance led Hopkins to envision the universe, according to Hillis
Miller, as "a great multitude of strongly patterned things." But while there are
"throngs of each kind, and all of each kind are alike and rhyme," Miller correctly
indicates, "each throng is apparently unrelated to any of the others."[153] Things
are most like Christ only when they are their fullest selves and chime univocally.

Hopkins's notion of "being" remains clearly at odds with Darwin's. He
indicated that "human nature, being more highly pitched, selved, and distinctive
than anything in the world, can have been developed, evolved, condensed, from
the vastness of the world . . . but only by one of finer or higher pitch and
determination than itself." He felt that his own inscape, what he otherwise called
his "tankard," is unique and "more distinctive than the smell of walnutleaf. . . .
Nothing else in nature," he contended, "comes near this unspeakable stress of
pitch, distinctiveness, and selving, this selfbeing of my own. Nothing explains
it or resembles it." In "searching nature," he confessed, "I taste 'self' but . . . that
of my own being," not some other self, because the "development, refinement,
condensation of nothing shews any sign of being able to match this to me or give
me another taste of it, a taste even resembling it." Thus, "when I compare my
self, my being–self, with anything else whatever, all things alike . . . rebuff me
with blank unlikeness."[154] In "As kingfishers catch fire," then, every mortal
being flames out its "haecceity," its individuation, and so "speaks and spells"
itself, forming, according to Said, "a sort of lexical unit."[155] So insistent is
Hopkins on separateness that he regarded even his verses selved entities. They
were the legitimate offspring of his mind, the "mother of immortal song," sired
by the poet and were apparently the "innocents" later slaughtered. But they can
also be prodigals that "stand or fall by their simple selves,"[156] a remark

resembling the self–generating, self–evolving fiction of Dickens's David: "They express themselves, and I leave them to themselves."[157] Jane Austen, too, was to regard her novels her children, though in her case the metaphor speaks more to the emphasis on familial relations in her novels. Hopkins, like Austen, Dickens, and even Emily Brontë, was concerned with text and selving, and as these pertain to literary orphanhood.

Hopkins's was a universe governed by infinite purpose, a belief advanced through his notion of inscape and tied with his ecological concerns. While Darwin too was concerned with ecology, he was apparently more interested in the interdependence nature affords, in the mutual and reciprocal relations between man and nature. Hopkins was not particularly anxious about the destruction nature exerted on itself as he was with the effects of industrialism on the inscape of nature, and especially with the aesthetic, moral, and religious implications of such destruction. Inscape to him was the distinctive individual-izing feature of a thing, the unique design of which bears testimony to its designer, God. Thus when nature is maliciously destroyed, a common event in Hopkins's day, he envisioned the loss as the riddance of witnesses of and for God. When, for instance, the landscape of "God's Grandeur" is being torn apart by man, God's presence in "the deep down things," though still perceptible, becomes less so, because the inscape of a thing bears the mark of God. That same complaint is made in "Duns Scotus's Oxford" and its companion "Binsey Poplars," though in both of these poems beauty and memory are the things forfeited. But "Binsey Poplars" does advance an ecological concern in the rejoinder that man seems ignorant of the extent of his destructive actions on nature. Expressed here is the concern that with the senseless felling of trees the earth is left naked to the piercing rays of the sun, the ramifications of which we remain ignorant.

Because of all of this purpose to nature, Hopkins is not only pained when he witnesses "the inscapes of the world destroyed," but further rules out chance as "a cause or principle or explanation of being." Catching sight of "the random clods and broken heaps of snow made [as if] by the cast of a broom," he notioned that "All the world is full of inscape, and chance left free to act falls into an order as well as purpose."[158] Inscape, then, answers chance or atomism. Chance, Hopkins posited, is "the stress, of the intrinsic possibility which things have. . . . And as mere possibility, passive power . . . cannot of itself come to stress, cannot instress itself." "No man," he therefore reasoned, "can believe that his being is due to chance," because nothing finite can exist of itself: "For being finite it is limited and determined in time and space." The "being" a thing possesses, accordingly,

has a great perfection and higher selved, than anything else I
see. . . . [T]o be determined and distinctive is a perfection,
either self–bestowed or bestowed from without. In anything
finite it cannot be self–bestowed; nothing finite can determine its own being. . . . Nothing finite then can either begin
to exist or eternally have existed of itself, because nothing can
in the order of time or even of nature act before it exists or
exercise function and determination before it has a nature to
"function" and determine, to selve and instress, with.[159]

Thus this world, Hopkins concluded, "must have been determined by the
universal being out of all possible worlds, for . . . it could not determine its own
being or determine itself into being. . . . No thing then, including myself, is in
any sense selfexistent except this great being."[160] But while design or inscape
denotes the outward feature of a thing, reinforcing that thing is some law or order
inherent in nature and the self that Hopkins was fond of calling instress.

Here Hopkins assumes the old argument from design, which presupposed
that the complex network within the creation was effected by Divine Fiat and
that design was the means to specie adaptation. Paley's *Natural Theology; or,*
Evidences of the Existence and Attributes of the Deity, Collected from Appear-
ances of Nature, 1802, had presented happy animals in a universe designed with
purpose by an equally beneficent Designer. And the assumption fitted nicely the
Victorian impulse to duty, regulated behavior, and a system of rewards and
punishments tantamount to those behaviors. Darwin himself acknowledged this
supplanting. He writes in his *Autobiography*: "The old argument of design in
nature, as given by Paley . . . which formerly seemed to me so conclusive, fails,
now that the law of natural selection has been discovered. We can no longer
argue that, for instance, the beautiful hinge of a bivalve shell must have been
made by an intelligent being, like the hinge of a door by man. There seems to
be no more design in the variability of organic beings and in the action of natural
selection, than in the course which the wind blows."[161] Darwinism, in the form
of natural selection, argued that adaptation was a result not of design but of
natural causes, and so ruptured the design argument, dealt it a "fatal blow," a
"wedge," to use one of Darwin's favorite metaphors, and replaced it with a
"completely mechanistic alternative to design as an explanation of the phenomenon."[162] At stake, as Don Cupitt points out, was the design argument, which for
two centuries "had been central to English religious thought, and Darwinism
was a calculated and powerful assault upon it."[163]

But Darwin's position on whether or not purpose rules the creation remains equivocal or, in his words, a "hopeless muddle," a "complete jumble." From the years 1838 to 1859 when he was at work on the *Origin*, he had arrived at the conclusion that it was almost inconceivable to imagine "this immense and wonderful universe, including man with his capacity of looking far backward and far into futurity, as the result of blind chance or necessity," a position somewhat consistent with the arguments of the *Origin*. In a 22 May 1860 letter to his Harvard friend and supporter Asa Gray, Darwin admitted not being as totally convinced about design as was Gray: "I cannot see as plainly as others do . . . evidence of design and beneficence on all sides of us." His reason: "There seems to me too much misery in the world. . . . On the other hand, I cannot anyhow be contented to view this wonderful universe, and especially the nature of man, and to conclude that everything is the result of brute force. I am inclined to look at everything as resulting from designed laws, with the details, whether good or bad, left to the working out of what we may call chance," by which Darwin almost always meant unknown causes as opposed to blind forces. "Not that this notion *at all* satisfies me. I feel most deeply that the whole subject is too profound for the human intellect." Darwin again expressed this sentiment to Gray six months later, on 26 November 1860: "I cannot think that the world, as we see it, is the result of chance; and yet I cannot look at each separate thing as the result of Design." A year later he told John Herschel: "One cannot look at this Universe and man without believing that all living production has been intelligently designed; yet when I look to each individual organism, I can see no evidence of this. . . . I cannot see design in the variations of structure in animals in a state of nature,— those variations which were useful to the animal being preserved & those useless or injurious being destroyed."[164] Rejecting Herschel's position on design, Darwin said to Lyell, also with Asa Gray in mind, that while he, Darwin, did not allow "enough for the stream of variation having been guided by a higher power," the idea that "each variation has been providentially arranged" makes his theory of natural selection "entirely superfluous," and so "takes the whole case of the appearance of new species out of the range of science,"[165] allowing it, then, to operate within the purview of theology.

During July and August 1861, Darwin continued to vacillate on the subject of design. He told Julia Wedgwood in an 11 July letter: "The mind refuses to look at this universe, being what it is, without having been designed; yet, where one would expect design, viz. in the structure of a sentient being, the more I think on the subject, the less I can see proof of design."[166] Darwin finally admitted his equivocation, first in a 12 July 1870 letter to J.D. Hooker: "My theology is a simple muddle; I cannot look at the universe as the result of blind chance, yet

I can see no evidence of beneficent design, or indeed of design of any kind, in the details";[167] three years later, on 2 April 1873, he told a Dutch student: "But I may say that the impossibility of conceiving that this grand and wondrous universe, with our conscious selves, arose through chance, seems to me the chief argument for the existence of God; but whether this is an argument of real value, I have never been able to decide." Darwin's reticence was aggravated by the reality of immense suffering in the world, which he believed was the most practical challenge to the design argument.[168] His equivocation on chance and design gave rise to his "Essay on Theology and Natural Selection," meant to formulate a theory that would accommodate natural and divine laws, natural selection and natural theology. This essay that seems not so much a revision of Darwin's views as a clarification of them admits a higher law than the law of adaptations at work in the universe.[169]

Hopkins's embracing of the design argument demonstrates that Darwinism served often to reinforce his personal faith. He was, as one critic observes, "singularly free from the anxious trepidations which assailed so many orthodox Victorian minds,"[170] once admitting being "amused to find how very far the advance of thought or science is fr. being on every side an encroachment on Christianity."[171] Here he is much like his mentor Newman, who also felt that the *Origin* does not advocate an "antichristian theory," that it is not "against Theism," and that "Darwin does not 'profess' to oppose Religion." Newman added: "I don't know why Adam needs be immediately out of dust . . . i. e. out of what really was dust and mud in its nature, before He made it what it was, living." Newman's reaction to the *Origin* was, says Charles Frederick Harrold, "strikingly unlike most mid–Victorian clergymen, who . . . took an indignant, frightened, and belligerent attitude toward the new biological theories." And while he would have "sternly rejected any 'Darwinian' interpretation of dogmatic developments in Revealed Religion, his faith in supernature was so firm that he had no fear of genuine scientific inquiry into nature."[172]

Unlike Hopkins, Newman had more serious reservations about the persuasiveness of the design argument. In that classic passage from the *Apologia*, he looks to the world and finds in it no reflection of its creation. He points out, as did Wordsworth before him and as Hopkins would later do, that the "human race is implicated in some terrible aboriginal calamity" (Wordsworth's "Pagan suckled in a creed outworn") and that the world is "out of joint with the purposes of its Creator" (Hopkins's "bent world"). Newman's empty mirror (looking into "this living busy world" and seeing "no reflexion of its Creator") and Hopkins's "Vacant creation's lamps appal" reflect the failure of natural theology, to be replaced by an existential inner voice, what Newman's Callista calls "this inward guide of mine," whispering to the heart and conscience. In her defense, Callista provides from her own experience proof of what Coleridge calls that "Faith that only *feels*":

> "I feel that God within my heart. I feel myself in His presence. . . . You may tell me that this dictate is a mere law of my nature, as to joy or to grieve. I cannot understand this. No, it is the echo of a person speaking to me. Nothing shall persuade me that it does not ultimately proceed from a person external to me. It carries with it its proof of its divine origin. My nature feels towards it as towards a person. When I obey it, I feel a satisfaction; when I disobey, a soreness—just like that which I feel in pleasing or offending some reverend friend. . . . I believe in what is more real to me than sun, moon, stars, and the fair earth, and the voice of friends. You will say, Who is He? Has He ever told you anything about Himself? Alas! no!—the more's the pity! But I will not give up what I have, because I have not more. An echo implies a voice; a voice a speaker. That speaker I love and I fear."[173]

Natural theology, Newman felt, provides neither heat nor light, comfort nor enlightenment; it does not "take away the winter of my desolation, or make the buds unfold and the leaves grow within me."[174] While the "new and further manifestations of the Almighty" remain "in perfect harmony with the teaching of the natural world," he pointed out in *The Idea of a University*, these cannot be gleaned from nature. But in a scientific age as ours is, "there will naturally be a parade of what is called Natural Theology,"[175] since natural theology was the means by which science was attempting to shore up the view of a God whose designs were thought benevolent. Newman's suspicion, even rejection, of natural theology was again voiced in his *Philosophical Notebook*:

> I cannot comprehend how anyone can deduce the Being of God from the visible world, taken by itself, for this reason, that (putting aside the difficulty of assuming design because there is order) order has only reference to form, not to matter, and if order proves Mind, phenomena quite as forcibly prove Matter. In other words, the visible world leads to a Dualism — [– but] for when do we learn from the visible world that Mind can create Matter?[176]

However, judged singularly, as was rarely done, Darwinism never appeared enervating to Newman or for that matter to Hopkins. Still Hopkins's nature poems, where, according to Cosslett, science is "most obviously relevant, most akin,"[177] demonstrate subtle revisions of Darwinism. The metaphysical assumption underlying them—"that language and nature are mirrors reflecting each other in a simple and undistorted manner"—must have influenced a poet like Hopkins who, as Michael Sprinker suggests,"sought, especially in the nature sonnets of the 1870's, to affirm the immanence of God in creation by miming God's presence in language."[178] Hopkins's incessant appeal in these poems serves to counter Darwinism and to revive the faith that it was assailing. Yet because Hopkins resisted publication of his poems, that effort was compromised and his, not even Bridges's, was the only faith revived. Still the poems operate as sermons. The world of "God's Grandeur" is accountable for stressing ("charged") the resplendent beauty of God; and the abiding energy of the Holy Ghost redeems the "bent world" from a joint industrial and Darwinian randomness, purposelessness, and chaos. The windhover willingly empties itself of its natural and Godlike mastery to be broken for a mission "lovelier," albeit "more dangerous." And each thing in creation ultimately communicates its best self when it "speaks and spells" Christ. But the religious underthought present in these poems is suspended in "Spelt from Sibyl's Leaves." In this twilight poem, evening, with the sun "wound to the west" and the moon "hung to the height," strains to assemble in one significant moment an entire lifetime as though it were the world's last breath. Apparent celestial harmony—the stars as "Fire–featuring heaven"—contrasts terrestrial chaos; earth's inscape is disfigured and its dappleness diminished—"her being's unbounded" and "self in self steeped and pashed." This infernal condition (concealed in a Dantesque pun in the prefix of "Disremembering" and "dismembering") marked by the absence of natural piedness forges an antithesis between "spools" and "flocks." Within this polarization, things bond with their negations ("black, white; right, wrong"), but only to immolate each another, including the intellectual warfare of "thoughts" in civil conflict with "thoughts in groans grind."

The religious counterargument familiar in Hopkins's quasi-nature, quasi-religious poems reappears in "That Nature Is a Heraclitean Fire and of the Comfort of the Resurrection," a poem that manifests the poet's lifelong interest in science. Hopkins's title could have come from Pater, who quotes Heraclitus: "TO REGARD ALL THINGS and principles of things as inconstant modes or fashions has more and more become the tendency of modern thought."[179] Later in *Plato and Platonism* (1893), Pater made the Heraclitean connection to Darwinism even clearer, pointing to the presence of Heraclitean doctrine in

Darwinian thought. In "Darwin and Darwinism," wrote Pater, "'type' itself properly *is* not but is only always *becoming*. The bold paradox of Heraclitus is, in effect, repeated on all sides . . . in illustration of the very law of change which it asserts, may itself presently be superseded as a commonplace." As in *The Renaissance*, here again Pater pointed to the constant change occurring in nature and applied it to Darwinism: "that 'species,' immutable though they seem now, as of old in the Garden of Eden, are fashioned by slow development . . . the idea of development . . . is at last invading one by one." The cultural implications of both theories are also broached: "In Plato's day, the Heraclitean flux, so deep down in nature itself—the flood, the fire—seemed to have laid hold on man, on the social and moral world, dissolving or disintegrating opinion, first principles, faith."[180]

Pater's atomistic philosophy, closely related to Darwin's theory of natural selection, distinct from it only because Pater suggests recombination rather than annihilation, informs Hopkins's poetic revision of Heraclitus and Pater in "Heraclitean Fire." Hopkins's fear of atomism, implicit in the frequent images of connectedness in his poetry ("finger," "vein," "bound," "strand," "rope," "laced"), was expressed as early as 1867 in an undergraduate essay, "The Probable Future of Metaphysics." Hopkins indicated that a "form of atomism like a stiffness or sprain seems to hang upon and hamper our speculation: it is an overpowering, a disproportioned sense of personality."[181] In a second undergraduate essay, "The Connection of Mythology and Philosophy," Hopkins wrote, this time with specific reference to Heraclitus: "Heraclitus, who felt beyond any of his predecessors the chaos, uncertainty, and illusion of all things, spoke nevertheless of a rhythm, something imposed by mind as an air on the notes of a flute."[182] The ideas contained in these two undergraduate essays directly shaped "Heraclitean Fire," which addresses the fear of atomism in the context of Dublin's inhospitability to Hopkins where such treasured concepts as "dapple," "being," and "self" become devalued.

The poem's title indicates bipolar concepts: nature's conflagration, a hypothesis Hopkins apparently accepts (the fire refining base properties into a diaphanous "immortal diamond"), and the religious counterargument in Christ's resurrection. In fact, both pagan and Christian elements are conflated in the poem. The idea of flux was not particularly troubling to Hopkins, if regulated by a Platonic sequence of movement from and a return to God, as in the poem "Thee, God, I come from, to thee go": "like fountain flow/ From thy hand out." In the first part of "Heraclitean Fire," a powerful, hot wind "beats earth bare" into "dough, crust" and then "dust," consuming all former signatures ("manmarks") of man in "nature's bonfire."[183] Part 1 ends with the lament: "O pity and indignation." In part 2, the resurrection answers both nature's and man's consummation; for while "Flesh fade, and mortal trash / Fall to the residuary worm," and "world's wildfire, leaves but ash," instantaneously, "I am all at once what Christ is, since he was what I am"; now mortality succumbs to immortality, imperfection to perfection, and the slime, "This Jack, joke" and "potsherd," is transformed into "immortal diamond."[184] In this poem, says Gillian Beer, Hopkins "images the profusion and decay, the endless energy of the natural world, and stays it with the image of Resurrection, man's leap...." To Darwin, however, the belief that "nature does not make leaps opened into some of his most radical insights, leading him away from the idea of the chain of being or the ladder, with its hierarchical ordering of rungs."[185] The Incarnation, then, and ultimately Christ's Resurrection, to Hopkins, provide hope for this life of "perpetual motion." But Darwin pushed the perfection of man to some uncertain, teleological point, the "distant future," at which time, and after such "long–continued slow progress," the potential exists for "complete annihilation." He maintained that to "those who fully admit the immortality of the human soul," suggesting that he apparently did not, "the destruction of our world will not appear so dreadful."[186] In a related way, Darwin's insistence that novels end happily might account for a desire to have art achieve what life cannot promise; and that the tragedy he saw inherent in natural selection and in life led him to look to art for its comedy.

Hopkins's 1867 auguring of modern atomism anticipated by six years Max Müller's own assessment of atomism in Darwinian thought, but Müller's evaluation predates "Heraclitean Fire" by some fifteen years. Heraclitus wrote, "'All is moving and nothing is fixed,' or as we should say, 'All is growing, all is developing, all is evolving.'" Heraclitean thought, Müller claims, is "now again in the ascendant. All is changing, all is developing, all is evolving."[187] Hopkins, however, rejected all forms of atomism, whether Paterean or Darwinian; for while Epicureanism maintains that individual perfection is unattainable (nothing is, for everything in the universe is in a state of becoming) and Darwinism that it is progressionistic (change in natural selection is accidental, random, directionless, therefore, no organism is as perfectly adapted as it might be),[188] Hopkins held that the Incarnation effects immediately the potential for the perfection of self. Thus, while "The Valley of the Elwy" on the one hand concedes the completion of nature and on the other hand confesses the imperfection of the individual who "does not correspond" to nature, it also avows a perfection effected only by and in Christ ("Complete thy creature dear O where it fails"), an ontological position at one with Hopkins's conviction that "nothing finite can determine its own being."[189]

Like Darwin, Pater discovered ecstasy from emersion in the flux—burning "always with this hard, gem–like flame"—or from "expanding that interval, in getting as many pulsations as possible [mostly through art and music] into the given time."[190] Connecting Pater's atomism with Darwin's, Peckham notes that the basic assumption of Pater's injunction to "burn with a hard, gem–like flame" is similar to Darwin's "whole mechanism of natural selection and the origin of species, which depended upon the imperfect, or less than perfect, adaptation of organism to environment."[191] Though "Heraclitean Fire" falls short of discrediting Pater's Epicureanism, thus retaining its distillation of "a great deal of early philosophical thought,"[192] the poem's answer for a meaningful life is altogether Christian: "the comfort of the Resurrection." Indeed, Lucretian atomism does find consolation in death, but it is one marked by the death of consciousness:

> If the future holds travail and anguish in store, the self must
> be in existence, when that time comes, in order to experience
> it. But from this fate we are redeemed by death, which denies
> existence to the self that might have suffered these tribula-
> tions. Rest assured, therefore, that we have nothing to fear in
> death. One who no longer is cannot suffer, or differ in any way
> from one who has never been born, when this mortal life has
> been usurped by death the immortal.[193]

Hopkins's offering the resurrection as answer to atomism finds a suitable model in Acts 17 in the Apostle Paul's discourse with the Epicureans; he too partially embraces atomism, but also charges it with potential ennui and incompleteness.

"The Sea and the Skylark" (1877), like "Heraclitean Fire," also laments changes in nature. The octave treats the longevity of two ancient sounds: the "flood" or "fall" of the "Frequenting" tide (as it contrasts the unstable moon that "wears and wend") and the renewed "rash–fresh . . . score" of the lark discharging its music until none remains "to spill nor spend."[194] These treasured relics of nature embarrass the sordid, industrialized Rhyl, a place devoid of piedness. Formerly nature's regal head, "eye," "tongue," "heart" ("Ribblesdale"), and "life's pride and cared–for crown," man has now forfeited "that cheer and charm of earth's past prime." Consequently, his very self ("make") and fruits of his labor ("makings") experience disintegration. Rather than having evolved upwards, man is now, in the words of Norman MacKenzie, "the dregs of a once noble race."[195] But while this entropy is teleological—toward "man's last dust"—it is also cyclical— "towards man's first slime." Hopkins might well be citing the Douay version of Genesis 2:7 which uses "slime" for "dust,"[196] but one can hardly resist the temptation to render "slime" not only as the dust in the hand of the Creator but as Darwin's inorganic matter, his primordial germ or, as Hopkins writes on Parmenides, "Men, he thought, had sprung from slime."[197] Newman, we might recall, rendered a similar reading. But in contrast to Darwin, the degenerationist Hopkins maintained that earth's "prime" was "past," that "earth's sweet being" was "in the beginning / In Eden garden" ("Spring"), and that the tendency is not progressive but regressive, not toward perfection but toward deterioration: "Our make and making break, are breaking, down." Or as he again comments in a similar vein in "The Leaden Echo and the Golden Echo": "Age and age's evils, hoar hair, / Ruck and wrinkle, drooping, dying, death's worst, windingsheets, / tombs and worms and tumbling to decay."

These poems all show that Hopkins at times queried impulses from vernal woods, witnessing, for example, "the glories of the earth / But not the hand that wrought them all," or admitting that earth has been denuded of its former "cheer and charm." However, other poems furnish sufficient examples of God's manifestation of himself in nature. The first of these, "The Starlight Night," attests to Hopkins's lifelong interest in the constellations. On the evening in which this poem was written, a paper entitled "The Nebular Theory of Creation" was delivered to the Essay Society at St. Beuno's. Its thesis was, MacKenzie speculates, the gradual evolution of the stars through "gravitational and other forces acting upon luminous gases diffused in space."[198] A paper on "Evolution" was also presented to that same Society two months later, on 21 April 1877.[199] "The Starlight Night," Hopkins's "nocturnal reconnoitre" (Hardy's words), beckons the reader's gaze heavenward to the stars, personified mythologically as "fire–folk sitting in the air." Such pricelessness extends also to the earth, if one reads the remainder of the octave as a movement earthward and not as a continuation of that heavenward gaze. The continuation theory is more faithful to the poem's title. Quite relevant is the fact that Hopkins chose, as he seems always to do, earthy metaphors as natural explanations for heavenly phenomena. In an 1864 diary entry, for instance, he noted "The fields of heaven covered with eye-brights. —White-diapered with stars."[200] Yet, be the vision heavenward or earthward, "Down in dim woods the diamond delves," on the "grey lawns cold" lies "gold," "quick gold," stars ignite and seem to traverse the sky as startled "doves" take flight from a "farmyard." The currency required to purchase this rich "May–mess" is spiritual ("Prayer, patience, alms, vows"), not monetary, illustrating Hopkins's revulsion for the Victorian economic system. The tercet closes with metaphors again drawn appropriately from the natural world: the stars become the wooden planks of the barn through which slits of light ("piece–bright paling") disclose and enclose the wedding feast of Mary, Christ ("spouse"), and his Saints.

"Pied Beauty," Hopkins's psalmic, curtal sonnet, praises God for his variegated creation, an inclusiveness seen also in the numerous variations of piedness: "dappled," "brinded," "stipple," "plotted and pieced," "counter," and "freckled." The poem catalogues the variegated species in creation that, like the etymological nuances of "pied," derive from a single and original genus. The poet is stirred by the multitude of nature's piedness ("variegated coloring") and dappleness, excesses that act out individuationally, and flame out the Creator–poet who graciously disperses ("fathers forth"; here the creative act is again masculine) his unchangeable beauty. If Darwin's world is, according to Gillian Beer, "unruly superfluity" and "superfecundity without design,"[201] Hopkins's is predictable piedness and superfecundity with design. Piedness is proof that Hopkins's science of aspects and diversitarianism avoids pashing things; it shuns the too-near resemblances of species in Darwin. Things in nature are constantly rescued by Hopkins from becoming pashed, a device enacted when he names or particularizes individuals, flowers, plants, birds, insects, and animals. Nomenclature, as John Herschel pointed out, is critical to science. The strategy helps us from being lost in a "wilderness of particulars, and involved in inextricable confusion."[202] In an early letter to Baillie, dated 10 July 1863, Hopkins reminded him: "I think I have told you that I have particular periods of admiration for particular things in Nature."[203] Oxford's landscape, for example, is particularized as "*these* weeds and waters, *these* walls" (italics mine), a principle reminiscent of Wordsworth's "These plots of cottage–ground, these orchard–tufts," "These hedge–rows," and "these pastoral farms" ("Tintern Abbey"). "One of the most basic and revolutionary changes Darwin's concept of evolution brought about," Carol Christ rightly observes, "was the elimination of typological thinking."[204] But "Pied Beauty," in contrast to Darwin's uniformitarianism, retains and embraces types, which yet call up their distinctive and highly individualized patterns. And although things in nature retain their distinctiveness, their otherness, they yet share a recognizable similarity both in being pied and in having been fathered forth from a single genus. Speaking, for instance, of schools of thought and their influence, Hopkins felt that it will "always be possible to find differences, marked differences, between original minds; it will be necessarily so." He found in species a related analogous relationship: "So the species in nature are essentially distinct, nevertheless they are grouped into genera: they have one form in common, mounted on that they have a form that differences them."[205] Thus, whereas Hopkins's "sense of the unique inscape of every object seems to produce a world of particulars, like

Darwin's, without connection to types or species," writes Carol Christ, "this is not the case, however, because he does not see things as monochrome but as pied, so that each thing derives its peculiar existence, or inscape, from a unique interlocking or interweaving or coincidence of characteristics."[206] Consequently, things "swift" or "slow," "sweet" or "sour," "adazzle" or "dim" all buckle in Christ, in whom they are, to use Hillis Miller's term, "Logosimilar."[207] Indeed, Darwin had argued for a single genus, for a common origin, from which "individuals of the same species, wherever found, are descended."[208] But Hopkins, that common parent, that single progenitor, of all things in the creation within and across all variety of species is not inorganic matter but God, the fatherfortherer.

That Hopkins's interest in Darwinism never waned is evident in "In Honour of St. Alphonsus Rodriguez," the Dublin sonnet written a year before Hopkins's death. Other than the last line, the poem obscures the fact that it is in fact a tribute to the Jesuit Hall porter. For instance, the octave celebrates heroic exploits, both human and spiritual, which Hopkins apparently witnessed in Saint Alphonsus. More celebrated, however, is the successful waging of the war within, concealed to outsiders. Ultimately it is God with his in–sight who evaluates the success and presents the reward. But most intriguing in the poem is Hopkins's parenthetical characterization of God. In the sestet, he speculates that mountains originated from God, who "hews mountain, continent, / Earth, all, at last; who, with fine increment, / Trickling, veins, violets and tall trees makes more." Although he acceded to Bridges's skeptical suggestion not to retain the picture of God as "mountain–mason, continent– / Quarrier, earthwright," choosing instead to portray him as a stone sculptor who "carves" out or "hews" mountains and continents (both terms consistent, Hopkins believes, with what "to create" means), Hopkins held firmly to his view that continents are formed by "'trickling'; but what is on the whole truest and most strikes us about them and mountains is that they are made what now we see them by trickling *de*crements, by detrition, weathering, and the like," a point, incidentally, consistent with Lyell's notion on the mutability of mountains.[209] Hopkins's was not the Frenchman Alcide d' Orbigny's cataclysmic theory of mountain formation but instead, Lyell and Darwin's gradualistic one. In a footnote explanation, Hopkins cited Darwin's opinion regarding the end of all continents and dry land: they will all be "washed into the sea."[210] Darwin had felt that if landscapes undergo gradual change, why not species? And while Lyell made popular the idea of mountain elevation caused by earthquakes, Darwin, on the other hand, observing the rising Andes, felt that coral reefs are the last stages of drowning continents. Lyell soon renounced his volcanic crater theory and accepted

Darwin's explanation for mountain formation. Hopkins felt, then, that it was not a compromise to hold the apparent contradictory views of special creation and progressive evolution: while God originally created the earth, including the mountains, some continents continue to evolve by "trickling *de*crements, by detrition, weathering" and, Hopkins would include, seismic restructuring activities on the earth.

Evident in Hopkins's relationship to Darwinism is the reality that because his strict Jesuit vocation prevented him from complete immersion in formal scientific endeavors, he was hardly ignorant of prevailing scientific trends and their impact on religion, culture, and literary discourse. His letters confess a keen awareness of science and a knowledge of Darwinism; he was concerned with ways Darwinism fueled discussions in areas such as language and music; he was interested in the scientifically acclaimed journal *Nature*, for which he wrote four essays; his journals illustrate his philological and naturalistic speculations, all linked inextricably to Darwinism; and his poetry not only reveals an abiding love for nature but also reaffirms the creation as God's handiwork. Summarily then, Hopkins's relationship to Darwinism reveals that because he did not perceive the theory a grave assault on his belief, he was able to exploit it, employing and at times rejecting Darwinism in his poetics, poetry, and close scrutiny of the busy workings of nature. This "all–accepting fixed eye" led to Hopkins's poetic harmonizing and ordering of otherwise discordant views. And it is such deft artistic compromise that makes Hopkins so prophetic a Victorian figure and his poetry so rich a legacy of incandescent Victorian concerns that extends even to our modernity.

Chapter 4

The Handsome Heart:
Hopkins, Pater,
and Victorian Aesthetics

Darwin's most profound regret nearing the end of his life was the demise of his aesthetic passion—in his words, the "lamentable loss of the higher aesthetic tastes." Echoing the complaint of both Carlyle and Dickens against the personal and aesthetic consequences of Victorian industrialization, Darwin discovered that his mind had become "a kind of machine for grinding general laws out of large collections of facts." No longer did the Romantics, especially Wordsworth, Coleridge, and Shelley, give him "great pleasure." Shakespeare seemed "intolerably dull" and nauseating, art no longer evoked any of the old aesthetic tastes, music served only to plunge his mind deeper into his work instead of providing an outlet for pleasure, and natural scenery no longer held the "exquisite delight which it formerly did." If he had to live his life all over again, Darwin vowed, he "would have made a rule to read some poetry and listen to some music at least once every week; for perhaps the parts of my brain now atrophied could thus have been kept active through use. The loss of these tastes," Darwin concluded, "is a loss of happiness, and may possibly be injurious to the intellect." The injury might even be harmful to the "moral character, by enfeebling the emotional part of our nature."[1]

The aesthetic passion whose demise Darwin lamented was vital in his early life. As he recalled as though from the dead, he chronicles a life shaped by aesthetic passion. For instance, the word "pleasure" (not counting its synonyms) is used some fourteen times in Darwin's *Autobiography*. He associated pleasure with the customary sources of its positive sensations. He found pleasure in reading poetry, in music, in reminiscing about his Cambridge days, in the sale of his books, however momentary the sensation lasted, and in scenery, which he felt outlasted all other aesthetic experiences. Because of a profound Romantic influence on Darwin, morality assumes an aesthetic function. Darwin considered love of others "undoubtedly the highest pleasure on this earth."[2]

Pleasure also became inextricably tied to Darwin's vocation. His ornithological curiosity was fed from the pages of the celebrated *Natural History of Selborne* (1789), written by the eminent parish naturalist Gilbert White (1720–93), and one of the first books to record, in unusually literary and aesthetic ways, the behavior and migration of birds. Darwin also received immense pleasure from investigating and from collecting beetles, which provided the most memorable episode of his naturalistic passion. Wishing to snare more beetles than he could possibly hold, Darwin placed a prized one in his mouth, the result of which was a bitter secretion let off by the beetle. Darwin's entire *Autobiography* evidences an awareness of Wordsworth's "Preface to *Lyrical Ballads*," a work also inundated with the word "passion." Particularly significant is Wordsworth's association of the poet with the scientist: "The knowledge both of the Poet and the Man of Science is Pleasure."[3] When Darwin talked about sensations derived from the arts, nature, and from his scientific curiosity, he is, by definition, talking about a genuine philosophical aesthetic, for he locates the source of the sensations both in the sensuous and in the mental apprehension of and response to external objects.

I begin this chapter on Victorian aesthetics with Darwin because his life and occupation reflect the aesthetic concerns of nineteenth–century England. As the age became more positivistic, utilitarian, and mechanistic, a new aesthetic theory had to be forged to accommodate a changing epistemology, even ontology. Furthermore, Darwin's attempt to devise a Victorian aesthetic that engages the challenges of modernism is what both Pater and Hopkins sought to negotiate, however dissimilarly at times, through far more intricate and sophisticated processes.

Hopkins's first reference to Pater is a terse citation in his 2 May 1866 journal: "Coaching with W.H. Pater this term. Walked with him on Monday evening last, April 30. Fine evening bitterly cold. . . . Same evening Hexameron met here: Addis read on the Franciscans: laughter."[4] This was Hopkins's first reference to Pater, linking the commencement of his formal relationship with Pater to the Hexameron, the essay society founded to counteract Pater's Old Mortality. Quite typical at Oxford where students were provided special instruction from an outside tutor, Hopkins, during Trinity term 1866, walked from Balliol at the head of Broad Street down Turl to Brasenose to be coached by Pater. Pater had come up to Queen's College in 1858 from King's School (1853–58) near Canterbury. It was at the cathedral, forever in Pater's writings, that he met and became fond of A.P. Stanley, one of the canons, who had come down from Oxford in November 1851. At the end of 1856, Stanley was appointed Professor of Ecclesiastical History at Oxford but did not actually assume the position until 14 April 1858. When he did, he was united once more with Pater, who attended his Lectures on Ecclesiastical History and his social gathering on Sunday evenings at Christ Church, an event held concurrently with Liddon's lectures at St. Edmund's Hall. It was apparently there that Pater met and developed a friendship with C.L. Dodgson, then mathematical lecturer at Christ Church. Pater took his final examination in the Michaelmas term of 1862, and two years later on 5 February 1864 he was, boosted by his knowledge of German philosophy, elected a probationary Fellow at Brasenose. Exactly one year later he was elected Fellow.

Pater felt he owed much to Benjamin Jowett. While a Brasenose student reading for his degree, he was himself coached by Jowett (1860 to 1862). But when Jowett failed to support him for the coveted Proctorship at Brasenose, the relationship cooled. In a 6 May 1894 recollection, Pater, it appears, suspended temporarily his personal differences to offer this flattering tribute of Jowett for Evelyn Abbott's *Life and Letters of Benjamin Jowett*. Pater fondly recalled that Jowett was accessible to all undergraduates and was a very encouraging but really critical judge of their work. . . . When he lectured on Plato, it was a fascinating thing to see those qualities as if in the act of creation, his lectures being informal, unwritten, and seemingly unpremeditated, but with many a long–remembered gem of expression, or delightfully novel idea, which seemed to be lying in wait whenever, at a loss for a moment in his somewhat hesitating discourse, he opened a book of loose notes.[5] Hopkins's going over to Pater for coaching, then, was part repayment of Pater's debt to Jowett and part Pater's fondness for him. At that time, Pater was not a recognizable figure in the university. By "the end of 1866 or beginning of 1867," Humphry Ward records, "the Junior Fellow of Brasenose was almost unknown to the seniors of the University, and quite unknown to the undergraduates." He was some years away from becoming, in the words of John Buchan, "the greatest Brasenose name of the nineteenth century" and, since Arnold, "the most distinguished figure that Oxford has given to the world of letters."[6]

When Hopkins went to Brasenose to be coached, Pater entertained an interest in Plato, derived largely, no doubt, from his coaching by Jowett. Pater had also presented papers to the Old Mortality, the most familiar being "Fichte's Ideal Student" and "Diaphaneitè," the latter eventually published in *Miscellaneous Studies* (1895).[7] He had also just seen his first publication, "Coleridge's Writings," which appeared in the January 1866 *Westminster Review*. "Winckelmann" appeared anonymously in the January 1867 issue of *Westminster*, six months before Hopkins graduated from Oxford. While it is difficult to determine how much of Pater's work Hopkins actually knew, it would seem likely, from the nature of the essays Hopkins wrote for Pater and from his attendance at the Old Mortality when Pater read, that Pater would have shared much of his scholarship with Hopkins. To have been attracted to "the naturally innocent, guileless, upright, unstruggling character, of conservative tendencies," according to Michael Levey, Pater would have discovered Hopkins a prime candidate for friendship. John Buchan characterizes that attraction similarly. Pater, he alleges, "liked the rough, genuine young life around him."[8]

To assess Pater's relationship with his friends is a most challenging task; and it is not simplified even when directed to more intimate friends, such as Charles Lancelot Shadwell, Pater's companion on his first (1865) tour of Italy and the one to whom *The Renaissance* is dedicated. Pater was arguably the most private Victorian, liked it that way, and wished no biography of himself written. With that understanding, and valuing as he did the "hiddenness of perfect things" and the function of art to "conceal itself,"[9] Pater kept no journal or diary, burned all of his poetry, much of it religious and orthodox, and openly acknowledged a penchant for not writing letters, which, when written, yielded little of the personal and were, to put it bluntly, very uninteresting . The only letters with some life in them are the ones written to Violet Paget (Vernon Lee), mostly because they deal with Pater's criticism of her fiction, an aesthetic posture already familiar to us. But that slim collection of extant letters constitutes no coherent focus, provides little access to Pater's inner life, and gives no real sense of the extent of his relationships, forming the picture of a reclusive life notably similar to Pater's portrayal of Michelangelo. Consequently, there remains even today no authoritative biography of Pater. "Pater's would be a difficult life to write," says one early critic, "because in the ordinary sense it was so unfeatured and because he had few intimates."[10]

Attempts at a Pater biography, then, present formidable challenges. A.C. Benson's *Walter Pater* (1906), while receiving support from Pater's sisters, Clara and Hester, ignores the few letters then available and pursues, instead, a critical approach to Pater. Disregarding the little there is of the personal, the biography provides too little an impression of the person Pater. The next attempt at a biography is Thomas Wright's two volumes, *The Life of Walter Pater* (1907). But steeped in much unsubstantiated claims, the work remains dubious and is called by one critic a "volume of gossip" and "an outrage."[11] Wright received no assistance from Pater's sisters, who, despite their support of Benson mostly because of his focus, wished no close scrutiny of their brother's life. More recently, Michael Levey's *The Case of Walter Pater* (1978) very cautiously brings together the efforts of both Benson and Wright, using an approach that Gerald Monsman carved out in *Pater's Portraits* (1967) and *Walter Pater's Art of Autobiography* (1980). That is, both Levey and Monsman (Monsman more so) approached Pater not so much through the piecemeal remains of his poetry, letters, and memorials as through a psychological exhuming of his life buried among and within his numerous literary portraits. Mindful of Pater's own admission—that "it is necessary that there should be perceptible in [one's] work something individual, inventive, unique, the impress there of the writer's own temper and personality," and that in fact "the writer has for his aim the portraiture of his own most intimate moods"[12]—both Levey and Monsman insist that Pater's life is both deliberately and subconsciously fictionalized in his portraits, portraits, they believe, consistent with what Pater himself calls "a generous loan of oneself" in an attempt at "rectifying and concentrating [one's] impressions into certain pregnant types."

Given Pater's penchant for autobiographical fiction, masking himself in such fictional types as Florian and Marius, biographers of Pater are forced to catch a reflection of the man in the mirror of his texts (one type of the *solus cum solo* approach to autobiography) and not through the accepted conventions of letters and diaries, and the generic model of self–conscious autobiography. Such, to use Paul de Man's characterization, is Pater's autobiography of "de–facement," the use of prosopopeia ("to confer a mask or a face") as a "trope of autobiography."[13] The pleasure Marius finds in losing one's self in sleep might well be a metaphor for the anti–self–conscious life, the epitaphic autobiographical act, Pater pursued in his life and writings. Pater himself described his own writing as one "so exclusively personal and solitary as the kind of literary work, which I feel I can do best, must be."[14] In this Pater must have felt a particular kinship with Lamb, whom he celebrates for "forgetting himself in his subject" (achieving Negative Capability) and for pursuing "self–portraiture," the "real motive in writing at all." Through his own biographical acts, Lamb, like Pater, and in Pater's words, sought to "give you himself, to acquaint you with his likeness; but must do this, if at all, indirectly."[15] Monsman finds that "Pater's overriding strategy" was "to reveal himself covertly by deploying through critical or fictionalized critical utterances 'a self not himself.'"[16] Speaking of this in regard to Pater's typological penchant, John Buchan discovers too that it is precisely in this "conscientious type portraiture, in which Pater always enshrined a phase of his own thought, we can piece together some record of his development."[17] It is just such a stitching that I am attempting here in treating the similarities and divergences between Hopkins and Pater, and especially as these relate to their aesthetics. More significantly, my attempt here is to define, on the basis of Pater's writings and from the essays Hopkins wrote for him, an aesthetic that is at once Paterian and Victorian, and to show at what points Hopkins's own aesthetic theory and practice are consistent with or are a critique of Paterian and Victorian aesthetics.

We know for certain that the year after Hopkins came up to Balliol he knew of Pater. Pater was elected to the Old Mortality in 1862. A self–proclaimed radical essay society, the Old Mortality was founded at Balliol in November 1856 by John Nichol. The society was named as a sort of joke on the poor bodily health of some of its seven founding members, six of whom were Balliol students. But the society expressed no allegiance to any particular college, although Nichol personally supported the increased endowment of the Greek Chair at Balliol under Jowett, whom the society saw as "the chief intellectual power in Oxford, stimulating every one to do his best, and criticizing from an armoury which seldom failed, the weak points in his pupils."[18] The society, whose membership included Algernon Swinburne and T.H. Green (later one of Hopkins's Balliol tutors), met once a week during term to discuss religious and political topics mostly in opposition to conservative views. One stated goal of the Old Mortality was "the stimulating and promoting of the interchange of thought among its members, on the more general questions of Literature, Philosophy, and Science, as well as the diffusion of a correct knowledge and critical appreciation of our standard English authors."[19] Papers were read on Pope, Dryden, Byron, Carlyle, American Puritan settlements, and on support for the North in the American Civil War. With the society still meeting mostly at Balliol, Hopkins attended its meetings, and it was apparently there he first met Pater.

In a 7 March 1864 walk with Liddon, Hopkins told of Pater's 20 February essay on "Fichte's Ideal Student at the Old Mortality Club, in wh. he denied the Immortality of the soul." Weeks later, on two separate occasions, Liddon told the Bishop of Salisbury and Keble of the Old Mortality's goal of "propagating sheer unbelief, e.g. one Paper which obtained great notoriety at the beginning of this Term was directed against the immortality of the soul"; and "I told you [Keble] of the Essay Club at which last Term the immortality of the soul was denied outright as a vulgar notion (by one of your younger imitators of Fichte)." Liddon's fear was that "'nice pleasant fellows who believe in nothing at all' is a true definition of not a few of the cleverer men who are turned out hence into the London world."[20] S.R. Brooke, a conservative member of the Old Mortality soon to defect to become the Hexameron's first secretary, described Pater's essay as "the most thoroughly infidel productions," in which Pater "advocated

Self-portrait of Hopkins done as an undergraduate.
Courtesy of the Bodleian Library.

'self–culture'" and rejected any belief in "a future existence." "To sit in one's study," Brooke continues,

> and contemplate the beautiful is not a useful even if it is an agreeable occupation; but if it were both useful and agreeable, it would hardly be worth while to spend so much trouble upon what may at any time be wrested from you. If a future existence is to be disbelieved the motto "Let us eat and drink for tomorrow we die," is infinitely preferable.[21]

Brooke was most critical of what he saw in Pater as a preoccupation with inactivity and the non–utilitarian gratification of self–culture.

Fichte's "Divine Idea" lies "concealed behind all natural appearances." Spiritual or Learned culture, synonymous to Fichte for an educated mind, helps to extract part of this Divine Idea, and the one who accomplishes this is a Scholar of the Age. But from this scholar, "His person, and all personality in the world, have long vanished from before him, and entirely disappeared in his effort after the realization of the Idea."[22] In Pater, the type is permanent while personality, flame–like in its composition, is constantly being purged away, made ethereal. Pater's conception of "self–culture," privileging of "pregnant types," and indefiniteness of personality, even his refusal to attempt, except through the calculated selection of fictional types, self–conscious autobiographical acts, all relate nicely to Fichte's argument for the Divine Idea and for the absence of fixed personality. Gerald Monsman believes that "Diaphaneitè" was not a separate essay delivered to the Old Mortality but actually the revised essay of the earlier controversial one on Fichte and the soul's immortality. While "Diaphaneitè" shares remarkably similar ideas with the essay on Fichte, it is difficult to identify what in the essay so repelled Hopkins and others like Brooke. In "Diaphaneitè," Pater looks to that type of character within culture that is "rare, precious above all to the artist," which he describes as a "fine edge of light, where the elements of our moral nature refine themselves to the burning point." He finds that that character ("certain elect souls" he calls them in *Marius*) who participates in this intellectual and spiritual culture is formed by way of grace, not nature, showing that the Divine Idea is "indeed within the limits of man's destiny." And "Like all the higher forms of inward life," this character demonstrates a "subtle blending and interpenetration of intellectual, moral and spiritual elements. But it is a phase of intellect, of culture, that it is most striking and forcible. It is a mind of taste lighted up by some spiritual ray within."[23] While Hopkins's Catholic dogma and his many understated comments on the power of personality would have led him to reject Pater's conclusion that a majority of such types, possessing the "supreme artistic view of life, held by the few," would lead to "the regeneration of the world," he would not have disavowed Pater's assertion that the saint, artist, and philosopher, made exceptional by "order of nature," participate in that "intellectual culture," work "in and by means of the main current of the world's energy," but cross "rather than [follow] the main current of the world's life."[24]

Hopkins attended one such meeting of the Old Mortality on 31 May 1866 and noted in his journal: "Pater talking two hours against Xtianity."[25] Pater was remembered by a society member as one whose "speculative imagination seemed to make the lights burn blue."[26] Although from an old Catholic family, Pater was raised Anglican and was attracted early to Keble and his High Church views.[27] Many felt that Pater was heading Romewards because of the post–Tractarian fervor that later attracted Hopkins. Pater came up to Queen's College in 1858. His break with Christianity, according to Thomas Wright, occurred in 1859 and his attacks—what Wright, quoting Pater's friend Robert McQueen, calls "Mephistophelian sneers"—commenced that same year. Still by 1860 he felt he would take Holy Orders, a strange decision, since, according to Wright, Pater had only recently burned his manuscript of mostly religious poems. Up to this point, Liddon had apparently taken an interest in Pater and was, if Wright is to be believed, "kindly disposed towards him." Knowing this, John McQueen, Pater's estranged friend, appealed to Liddon, who suggested that McQueen write the Bishop of London, Archibald Tait, to oppose Pater's ordination. Pater, like Goethe, now "regarded religion as merely a department of art,"[28] related somewhat to the way both Florian and Marius, portraits of the artist as a young man, envision art and religion:

> He began to love, for their own sakes, church lights, holy days, all that belonged to the comely order of the sanctuary, the secrets of its white linen, and hold vessels, and fonts of pure water. . . . His way of conceiving religion came then to be in effect what it ever afterwards remained—a sacred history indeed, but still more a sacred ideal, a transcendent version or representation, under intenser and more expressive light and shade, of human life and its familiar or exceptional incidents.[29]

The young Marius, Pater tells us, "feels himself to be something of a priest, and that devotion of his days to the contemplation of what is beautiful, a sort of perpetual religious service."[30] In Pater, says A.C. Benson, is "always something holy, even priestly," about his "attitude to art."[31] Pater graduated in October

1862 and was not ordained. Still not clear is whether Liddon forestalled ordination or whether Pater on his own decided against it.

Hopkins and Pater had a prime opportunity to meet together in the summer of 1867. Had it occurred, that meeting would have left us invaluable information on the extent of their friendship and the precise points at which their ideas converge and deviate. Hopkins graduated from Oxford in June 1867, went to Paris in July with Basil Poutiatine, and had no firm plans between then and September when he was to join the staff at Newman's Oratory. But he was expecting an invitation from Pater to spend part of a summer vacation at the resort area of Sidmouth, a reading party Pater afforded his students. Humphry Ward spent such a vacation with Pater and might well have been the person who supplanted Hopkins. Ward, Pater's student at Brasenose and with whom he had become increasingly familiar, provided details of the 1867 vacation at Sidmouth. He recalled learning much from Pater during their long autumn walks at Oxford and

> more still in a delightful month that I spent, by his invitation, at Sidmouth in the Long Vacation of 1867. He lived in a little house overhanging the sea, and I had lodgings in the town, going to him every morning with an essay, or to hear him discourse on the *Republic* and the thousand subjects suggested by it. In two ways his teaching was immensely fruitful. His ideas, his view of life, were fresh and original . . . ; and his criticism of style . . . was convincing and final.[32]

Why Hopkins did not receive the invitation is uncertain. He gave no indication of there being a rift in the relationship, and in fact assigned the anticipated invitation top priority, rearranging his summer schedule around it. The decision was obviously Pater's, leading one to suspect that the rejection was either because of Hopkins's recent conversion to Roman Catholicism or, more likely, Pater's penchant for not sustaining close friendships. Not hearing from Pater by 15 August, Hopkins on 26 August went to see his Oxford friend Edward Urquhart, curate at Bovey Trace, from where he left on 10 September for the Oratory. Hopkins apparently had no further contact with Pater until 17 June 1868. Conceding the Oratory experience a failure, Hopkins had decided to join the Jesuits. From his home in Hampstead, he returned to Oxford, lunched with Pater, and then, no doubt accompanied by Pater, toured the studio of the artist Simeon Solomon, friend of Pater, an admitted homosexual, and a member of the Old Mortality.[33] Following a tour of Switzerland with Edward Bond, Hopkins entered his novitiate at Roehampton.

The relationship with Pater lasted for twelve years. David Downes is convinced that the friendship lasted longer. While "references to Pater do not stand out in [Hopkins's] letters and papers," says Downes, "they are there, sprinkled at such salient points that it is not too much to observe that their friendship lasted all of Hopkins' life."[34] In April 1878, Hopkins was pleased to hear from Bridges that Pater still remembered and took an interest in him. Naturally, then, when Hopkins returned to Oxford for a ten–month stint (from December 1878 to October 1879) at St. Aloysius' church, he saw much of Pater, at one point inviting him to dinner. Pater's typically short letter of 20 May 1879, his only extant one to Hopkins, expressed great pleasure at the invitation.[35] Writing to Baillie about that Oxford experience and of mutual acquaintances, Hopkins told him that though still fond of the place and of the university, it was "not to me a congenial field." Hopkins had lost much of his juvenile affection for Oxford. But Pater apparently made Hopkins's tenure at Oxford tolerable: Pater was, Hopkins told Baillie, "one of the men I saw most of";[36] on one occasion, 11 February, Hopkins dined with Pater.

The time Hopkins spent with Pater indicates that the two certainly had much to share. Both men, said Downes, "had artistic personalities which they found to be highly compatible to each other. . . . There is every reason to believe that undergraduate Hopkins found in Pater a most engaging person whose latent attitudes on life, art, and religion were quietly evocative and interesting; now returned to Oxford, Father Hopkins renewed his friendship at a time when Pater's views had advanced to stages wherein their main tendencies had been more elaborately demonstrated and impressively stated."[37]   From the time Hopkins graduated from Oxford to his return to Saint Aloysius, Pater had become celebrated in Oxford. He had *The Renaissance* to his name, along with several other essays of criticism in journals Hopkins knew and read. One must assume that, because of their frequent contacts and their mutual aesthetic interest, the two would have discussed Pater's scholarship and Hopkins's aesthetic views. In October 1879 when Hopkins left Oxford for good, he had severed all personal ties to Pater. Yet the influence of that early aesthetic education, however modified, remained with Hopkins. Poem after poem and in his other writings, whether the devotionals or the diary and journal, Hopkins remained fascinated by things aesthetic, which he saw as a beauty instressed by God that needed only to be witnessed, stressed.

To show what Hopkins's aesthetic theory owes to Pater's and where it departs radically from his, one must first attempt to define a Paterian aesthetic, not the easiest of enterprises. Pater's is a fluid and developmental aesthetic, which, to accurately represent, one must account for its progression, indeed its evolution. There is, for example, a sense in which art, to Pater, exists to and for itself, becoming heterocosmic; but art is also religious and at times seems to replace religion. There is also a sense in which art reflects and deals with the complexities of life, including, at times, when it speaks to moral issues. If Pater's aesthetic theory is at all constant, that stability lies in his assertion that art is preeminent and partakes of the indefiniteness of personality and the fluidity of the age; within this flux, art provides relative permanence to the moment. Becoming one with the flux—burning with its "gem–like flame"—a being at once participates in and produces something that withstands flux. The complexities of this transaction can best be witnessed in *The Renaissance*, an anthology of essays published in separate issues of the *Westminster* and *Fortnightly* reviews between 1867 and 1877.

Pater's own "Preface" to *The Renaissance* provides the paradigm by which to estimate how his aesthetic theory relates to personalities and schools of aesthetics. He claims, with Arnold in mind, that an aesthetic theory cannot be defined abstractly, as is the tendency. Beauty is relative, and an abstract approach to it compromises our appreciation and blurs our discriminating judgment about its lesser or greater aesthetic qualities. An aesthetic theory should approach the subject concretely, not abstractly, and should attempt to expose its particular formula, its own intellectual theorem. It is, and here Pater refers to Arnold, "To see the object as in itself it really is."[38] The first step in this transaction lies with the individual. In this subjectivizing of criticism, one must get to "know one's own impression as it really is, to discriminate it, to realize it distinctly." A true aesthetic, then, is located in the perceiver, not in the object of perception, and as that perception relates to the changing relationship between the subject and the object of perception. Pater's aesthetic, then, is jointly one of subjectivity and one of distancing, creating a dialectic in which beauty, to be found, must be located in the space between subject and object of perception. But before this relationship can be forged, one must first perform surgery of sorts on one's impression, "a clearing of the organs of observation and perfecting of analysis," says Pater, or, to use Hopkins's analogy, cleansing the eye from time to time. Again, according to Marius's dictum, one must "Beware of falsifying [one's] impressions"[39] in order to account for the effect the object has on the perceiving self and how that self is either influenced or changed. Pater's aesthetics, as Carolyn Williams observes, is not an entire turning away from the "'aim' of objectivity."[40]

From these objects of perception, whether from nature, art, or human life, in person or in books, come pleasurable sensations the aesthetic critic feels and wishes to explore. The duty of the aesthetic critic is "to distinguish, to analyse, and separate from its adjuncts" the process by which art produces its "special impression of beauty or pleasure, to indicate what the source of that impression is, and under what condition it is experienced."[41] The critic is obliged not to produce an intellectually abstract definition of beauty—even though Pater's aesthetic does not cater exclusively to the senses—but to cultivate the kind of temperament that responds excitingly and equally to the diverse forms of beauty. An important function of aesthetic criticism is "to estimate the degree in which a given work of art fulfills its responsibilities to its special material," whether poetry, painting, music, or architecture.[42] Applied to Wordsworth's poetry, this principle, Pater believes, would lead one to conclude that his best poems are the ones treating the mystical sense of life in things in nature, man's connection to nature, and the reciprocal ways in which nature's sights and sounds invigorate man. But in that same corpus, Pater finds, in language that echoes Hopkins's Parnassian charges against Wordsworth, a "great mass of verse" that "might well be forgotten." But the "heat of his genius" has deposited, as for instance in his "Ode: Intimations of Immortality," a "fine crystal here or there."[43] Insisting on the literary rebirth of the Renaissance as an expansive movement whose conception and development occurred in the Middle Ages and is thus of a piece with it, Pater's *Renaissance* seeks to counteract the medievalism of the mid–nineteenth century best represented in Ruskin's *The Stones of Venice* (1853), to assimilate a Hebraic and Hellenic conception of beauty, to argue for the fluidity of personality and moving form, and to propose a subjectivist aesthetic to bridge perceiver and object.

Pater asserts that the Renaissance had its conception and culmination in late twelfth–century France, and that new experiences, new poetic subjects, and new artistic forms—the attributes of the Renaissance—witnessed an outbreak at the end of the twelfth and beginning of the thirteenth century, the period historically of the Middle Ages. Arguing obviously with Ruskin, Pater asserts that the so–called rupture between the ideas of the Middle Ages and those of the Renaissance is exaggerated. Even in Dante, the bard of the Middle Ages and his work the "peculiar and perfect flower" of its time, one finds, says Pater, a "large–minded treatment of all forms of classic power and achievement" bearing the marks of a "stage of progress, from the narrower sentiment of the Middle Ages, towards 'humanism,' towards," that is, "the mental attitude of the Renaissance and of the modern world."[44] The Renaissance spirit is evident in the ecclesiastical art, sculpture, and painting of the Middle Ages, and nowhere is this spirit more evident than in its poetry. Committed, then, as he was to an understanding of the Classical spirit of his own times, Pater saw the eighteenth and nineteenth centuries as the completion of the *eclaircissement* initiated by the Renaissance, a time when art was reconciled with religion and the pursuit of art so devoutly undertaken that the enterprise itself became religious, when the religion of the Middle Ages became "the subject of a purely artistic or poetic treatment." The "religion of antiquity," says Pater, was reconciled with "the religion of Christ"; the old Greek gods reasserted themselves and competed with the monotheistic God of Christianity; and Plato and Homer were "made to speak agreeably to Moses." Blind to the historic sense and the theory of development, and unable to harmonize the two religions, the Renaissance scholars turned to the quagmire of allegorical interpretation. That truce, that "scientific reconciliation of Christian sentiment with the imagery, the legends, the theories about the world, of pagan poetry and philosophy,"[45] was manifested in the life and work of the Italian scholar and mystic, Pico, Pater's model of a humanist, who sought to keep alive everything human. Pater saw Botticelli attempting to forge the same union in going beyond the simple religion of Giotto. The Renaissance was the rebirth of feelings, sensations, and thought not contradictory to but independent of and beyond the existing spiritual system.

But it is in Winckelmann's career (to study the Classics rather than theology) and work one finds, according to Pater, the perfect merger of religion and aesthetics, the reconciliation of Hebraism and Hellenism. Winckelmann is represented by Goethe as a thoroughly Greek figure, "alien from the Christian world," who discovered the "end of all endeavor in the aspects of the human form, the continual stir and motion of a comely human life."[46] Pater's principal argument is that Greek art evolves naturally from its religion and is "entangled" with it—to the Greeks beauty was one with religious ritual and the beauty of that ritual was experienced through the senses, a medium that separates the Greek experience from the Christian one. In the rejection of the senses lies the main point of difference between Greek art and the Christian art of the Middle Ages, in which Christianity is perceived to be in a struggle to "express thoughts beyond itself." To the medieval artist, dependent as he was on pagan models, a thing in nature was to be apprehended not as an object but as a "symbol or type of a really inexpressible world."[47] But in Greek art, says Pater, the object stands on its own merit and exists for its own purpose. The symbol does not suggest "anything beyond its own victorious fairness. The mind begins and ends with the finite image, yet loses no part of the spiritual motive," a motive not "lightly and loosely attached to the sensuous form, as its meaning to an allegory, but saturates and is identical with it." While the spiritualist relishes in the gradual fading away of the sensuous elements "as the dyed garment bleaches in the keen air," the artist, on the other hand, "steeps his thought again and again into the fire of colour." In "discrediting the slightest touch of sense," the ascetic is then at odds with his own nature; but in grounding his "intellectual and spiritual ideas in sensuous form," the aesthete is in complete unity with himself, with nature, and with the world.[48]

What was eventually realized in the Renaissance was also pursued in the Middle Ages. In this earlier period, a sort of "medieval Renaissance," Pater detects an antinomianism, an "assertion of the liberty of the heart," a "spirit of rebellion and revolt against the moral and religious ideas of the time." Renegade medievalists, chronicled in Pater's "Two Early French Stories," pursued sensuous and imaginative pleasures, valued beauty, and worshiped the body, concerns extending "beyond the bounds of the Christian ideal; and their love became sometimes a strange idolatry, a strange rival religion." But the unbridled celebration of the sensuous is found in the Hellenic spirit, when suddenly "the imagination feels itself free" and when "this life of the senses" recognizes its facile and direct characteristics.[49] All true aesthetic criticism, says Pater, must begin with the contemplation of the sensuous aspect of beauty, the belief that we must respond to art in a feeling way. There are also differences in kinds of aesthetic beauty because each work of art addresses the "'imaginative reason' through the senses," each has its own "special mode of reaching the imagination, its own special responsibilities to its material." Thus works of art "must first of all delight the sense, delight it as directly and sensuously as a fragment of Venetian glass," a veiled reference to Ruskin; and "through this delight alone become the vehicle of whatever poetry or science may lie beyond them in the intention of the composer." Because art evokes pleasure, then, the fundamental function of a masterpiece possesses no greater moral or ethical value than "an accidental lay of sunlight and shadow for a few moments on the wall or floor: is itself, in truth, a space of such fallen light . . . refined upon, and dealt with more subtly and exquisitely than by nature itself." [50]

But Pater's is an aesthetic that also celebrates the ascesis, "Self–restraint, a skilful economy of means," which has too a "beauty of its own."[51] Pater traces the aesthetic and the ascetic back to the time before Plato when Pythagoras stressed "abstinence, the repression of one's carnal elements" in order that the pilgrim soul might "secure full use of all the opportunities of further perfecting . . . in the many revolutions of its existence." Thus anticipating Plato, Pythagoras already had "something of the monk, of monastic *ascesis*, about him" to "fit him for, duly to refine his nature towards, that closer vision of truth."[52] *Ascesis*, then, becomes essential to perfection, in art as in life. The early phases of the Renaissance revealed, says Pater, "the freshness which belongs to all periods of growth in art, the charm of *ascesis*, of the austere and serious girding of the loins in youth." He talks repeatedly of the ascetic impulse, a "law of restraint," in

Hellenic art, of the beauty of "moral sexlessness," a subject, according to Thomas Wright, Pater addressed in a schoolboy poem, "St. Elizabeth of Hungary." Written in January 1856 to answer Kingsley's dramatic poem, *The Saint's Tragedy, or the True Story of Saint Elizabeth of Hungary* (1848), the poem advocates the beauty and sanctity of celibacy.[53] In another of Pater's self–portraits, "Emerald Uthwart," this "rather sensuous boy" felt too "the beauty" of the *ascesis*: "He found himself in a system of fixed rules. . . . The confident word of command, the instantaneous obedience expected, the enforced silence, the very games that go by rule."[54] Likewise, Pater's young Wordsworthian child, Florian Deleal, comes to realize a beauty mixed with pain and sacrifice. From "the larger world without, as at windows left ajar unknowingly," comes to Florian "two streams of impressions, the sentiment of beauty and pain. . . . From this point he could trace two predominant processes of mental change in him––the growth of an almost diseased sensibility to the spectacle of suffering, and, parallel with this, the rapid growth of a certain capacity of fascination by bright colour and choice form." This "desire of physical beauty" mingles early in Florian with "the fear of death intensified by the desire of beauty."[55] Wrestling with the ideal of asceticism and the ideal of culture, with how the church and society espouse a better life, Marius concludes that the "ideal of asceticism represents moral effort as essentially a sacrifice, the sacrifice of one part of human nature to another." This attempt to "live more completely" means finding that completion only within a severed self. However, the ideal of culture—and Pater would have in mind Pico, Botticelli, or Winckelmann—represents morality not in living as a divided self but in a "harmonious development of all the parts of human nature, in just proportion to each other."[56]

Because Pater valued the epiphanic nature of sensuous apprehension, he privileges "measured motion," whether it occurs when a "sudden light transfigures some trivial thing," or whether it be "a weather–vane, a windmill, a winnowing–fan, the dust in the barn door." But pleasurable moments are only evanescent, leaving behind a "relish," a desired recurrence of epiphanic moments. Arrested in these "ideal" and "animated instants," these "caprices of a moment," "fiery friendships" ("a mere gesture, a look, a smile, perhaps—some brief and wholly concrete moment"), when past and future are absorbed "in an intense consciousness of the present," we become mere "spectators of all the fulness of existence."[57]

With life a fleeting thing and beauty always on the wing, leaving beholders as mere observers of life, Pater is particularly interested in strategies that might fix the moment. "This attempt to recreate a sense of objectivity," as Carolyn Williams discovers, "places Pater directly in the mainstream of Victorian poetics, but his temporalizing of the ecstatic stance represents one of his crucial shifts toward the 'modern.'"[58] One strategy to stabilize the moment is the art of contemplation. Before examining this in Pater, I turn for a moment to Hopkins, who also values contemplation, but not as a substitute for the active life; his "heart in hiding" too often "stirred for a bird." But, for Hopkins, contemplation, either of beauty or nature, is seldom if ever an end in itself; rather, contemplation always assumes an Ignatian quality, whose "absoluteness is impossible unless in a trance."[59] But whether in its normal of absolute state, contemplation moves one to worship, gratitude, and praise. Hopkins discovered two kinds of energy in the mind, "a transitional kind" and "an abiding kind." In the latter,

> the mind is absorbed (as far as that may be), taken up by, dwells upon, enjoys, a single thought: we may call it contemplation, but it includes pleasures. . . . Art enacts this energy of contemplation. . . . The more intellectual, less physical, the spell of contemplation, the more complex must be the object, the more close and elaborate must be the comparison the mind has to keep making between the whole and the parts, the parts and the whole. . . . The further in anything, as a work of art, the organisation is carried out, the deeper the form penetrates, the prepossession flushes the matter, the more effort will be required in apprehension, the more power of comparison.[60]

This is Hopkins's joint discourse on contemplation and inscape, "individually–distinctive beauty," a discourse that, according to Hilary Fraser, places him "very centrally in the post–Romantic religio–aesthetic tradition which defines Victorian aesthetic thought."[61] Not the mere outward characteristics of a thing but the form that resides somewhere within it, inscape must be culled out, and contemplation, the microscopic eye, must uncover the form, the design. Hopkins's ideas on the complexity of form and its challenge to the discriminating faculties of perception echo ideas in George Eliot's essay, "Notes on Form in Art," written in or before 1868. Additionally, Hopkins's ideas on inscape, on how inscape is detected ("inscape must be dwelt on"), and on likeness and unlikeness in species, and in particular how these are presented in poems such as "As kingfishers catch fire," "Pied Beauty," and "Spelt from Sibyl's Leaves," closely resemble Eliot's. In other words, Eliot's comments might be the source for Hopkins's ideas on diatonicism, associated at times with "marked parallelism"– abrupt, intervallary kind. The passage from Eliot reads:

> Form, then, as distinguished from merely massive impression, must
> first depend on the discrimination of wholes & then on the discrimina-
> tion of parts. Fundamentally, form is unlikeness, as is seen in the
> philosophical use of the word Form in distinction from Matter: & in
> consistency with this fundamental meaning, every difference is form.
> . . . But with this fundamental discrimination is born in necessary
> antithesis the sense of wholeness or unbroken connection in space &
> time. . . . And as knowledge continues to grow by its alternating
> processes of distinction & combination, seeing smaller & smaller
> unlikeness & grouping or associating these under a common likeness,
> it arrives at the conception of wholes composed of parts more & more
> multiplied & highly differenced, yet more & more absolutely bound
> together by various conditions of common likeness or mutual depen-
> dence. And the fullest example of such a whole is the highest example
> of Form: in other words, the relation of multiplex interdependent parts
> to a whole which is itself in the most varied & therefore the fullest
> relation to other wholes. . . . The highest Form, then, is the highest
> organism, that is to say the most varied group of relations bound
> together in a wholeness which again has the most varied relations with
> all other phenomena.[62]

If these remarks are compared to Hopkins's "any two things, however unlike,
have something in common," "Likeness therefore implies unlikeness," and
"nature is a string all the differences in which are really chromatic but certain
places in it have become accidentally fixed" (diatonic),[63] one gets a sense of how
remarkably close Hopkins's ideas are to Eliot's.

An undergraduate essay of Hopkins, entitled "Poetic Diction," defines
parallelism. Parallelism, according to Hopkins, takes on not only the attribute
of the "clearly marked," diatonic, but also of the transitional attribute of the
chromatic. Under the rubric of parallelism (diatonic beauty) come likeness
(simile and metaphor) and unlikeness (antithesis and contrast). Marked or
diatonic parallelism is evident in such devices as verse structure, rhythm, and
alliteration. In the area of thought, abrupt parallelism determines such figurative
features as simile, metaphor, and antithesis. Chromatic parallelism, on the other
hand, deals with the musical contrivances of tone, intensity, expression, and
climax.[64]

The complex nature of form that requires trancelike contemplation is
catalogued repeatedly in Hopkins's journal and poetry. The "spraying" of beech
woods against the side of the Swiss mountains, for example, was "baffling"

because it was "beautiful"; bluebells "baffle you with their inscape, made to
every sense"; a "puzzle of very slight clefts branched with little sprigs" describes
a pond; and "a budded lime against the field wall: turn, pose, and counterpoint
in the twigs and buds—the *form* speaking." With contemplation as the access
to beauty and the means to worship, Hopkins noticed never having seen
"anything more beautiful than the bluebell I have been looking at." In or (and)
through them he found the "beauty of our Lord"; and when the stars came out
in abundance, Hopkins "leant back to look at them and my heart opening more
than usual praised our Lord to and in whom all that beauty comes home."[65] In
other words, inscape in things, and with it beauty, arrives by way of the senses
and through contemplation. Christopher Devlin sees this in a similar light. In
several of Hopkins's poems, writes Devlin, "there seems to be the attempt to *re-
trace* the transition from innate memory to insight through the senses." The
opening lines of "[Ashboughs]" might corroborate this, according to Devlin.
Words such as "boughs break," "combs creep," "touch," and "grouping" all
seem suggestive of "inchoate sensation beginning to burgeon." And more
striking expressions in other poems "seem to be those in which sight and sound
recover their common origin in touch."[66]

   For Pater, however, contemplation is always end in itself and in contemplation, not in activity, dwells the genuine source of pleasure. Thus Marius's entire
boyhood was "more given to contemplation than to action," conceiving himself
as "the passive spectator of the world around him."[67] Believing that one can
never get beyond "the walls of the closely shut cell of one's own personality,"
that the mind, as Pater elsewhere claims, is but a "solitary prisoner" of "its own
dream of a world,"[68] because the ideas of the outer world are too unstable, too
evanescent, Marius's was an attempt to construct "the world for himself in great
measure from within, by the exercise of meditative power." Pater calls this "A
vein of subjective philosophy, with the individual for its standard of all things."[69]
So valuable then is contemplation to Pater that in his essay on "Wordsworth" he
valorizes the "art of impassioned contemplation" as the avenue to beauty, even
morality. "Contemplation—impassioned contemplation"—is the "*end–in–itself*, the perfect end" (my italics):

> That the end of life is not action but contemplation—*being* as distinct
> from *doing*—a certain disposition of the mind: is, in some shape or
> other, the principle of all the higher morality. In poetry, in art, if you
> enter into their true spirit at all, you touch this principle, in a measure:
> these, by their very sterility, are a type of beholding for the mere joy of
> beholding. To treat life in the spirit of art, is to make life a thing in which

means and ends are identified: to encourage such treatment, the true
moral significance of art and poetry.[70]

When in the same breath, then, Pater calls contemplation an end in itself and
states that "the supreme importance of contemplation is the conduct of life,"[71]
that conduct begins and ends with the self and seems to have no connection
whatsoever to outward or communal behavior. But Pater's is not an aesthetic
that dismisses altogether the value of communal relationships, the argument for
which is found in his ideas on how we respond to suffering. Through Marius,
Pater finds suffering "so large a principle in things—since the only principle,
perhaps, to which we may always safely trust is a ready sympathy with the pain
one actually sees." Logically, then, the significant differences among men
reside in their "power of insight," their "power of sympathy." And it is in
sympathy, that "pitiful contact," the "mere clinging of human creatures to each
other," that we somehow "seem to touch the eternal" and find satisfaction to our
"moral sense."[72]

To Hopkins, however, *being* and *doing* are concepts equally valued. But the
two, we will discover, function not independently of each other but jointly:
being in Hopkins induces *doing*, the two operating dialectically. In Pater,
however, *being* and *doing* remain distinct: the "office of the poet is not that of
the moralist," the duty of great artists is "not to teach lessons, or enforce rules,
or even to stimulate us to noble ends." Rather, the goal is to free our thoughts
from "the mere machinery of life" in order only to witness the spectacle of life.[73]
In this way, as Wolfgang Iser points out, art for Pater is "no longer tied to a
definite sacred or profane setting or service, but allows instead a perception of
the manifold forms of human self–realisation."[74]

"Ideal" or "animated" instant is Pater's metaphor for life and personality.
The metaphor also accounts for Pater's notion of the shifting or indefinite nature
of the self and his numerous self–portraits. "Generality" and "breadth," says
Pater—aware that the scientific approach involves framing general principles
(formulating "intellectual theorems") for particular discoveries—are "the supreme characteristics of the Hellenic ideal." And these arise from a culture that
is constantly renewing, "rectifying and concentrating its impressions into
certain pregnant types."[75] This desire to find "pregnant types" in the general is
Pater's approach to the self and personality. Among Victorians such as Carlyle,
Ruskin, and Newman, Pater especially avoided formal autobiographical strategies, choosing instead to conceal himself in pregnant types such as Florian,
Emerald, Marius, and in many of the Renaissance figures. For example,
Botticelli, like Pater, "usurps the data," and plays "fast and loose" with them,

"rejecting some and isolating others, and always combining them anew." He, like Pater, worked not merely to translate but to catch his own vision. Luca sought after "the type in the individual to abstract and express only what is structural and permanent, to purge from the individual all that belongs only to him, all the accidents, the feelings and actions of the special moment, all that (because in its own nature it endures but for a moment) is apt to look like a frozen thing." Like Michelangelo, all these sculptors "fill their work with intense and individualised expressions." Like Pater's too, "Their noblest works are the careful sepulchral portraits of particular persons."[76] Leonardo's "curiosity" and "desire for beauty," at times in conflict, is also Pater's, and especially so in his plunge into "human personality" and becoming a "painter of portraits." For "all artistic genius," Pater believes, "lies in the power of conceiving humanity in a new and striking way," of "selecting, transforming, recombining the images it transmits, according to the choice of the imaginative intellect." Thus the "all–important" goal of the artist is to "choose from a select number of types intrinsically interesting" and to purge away from them all that is "accidental, all that distracts the simple effect upon us of the supreme types of humanity, all traces in them of the commonness of the world," leaving only "the type, the general character of the subject."[77]

Pater's most profound comment on the indefiniteness of personality and the self, made so because of the flux in which they are immersed, comes in his famous "Conclusion" to *The Renaissance*. Pater's asserts that all things, whether it be "our physical life," "this world," or our "inward world of thought and feeling," are marked by instability.[78] Or as he remarked earlier in "Diaphaneitè," "Our collective life, pressing equally on every part of every one of us, reduces nearly all of us to the level of a colourless uninteresting existence."[79] Relegating life to the mere material, Pater finds that our entire physical life is "but a combination of natural elements to which science gives names" and is "a perpetual motion of them." And the visible manifestations of the elements on forces external to us manifest similar "flame–like" effects on our life, "renewed from moment to moment." The "whirlpool is still more rapid, the flame more eager and devouring"; and even our "inward world of thought and feeling," when examined, also manifests "momentary acts of sight and passion and thought."[80]

With no definite and stable self, no fixed point of reference and basis for judgment, the "whole scope of observation is dwarfed into the narrow chamber of the individual mind." Experiences, now reduced only to "impressions," are confined to that "thick wall of personality." And every one of these impressions is "the impression of the individual in his isolation, each mind keeping as a solitary prisoner its own dream of a world." Analysis only reveals these experiences in "perpetual flight," and each of them is "limited by time," "constantly re–forming itself on the stream," and "gone while we try to apprehend it," a "relic more or less fleeting"; thus it "may ever be more truly said," wrote Pater, employing a Darwinian epistemological stance that change is the only reality, that each experience "has ceased to be than that it is." With one's very self immersed as in a whirlpool, thrown into the stream, in that "continual vanishing away, that strange, perpetual weaving and unweaving of ourselves," analysis is at best provisional; and truth, if at all discoverable, is recognized only as "a power of distinguishing and fixing delicate and fugitive detail." Philosophy's real contribution is either to re–ignite or to stabilize observation that lasts only for a moment. Success in life comes only when we can "maintain this ecstasy" ("intellectual excitement"), to "burn always with this hard, gem–like flame"; our failure: "to form habits," and not attempting to "discriminate" in "every moment some passionate attitude." For, says Pater, "we have an interval, and then our place knows us no more." Thus we should be preoccupied with "ever curiously testing new opinions and courting new impressions" and "never acquiescing in a facile orthodoxy."[81] In the words of Philip Toynbee, during this "high–tide of Victorian moral earnestness," Pater had "hurled down an almost contemptuous challenge to the whole of educate English society," announcing that "aesthetic passion ought to be given priority over ethical values, social conventions and religious faith; a claim which must have been as astonishing as it must have seemed bold and original."[82]

Pater's claim in the "Conclusion" did not go unacknowledged, and espe- cially its seeming capitulation of all religious and moral absolutes. I say seeming because it is entirely conceivable to read Pater's claim as an insistence on a muscular rather than an enfeebled orthodoxy. One divine and former private student of Pater, John Wordsworth (grandnephew to the poet), wrote to Pater in a 17 March 1873 letter applauding the style and thought of *The Renaissance*. But lamenting Pater's epistemological conclusion, Wordsworth expressed grave concern that the philosophical assumption maintains that "no fixed principles either of religion or morality can be regarded as certain, that the only thing worth living for is momentary enjoyment and that probably or certainly the soul dissolves at death into elements which are destined never to reunite." Fearing the effect that Pater's claims might have on the minds of impressionable Oxford students, Wordsworth further reprimanded him for not choosing anonymity and thus self–censorship.[83]

Pater had made the same claims three years earlier, but they had gone virtually unnoticed at that time. In his less than flattering positivistic approach to Coleridge, an individual he saw as one of those "leaders of lost causes in philosophy and in religion," Pater asserts that "To the modern spirit nothing is, or can be rightly known, except relatively and under conditions. The philosophical conception of the relative has been developed in modern times through the influence of the sciences of observation. Those sciences reveal types of life evanescing into each other by inexpressible refinements of change." And because the "moral world is ever in contact with the physical," the "relative spirit has invaded moral philosophy." Thus "Hard and abstract moralities are yielding to a more exact estimate of the subtlety and complexity of our life." Coleridge's, however, was a "disinterested struggle against the relative spirit," ever "restlessly scheming to 'apprehend the absolute,' to affirm it effectively, to get it acknowledged." And while "Scientific truth is a thing fugitive, relative, full of fine gradations," Coleridge, on the other hand, attempted "to fix it in absolute formulas," to "reclaim the world of art as a world of fixed laws."[84] Coleridge's failure, then, according to Pater, who privileges the individual and not some accepted fixed value, was in attempting to fix an absolute in the face of current moral relativity, to exhibit a "passion for the absolute, for something fixed where all is moving." To use the word "scheming" to describe Coleridge's efforts, Robinson correctly detects, is to accuse him of "not simply duplicity but a fundamental untruth to life."[85]

Given Hopkins's stated preference for the diatonic rather than the chromatic, realism/idealism rather than materialism, fixity rather than continuity, Pater would have charged Hopkins with similar disingenuousness. On the other hand, Plato, less rigid, according to Pater, "holds his theories lightly, glances with a somewhat blithe and naive inconsequence from one view to another, not anticipating the burden of importance 'views' will one day have for men."[86] Hopkins no doubt read Plato differently than did Pater. Hopkins saw Platonism one with realism and therefore opposed to the philosophy of flux. But he felt that the emerging realism, like Pater's spirit of relativity, will "probably encounter this atomism of personality with some shape of the Platonic Ideas." Hopkins saw, then, the prevailing philosophy as one of "continuity or flux." And because of this relativity, "A form of atomism like a stiffness or sprain seems to hang upon and hamper our speculation: it is an over–powering, a disproportioned sense of personality." Pater, however, read the spirit of modern relativism similarly. "To the modern spirit nothing is, or can be rightly known, except relatively and under conditions. The philosophical conception of the relative has been developed in modern times through the influences of the sciences of observation. Those sciences," says Pater, "reveal types of life evanescing into each other by inexpressible refinements of change."[87]

Pater's epistemological stance—that life, in its physical and even meta-physical composition, is momentary, evanescent, unstable, fluid, perspectival––influenced greatly his claims for art. Marked only by the certainty that "all melts under our feet," we are left grasping for "any exquisite passion." One such passion comes in filling up our moments with art. While some choose ennui, some "high passions," the most intelligent opts for "art and song," in some form of listening. The sole option left us is in "expanding that interval, in getting as many pulsations as possible into the given time." [88] Marius thus accepts the melancholy advice to "seek in literature deliverance from mortality"; and Gaston's goal in reading poetry is to expand it "to the full measure of its intention." Conceived this way, poetry becomes "mere literature in exchange for life." This aesthetic doctrine is the "art of placing the pleasantly aesthetic, the welcome, element of life at an advantage." [89] Such an aesthetic theory asserts, then, "the love of art for its own sake." Concluding *The Renaissance*, Pater remains convinced that "art comes to you proposing frankly to give nothing but the highest quality to your moments as they pass, and simply for those moments' sake." [90] While Pater's aesthetic theory does insist on art for its own sake ("beholding for the mere joy of beholding"), promising us nothing but expanding the poetic passion of the ecstatic moment, his theory of art, as we will see, also advances moral claims.

Pater's theory of art for art's sake—the contemplation of beauty as an end in itself, that art and life are even interchangeable—is a consistent epistemological stance throughout *The Renaissance*. Even the character of the medieval Renaissance created in the human mind sensations and thoughts not opposed to but "beyond and independent of" the existing "spiritual system" and produced in Renaissance literature a "direct, aesthetic charm in the thing itself." In Botticelli, Pater finds art "undisturbed by any moral ambition," except "sympathy," concerned only with the mixed and uncertain condition of men and women, and it is in this condition that it "does its most sincere and surest work." For "all artistic genius" comes from the ability to conceive of humanity in a "new and striking way." [91] Pater sees in Da Vinci, in spite of his frequent workings with sacred subjects, the pursuit of "purely artistic ends." And Winckelmann's works of art, according to Goethe, are "a life, a living thing." The life and work of these figures demonstrate, says Pater, "the desire for beauty, the love of art for its own sake." [92]

These claims notwithstanding, Pater's is also an aesthetic that attempts to salvage the individual, and with him culture, from the chaos of life and experiences. Thus he asserts a moral purpose to art, one that works toward the perfection or completion of the individual. Marius believes that his Epicureanism seeks not pleasure but "a general completeness of life," and "towards such a full or complete life, a life of various yet select sensation," insight becomes the key. To pursue culture is the same as pursuing an "'aesthetic' education," in which art, literature, and music play vital roles. Looked at in this way, "the true aesthetic culture would be realisable as a new form of the contemplative life, founding its claim on the intrinsic 'blessedness' of 'vision.'" Marius thus resents the charge made by some that his Epicureanism is tantamount to hedonism, that he, Marius, was courting pleasure as "the sole motive of life." In his apology, he insists that "Not pleasure, but fulness of life, and 'insight' as conducting to that fulness" comprise his aesthetic philosophy, which includes too energy, variety, selected experiences, and, even, "noble pain and sorrow."[93] The rightful aim of our culture, he concludes, "should be to attain not only an intense but as complete a life as possible."[94]

Pater's search for perfection within culture is of a piece with the claims Arnold makes in *Culture and Anarchy* (1869), and it is not coincidental that the two (including Hopkins) were influenced by what Hopkins saw in Wordsworth as his spiritual insight on nature and life. The "key issue," according to Downes, "on which to examine Hopkins and Pater is the good and the beautiful. Both held views in which these notions are strikingly similar, yet each approached them from different ways. Pater worked through a moral system by way of art, and Hopkins sought art by way of a moral system."[95] The preeminent advocate of a connection between ethics and aesthetics, Arnold alleges that culture, not religion, is the study of perfection. "The total effect of Arnold's philosophy," as T.S. Eliot reads it, "is to set up Culture in the place of Religion, and to leave Religion to be laid waste by the anarchy of feeling." Pater, says Eliot, is that direction from Arnold.[96] For example, in his essay "Diaphaneitè," Pater insists on a simplicity that should constitute the personality of the artist. He calls it "a kind of moral expressiveness . . . characteristic of the repose of perfect intellectual culture." The rare artist who treats life in "the spirit of art" approximates verisimilitude and so approaches nearer to that desired perfection. Thus people will continue to look to literature and other fine arts for "a refuge, a sort of cloistral refuge, from a certain vulgarity in the actual world." And art will present them with "something of the uses of a religious 'retreat.'"[97] In Pater's post–Romantic aesthetic, one commencing in late Romanticism— through Keats in particular—"real life becomes aesthetic life, and real conduct becomes aesthetic conduct," says Wolfgang Iser, and art is granted an autonomy in which it functions "as an escape from the melancholy of human finiteness."[98] But these qualities in which art and morality converge, when art as yet retains a connection to morality, are best attested by Wordsworth, whose "inborn religious placidity," handling of natural objects whereby they "seemed to possess more or less of a moral or spiritual life," sacramental treatment of nature, and, most of all, whose treatment of "life in the spirit of art" captures "the true moral significance of art and poetry."[99]

Recalling too his claims for art and asceticism, Pater calls the beauty of Greek statues a "sexless" one, "a kind of impotence, an ineffectual wholeness of nature, yet with a divine beauty and significance of its own."[100] Pater's Winckelmann chapter again focuses on the connection in Greek art between the beauty of sexuality and religion: "The beauty of the Greek statues was a sexless beauty: the statues of the gods had the least traces of sex. Here there is a moral sexlessness, a kind of ineffectual wholeness of nature, yet with a true beauty and significance of its own." Focusing, then, on Winckelmann's "exercise of sight and touch," especially touch, Pater points to his "handling of the sensuous side of Greek art," though without "any sense of want, or corruption, or shame." Consequently, because Greek sensuousness "does not fever the conscience," making it "shameless and childlike," Winckelmann is saved from any homosexual "intoxication," freed from any sexual perversion: "he fingers those pagan marbles with unsinged hands, with no sense of shame or loss," with, in other words, an "ineffectual wholeness of nature." When Plato is then presented to Winckelmann, he comes across not as Christian but as pagan, "wholly Greek, and alien from the Christian world." And that representation is best witnessed in "that group of brilliant youths in the *Lysis*, still uninfected by any spiritual sickness," that is, still free from the taint of Platonic homosexuality. Richard Jenkyns finds in all of this Pater's sublimation of Platonic homosexuality.[101]

Winckelmann also established similar friendships and from those originate his interest in the human form. Thus his affinity with Hellenism was "not merely intellectual, that the subtler threads of temperament were interwoven in it, is proved by his romantic, fervent friendships with young men," knowing many of them "more beautiful than Guido's archangel." And it was these friendships, an intimacy with the "beauty of living form," that brought him "into contact with the pride of human forms" and "perfected his reconciliation to the spirit of Greek sculpture."[102] Association of beauty with morality, then, is especially developed in the life and work of the Classical votarist, Winckelmann, in whom "the moral instinct, like the religious or political, was merged in the artist." While the religion of Rome has come around to accepting the Renaissance, the German Protestant "principle in art" maintained a separation from the "supreme tradition of beauty." Winckelmann dismissed the aesthetics of his religious culture, merging the "moral instinct, like the religious," with the "artistic." And has shown us that the "aim of our culture," indeed all cultures, should be to "attain not only as intense [maintaining ecstasy] but as complete a life as possible," to "cultivate many types of perfection."[103] Marius will also discover physical beauty as a thing "morally salutary," and through the story of Cupid and Psyche will envision a "perfect imaginative love, centered upon a type of beauty entirely flawless and clean. . . . The human body in its beauty, as the highest potency of all the beauty of material objects, seemed to him just then to be matter no longer, but, having taken celestial fire, to assert itself as indeed the true, though visible, soul or spirit in things." And he will see Flavian as one with that former "band of 'devoted youth,'" worshippers of the Greek gods, "bearing the sacred flame."[104]

In an attempt to locate the intersecting points between Classical male sexuality and aesthetics, Pater appears to be formulating some distinction, not always lucid, between the "wholeness of nature" and the "spiritual sickness" of male homosexuality. If the desire is, to use Eve Sedgwick's term, "homosocial"––male bonding or men loving men for personal, social, and educational development—then the transaction advances the wholeness of nature, which permits someone like Hopkins to enter, says Richard Dellamora, "into a range of 'safe,' male homosocial relations."[105] If, however, the relationship is exploitive, reductive, and guilt–ridden, then the drive assumes spiritual sickness. The Classical culture out of which Pater was exploring male attraction to other males was a culture in which male homosexuality was important to the social and economic aspects of life. Plato's *Symposium*, along with any number of other texts, according to David Halperin, "vouches for the existence of homosexuality as an ancient (if not a universal) category of experience."[106] And if K.J. Dover is right in his seminal study on *Greek Homosexuality*—and the abundant evidence he cites from Greek literature, art (especially vase–painting), and sculpture support him—then Greek culture considered licit male homosexuality without finding that such "alternation or coexistence created peculiar problems for the individual or for society."[107] In an essay on Pater and nineteenth–century anthropological Romanticism, Robert Crawford finds that both Pater and Hopkins employing similar homoerotic codes:

> In Pater's pupil, Hopkins, for example, the great imaginative cluster at the heart of his work centers around the Greek term *poikilos*, which is used to refer to homosexual love in Plato's *Symposium* (a text familiar to undergraduates), and which has a range of meanings including "pied," "dappled," "flashing," "intricate," "ambiguous." So the poet of "Pied Beauty" is able to interweave Christian and homoerotic experience, just as his teacher, Pater, before talking of Dionysus's

"mystic rod" (which he sees representing "all wreathing flowery things whatever, with or without fruit"), is drawn to the Euripidean detail of the god's "white feet, somewhat womanly, and the fawn-skin, with its rich spots."[108]

Despite how credible Crawford's reading might be, I am more prone to agree with Linda Dowling that the evidence, biographical or otherwise, is just not there to unequivocally substantiate any firm claim of male homosexuality in the writings of Pater and Hopkins.[109] However, given their full participation, educationally and professionally, in the patriarchal aspects of their culture,[110] neither Pater nor Hopkins could be exempt from the assertion of (at least) male homosocial desire and relations and an accompanying aesthetic that reflects those relations.

Both Pater and Hopkins affirmed the significance of something spiritual in male beauty. They both understood, in the words of Dover, "the response of a male to the beauty of another male . . . as the starting–point of a co–operative philosophical effort to understand ideal beauty."[111] But while Pater is less reserved in what Richard Dellamora calls his "cultural critique based in sexual desire directed toward other men,"[112] however much he may have "delighted to hide in his obsessive refinements traces of pagan erotic energy,"[113] Hopkins's own sexual–aesthetic code remains more disguised. His cautious attitude to male homosocial desire is indicative of the way in which he displaces the poet's attraction to male bathers to a projected other, the "listless stranger," in "Epithalamion." Hopkins, however, does employ this sexual–aesthetic discourse in his handling of male portraits. One example of it is his use of the beauty of young English male slaves as the source of their attraction to Pope Gregory, who was moved to their spiritual plight. However, his most profound execution of the code appears in the poem "Epithalamion." Hard pressed to find a suitable wedding–gift for his brother Everard and his wife Amy, married one month earlier, and at the time of the poem's composition "in ecstacy" in Paris, Hopkins sat down while supervising an examination at University College, Dublin, and composed this gift. In a supposed contrived ("make believe") experience, the poet beckons a hearer to imagine that both of them are "leaf–whelmed some-where with the hood / Of some branchy bunchy bushybowered wood" espying on a group of city boys frolicking in a "Marbled river." From their secluded spot, their own bower, the poet and his companion observe an aimless stranger who, drawn to the homosocial activity of the "bevy" boys, also sets about to spy on them. With "bellbright bodies huddling out," they hurl off the cliff and plunge into the "heavenfallen freshness" of the "waterworld."[114] Like Lancelot's bright armor flashing into the Lady of Shalott's crystal mirror, the "garland of their gambol flashes" in the breast of the hidden stranger who soon changes location for a more generous "feasts" of his eyes. The stranger's immersion in the scene climaxes when he undresses and joins the swimming party, though remaining at some distance from the boys. His "apartness," Richard Dellamora finds, "suggests that the immanent subject may be Hopkins himself as a male sexually attracted to other males, but one who chose to immure himself within a male homosocial institution."[115] A clear projection of the poet's uninhibited self, the stranger is allowed to participate, however detached, in an activity the poet finds appealing. No longer "listless," the stranger is, when the poet and hearer regretfully leave him, "froliclavish."

With a sort of volta in "Enough," the poet turns from "this only gambolling and echoing–of–earth note" to engage the otherworldly occasion for the poem, the "sacred matter." But his tea–tabling, his desire to make us believe that the first part of the poem (the longer of the two) is "only gambolling," is not at all successful. The syntactic relationship that the word "gambolling" shares weds the boys' activity to the poet's guarded immersion in their play. Like the volta that signals a shift in "Heraclitean Fire," the volta here conveys not a rejection but an acceptance of the earlier transaction, and in fact the earlier scene is meant to illustrate the latter. The "delightful dean," the "bushybowered wood," where the boys' frolicsome play occurs is made analogous to a marriage, "Wedlock," and the water in which they plunge to the seminal fluids of "Spousal love." Both are tributes to the poet's brother Everard, "Sparkled first in Amy's eyes." Hardly an unfinished fragment as was for years alleged, the poem ends by returning to the sylvan scene of the opening, forming a ring–like shape. The closing line "Ranked round the bower" creates a circle comprised of family members and friends that in turn encloses, forms a "bower" for, the wedded couple. Similar to the kinds of metamorphosis that occurs in "The Starlight Night," here parents, siblings, and friends of the bridal party are transformed into "fairy trees, wildflowers, woodferns" around the "bower," now both the "bushybowered wood" of the bathers and the boudoir of the newly–married couple. Hopkins's "Enough" is not a rejection of homosocial for heterosocial love. The poem does not privilege the union of Everard and Amy over that of the bathers. Rather, what we are presented are two equally licit sexual desires, separate, analogous, and equal. In fact, the word "bevy," while it could denote a company of any kind, is, according to the *OED*, more commonly used to characterize a company of ladies. Both accounts are distinct, though not bifurcated, forms of "Wedlock" and "Spousal love." In a related way, Hopkins, in the autobiographical poem "At the Wedding March," represents his Jesuit vow, his own lacing with fire of stress, as a marital wedlock to Christ, a turning in tears to Christ "Who to wedlock, his wonder wedlock, / Deals triumph and immortal years."[116]

Both epithalamions, expressing Paterian notions of the wholeness of male sexuality, clearly indicate ways in which Hellenic art aspires to a reconciliation between the ascetic and aesthetic, between the Christian and the pagan; most crucially, it is a reconciliation in which man, rather than being divided, is "at unity with himself, with his physical nature, with the outward world."[117] When it comes to morality in literature, however, Pater reverses himself, valuing matter over form and subverting, as he does at the close of his essay on "Style," the formalist argument (estimating the "essential beauty in all good literary style," privileging prose style as conducive to the "chaotic variety and complexity" of the modern world, and considering structure "all–important") he had been waging throughout the essay. He concludes the essay on "Style" by differentiating between good art and great, distinctions along the same lines as the ones Thomas De Quincey made in 1848 between the "literature of knowledge" and the "literature of power." Ultimately, says Pater, the differentiating characteristic of great art from good art, at least in literature, is not form but matter. Thus Thackeray's *Henry Esmond*, because of "the greater dignity of its interests," is, in Pater's estimation, a better novel than *Vanity Fair*. For "It is on the quality of the matter it informs or controls, its compass, its variety, its alliance to great ends, or the depth of the note or revolt, or the largeness of hope in it, that the greatness of literary art depends." Additionally, "if it be devoted further to the increase of men's happiness, to the redemption of the oppressed, or the enlargement of our sympathies with each other, or to such presentment of new or old truth about ourselves and our relation to the world as may ennoble and fortify us in our sojourn here, or immediately, as with Dante, to the glory of God, it will be great art." Meeting these criteria, the work of art will have something of the "soul of humanity" in it and will find its "logical, its architectural place, in the great structure of human life."[118]

Pater's argument for morality and beauty finds support not only in Wordsworth and Arnold but also in George Eliot, who, in fact, might have read Pater's "Winckelmann." In *Middlemarch*, Will Ladislaw's German friend and artist, Adolf Naumann, comparing Dorothea to an Ariadne (Cleopatra) figure, recognizes in the comparison a "fine bit of antithesis." The Ariadne, represents "antique beauty, not corpse–like," but "arrested in the complete contentment of its sensuous perfection." Dorothea, however, represents "beauty in its breathing life, with the consciousness of Christian centuries in its bosom." But in fact Naumann, upon closer scrutiny of this "most perfect young Madonna," so longer sees an antithesis. Instead, Dorothea, to him, now comprises both the pagan and Christian. Now, more correctly, and from the point of view of Eliot's characterization, the artist Naumann sees Dorothea as "antique form animated by Christian sentiment—a sort of Christian Antigone—sensuous force controlled by spiritual passion." An arch–reformer who admits knowing little about the formal aspects of art, Dorothea aspires to "make life beautiful" for everyone; consequently, she is pained when she witnesses "all this immense expense of art, that seems somehow to lie outside life and make it no better for the world." She believes that art should somehow touch the lives of all people; thus her enjoyment of anything is ruined when she is made to think that "most people are shut out from it." Later when cross–examined about the nature of his religion, Will, representing, as did Dorothea, Eliot's own view, remarks: "To love what is good and beautiful."[119] The views of art expressed in Eliot's fiction are more clearly articulated in an October 1841 letter Eliot wrote, a letter predating both Arnold's and Pater's views on art and perfection:

> Much is said about the love of the beautiful, and the idea of perfection
> as a characteristic of the refined mind, and as being the spring of all
> high attainment in the triple sisterhood, painting, poetry, and music.
> But there is a more important application of the terms, a moral one,
> which I trust we shall ever have before our mind's eye—the love of the
> beauty of holiness, and a continual yearning after a conformity to it, an
> habitual contemplation or Moral Perfection, and a dissatisfaction with
> all that falls short of that standard.[120]

The final aspect of Pater's aesthetic theory relevant to Hopkins's is the idea of form and its relationship to the arts, especially music. To Hopkins, form is inscape, the "very soul of art," he calls it;[121] and as inscape, form, not easily detected and forever being perceived anew ("The sun on falling waters writes the text"), must be caught afresh each time, as in the case of the windhover. While flaunting its natural form, the bird is at the same time engaged in a desperate struggle to preserve that form, to rebuff all attempts against the referentialness with which the poet's perceiving mind is all too willing to assign it. In not entirely dissimilar ways, Pater believes that art must resist the hardness of form against which it is forever working, a part of his aesthetic theory again consistent with his multitudinous self–portraits and with his emphasis on perspectivism and flux. "Discourse and action," says Pater, "show man as he is, more directly" than rigid form, the "play of muscles and the moulding of the flesh," which is why poetry achieves the beauty of living form that sculpture, for example, does not. Thus, in the best of Greek sculptures, "forms are in motion;

but it is a motion ever kept in reserve."[122] Good art, like Michelangelo's
sculptures, avoids "heavy realism, that tendency to harden into caricature" what
is being represented. For great art "suggests rather than realises actual form";
great art etherealizes pure form, "relieving its stiff realism, and communicating
to it breath, pulsation, the effect of life." The pursuit of form, should, Pater
believes, be the goal of all art, even an end in itself, and in one place, quoting
Flaubert, claims that "There are no beautiful thoughts . . . without beautiful
forms."[123] Understandably, Pater, like the Romantics before him, considers
lyrical poetry the supreme poetic type. In it form is indistinct from matter mainly
because of a "certain suppression or vagueness of mere subject"; meaning,
therefore, comes in ways not "distinctly traceable by the understanding," and the
most meaningful comes across as though it were to "pass for a moment into an
actual strain of music." Form and matter are, thus, inextricably bound in what
Pater called an "electric affinity. " In this way art, because it can so "rearrange,"
even re–represent, "the details of modern life," enables us to deal with "the
conditions of modern life."[124]

While the pleasure of poetry derives from the success of combining form
and matter, it is music, Pater believes, that most thoroughly and consistently
accomplishes this goal. Pater's music is a metaphor for life, "a sort of listening,"
whether to music, water, or time. Our best moments are our "moments of play,"
for it is to them we apply ourselves and it is in them we are most relaxed,
affording our "happier powers" "free passage." Thus life evolves into play and
play into music. Pater finds that all arts tend to the condition of some other art:
music, and even architecture, can be seen approaching "to figure, to pictorial
definition"; sculpture "aspires out of the hard limitation of pure form towards
colour," poetry finds "guidance from the other arts," and all the arts in common
aspire "towards the principle of music; music being the typical, or ideally
consummate art." For while the other arts—poetry a slight exception—separate
matter from form, only in music can be found such "interpenetration of the
matter or subject of a work of art with the form," such a perfect wedding of matter
and form, fully realized; in music "the material or subject no longer strikes the
intellect alone; nor the form, the eye or the ear only. . . . It is the art of music which
most completely realises this artistic ideal, this perfect identification of matter
and form." In music's best moments, "the end is not distinct from the means,
the form from the matter, the subject from the expression; they inhere in and
completely saturate each other; and to it, therefore, to the condition of its perfect
moments, all the arts may be supposed constantly to tend and aspire." In music
rather than in poetry one locates the "true type or measure of perfected art," and
while all art has its own "incommunicable element, its untranslatable order of

impression," its special way of achieving "imaginative reason," still all art can be seen "continually struggling after the law or principle of music"; and one of the functions of aesthetic criticism is to determine the degree to which the arts approach "musical law."[125]

Before turning to Hopkins's conception of poetry and where it either corroborates or rejects Paterian aesthetics, I wish first to examine the more meaningful aesthetic discourse in the undergraduate essays thought to be supervised by Pater. It is not known how many Greats essays Hopkins wrote for Pater. The cataloging of those essays at Campion Hall seems to suggest six: "The Origin of Our Moral Ideas"; "Plato's View of the Connection of Art and Education"; "The Pagan and Christian Virtues"; "The Relations of Plato's Dialectics to Modern Logic and Metaphysics"; "Shew Cases in which Acts of Apprehension Apparently Simple are Largely Influenced by the Imagination"; and "The History and Mutual Connection in Ancient Ethics of the Following Questions—Can Virtue be Taught? Are Virtue and Vice Severally Voluntary and Involuntary?" This last essay and the one on Plato's dialectics were initialled by Robert Scott, Master of Balliol (1854–70) and famous co–author of the Greek Lexicon. It matters little who actually supervised the essays. The fact remains is that to Hopkins, as Carl Schmidt rightly claims, "the function of 'mortal beauty' is that it *can* lead to virtue and truth and 'keeps warm / Men's wits to the things that are,'" and that the essays foreshadow Hopkins's "later preoccupation with 'God's better beauty, grace.'"[126] Of Hopkins's thirty–eight extant Greats essays, as Carl Schmidt points out, twenty–eight are philosophical, proving that Greats "was overwhelmingly a school of philosophy."[127] These philosophical exercises, although written when Hopkins was an undergraduate to fulfill requirements for Greats, chart the direction Hopkins's approach to beauty, and with it truth and morality, will assume.

Hopkins's most recognized essay for Pater is "The Origin of Our Moral Ideas," a title Lockean and Darwinian in intention: moral ideas have an origin and that origin is discoverable. The essay sketches three approaches in determining that origin: innate ideas (of Plato and Descartes), utilitarianism (of Bentham and Mill), and the historical theory (of, possibly, Comte and Darwin), the latter, the historical theory, stating that "an idea of morality or of good is evolved and receives localisation and recognition in the process of time." Hopkins only gestures to the historical or evolutionary theory, attending more to the first two, innate ideas and utilitarianism. He takes the side of innate ideas, which asserts that human beings have a moral sense that is the source of moral ideas. The essay appears to have been informed in a number of areas by eighteenth– and nineteenth–century philosophical treatises on the search for the source of beauty

and morality, and the equating of the two. Hopkins's three theories seem related
to Henry Sidgwick's three systems of classification: Intuitionism, Utilitarianism, and Egoism.[128] Hopkins probably did not read the Scotsman Francis
Hutcheson's widely acclaimed *Inquiry into the Original of Our Ideas of Beauty
and Virtue* (1725), though he was familiar with Hutcheson's disciple, David
Hume.[129]

   Hopkins's argument for the origin of our moral ideas approximates
Hutcheson's, though without the notion that the moral sense is not the same as
reason but, rather, result from some sensible qualities within us: we respond to
objects in a feeling way, either from pleasure or from pain, and the things that
best please us possess regular form that match an idea present in our minds. In
essence, Hutcheson argues that human nature was not left unaided in determining matters of virtue and conduct. Was Hopkins, one has also to ask, aware of
Richard Price's important eighteenth–century treatise on ethics, *Review of the
Principal Questions in Morals* (1758)? While not denying that feelings and
emotions have some role in the morally beautiful, Price, like Sidgwick, opposed
both Hutchesonian and Lockean epistemology, maintaining that right actions
have something innately to do with cognition; that we can somehow intuit truth;
that right and wrong are based on some innate understanding we have of certain
objects; and that moral feelings in fact assist reason and are not substitutes for
it. This is probably what Hopkins alludes to when he refers to innate ideas as a
source of moral ideas, that "an objectively good idea is logical" and that the
morally right seems to follow "a correct logical form." This view differs from
a utilitarian approach to right moral action, for "the happiness of the greatest
number fulfils an ideal in the mind," pleasing the subject, and is not
consequentialist, whereby good and bad, right and wrong are determined by the
results achieved.

   In this brief essay for Pater, then, Hopkins seeks to explore the relationship
of the beautiful and the good. The more educated one becomes, the clearer
beauty is perceived but the less it is appreciated. In other words, in acquiring the
language of beauty we lose the intuition, a philosophical dilemma that keeps
distant, for example, Margaret's "fresh thoughts" with "sights colder" ("Spring
and Fall"). Education provides the discourse ("you *will* weep and know why"),
the ways of talking about beauty ("apprehension of beauty comes of education"), but it also causes one to forfeit intuition ("the innocent eye ... free from
fallacies implying some education"). Pater makes a related comment in "The
Child in the House": "earlier, in some degree, we see inwardly," and the sensible
things that fall around the child lie about unnoticed; later, however, these things
become "the texture of his mind," and "indelibly, as we afterwards discover,

they affect us; with what capricious attractions and associations they figure themselves on the white paper [of the mind], the smooth wax, of our ingenuous soul."[130] What both Hopkins and Pater share is that Wordsworthian idea of innocence: the child comes not in total nakedness of ideas but in trailing clouds of glory. To all three—Wordworth, Pater, and Hopkins—memory becomes a storehouse of experience. Beauty, then, resides in the ways in which the parts of a sensuous object relate each to the other. That relationship is temporal, for the arts nearest to morality are the ones whose effect relates to time as opposed to space, since "action lies in time." Therefore, the most excellent moral action is the most latent. Is the source of morality located, then, in the relationship between acts or in the parts of the action? "Is it," Hopkins asks, " a sequence of action?" Is there, then, an objective and a subjective morality? And does morality, like justice, have antecedent conditions, hence sequence? And what type of sequences does morality have, and are they the same as those of beauty?

Sensuous apprehension of beauty comes arbitrarily by way of proportion in intervals. The question put to morality is whether, like beauty, it is arbitrary or whether is a matter of logic. Hopkins concludes that an objectively good deed is logical. But, ironically, the exercise of logic in morals creates dichotomous positions, and in the dichotomy (of virtue and vice creating stress on the mind) resides the essence of right and wrong. Does virtue, then, have an exact logical form? If so, what are its universals since its particulars at times do not impinge on logic? And are virtue and vice similar? The remainder of the essay probes the utilitarian approach to the good: what is advantageous to the greatest number. But this formula, says Hopkins, requires "much exception," a point that Pater in reading the essay emphasized, for it explains not morality but only the objective form of morality—the ends—and not the antecedent conditions. What is required, then, is not only a good deed (the object benefiting) but also a knowledge of antecedent conditions, the sponsor benefiting as well from the deed. The purest of morality is when both the subject and the object derive joint (though, I suspect, not necessarily equal) pleasure.

Hopkins concludes that utilitarianism fails to account for right moral actions because it neglects the complex conditions or hidden assumptions behind which ends are reached. The only possible explanation—and at that an appropriate beginning point—is to consider that what is good for the greatest number satisfies some mental ideal, that is, innate ideas. This ideal strives to achieve unity, a principal pertinent to art as to morality. And art that tends after this unity, this ideal, "will satisfy the historical phenomena of morality."[131] Beauty, then, requires unity. The "collective effect" of each aspect of art, Hopkins remarks in another essay, "On the Origin of Beauty," "is due to the effect of each part on the rest," and the "addition or loss of any act or stanza" of a play or poem "will not be the addition of loss of the intrinsic goodness of that act or stanza alone, but a change on the whole also." Unity affects both the spirit and the structure of all art.[132] Not only are unity and pattern pursued in art, but so too are such concepts as difference, variety, and contrast. Thus we strive after rhyme and not mere echo, harmony and not mere unison. The dialectic, perfect instress, in which these concepts operate holds together perfectly in "Pied Beauty" and falls apart woefully in "Spelt from Sibyl's Leaves." The desire for unity, Hopkins maintained, is antecedent to the desire for difference; and while unity and difference can be realized in art, in moral action the two cannot be perfectly realized, harmonized. We desire unity because it allows us to apprehend who we really are, a self whose being and thoughts are fractured and dissipated by vice.

A second undergraduate essay, "On the Signs of Health and Decay in the Arts," also initialled by Robert Scott, again spells out essential parts of Hopkins's aesthetic theory. Avowing a Platonic aesthetic dictum, coming by way of Keats and modified drastically by Pater, Hopkins finds that the proper objects and ends of art are truth and beauty. But rather than finding them coeval, as did Keats, Hopkins privileges beauty over truth.[133] Truth in art is determined on the basis of comparison, parallelism, contrast, antithesis, and, especially, the degree of the mimetic representation of reality discoverable not through the senses but from intellectual apprehension: the more precise the parallel the greater the pleasure derived. And "As soon as composition becomes formal and studied, that is as soon as it enters the bounds of Art, it is curious to see how it falls into parallelisms." But this type of beauty is only extrinsic, having nothing whatever to do with the intrinsic or formal aspects of beauty. "Truth," writes Hopkins, "is not absolutely necessary for Art; the pursuit of deliberate Beauty alone is enough to constitute and employ an art." Deliberate beauty—relations in art—is determined by proportion. Proportion has a certain scientific ground or character to it and applies more to music and architecture than it does to painting and poetry; yet, "some scientific basis of aesthetic criticism is absolutely needed; criticism cannot advance far without it; and the beginning of any science of aesthetics must stand the analysis of the nature of Beauty."[134]

However, proportions and unity can be applied to poetry. Commenting on the composition and success of sonnets, Hopkins remarks that "in form of any work of art the intrinsic measurements, the proportion, that is, of the parts to one another and to the whole, are no doubt the principal point"; yet "the extrinsic measurements, the absolute quantity or size" has value. And if the form of the Italian sonnet is successful, that success seems tied to the perfection of its "proportion, inward and outward." Hopkins would again talk about unity in the context of Greek plays. When unity of action, unity of place, and unity of time are observed, the plot, as in *Agamemnon*, assumes simplicity; when ignored, as in the *Eumenides*, the plot becomes complicated.[135]

To know what is healthy and what is decadent in art, then, we must first know "what Art ought to be doing and pursuing"; we must, that is, have a clearly defined aesthetic. Realism pursues truth in art, idealism beauty, and proportion is "the source or the seat of Beauty." Proportion can have either the attribute of interval or continuance, concepts in the Darwin chapter we saw connected to the diatonic or chromatic, special creation or evolution, fixity or fluidity. Interval is marked by abrupt, parallelistic, and quantitative beauty, continuance by gradualistic, continuous, chromatic, and qualitative beauty. The codifying or determining feature of beauty is parallelistic; when beauty cannot be so distinguished it is chromatic. Art combines both kinds of beauty, but "some arts have more of the one, some of the other." All art comprises continuous or noncontinuous lines or both; notes either follow one another or pass from one note to the other; things are either abrupt or transitional. And the type of beauty, whether diatonic or chromatic, is linked to the aesthetic temper of the age and of the artist.

Hopkins applied these distinctions to architecture, finding in Greek architecture a diatonic or intervallary kind of beauty and in Teutonic a chromatic or qualitative kind. To separate the elements of truth and beauty in art is to destroy the balance and with it the success of art; a legitimate attempt at aesthetics includes a hierarchical ordering of the two—truth and beauty. It would seem, Hopkins speculates, that in the early stages of art the deliberate pursuit of beauty would have had some connection to the faithful rendering of the object represented; hence the pursuit of truth would be tantamount to the pursuit of beauty. Much of early art shows a compromise, one between faithfulness to conventional expectations, which makes for much neglect of truth, and "a little–indulged realism" to faithfully represent things in ways they are perceived, of art yielding "its own language" and "appealing to a critical body of its own state of civilization to accept and allow its conventionalities." There is little regard here either for tradition or for the individual talent until we come to early Greek and medieval art, where we find "completer instances of the coexistence of realism with broad conventionalism." But when artists yield too much to conventionalism, becoming mere "imitators of manner not of spirit," details are "subordinated, neglected, falsified," and art "degenerates into mere touch, trick and mannerism." This distinction Hopkins would again make in his attempt to group poets under the categories inspirational, Parnassian, and Delphic. It is apparent, Hopkins concludes, that early art succumbs to conventionalism by its fidelity to "the chief, the characteristic points of a thing, the prominent details"; thus it becomes "too stiff, too much abbreviated," and loses its essential realism when it disregards carefully wrought treatment.[136]

Late art is marked from early art in its desire for perfection, as is the case, says Hopkins, with the Renaissance. In that art, "Perfection presented itself with irresistible attraction to men's minds," a desire found in the Greeks rather than in the artists of the Renaissance who turned not to their own time and material for models of perfection but rather to the Greeks. Art presents things to us that in their best representation is idealism, in their worst conventionalism. And to judge the health of the best art of any age, one must analyze the nature of its idealism, that is, its claim on beauty. And a "sure sign of decay and weakness" in art is, according to Hopkins, "the love of the picturesque, the suggestive, when developed to the exclusion of the purely beautiful."[137]

In his attitude toward the Greeks, Hopkins reveals a mixture of attraction and repulsion, a tension, according to Richard Jenkyns, characteristic of the Victorians: "A sense of the close alliance between Christianity and the study of the classics, strangely but eloquently blended with an awareness of tension between them, runs right through the nineteenth century."[138] Hopkins was, for instance, mindful of the Greeks when he situated poetry under the rubrics Parnassian and Delphic and of the concept of the body politic (combining here Plato's and Saint Paul's idea of the commonwealth) in his organization of the poem "Tom's Garland." Additionally, the rhythm of "The Leaden Echo and the Golden Echo" sought to imitate that of the "Greek tragic choruses or of Pindar: which is pure sprung rhythm."[139] In *The Wreck*, as Jenkyns points out, one locates the familiar Pindaric address to a muse or deity and the partnership of man, god, and the poet in the heroic narratives. Like Pindar's poems, *The Wreck* is "a victory ode, a celebration of the human spirit triumphant," and this poem, however original, shows that "Pindar pointed the way for [Hopkins] to the style that he was to make distinctively his own."[140]

Hopkins, it must be recalled, received a Classical education, and Greats consisted of five terms of ancient literature. Of the few Victorians who, according to Jenkyns, took Greek seriously,[141] Hopkins remains a striking exception. He was one of the rare Victorians to have learned both koine (see, for example, his notes from Liddon's Sunday evening lectures) and classical Greek, writing two poems, "Tell me where is Fancy bred" and "Orpheus and his lute made trees," in classical Greek, the organization and cadences of which are Pindaric. Later, with Jowett's high recommendation, he went on to Dublin to become professor of classics at Newman's University College. During his winter world in Dublin, his supposedly uninspirational period, he was pursuing a book on Dorian measure, a "quasi–philosophical paper on the Greek Negatives, and had, with Bridges's prompting, restored nearly all of the text and sense of the choral odes of Aeschylus's *Choephori*, which he began at Stonyhurst in 1882, desiring even to have parts of the restoration published. He applauded Aeschylus's "noble genius," his oxymoronic "manly tenderness," and his "earnestness of spirit," qualities clearly Victorian.[142] Additionally, he felt that English poetry, though superior to the Greeks in "poetical insight and inspiration," fell short of theirs in rhetoric, the "common and teachable element in literature."[143] Hopkins also attempted to employ the metrical structure of Greek choruses in a poem now lost, wrote the music for part of the chorus from *Prometheus Bound*, and distilled a great measure of Greek philosophical thought in the poem "Heraclitean Fire." He felt too that while Milton was the stylist extraordinaire ("the central man of the world for style"), surpassing all ancients and moderns, he fell short of the Greeks.[144]

While Greek style and rhythm, then, were acceptable to Hopkins ("I pay most attention to . . . the art of the choric parts . . . including of course the lyric parts of dramatic poets"[145]), not so was Greek religion. Characteristic of the Victorians, "or of its more enquiring members," was the feeling, if not the belief, that "between faith in Christianity and the love of Greece there must be a tension" and the need to justify "the study of a pagan culture by a Christian people."[146] Revolted, then, by the fact that in his play *Ulysses* Bridges included "a goddess among the characters," Hopkins called their gods a "totally unworkable material" that "chill and kill every living work of art they are brought into," a stark contrast to Pater's Greek gods walking arm in arm with us. There are, according to Hopkins, three acceptable departures from truth in a play: the first, in a historical play, when, for accuracy, changes and conventions must be observed; the second, a plot of fiction whereby elements of it did not actually occur but could have; and third, allegory, when a thing without being and action is employed to represent or mask something that is or does.

Hopkins felt that *Ulysses* belonged to the second category, the fictional, not the third, and as such should not possess elements of the allegorical. Ulysses, and not the gods, participates in the human, and so should be made "to act; and in earnest," unlike the Greek gods that are impliable and frigid.[147] "I cannot take heathen gods in earnest," Hopkins told Patmore, "and want of earnest I take to be the deepest fault a work of art can have."[148] However intolerant of the Greek pantheon, Hopkins's was not a total disregard of the Greek system. The criticism must be understood mostly as a distinction Hopkins was attempting to establish between art and life. For a year later he told Canon Dixon that there is a beauty and a resilience to Greek mythology. "But mythology is something else besides fairytale: it is religion, the historical part of religion,"[149] a position along the same lines of what Pater stated in *The Renaissance*: "Always, the fixed element is the religious observance; the fluid, unfixed element is the myth, the religious conception."[150] As history, Greek mythology is "untrue." Coming more specifically to his complaint, Hopkins cites the "heathenism" of the Greeks as most repugnant, of "man setting up the work of his hands," and especially "of that hand within the mind of the imagination, for God almighty who made heaven and earth."[151] It is acceptable, Hopkins felt, for the artist to establish perfect beings like the gods. But the Greek gods, as represented, are "rakes, and unnatural rakes," whose "wickedness" is allowed, in Homer, for instance, to go unchecked. However, mythology as mythology—not as the historical part of religion—remains "susceptible of fine treatment, allegorical treatment for instance, and so treated gives rise to the most beautiful results." But "heathen gods," informing Dixon of that earlier position he assumed when Bridges brought in Athene in the prologue of *Ulysses*, "cannot be taken seriously on our stage. . . . So I damped and damned and must have hurt Bridges."[152]

Hopkins felt the same oscillation between attraction and repulsion to the Greeks as did his mentor Newman. In an 1833 sonnet written at Messina, Newman asks:

> Why, wedded to the Lord, still yearns my heart
> Towards these scenes of ancient heathen fame?

Newman feels that there needs to be no guilt nor tear over the wayward adventures in Greek art, over "the mad deeds that set the world in flame." The tears in his eyes stem from "no fount impure," but, rather, from "sympathy with Adam's race / Which in each brother's history reads its own."[153] Concerned as he was with the argument from Antiquity, and consistent with his overall liberal posture, Newman saw the Christian and pagan hearts as one, united in "Adam's race," each reading its own history from the light of the other's. This was the same moderate stance Newman assumed thirty–one years later in the *Apologia*, discovering in "pagan literature, philosophy, and mythology, properly under-stood . . . a preparation for the Gospel," and going so far as to claim that "The Greek poets and sages were in a certain sense prophets."[154] Newman's aesthet-ics, like Pater's, was a more welcome reception of the challenges of modernity than was Hopkins's. Carolyn Williams tells us that Pater's aesthetic historicism "prefigures the bridge between science and mythopoeia that early–twentieth–century modernism was concerned to construct."[155] However tolerant of the

Greeks, Hopkins did not so warmly embrace them. And so central are the Greek gods to the Classical Ideal that his rejection of them is tantamount to (and Hopkins would deny this) a repudiation of the entire Classical system. Newman's "prophets" are a far cry from Hopkins's "rakes."

Hopkins's most comprehensive treatment of beauty appears in his 12 May 1865 essay "On the Origin of Beauty: A Platonic Dialogue." This discourse on aesthetics is arranged as a fictional account of a conversation between an unnamed professor of a newly founded chair of aesthetics at Oxford and two other participators, a student Handbury and a fresco painter Middleton, who enters the conversation surreptitiously. The question before them is whether ascertainable laws exist by which aesthetic taste can be judged. Hanbury believes there are no such laws of aesthetic criticism and no "logical grounds for one's belief." Contrarily, the professor believes there are, and pursues an aesthetic system altogether consistent with Hopkins's earlier position on innate ideas and on diatonicism. The professor argues that while symmetry and regularity (the Renaissance ideal) are important aspects of beauty, so too are rugged and bold irregularity (the Medieval ideal) and the preference for "variety over absolute uniformity." True beauty, then, is a "mixture of regularity and irregularity," as long as that regularity follows a certain law, for when things "differ by a law" they are "more beautiful than if they differ irregularly."[156]

The professor's insistence on a law that governs the behavior of things in nature and that culls out beauty is the same as Hopkins's emphasis on finding order or design in nature, which is what inscape in part designates: the belief that "All the world is full of inscape and chance left free to act falls into order as well as purpose." Thus, Hopkins puzzles over the behavior, or inscape, of the flag flower, when "each term you can distinguish is beautiful in itself," and if the "whole 'behaviour' were gathered up and so stalled it would have a beauty of all the higher degree." He finds a yellow flower like that from a potentialla, but whether it belongs to that plant he remains unsettled. The "great richness of the membering of the green in the elms" is conspicuous, but only art best captures its beauty, and then only after studying it. Finding beauty, Hopkins discovers, is "almost synonymous with finding order," and is understandably delighted when he finds "the law of the oak leaves."[157] That law or behavior present in nature is inscape, the "something mystical," for which Hopkins's professor of aesthetics cannot yet name.

Beauty, to return to the professor's aesthetic dialogue, is "a mixture of likeness and difference or agreement and disagreement or consistency and variety or symmetry and change," a balancing of the symmetrical with the asymmetrical, or the "contrast of two opposite things, symmetry and the violation of it," or the "contrast of regularity with variety." Throughout Hopkins's poetry and especially in *The Wreck*, "Pied Beauty," and "Spelt from Sibyl's Leaves," we discover the elements of contrast, balancing, parallelism, and antithesis, all characteristics of the diatonic.[158] For "not the excellence of any two things (or more) in themselves" makes beauty, but, rather, "those two things as viewed by the light of each other." The professor concludes that beauty is "a relation, and the apprehension of it a comparison. The sense of beauty in fact is a comparison."[159] Hence the poem "Pied Beauty" is built entirely on comparison, on likeness and unlikeness (antithesis), and on symmetry and asymmetry. The participants in the conversation argue, in different ways, for the importance of comparison (likeness), contrasts (unlikeness), and antithesis (the joint consideration of likeness and unlikeness). Rhythm, meter, and rhyme all reveal the same "likeness tempered with difference." Rhyme (in general "agreement of sound") illustrates not only the principle of agreement and disagreement jointly but also identifies the points at which "the principle of beauty is to be strongly marked, the intervals at which a combination of regularity with irregularity with disagreement" are most pronounced. Thus "All beauty may by a metaphor be called rhyme."[160] Here Hopkins returns, as did Pater, to music as the art to which all the other arts tend.

Hopkins resumes his discourse on diatonicism and chromaticism in another undergraduate essay, "The Probable Future of Metaphysics," applying the terms this time to the atomistic tendency of the nineteenth century. "Purely material psychology," Hopkins felt, "is the [conqueror] foretold and feared." But however formative an influence materialism exerted on the age, it remains still unprepared to explain thought and the mind. Hopkins's real fear is that with advances in science, metaphysics will be marginalized and psychology will replace metaphysics. In that case, science without metaphysics will remain atomistic, loose, even incomprehensible ("scopeless"), for metaphysics provides science with explanations for causes and developments. There will forever be, says Hopkins, a pull between idealism and materialism. And the way culture is progressing, the new metaphysics will be one of development that speaks not to the received tradition of right and wrong but to its own history and growth. Set against this philosophy of flux and chromaticism, and seeking to replace it, is Platonic diatonicism, adversary to the philosophical materialism of Epicurus. The new realism will call for a return to fixed and permanent forms, to a unity that can never be dismembered, and will encounter an "atomism of personality" bearing "some shape of the Platonic Ideas."[161]

Hopkins was drawn to Plato because of Plato's fixed forms ("the discovery of a few first principles from which systems might be properly drawn"), the given Idea, and the privileging of metaphysics over materialism. With Jowett as tutor, and preoccupied as he was, especially during 1864, with translating the works of Plato, Hopkins would have been bombarded with information on Plato. In "The Position of Plato to the Greek World," an essay written for T.H. Green, Hopkins looks to Plato as one who both represents and contradicts the times in which he lived. In language resembling Pater's, Hopkins talks of Plato as one who "stands to the general culture of his age," an age marked by "Intellectual-ism" that regarded "works of genius less for themselves than for the intellect implied in them" and that disregarded the "objective interest of things."[162] Other Greats essays of Hopkins also reveal the prominence of Plato. One, "Plato's view of the connection of art and education," argues that art has a causal relationship to the development of character. But Plato feared the dismembering effect art (plays, poetry, music) has on personality. Education, Plato felt, must "preserve unity in the distracting multiplicity of life." And art, if it is to be useful, must turn to its "order and law . . . expressed in the plainest possible way," and the presence of law, order, and unity must affect "every association of life like breathing a wholesome air." According to Hopkins, Plato "regards goodness as a unity of character and thinks every quickening of the sense of unity will act on morals."[163]

"The Pagan and Christian Virtues," another essay written for Pater, also invokes Plato and points again to the innate value in right moral action. Hopkins points out that Plato "only once includes piety among the cardinal virtues and Aristotle gave little notice to it." Thus good Greeks would not have been surprised to learn that an upright individual did not say his prayers every morning and evening. It is in that "new relation of the soul to God," says Hopkins, "that we trace all the peculiar forms of Xian morality." And disclosing an early attraction to Roman Catholicism, he points out: "For those we look naturally to Catholicism, the consistent acceptance of Christianity," and to the saints as the "great types or success of Xtianity. In them we see one clear distinction of pagan and Xian virtues." Christianity and paganism assign different values to "the subjective and objective sides of morality." From "will and deed or conscience and law or spirit and letter," Christianity has established a system whereby we can turn to the "ethics of the ancients and see the slow and winding or moral fr. mental excellences and the far greater prominence given to the fulfilment of the outward ideal of right conduct." To act rightly, says Hopkins, the "purpose and the carrying out must be right." However, pagan ethics undervalues right action and when "morals are vague, unfixed, or broken up the moral instinct, and not a well recognised rule, give its shape to action."[164]

Hopkins's criticism reflects the subjectivity, contemplation, indeterminacy, and fluidity that compose both Pater's and nineteenth–century aesthetics. Hopkins's ensuing comment—because of the emphasis on teleology and on staking out a firm conviction—clearly separates his religious ethics and aesthetics from Pater's: "Xtianity however has thrown the two sides of morality with clearness and strength to a distance fr. each other: on the one hand, the subjective side, it has refined motive, on the other it has raised the outer supports to devotion, the sacraments, prayer, ritual, fasting and other discipline, and taken the utmost pains to present them as existing independently of the wishes or emotion of the soul." Hopkins turns to the word *act* to underscore the varied significations given to intention by Christianity: "Acts of love, faith, or the like being the name used in bks. of devotion not for deed springing fr. these graces but formally made professions and protestations of love or faith."[165] The Christian faith is a thing acted out, demonstrated. The "just man justices," we might recall, "Acts in God's eye what in God's eye he is." An even greater determiner of Christian morality, says Hopkins, is "dogma," from which derives such concepts as "the Christian virtue of faith."[166]

Another undergraduate essay, "The Relations of Plato's Dialectic to Modern Logic and Metaphysics," opens with Plato's notion of "the one and the many," a general description that applies to "many individuals and many individuals being called or becoming some kind of unity." Hopkins ties this further to the particular and the universal in Plato, and finds the discourse relevant to nineteenth–century concerns with the *subjective* and the *objective*.[167] Hopkins's curiosity with the one and the many involves his search for the true identity of the self. In Hopkins's essay on "Parmenides," we locate the first reference to his coinages "inscape" and "instress" and their connection to Plato and the one and the many. According to Hopkins, Parmenides's notable claim that "Being is and Not–being is not," however "over–defining," means that "all things are upheld by instress and are meaningless without it. . . . His feeling for instress . . . and for inscape / is most striking and from this one can understand Plato's reverence for him as the great father of Realism." We might recall that in other essays, "The Probable Future of Metaphysics" especially, Hopkins associates Platonism to Realism, further connects them to diatonicism and the fixity of being, and presents them as the philosophical contrast to chromaticism or materialism, which in his time was represented by the atomism of Darwin and Pater. The word *esti* (*it is* or *there is*), says Hopkins, "may roughly be expressed by *things are* or *there is truth*." And "I have often felt when I have been in this mood and felt the depth of an instress or how fast the inscape holds a thing that nothing is so pregnant and straightforward to the truth as simple *yes* and *is*."

The *yes* in Hopkins always deals with a religious assent, to action as the completion of, or the at–oneness with, faith. Hopkins's *is* is the certainty, the definiteness, the *ecceitas*, the self, my *me*. In Parmenides, says Hopkins, the contrast is between "the one and the many," of two principles that "meet in the scape of everything—probably Being," of "particular oneness or Being, and Not–being, under its siding of the many. The two may be called two degrees of siding in the scale of Being. Foreshortening and equivalence will explain all possible difference. The inscape will be the proportion of the mixture."[168] On the scale of Being in the Parmenidean copula, Being in the world of phenomena deals with particular oneness and Not–being with the universal Many. Plato uses dialectic, to return to Hopkins's essay on Plato and modern metaphysics, to separate the "materials for the syllogism"—whether Being and Not–being, the particular and the universal, the subjective and objective—from the complexities of speech and other accidents and to make them metaphysical properties, to present these to the thought, to get, that is, at the idea. The siding, as far as beauty is concerned, is from the one to the many. For according to Plato, says Hopkins, philosophy springs from love: "fr. loving beauty in one the mind goes on to love it in more and in many, then to love beautiful action, then beautiful knowledge, lastly the knowledge of the beautiful itself."[169]

Because of the functional purpose of beauty to Hopkins—that beauty should be put to some service ("To what *serves* Mortal Beauty," my italics)—it is not at all surprising that he cites first the love of the one, presumably God or each other, then love of others, a love that in both cases prompts action. Love of beauty for its own sake is not, unexpectedly, the final act of love. Earlier in "The Pagan and Christian Virtues," Hopkins found in Plato's ideas a suitable precursor to Christian doctrine:

> In Xtianity the all–important relation is to God, the next—"and the second is like unto it" [here employing intertextually the language of the greatest commandment]—is to man, but here too one sees that the basis of relation is somewhat changed fr. that of Greece and as Aristotle says love each other fr. having the same relations to their parents so Xians are to love each other fr. all having the same God. . . . It is to this principle however, the new relation of the soul to God, that we trace all the peculiar forms of Xian morality.[170]

Love of others and love of beauty for its own sake are joint concerns in Pater's *Marius*. Commenting on this work, A.C. Benson finds that the real failure of the novel's premise is that rather than "emphasising the power of sympathy, the

Christian conception of Love, which differentiates Christianity from all other religious systems"—the very distinction Hopkins makes—"Marius is after all converted, or brought near to the threshold of the faith, more by the sensuous appeal, its liturgical solemnities; the element, that is to say, which Christianity has in common with all religions, and which is essentially human in character."[171] Marius was attracted to the "wonderful liturgical spirit of the church, her wholly unparalleled genius for worship." In other words, he was drawn to Roman Catholic "serenity and its detachment, not its vision of the corporateness of humanity and the supreme tie of perfect love."[172]

While in theory Hopkins espouses love as the attraction to Christianity, in practice, he as well as Newman were, like Marius, not immune to the sensuous appeal in Christianity, especially in Roman Catholic worship. Hearing of Gerard's conversion, his father, in a letter to Liddon, identified his growing love for high ritual. In his defense, Gerard denied that "aesthetic tastes have led me to my present state of mind."[173] Less reticent and a great deal more honest as to the aesthetic attraction to Roman Catholic rituals, Newman, in a series of sermons Hopkins knew, stated unequivocally:

> Catholic truths and rites are so beautiful . . . that they draw one to love and admire them with a natural love, as a prospect might draw them on. . . . Hence men of lively imagination profess this doctrine or that, or adopt this or that ceremony or usage, for their very beauty–sake, not asking themselves whether they are true, and having no real perception or mental hold on them. Thus too they will decorate their churches, stretch and strain their ritual, attempt candles, vestments, flowers, incense, and processions, not from faith, but from poetical feeling.

But while Catholic doctrines and worship, Newman believes, are aesthetically appealing, possessing "beauty, sublimity, and sanctity," that attraction must be met with a firm commitment.[174]

Another of Hopkins's Greats essays, "On the True Idea and Excellence of Sculpture," initialed by Robert Scott, addresses how aesthetic criteria should be determined. It argues that the "laws of criticism in aesthetics" cannot be applied equally to all the arts but must be applied singularly and independently to each particular art; these laws must derive from "the condition under which each art works: this alone will direct criticism to its point and ensure its justice." Thus one must be careful with generalizations, and factors that on first blush seem worthless might in fact prove useful to aesthetic judgment. Only by understanding the necessary conditions under which each art is produced does perfection become attainable. There have been some artists, however, who, failing to regard those conditions, have been able to "express in their art what cd. never be expressed in that art or in any art at all," and their failures have been met with greater acclaim than the success of others. Yet, Hopkins believed, these artists should not be emulated. Emphasizing the need for particular aesthetic criteria for particular forms of art, Hopkins urges a scientific approach, with each form of art possessing "its own definitions and postulates." This approach, says Hopkins, is best found in Lessing. However, Hopkins censures Lessing for excluding religious art (statues in ancient temples) because it did not, Lessing felt, "labour on its own account, but was a mere helpmate to religion." Because of this religious art espoused a teleology other than pure beauty.[175] Hopkins is here again attacking the privileging of art for art's sake and the demeaning of religious art (because it "serves") as inferior, Lessing's "mere helpmate."

In Hopkins's estimation, true art should and does serve some higher, nobler, even moral, cause. True art "keeps warm / Men's wits to the things that are; what good means." Contrary to Lessing, Hopkins maintains that "the need of worshippers and the nature of its difficult materials, is the best possible instance of Art made vigorous and efficient by being, not its own mistress, but the helpmate of religion."[176] In the now familiar analogy between beauty and truth, Hopkins finds that in architecture, bronze, not stone, for example, is the most suitable material for equestrian statuary because the metal "pleases the beholder with a better sense of reality [truth] and security in the free action." And he finds that working with stone is further complicated because the hardness of the material means that the "realism [truth] aimed at . . . shd. so be deeply studied and very complete; that the idealism [beauty] aimed at, that is the modification of nature or truth so as to attain to the beautiful." It is the statue, says Hopkins, that "sets the standards of the perfection of beauty in the human figure." And because "practically the capacities of an art are its *duties* : hence the study of anatomy for which marble offers so great a field has become so peculiarly the pursuit of sculpture" (my italics). Hopkins turns also to simplicity and unity in sculpture, finding the two natural to this art form, which—and here his assumption might encounter great disagreement—lacks passion and drama. He soon modifies his judgment, however, finding in sculpture the expression of "single, severally simple, passion." Used almost exclusively for religious and monumental purposes and revealing a penchant for unity and perfection from its simplicity, sculpture, Hopkins finds, is on the one hand almost immune from the factors that lead to the degeneracy of painting, poetry, and architecture, and, on the other hand, the art form least accommodating to aesthetic revivals: "it is the accessories which first feel and shew a change in aesthetic temper, and these are in sculpture very much less important than elsewhere."[177]

Hopkins's undergraduate essays, then, remain integral to his aesthetic discourse. They determined, however early and without significant variation, the direction his approach to beauty would take. One way or another, the essays are all preoccupied with beauty and its connection to form, unity, self, right moral action, and function, preferably a religious one. His Jesuit training and priestly vocation further shaped that aesthetic, but without effecting any radical change. Poems from "The Kind Betrothal" to "To What Serves Mortal Beauty" all deal with aesthetic form and the reallocating of the senses to allow for the true expression of beauty. Hopkins's obsession with beauty was admitted rather pointedly in a letter to Bridges on the death by drowning of Digby Dolben, Bridges's cousin: "You know there can very seldom have happened the loss of so much beauty (in body and mind and life) and of the promise of still more as there has been in his case." Hopkins's admission of attraction to physical beauty has sparked the charge that Hopkins had a homosexual attraction to Dolben and also, critics maintain, to Bridges himself, akin to the kind of feverish attraction Marius had to Flavian: "How often, afterwards, did evil things present themselves in malign association with the memory of that beautiful head, and with a kind of borrowed sanction and charm in its natural grace." Flavian's "perfection of form," voice, and glance "were like the breaking in of the solid world upon one, amid the flimsy fictions of a dream. A shadow, handling all things as shadows, had felt a sudden real and poignant heat in them."[178] Possessed by the same attraction to physical beauty and perfect form, Hopkins, in a related way, admitted frankly that "no one can admire beauty of the body more than I do, and it is of course a comfort to find beauty in a friend or a friend in beauty," here echoing jointly, it seems, Keats's and Tennyson's declaration of the joyousness of beauty and its friendship to man. "But this kind of beauty," Hopkins continued, "is dangerous. Then comes the beauty of the mind, such as genius, and this is greater than the beauty of the body and not to call dangerous. And more beautiful than the beauty of the mind is beauty of character, the 'handsome heart.'"[179] Sufficient to say here that in Hopkins's hierarchy, beauty of character, and under its rubric virtue, motive, and action, is the supreme act of beauty. Less esteemed are mental and physical beauty. Hopkins once told Baillie he wanted to be a painter, but gave it up "for the fact is that the higher and more attractive parts of the art put a strain upon the passions which I shd. think is unsafe to encounter."[180]

So concerned was Hopkins with theories of beauty that a vast number of his poems in one way or another address the subject. Some, like "Brothers" and

"Harry Ploughman," speak to the physical beauty of male sexuality we have come to associate with Pater. In the expression "what once I well / Witnessed," the poet recalls an experience of seeing a play, a "little scene," performed at Mount St. Mary's school in which two brothers were linked in a filial bond. Henry, the older boy, was so emotionally fettered to his young brother, John, that he became apprehensive over John's part in the play. Two plays, then, as Jeffrey Loomis points out, are occurring simultaneously, "John's onstage and Henry's ('byplay') in the audience."[181] The poet seems critical of Henry's play ("wrung all on love's rack"), his too sympathetic attachment to his brother ("lost in Jack"), disclosing his "heart's stress" "hung on the imp's success" (A similar filial attachment can be seen in Teryth and his daughter Winefred in "St. Winefred's Well"). Jack's over–acting, his "brass–bold" behavior, his hubris, also receives criticism. As Loomis again notes, Hopkins well knew that "art and beauty can be, for all their humanizing virtues, morally limited and dangerous." But, as Loomis is quick to remind us, "Hopkins is not here devoting himself to a degrading of art in itself." Rather, it shows his commitment during this period to "values of religious renunciation," when art, at that time, was "displaced from an ultimate position in his hierarchy of values." [182]

Poems like "The furl of fresh–leaved dogrose," "Duns Scotus's Oxford," "Binsey Poplars," and "Ribblesdale" commemorate nature's beauty and vulnerability without any noticeable sacramental import. In "The furl of fresh–leaved dogrose," the poet uses the beauty of nature to describe another "limber liquid youth," whose hair is likened to "a juice and jostling shock / Of bluebells sheaved in May" or like shorn "wind–long fleeces on the flock." On the edges of his temple the sunlight through his hair appears "like dewdrops, like dandled diamonds," images related to ones in "Binsey Poplars": "That dandled a sandalled / Shadow that swarm or sank." "Duns Scotus's Oxford" and "Binsey Poplars" are companion poems. The first, an Italian sonnet, recalls the medieval charm Oxford held during the time of Duns Scotus. Then, country and town were in perfect equipoise: "country and town did / Once encounter." Now, however, Oxford's native beauty is "grounded / Best in" and her modern growth is "graceless." "Binsey Poplars," a "little lyric," laments the wanton violation of tender nature. The poem memorializes the "beauty been" of the landscape of the Binsey area west of Oxford along the Isis where elegant aspens once lined the river and added to the charm of this otherwise unattractive landscape. Most lamentable to the poet is the potential ecological disaster and the personal displacement of one's place in the landscape of history. "Ribblesdale" makes an ecological plea recognizable in "God's Grandeur" and "Binsey Poplars." Man deals (gambles away) nature's "lovely dale down thus and thus bids reel / Thy river, and o'er gives all to rack or wrong." Committed to his own warped selfish–interest ("selfbent"), "To thriftless reave both our rich round world bare," man cares not if anyone "reck of world after"; so earth's "brows" bear "such care, care and dear concern."

"Harry Ploughman" celebrates immense strength and rugged anatomical beauty, void, it seems, of any homoerotic attraction. But superior to and less dangerous than physical beauty is the beauty of the soul, seen, for example, in "The Handsome Heart."[183] The younger of the two boys who answers the priest, "Father, what you buy me [presumably prayers] suits me best," the same type of spiritual bartering Hopkins affirms in the sestet of "The Starlight Night": "Buy then! bid then!—What?—Prayer, patience, alms, vows." Such a mature choice of remuneration solicited by the lad makes the poet feel that he, the lad, had been catechized for ten years. He possesses, then, a right heart, a "Mannerly," one, the true estimation of beauty, and therefore "handsomer than handsome face," as an earlier version of the poem reads. That "little hero of the Handsome Heart" would later follow the priestly vocation, Hopkins boasted to Bridges, and is "bent on being a Jesuit."[184]

In several poems, Hopkins argues the sacramental aspect of physical beauty. "The Bugler's First Communion" is a portrait of "Breathing loom of a chastity in mansex fine." Here in Hopkins is an unsinged celebration of the innocence of male sexuality; the fineness of male sexuality and manly beauty are tethered, as they were in Pater, to the ascetic principle. And as Winckelmann's "fiery friendships" with limber, liquid youths sought to rival the Greek gods, so in Hopkins's "fresh youth fretted in a bloomfall" is the true realm of Christ: "there reigns." The soldier's youthful innocence, the poet–priest finds, "does my heart good, visiting at that bleak hill, / When limber liquid youth, that to all I teach / Yields tender as a pushed peach." Celebrated here are the soldier's innocence, beauty, and malleableness: "Nothing else is like it." The poet's prayer, which he hopes does not go "disregarded," is that the sacrament, once administered, "charms, arms," "bans off bad, / And locks love ever in a lad"; and "may he not rankle and roam / In backwheels." This wish is the same for Felix Randal, whom the priest "fettle[ed]" for the rough road ahead. Hopkins's celebration of physical beauty in "The Bugler's First Communion" is made entirely sacramental. And, in fact, his premonition that the "Hero" of the poem "may be killed in Afghanistan" indeed makes the young man's life a sacrament. One can argue a similar expense of self for another in Marius's sacrifice of himself that Cornelius might live: "So far, he had but taken upon himself, in the stead of Cornelius, a certain amount of personal risk; though he hardly supposed himself facing the danger of death. . . . [T]he hope that Cornelius had seemed to bear away upon him the strength, with a buoyancy which had caused Marius to feel, not so much that by a caprice of destiny, he had been left to die in his place."[185]

Not to be ignored is the fact that Hopkins's Bugler is a soldier whose life becomes expendable, not for Christ, but for nation, although in the poem, as in Hopkins's nationalism, both are wedded: "And do serve God to serve to / Just such slips of soldiery Christ's royal r[n?]ation." Church and State are also linked because chivalry, whether religious or monarchical, has always meant a great deal to Hopkins. Even works of art, to Hopkins, assume national significance. Hopkins so privileges the beauty of chivalry in the poem that he slights the disaster awaiting the Bugler and even the premonition granted the priest that the Bugler will not survive Afghanistan. Hopkins's sympathy in his handling of beauty returns in "Tom's Garland," a poem written on the plight of the unemployed. Now the poet holds England fully answerable to its economic subalterns, its "Undenizened" people beyond the reaches of "earth's glory, earth's ease." Later explaining to Dixon the social condition that occasioned "Tom's Garland," Hopkins noted:

> My Liverpool and Glasgow experience laid upon my mind a convic-
> tion, a truly crushing conviction, of the misery of town life to the poor
> and more than to the poor, of the misery of the poor in general, of the
> degradation even of our race, of the hollowness of this century's
> civilisation: it made even life a burden to me to have daily thrust upon
> me the things I saw.[186]

Here lies a significant difference between Hopkins and Pater. While for Pater, the onlooker, the aesthete, sheltered as he was from the social sordidness of nineteenth–century industrialism, social ugliness, as far as I can recall, was never a topic broached. In fact, Pater saw it unfit for artistic expression. In his review of Oscar Wilde's *The Picture of Dorian Gray*, Pater criticizes Wilde's "intrusion of real life and its sordid aspects—the low theatre, the pleasures and griefs, the faces of some very unrefined people."[187] However, to Hopkins, assigned frequently to the parishes of these social undenizens of the nation, beauty assumed an added moral and social dimension, forged in the kind of social conscience that called itself, half–apologetically, a "Communist."[188] Only that conscience—certainly not Pater's—could have fathered the truly beautiful lines:

And all is seared with trade; bleared, smeared, with toil;
And wears man's smudge and shares man's smell: the soil.

The beauty of sacrifice—indirectly Christ's—is the subject of "The Lantern out of Doors." The poet queries the identity of a lantern carrier and uses that anonymity to generalize about men he meets who, in spite of their "Rich beams" of "beauty bright / In mould or mind" (the exact words Hopkins used to describe Dolben), leave little of a lasting impression on anyone. However, they concern Christ, who "minds," "eyes," "wants," and "haunts" them, for he is their "ransom" and they are his investment ("interest"). To Hopkins, "The Handsome Heart," or true beauty, is "Heart mannerly," a thing "more than handsome face." The architect in "Who shaped these walls has shewn / The music of his mind, / Made known, though thick through stone, / What beauty beat behind." Not even the insights of angels, whom we are told seek to inquire into the things of man, know how this gift comes, since "This piece of perfect song" comes indiscriminately. Mindful no doubt of his own personal artistic and religious choices, seeming himself as eunuch, unable to "breed one work that wakes," Hopkins finds that "What makes the man and what / The man within that makes" comes from whom he serves or not serves and "what side he takes." And even though there is some visible fruit for artistic expense, still the artist's "brightest blooms lie there unblown / His sweetest nectar hides behind."[189]

The sonnet "Felix Randal," which subverts normal chronology—the poem opens with Felix's obituary and ends with his early life—is a similar celebration of brute beauty and its brokenness as prelude to spiritual restoration. Here the poet–priest administers the sacrament not to "limber liquid youth" this time, but to an already broken and spent farrier. Hopkins seems to be suggesting that while rugged physical beauty is to be admired, more to be admired is the brokenness of that beauty for one "a billion times . . . lovelier," a refining of beauty promoted in poems such as *The Wreck*, "The Windhover," and the dark sonnets. "On the Portrait of Two Beautiful Young People" is just that, a poem whose subject is a picture of a brother and sister Hopkins saw while visiting Monasterevin. Residing in the vicinity at the time of the poem's composition, the siblings possessed "favoured make and mind and health and youth." This the poet admires. His sorrow, however, lies in his inability to forecast their uncertain future, their "landmark, seamark, or soul's star,"[190] for which "none but truth can stead" them. "Christ is truth," wrote Hopkins, in a deliberate substitution of Keats's adage, "Beauty is truth."

Other poems treat the beauty of the creation and the sacramental quality of that beauty. "God's Grandeur" recognizes, amid the sordid industrial landscape of Victorian England, a divine energy in the "deep down things" of nature that preserves it from being "spent." "The Starlight Night" sees a just as resplendent grandeur in the heavens where "gold, where quickgold lies," and considers the sight a "purchase" and a "prize." This gift, however, is bought not with money but with "Prayer, patience, alms, vows." And the sight becomes a barn within which is housed Christ, Mary, and the saints. In "Spring" the poet celebrates the vitality of new, though fragile, life and locates genuine rebirth not in the season, nor even in a presumed return to paradisiacal innocence, but in the person of Christ. "Pied Beauty" praises God for the motleyness and mystery of creation, even, surprisingly for Hopkins, the motleyness of industrialism. An early advocate for multiculturalism, for "dappled things," and for the sacredness and dignity of the individual, Hopkins celebrates not sameness but differences. For it is in the dappleness that distinct beauty resides, and the things about us that are "counter, original, spare, strange" make us more ourselves and at the same time more like God. Thus, the more we ring ourselves the more we chime Christ. "Hurrahing in Harvest" relishes in the "barbarous . . . beauty" of autumn and the "lovely behaviour / Of silk–sack clouds" in their march across the skies. The poet's uplifted heart seeks God in nature and finds him in the landscape, the contours of which are his "world–wielding shoulders." And when the subject and object bond, when the perceiver and object of perception become one, true ecstasy results; the heart (sick with desire in "The Windhover") now takes flight and flings the "beholder" heavenward.

There is in Hopkins too the beauty of being broken, the beauty of self–sacrifice, explored in *The Wreck*, "The Windhover," *The Loss of the Eurydice*, "St. Winefred's Well," "Not, I'll not, carrion comfort," and the dark sonnets. The theory is that the more highly pitched the self and the more that self is loved by God the more it suffers, a challenging concept in Hopkins. In *The Wreck*, the beauty of sacrifice is threefold: the poet, Christ, and the tall nun, respectively. In the autobiographical part 1 ("what refers to myself in the poem is all strictly and literally true and did all occur"[191]), the poet discusses his own spiritual impediments on the road to his priestly vocation, his religious assent, saying "yes," coming only after "lightning and lashed rod." His heart is swept, hurled, and trod "Hard down with a horror of height," and his only escape from the "flame" of hell is to the "flame" of the Holy Ghost. He pictures his life "soft sift / In an hourglass." The history of Christ's own self–sacrifice, from the "womb–life grey" to "Manger," to "maiden's knee," to his "driven Passion," to "the discharge of it," and finally to the "Warm–laid grave," is chronicled in the last five stanzas of part 1. Except for instances where both Christ and the poet participate vicariously in the nun's own self–sacrifice, all of part 2 treats the religio–political, narrative, and climatal events in which the nun's actions occupy center stage. To quell the "heartbreak hearing a heartbroke rabble," a "lioness [the nun] arose breasting the babble, / A prophetess towered in the tumult, a virginal tongue told." Amid the "swirling and hawling," the "rash smart sloggering brine," the nun "that weather sees one thing." Reading the "unshapeable shock night," "Wording" Christ's immanence, and grasping "God, throned behind / Death," the nun expended her last "fetch" and "rears herself to divine / Ears" "calling 'O Christ, Christ, come quickly': / The cross to her she calls Christ to her, christens her wild–worst / Best." Her solicitation is also for the "crown then, / The keener to come at the comfort for feeling the combating keen." But such pangs are, ironically, a harvest: "What was the feast [that] followed the night," the poet exclaimed. Even the "Comfortless unconfessed" of passengers and crewmen did not go "uncomforted." The same touch from Christ that the poet felt repeatedly in the opening is here experienced by the shipwrecked passengers: "Finger of a tender of, O of a feathery delicacy." With a Paterian image of a gem–like re–formation of the self through fire, the penultimate stanza of *The Wreck* celebrates Christ's rebirth, the Burning Babe:

> Now burn, new born to the world,
> Double–natured name,
> The heaven–flung, heart–fleshed, maiden–furled
> Miracle–in–Mary–of–flame.

Committed entirely to Christ's self–sacrifice—the poem's subtitle providing the only frank admission of that—"The Windhover" becomes the perfect symbol of Christ. Not flagrantly co–opted for its symbolic importance—though co–opted nonetheless—the windhover is allowed to operate in the octave with its entire natural being intact. One early morning, the bird is inscaped by the poet; its heroic mastery of turbulent forces and its "Brute beauty and valour and act" evoke envy from the poet whose sequestered self "Stirred for a bird." But "lovelier," albeit "more dangerous," than the windhover's superb control is its incarnated descent, its "Fall," its self–sacrificial willingness to be spent, to be "gash[ed]," into precious "gold–vermilion." Self–immolation as enacted by the windhover pertains not only to the kind Christ himself experienced but applies equally to us. In *The Wreck*, for instance, the poet is "laced with fire of stress," and his flight is "from the flame to the flame" only to have himself "forged" in fire to God's will. As to the nun, in expending herself, in aspiring to "breathe in his all–fire glances," she bears Christ's "cipher," "Stigma, signal, cinquefoil token," the reddening vermillion ("ruddying") of his suffering.

That threatened conflagration of the self magnifies in a universe where "nature's bonfire burns on." Recognizing in atomism the potential for the self's annihilation as well as its re–creation,[192] that weaving and unweaving of the self as Pater (quoting Heraclitus) describes it in the "Conclusion," the poet in Hopkins's "Heraclitean Fire" (relying too on Heraclitus) sees that the mind, its signatures on earth, and nature's most privileged specimen, man, are soon blotted out, "Drowned." But while his "mortal trash" becomes mere incendiary material, "matchwood" in the "world's wildfire," at the resurrection a self, an "immortal diamond," is forged anew out of the ashes. Pater's informing influence on "Heraclitean Fire" is evident in the reorganization of the properties of the self. According to Pater, as Carolyn Williams keenly perceives, the "problematized notion of a stable, unified self will be replaced not by dissolution but by a rhythm of dispersal and gathering."[193] An early poem by Pater, "Watchman, what of the Night?" speaks to a similar threat of self–conflagration. As bleak as the situation seems, in contrast to Hopkins's, there is yet again in Pater not dissolution but reorganization of the self. Faced with the question of the habitation of the dead, the speaker, unwilling to accept their nonexistence ("nowhere"), clings to Christ who had himself experienced the "abyss" of death. The speaker desires either life in Christ or life in hell rather than nonexistence: "it seems so awful not to be." Yet at insomniac moments, the soul itself seems to prophesy that "all things verge to their decay"; and the soul that seems immortal, "mistress" in "the round / Of nature," shall one day return to some triumphant primeval state of chaos; however, unlike a Christian reading of the resurrection, the soul will not awaken to "the trumpet sound . . . nor the high Archangel's call."[194] Instead, emptied of its Christian import, as Pater, following Hegel, reads it, the resurrection is a mere "symbol for the developing life of the mind."[195]

Hopkins's "Spelt from Sibyl's Leaves" speaks to a similar unfastening of the earth, a similar loss of dappleness, that is of consequence to the self, fastened as we are to nature. The self disentangles, succumbing to stress and slack, "Disremembering" and "dismembering," is "steeped and pashed," and is left "selfwrung, selfstrung, sheathe– and shelterless." A similar unfastening of the self, the slackening of "these last strands of man / In me," is again voiced in the sonnet "Not, I'll not, carrion comfort" prompting the poet to hope, to "not choose not to be"; in other words, the goal is to reject the self–annihilation that drowns the self "in an enormous dark." All three poems present Hopkins wrestling with his own self–definition set against Parmenidean and Heraclitean notions of the self. Parmenides's "great text, which he repeats with religious conviction," Hopkins recalled, states that "being is and Not–being is not," which in his own neologism Hopkins interprets to mean that "all things are upheld by instress and are meaningless without it."[196]

These poems of Hopkins take us logically to his discourse on the self, a significant point in the aesthetic relationship between himself and Pater. While Hopkins's self, like Pater's, seems at times fluid, its fluidity and indefiniteness are so only to a point. Hopkins's self has a fixed source, flowing from God to whom it returns, a process through which the self moves from "one cleave of being to another and to a vital act in Christ."[197] But between these events is the process toward redefinition and redemption of that self, what Hopkins calls "*freedom of pitch* and *freedom of play*," both of which "express moral freedom." But Hopkins's is a mostly fixed self: "a self is an absolute which stands to the absolute of God."[198] That determined quality of the self is spelled out in his poem "The earth and heaven, so little known":

> The unchanging register of change
> My all–accepting fixed eye,
> While all things else may stir and range,
> All else may whirl or dive or fly.

And in "A Vision of Mermaids," the eye "fix'd, fled the encrimsoning spot, / And gathering, floated where the gaze was not."

But Hopkins's theory of self and selving, what in reference to Scotus he called *ecceitas* (the "thisness" of any thing), is most poetically explored in "As kingfishers catch fire." In this poem, each part of the creation "speaks and spells" itself, "Acts in God's eye what in God's eye [it] is," and "finds tongue to fling out broad its name": "kingfishers catch fire," "dragonflies draw flame," "Stones ring," "each tucked string tells," and "the just man justices." In Hopkins's verbalness of being, whereby "*the doing* be, *the doing* choose," every created thing cries out, "*What I do is me*," demonstrating a distinctiveness that characterizes Hopkins's notion of both inscape and grace. "Self is the intrinsic oneness of a thing," and grace is "any action, activity, on God's part by which, in creating or after creating, he carries the creature to or towards the end of its being, which is its selfsacrifice to God and its salvation." When a just man acts justly, to return to "As kingfishers catch fire," he "Keeps grace: that keeps all his goings graces," and "Acts in God's eye what in God's eye he is— / Christ: For Christ plays in ten thousand places," not with his own limbs and eyes but in the "features of men's faces." Acting in harmony with one's true nature, then, is being one's best self; that action is maintained through grace and that self participates in the very play of the Incarnation: "That is Christ playing at me and me playing at Christ, only that it is no play but truth; That is Christ *being me* and me being Christ."[199] Thus in the poem "The Blessed Virgin," Christ "comes to be / New self and nobler me / In each one and each one / More makes." Even in Christ the distinctiveness and sacredness of the self is preserved. The danger, according to Hopkins, is when the self is totally absorbed, drowned. That unfastening applies to all selves, even nature's. This is why Hopkins resented the effects of industrialism in "God's Grandeur." So violated, the earth's self, disrobed of its own natural garment, its *thisness*, now "wears man's smudge and shares man's smell."

Hopkins's self, then, is unlike any other. His "selfbeing," that "conscious-ness and feeling of myself, that taste of myself," he finds, is "more distinctive than the taste of ale or alum, more distinctive than the smell of walnutleaf or camphor," and remains "incommunicable" to anyone else. "Nothing else in nature comes near this unspeakable stress of pitch, distinctiveness and selving, this selfbeing of my own. Nothing explains it or resembles it . . . searching nature I taste self but at one tankard, that of my own being. The development, refinement, condensation of nothing shews any sign of being able to match this to me or give me another taste of it, a taste resembling it." And although, according to Hopkins's ontology, two dissimilar things often share something in common, "when I compare my self, my being–myself, with anything else whatever, all things alike, all in the same degree, rebuff me with blank unlikeness."[200] Hopkins believes that the "universal mind" of, say, the Hegelians, "being identified not only with me but also with all other minds cannot be the means of communicating what is individual in me to them nor in them to me." Of that "selftaste which nothing in the world can match," the "universal cannot taste this self as I taste it," for the universal is "altogether outside of my self, my personality / one may call it, my *me*." The universal mind is "outside of my inmost self and not within it; nor does it share my state, my moral standing, or my fate."[201] Wendell Johnson finds that this pursuit in Hopkins of the distinct-ness of personality, of "personal identity," is in fact his "poetry of inscape."[202]

While Pater and Hopkins were both pursuing an understanding of the self, Pater was after the personality, how individuals relate to, say, intellectual culture, and Hopkins after the person, the distinctive pitch of the self, the univocity of each individual thing, its *ecceitas*. Thus, for example, the seven-teenth–century English composer Henry Purcell is portrayed in Hopkins's sonnet not as he fits into the particular myth of personality that characterizes the seventeenth century—as Pater would have read him—but for how his self stands out distinct from all others of that time and from all periods. The poem is dedicated to an artist who captured a sort of musical inscape, recreating in notes "the very make and species of man" that is at once distinct and universal. Hopkins celebrates Purcell's "arch–especial" spirit, his own "forged feature," the "rehearsal / Of own, of abrupt self."[203] In brief notes made on Brahman religion when he was an undergraduate, Hopkins found not only a structure analogous to the Christian Trinity (Śiva, Vishnu, and Brahma) but also that force of self; the concept of Atman, "originally breath or spirit," is in fact "constantly signified *self.*" And, as the Rig–veda points out, with reference to what Hopkins would see as God, "Self is the lord of all things, Self is the king of all things. As all the spokes of a wheel are contained in the nave and the circumference all things are contained in this Self. Brahman itself is but Self."[204] Hopkins's "Pied Beauty" presents the Christian correlate to Brahman religion; in the poem, God is that central self around whom ten thousand vertiginous selves play.

The beauty of the sacrificial self, of being broken, is again taken up in other poems. Of the "Three hundred souls" aboard the *Eurydice*, felled uncaringly like Hopkins's aspens, only two survived, Sydney Fletcher and Benjamin Cuddiford. But Hopkins makes a hero of the younger Fletcher, "all of lovely manly mould, / Every inch a tar, / Of the best we boast our sailors are," whose bravery ("strung by duty") and tanned beauty ("strained to beauty, / And brown–as–dawning– skinned / With brine and shine and whirling wind") do not go unheralded. Comparable only to the self–sacrifice of the tall nun of *The Wreck* is that of yet another woman, St. Winefred, a legend particularly fascinating to Hopkins. Hopkins was also intrigued by other women martyred for their faith. "St. Dorothea," "St. Thecla," and "Margaret Clitheroe" all memorialize the martyr- dom of these women. Dorothea's life and death resemble that of Newman's Callista; Thecla, except for the fact that she was drawn from actual history, could be called Hopkins's Andromeda; and Margaret Clitheroe recalls in many ways Hopkins's tall nun of *The Wreck*.

But from no one in Hopkins's list of violated women comes a voice so inviolable as from the fond Gwenvrewi of "St. Winefred's Well." So precious to her father Teryth, who has a presentiment that she will be killed ("this bloom, this honeysuckle" will be "sheared away"), Winefred is shortly thereafter beheaded by Caradoc when she refuses his sexual advances: "for passion–sake. Yes, / To hunger and not have, Yet hope on for, to storm and strive and / Be at every assault fresh foiled, worse flung, deeper disappointed." Throughout "all her beauty" blooming, nothing haunts the unrepentant and unreconciled Caradoc like her eyes, a damnation akin to the look Othello received from the eyes of the murdered Desdemona. If Winefred represents the sacred beauty of sacrifice, then Caradoc is a picture of the beauty of internecine evil. Winefred pays a truly exorbitant price for offering her "fresh, her fleeced bloom," to God. But in spite of Hopkins's condemnation of Caradoc's crime and approval of Winefred's saintliness, one cannot help but admire Caradoc's demonic defiance and bold rejection of all moral and societal values, seeing virtue only in "Valour" and "the heart valiant" and right "Only [in] resolution." Caradoc's crime—a violation of the handsome heart—arises from a corruption of the will, a point Hopkins argues in a letter to Coventry Patmore that fittingly contextualizes Winefred's beauty and Carodoc's ugliness:

> It is certain that in nature outward beauty is the proof of inward beauty. Fineness, proportion, of feature comes from a moulding force which succeeds in asserting itself over the resistance of cumbersome or restraining matter; the bloom of health comes from the abundance of life, the great vitality within. The moulding force, the life, is the form in the philosophic sense,   and in man this is the soul.... But why do we find beautiful evil? Not by any freak of nature, nature is incapable of producing beautiful evil. The explanation is to be sought outside nature; it is old, simple, and the undeniable fact. It comes from wicked will, freedom of choice, abusing the beauty, the good of its nature.[205]

Caradoc's action, then, is so utterly self–gratifying that he can even taste his own evil tankard. The act is also given "a zest, an edge, an ecstasy," and him a "keen self–feeling" and "dreadful distillation of thoughts."

Though admitting his evil and Winefred's purity, his blood to hers as "sewers with sacred oils," Caradoc, to the end, remains totally unrepentant of his crime and stoically awaits his fate. However, where Winefred's head came to rest there sprouted a "moist and musical" fountain whose healing waters drew pilgrims and the physically infirm continent–wide.[206] Pater's Marius, however, entertains no such redemption through his martyrdom: his would be but "a common execution: from the drops of his blood there would spring no miraculous, poetic flowers; no eternal aroma would indicate the place of his burial; no plenary grace, overflowing for ever upon those who might stand around it."[207] Hopkins's theory of suffering that all of his martyred women share is best explained from an account of one woman he knew well. When Mrs. Plow (Bridges's sister) died of grief a year after she had lost her husband and infant to a heinous crime, Hopkins's words of comfort to Bridges recalled that "sufferings falling on such a person as your sister was are to be looked on as the marks of God's particular love and this is truer the more exceptional they are."[208]

When Hopkins wrote this tribute, he had in mind all these truly exceptional, martyred types.

The poem "Not, I'll not, carrion comfort" and the terrible sonnets also portray the beauty of sacrifice and again recalls Marius's martyrdom. In "Not, I'll not," the poet is mired in a wrestling match with melancholy, which seeks to unravel the "last strands" of his very being. He vows, in the words of other poems, not to yield to melancholy's sultry siege, but finds, at the same time, no relief in tears, "beauty's dearest veriest vein." Hopkins concludes that this stem of stress, initiated when he assented to his priestly calling, is but a winnowing, employing here the same harvesting metaphor he used earlier to describe the passengers who perished aboard the *Deutschland*: "is the shipwreck then a harvest, / does tempest carry the grain for thee?" However, whereas *The Wreck* ends with the birth of a new day and the anticipated rebirth of a lost era, the sonnet "Not, I'll not, " ends with the poet still in darkness, still wrestling with "my God." In "To seem the stranger," the poet, in Ireland, feels a "third / Remove" from parents, siblings, and nation. Asserting once more the idea that the creative gift is masculine, the poet sees England as "wife / To my creating thought," and because he is distant from England and simultaneously, it seems, from God, his pleas to country and Christ go unheard and when heard "unheeded." Ironically, the absence of inspiration the poet expresses is not borne out by the immense creative power of these Dublin sonnets. In "I wake and feel the fell of dark," the despair and spiritual battle of "Not, I'll not" and the unheeded cries and estrangement of "To seem the stranger" return. The poet is now an insomniac whose "countless" cries are like "dead letters" mailed to a friend who is alive elsewhere. So dire is the poet's condition that he can even taste his bitter self, his "Selfyeast of spirit" that makes sour "dull dough." This, he concludes, is the condition too of the spiritually lost, "their sweating selves," whose state, however, is far "worse."

In "No worst, there is none," the poet finds himself "past pitch of grief" with ever–increasing pangs. Finding no assistance from the "Comforter," the Holy Ghost, and none from his intercessor Mary, he discovers that his cries have the effect of blows that only "wince and sing" off a seasoned anvil. The poet sees the mind poised on a precipitous cliff, and, unable to endure that "steep or deep" for any length of time, it must creep around in search of comfort. His only assurance, echoing Keats, is that death ends all life and "each day dies with sleep." Pater's Marius seeks a similar recourse nearing his death, that "blessedness of physical slumber. To sleep, to lose one's self in sleep—that, as he had always recognised, was a good thing."[209] Recalling earlier accounts of spiritual despair in poems such as "Myself unholy" and "Nondum," the sonnet "Patience, hard thing," another of Hopkins's "thin gleanings of a long weary while,"[210] also deals with a beauty characteristic of spiritual suffering and validates patience. The poet finds patience a "Rare" and "hard thing," but still bids for it, knowing fully well, and from experience, that the asking of it invites continued intellectual warfare ("We hear our hearts grate on themselves: it kills / To bruise them dearer"); for patience finds its "roots" in conflict, masking even "Our ruins of wrecked past purpose" as ivy does to a dilapidated wall.[211] The image of a shipwreck, Hopkins's metaphor for spiritual disaster, is here invoked. The purple berries of the ivy among the leaves are like the "eyes" of swimmers bathing in "seas of liquid leaves." Yet our "rebellious wills" do "bid God bend" to patience, which comes, the poet remains assured, in regular ways; patience sprouts from the parched soil of suffering and in time produces fruit.

Sonnets like "The Windhover," "Not, I'll not," "I wake and feel the fell of dark," and "Patience, hard thing" all deal with the beauty of suffering that in one way or another engages the heart, Hopkins's metonymy for the self. "My own heart," the last of the dark sonnets, again involves the heart in suffering. The poet requests pity and love for his own heart, his own "sad self," rather than continuing a life with his "tormented mind tormenting yet." Heart and mind are here set in opposition, and the poet seems to prefer the pain of the heart to that of the mind. In a dark and comfortless world, the poet, like a hopeful angler, casts about for some means of comfort, and, like Coleridge's distressed mariner, searches for some means to quench his spiritual thirst even though surrounded by water. To find any comfort, the poet calls upon his comedic self, "Jackself," to suspend all uses of the mind, an interval that will grant comfort the space it needs to take root. Then joy ("God knows when") will take hold of some uncertain hope ("God knows what"). And God's smile, not "wrung," though at times "unforeseen," will enlighten the way as clouds that part to reveal a bright sky or as skies seen by one who from the valley looks up through the crevice of dark, massive mountains.

In *In Extremity*, John Robinson raises the question as to the subtle aspects of the relationship between Hopkins and Pater that I have been pursuing, the prevailing irony that "a poet who practised austerities at Oxford and who afterwards made over the whole of life in disciplined obedience should have been taught while at university by a man such as Walter Pater."[212] The correctness of Robinson's claim, notwithstanding, Pater and Hopkins are not remarkably dissimilar. That they are in many ways different, ways I have sought to elucidate, is, I trust, abundantly clear. Pater's world of flux is one in which any still point is at best momentary, any claim to certainty is perspectival, and the self is forever being subjected to the "irresistible . . . changes of the human spirit on its way to perfection."[213] Hopkins's is a also a world of flux, in keeping with nineteenth–century epistemology; but he does locate a still point in the Christological, finding there a palpableness of personality and the self. Finally, unlike Pater who favors the Hellenic and Renaissance, Hopkins more often prefers the Hebraic and Gothic. As different in many ways, then, as Pater's aesthetic theory is from Hopkins's, there are points at which the two are not at all dissimilar in approach. In fact, Pater and Hopkins were, as Robinson alleges, "ultimately in opposition, but that opposition is better understood as a divergence than as a confrontation." Pater, Robinson correctly estimates, is for Hopkins "both mentor and foil."[214] Both writers value the beauty of sacrifice in art, both value the use of the senses (Hopkins in their spiritual reallocation), both were strongly attracted to physical beauty, and both esteemed music, because of the interpenetration of matter and form, as the art to which all other arts tend. But where the two are most dissimilar are in the claims they make for art.

Pater saw art and the artist integral to culture, lending it intelligence and morality. Hopkins and Pater agreed on the ends of art in so far as art serves some morally democratic teleology: "to educate, to be standards. Education is meant for the many, standards are for public use."[215] For Pater, however, art more often than not replaces religion and at times replaces, when it becomes a metaphor for, life itself. Pater rejected, says Iser, "the exclusively theological concept of art," a conception of art advocated by Ruskin and Hopkins. "For him, art had no fixed place in the hierarchy of a fixed world order, and its function was not to imitate but to extract experiences and impressions from the flow of time."[216] While Hopkins, like Pater, also worked at defamiliarization, he did so not by defamiliarizing the subject but through linguistic displacements and decenterings––by reordering the normal encoding processes of reading out of which a new text is always being encountered. "His is a theory of decentered form," as Michael Sprinker points out, "similar to contemporary deconstructive theories of interpretation."[217] To Hopkins, beauty in nature is already accessible: "the world is full of things and events, phenomena of all sorts, that go without notice, go unwitnessed"; "The rainbow shines, but only in the thought / Of him that looks."[218] But while beauty cannot be created ("For who makes rainbows by invention?"), it must be recognized, inscaped, comprehended, valued, from which engenders praise to God. Such a notion of art in "pious submission to Nature" Pater rejected, refusing as he did to believe in "Nature as substance" and in "an overall coherence of things.[219] There is a clear difference, then, between Pater's and Hopkins's understanding of contemplation. While Pater's was to locate temporarily the nature of the "real" among tenuous and flickering impressions, Hopkins's was to apprehend the energy, the instress, in the "real."

But this exchange between perceiver and the object of perception in Hopkins forges, like Pater's privileged moment, an ecstatic moment, and thereby beauty is returned to God:

> These things, these things were here and but the beholder
> Wanting; which two when they once meet,
> The heart rears wings bold and bolder
> And hurls for him, O half hurls earth for him off under his feet.

This aesthetic process, however, was not always lucid to nor readily attainable by Hopkins. Throughout his life he can be witnessed wrestling with the claims of art and those of religion. And quite frankly he did not always require that art serve the mandates of religion. In other words, the aesthetic in Hopkins often capitulated to the ascetic, the poet to the priest, the two tendencies not always perfectly poised. An ironic instance is "The Kind Betrothal." The poem's plea is for the redirection, the reclothing of the senses from sensual pleasures and to be put to the service of Christ. But that plea is formulated entirely in sensuous language. Hopkins, then, similar to Pater, pursued the sensuous appreciation of beauty but desired also to experience it religiously. He did not wish to silence the senses, but sought to reemploy them to worship, to adoration.

The poem "Morning, Midday, and Evening Sacrifice" seems to confront directly the Paterian notion that in the face of life's chaos, uncertainty, and brevity, one's only recourse is to saturate the moments with beautiful sensations. In contrast, however, Hopkins insists that the prime of one's life must not be toyed with but must be put to "Christ's employment." Because the hoariness of age soon puts an end to all dappleness, "all this beauty blooming," "all this freshness fuming" must, "while worth consuming," be surrendered to God. Even mental acumen, while still warm and ripe, though on the verge of being possessed by death and hell, must be yielded to God.

Spelling out more fully Hopkins's Christian poeticizing of beauty are the poems "The Leaden Echo and the Golden Echo" and "To what serves Mortal Beauty?" Sung by the maidens from "St. Winefred's Well," the former is divided into two echoes and treats two responses, the first utterly hopeless, the second equally hopeful. The first echo mourns the early demise of Gwenvrewi, and the second affirms the expended life, the life broken and extravagantly spilled for the cause of Christ. The "Leaden Echo" begins with the question of whether it is known by anyone how to retain beauty, what is the "latch or catch or key" to keep beauty from "vanishing away." In other words, how can beauty be forever preserved when the wrinkled face ("wimpledwater–dimpled") stands in stark contrast to "morning–matched–face." The question is the very one Keats asks in his "Ode to a Nightingale": how, from the ravages of aging, time, and sickness, can Beauty "keep her lustrous eyes," how can we preserve our "last gray hairs"? Hopkins's poem is just as keenly interested in aging:

> O is there no frowning of these wrinkles, ranked wrinkles deep,
> Down? no waving off of these most mournful messengers, still
>   messengers, sad and steeling messengers of grey?

Convinced that there is no way to arrest the demise of the dapple, to preserve, in the words of another poem, "all this beauty blooming," "all this freshness fuming," the "Leaden Echo" laments: "No there's none, there's none, O no there's none." Nor can what we now are, that is "fair," be that for long, whatever we might choose to do; and even as wisdom begins so quickly it is ever "early to despair"; "nothing," the poet mourns, "can be done"

> To keep at bay
> Age and age's evil, hoar hair
> Ruck and wrinkle, drooping, dying, death's worst, windingsheets,
>   tombs and worms and tumbling to decay.

The degenerationist poet ends the "Leaden Echo" with a mournful, repetitious whimper that attempts an incantation to preserve beauty from fleeting. As the section ends, the voice fades into despair.

However, the incantation does in fact succeed. The word "Spare" that commences the "Golden Echo" rejects the "de*spair*" (my italics) that ends the "Leaden Echo." Requesting a cessation, the word "Spare," a derivative of "despair," links structurally and thematically the two echoes with an echo. In answer to the question posed by the "Leaden Echo" of whether there is some way to preserve beauty from decaying and youth from aging, the "Golden Echo" affirms the existence of *one* such "key," *one* such "place," where "whatever's prized and passes of us, everything that's fresh and fast flying of us, seems to us sweet of us," "dearly and dangerously sweet / Of us," where all these and "The flower of beauty, fleece of beauty" "Never fleets more." Physical beauty is again characterized by Hopkins as both dear (costly, precious) and dangerous; but like flower and fleece it soon withers or evaporates. That key, that place, not within sight or the scorching heat of the sun, but beyond it, "yonder," is held fast "with the tenderest truth / To it own best being and its loveliness of youth: it is an everlastingness of, O it is an all youth!" That key or place, challenging the reality of things that "swiftly away," that are "too too apt to, ah! to fleet," has permanence, and not gingerbread permanence. And that answer is found not in retaining beauty but in giving it away, in resigning all of its manifestations, in signing, sealing, mailing, even delivering it as through the gestures of a breath (blowing it away) and through "soaring sighs." As in "The Kind Betrothal," so here too the poet begs us to surrender everything: pretensions, conspicuous apparel, sexuality, and especially, it seems, the sexual allure of hair: "loose locks, long locks" that create "lovelocks."

The "Golden Echo" also shares remarkable similarities to "Morning, Midday, and Evening Sacrifice," for the poet, using compressed images of "beauty–in–the–ghost" (an image akin to Blake's "marriage hearse"), requests that beauty be delivered "early now, long before death." To effectively retain beauty is to surrender it to God, "beauty's self and beauty's giver." For God, who numbers every hair and lash, is both the quintessence and giver of beauty, and in him "not [even] the last lash [is] lost." And the imperishable tokens we have devalued ("lighthanded left") within our perishable clay soon come alive, mount, and leave us even as we sleep. Why, then, the poet asks, are our hearts so beleaguered, "so care–coiled, carekilled, so fagged, so fashed, so cogged, so cumbered," when the thing we "freely forfeit is kept with fonder a care," when he who keeps it cares more for it "than we could have kept it," and when, ironically, in our desire to keep it we in fact lose it? That "somewhere elsewhere" inquired about in the opening of the "Golden Echo" is at the end answered in "yonder," and there is our "care [best] kept."

The poem "To what serves Mortal Beauty?" begins with the now–familiar admission that mortal beauty is "dangerous," "dearly and dangerously sweet" as the "Golden Echo" has it, precisely because it sets the blood "dancing," perfectly renders the human features, and flagrantly declaims the human form. It surpasses even the music of Henry Purcell ("proud fire or sacred fear," "something necessary and eternal"[220]), which captures "the moods of man's mind" and "beyond that, uttered in notes the very make and species of man." Hopkins, we might recall, elaborated on this dangerous form of beauty, telling Bridges that while "no one can admire beauty of the body more than I do," "this kind of beauty is dangerous."[221] However, mortal beauty does serve a vital function. While it flaunts the too human and is to be considered dangerous, it also keeps alive our knowledge of the being and existence of things, even "what good means." And as the architect

Who shaped these walls has shewn
The music of his mind,
Made known, though thick through stone,
What beauty beat behind,

so the artist who endeavors in his art causes the "countenance" of that art to
render back, to mirror, even at a glance, the mind of the artist. Without art—
man's attraction to mortal beauty—how then could Father Gregory (subsequently Pope) have rescued ("gleaned") from the "swarm[ed]" slaves at Rome
a troop of England's "lovely lads," the angelic ("wet–fresh") "windfalls of war's
storms"?   That encounter led ultimately to the Christianizing of England by
Augustine. Hopkins recalled the even: that very day "God to a nation dealt . . .
dear chance" for a people renowned for idolatry, their "worship [of] block or
barren stone." Gregory's spiritual love for the lads, because it was stirred by the
beauty of male sexuality, could well have embodied a sexual attraction, the type
of Platonic union whereby beauty of the soul is often viewed in the same light
as physical beauty. Gregory's response could be viewed, using the words of K.J.
Dover, as that from "an older male to the stimulus afforded by a younger male
who combines bodily beauty with 'beauty of the soul.'"[222]

Whereas beauty in Pater more often than not begins and ends with the
subject itself, serves itself, in Hopkins's scheme of things beauty prompts an
exchange, a return, giving, hence grace. However dangerous, then, art is, it
serves practical and moral good. For it causes us to "Love what are love's
worthiest," and the "World's loveliest" are "men's selves" (elsewhere nature's
"bonniest, dearest to her, her clearest–selved spark"), the same "Self" that
"flashes off [the] frame [of a picture] and [the] face" that daily meets us. How
then do we "meet beauty?" Hopkins asks. His answer: "Merely meet it." Beauty
is "heaven's sweet gift; then leave, let that alone," but leave wishing above all
for "God's better beauty, grace."   The "grace" that ends the poem is, in
Hopkins's aesthetic hierarchy of values, the same as the beauty of character, the
end all, though not the *be all*, of art. Although Hopkins's understanding of
beauty is never far from morality and ethics, and however much the poem
explores our behavioral responses to mortal beauty, this poem does address the
function of beauty and is not, as MacKenzie puts it, solely "a matter of ethics,
not aesthetics."[223] In Hopkins, ethics and aesthetics are never separate. Beauty
to him always evokes action, behavior: the stars, for example, provoke gratitude
to God and bluebells engender praise. Employing, then, the words of Christ on
virtue, Hopkins applies it to art: "Let your light shine before men that they may

see your good works (say, of art) and glorify yr. Father in heaven (that is, acknowledge that they have an absolute excellence in them and are steps in a scale of infinite and inexhaustible excellence)."[224]

While the sacramental aspects of beauty are most often declared in Hopkins's poems and journal entries (the world possessing the energy of God's beauty, knowing the beauty of Christ through the bluebells, or opening the heart in unusual praise for God when a mass of stars appeared in the sky), his was a wrestle with the genuine claims of art set against the preoccupation with his priestly vocation. John Robinson makes what seems to me a correct distinction not so much between Hopkins's priestly and poetic lives but between publication and Hopkins's understanding of poetry. It would be a mistake to suggest, says Robinson, that "the Society of Jesus as such suppressed his creative impulses." Hopkins's "attitude to poetry remained consistent," says Robinson, but his attitude to publication reveals "more fluctuation." Thus it was not poetry but publication that created for Hopkins "the real problem for the spiritual life."[225] Much of these personal battles were chronicled in Hopkins's letters and journals.

For example, after Hopkins had converted to Roman Catholicism, he decided to surrender all beauty "until I had His leave of it." Months earlier, on 1 June 1866, he had incinerated his 1862 journal, a catalogue of possibly sensuous attraction to the beauty of body and mind, and less of character.[226] That incineration would two years later, on 11 May 1868, extend to some of his poems, though not before assuring himself that others had fair copies of them. "I cannot send my *Summa*," he told Bridges on 7 August 1868, "for it is burnt with my other verses: I saw they would interfere with my state and vocation." Yet, wrote Hopkins, "I kept . . . corrected copies of some things which you have."[227] While the conflagration was partial and might have been merely symbolic, such inconsistencies are indicative not only of Hopkins's stance on poetry writing, but also of not having time to write when all along great poetry was being written. He told Bridges, for example, that "far more than direct want of time, I find most against poetry and production in the life I lead. . . . I cannot produce anything at all, not only the luxuries like poetry, but the duties of my profession, its natural outcome." Yet in the very next breath he mentioned composing a paper on the Greek negatives, expressed the desire to have it published, and as the letter ended enclosed a copy of "Tom's Garland."[228]

All of this is not to say, however, that Hopkins did not experience great apprehension about his preoccupation with art. In only his fifth letter to Canon Dixon, Hopkins, on Dixon's query, admitted that he did write poetry, but that when he became a Jesuit he resolved to write no further, "as not belonging to my profession, unless it were by the wish of my superiors," consistent with his vow of 6 November 1866. Later he again told Dixon that the strictures placed on him by his vocation made writing difficult; and his choice is either between fame, on the one hand, and the severe judgment from God, on the other hand, for neglecting his religious duties: "for the waste of time the very compositions you admire may have caused and their preoccupation of the mind which belonged to more sacred or more binding duties, for the disquiet and the thoughts of vainglory they have given rise to."[229] To Bridges Hopkins remarked that he "cannot spend time on poetry," and makes, it appears, a distinction between love of God and self–love, associating the latter to literary composition.[230]

Hopkins, however, seems to have had second thoughts about burning his early poems. After Patmore had told him on 10 February 1888 that he had "committed . . . to the flames" his *Sponsa Dei* "without reserve of a single paragraph," Hopkins remarked that not only did Patmore's action remind him of his own taken many years earlier, but that "I wish I had been more guarded in making them. When we take a step like this we are forced to condemn ourselves: either our work shd. never have been done or never undone, and either way our time and toil are wasted—a sad thought; though the intention may at both times have been good." Hopkins had finally, it seems, come around to a correct perspective on art—that pursuing or not pursuing art at the expense of one's vocation is neither right nor wrong; one simply has to choose prudence and when in doubt consult one's superior, and not necessarily an earthly one.[231]

Yet Hopkins still wished to compose and felt tentatively that maybe poetry could serve the claims of religion. "It always seems to me that poetry is unprofessional, but that is what I have said to myself, not others to me. No doubt if I kept producing I should have to ask myself what I meant to *do* with it all; but I have long been at a standstill, and so the things lie."[232] The concern here, as was so often the case with Hopkins, is the functional aspect of art, what it does, whom it serves. It is that functional aspect, the pursuit of the sacramental in art, that generated *The Wreck*. He had just called poetry not conducive to his vocation, "unless it were by the wish of my superiors," and so proceeded to request that someone, and preferably he, elegize the nuns who perished in the shipwreck. This, in Hopkins's functional aesthetic, is a proper use of poetry, and consistent with his desire "to write still and as a priest," though "not so freely as I shd. have liked . . . but not doubt what wd. best *serve* the cause of my religion" (my italics).[233]

Hopkins was particularly concerned with the fame and attraction that publication, not necessarily composition, drew; and the wavering, if any, seems lodged between them; in his own words, "if I could but produce some work I should not mind its being buried, silenced, and going no further; but it kills me to be time's eunuch and never to beget. After all I do not despair, things might change."[234] Here the tension is between the artist's need to create, to give life to something, and the feared notoriety that the results of that creativity might generate. "[F]ame whether won or lost," Hopkins told Dixon, "is a thing which lies in the award of random, reckless, incompetent, and unjust judge, the public, the multitude," which is precisely why "The only just judge, the only just literary critic, is Christ," or, in rare cases, a best friend: "I do not write for the public. You [Bridges] are my public and I hope to convert you."[235] He warned his mother that should *The Wreck* appear in the *Month*, she should not disclose that it is his. He also warned Dixon, albeit equivocally, against much the same exposure: "Pray do not send the piece to the paper: I cannot consent to, I forbid publication.... Moreover this kind of publication is very unlikely to do the good that you hope and very likely to do the harm that I fear." For while the Jesuit Society "fosters literary excellence," Hopkins felt that that permission, unless otherwise he had some clear sense that what he wrote was in keeping with his profession (finding, for example, "within my professional experience now a good deal of matter to write on"), must come from his superiors.[236]

Hopkins seems all along to have been following the advice once given him: "a very spiritual man once told me that with things like composition the best sacrifice was not to destroy one's work but to leave it entirely to be disposed of by obedience." This position, finally arrived at, remained consistent. On 1 December 1881, Hopkins told Dixon that giving oneself over to God's service means relying on God for guidance, which comes partly from one's superiors and, granting himself some literary room, partly from "direct lights and inspirations." If he is to await directions through any of these channels, "I do more wisely in every way than if I try to serve my own seeming interest in the matter," here again connecting art, as we saw earlier, with self–interest. And it is finally Christ who "chooses to avail himself of what I leave at his disposal" to do so "with a felicity and with a success which I could never command . . . if I had taken things into my own hands and forced on publication."[237] During his 1883 retreat at Beaumont, Hopkins confessed much the same aspirations:

> Also in some med. today I earnestly asked our Lord to watch over my compositions, not to preserve them from being lost or coming to nothing, for that I am very willing they should be, but they might do me harm through the enmity or imprudence of any man or my own; that he should have them as his own and employ them or not employ them as he should see fit. And this I believe is heard.[238]

There remains little doubt that Hopkins's clearly equivocal comments—"I have never wavered in my vocation, but I have not lived up to it," of the "backward glances I have given [the artist] with my hand upon the plough" (the priest),[239] comments all made in the context of seeking to clarify the priestly vocation with the aesthetic avocation—reflect the tension he experienced between the impulses of the ascetic and aesthetic. That tension between the claims of religion and those of art was less in Pater than it was in Hopkins. Concerned as Pater was with the religious milieu of the nineteenth century, in which religion no longer held firm claims on the lives of people, art assumed that place, giving meaning, order, and relative fixity to otherwise unstable and flickering realities. Hopkins esteemed art equally. Yet, however much his aesthetic faces up to the instabilities of the nineteenth century, he believed that there is more to art that mere sensuous self gratification whereby art exists in and for itself with some chimera of communal relevance. He was not willing as was Pater, according to Philip Toynbee, to sacrifice everything "to the single visionary moment of aesthetic passion."[240] Though just as radical an aesthetic, Hopkins's embraces, among other things, service, action, renunciation, and grace.

Ultimately, Hopkins and Pater pursued dangerous beauty of the body, beauty of friendship, and friendly beauty. They also engaged the less–dangerous mental beauty. But far more vital to Hopkins, because he stressed personal commitment, renunciation, and service, and Pater, because he valued the singular beauty of personality, is the beauty of character, "the handsome heart." Significant is the fact that all four types of beauty in Hopkins and Pater inform the unparalleled beauty of character. In that Hopkins and Pater were not at all dissimilar. That the two diverged in significant ways is abundantly clear; but the similarities in their aesthetics are equally compelling.

Conclusion

I have attempted in this work on *Hopkins and His Contemporaries* to show Hopkins's personal relationship with four prominent Victorians. Through them, I argue for the historical and literary sources of his discourse on religion, science, and aesthetics. The Victorian figures examined—Henry Parry Liddon, John Henry Newman, Charles Darwin, and Walter Pater—were (Darwin the only exception) acquaintances of Hopkins and at the same time individuals whose lives and ideas shaped significantly English thought in the nineteenth century. Precisely how Hopkins relates to them and to their ideas shows how he resonated with nineteenth–century intellectual life. But Hopkins's modernity, as Claude Abbott pointed out so many years ago, "means not that he belongs, spiritually, to us, but that by transcending in great measure the dead conventions of his contemporaries he is free of all ages and entombed by none"; and that, indeed, "The measure of his greatness is often the measure of his apartness."[1] My study has been historically rooted—looking at Hopkins in relationship to the nineteenth century—and so involved exhumations and excavations. However, because the religious, scientific, and aesthetic issues examined are so feverishly modern and contemporary, this study of Hopkins, through Liddon, Newman, Darwin, and Pater, has, I trust, opened up new intellectual vistas of contemporary discourse.

Critical examinations of Hopkins over the last decade have emphasized the variety of religious responses to his poetry—mostly its Ignatian and sacramental character. Margaret Ellsberg's *Created to Praise*, Maria Lichtmann's *The Contemplative Poetry of Gerard Manley Hopkins*, and, more recently, Virginia Ridley Ellis's *Gerard Manley Hopkins and the Language of Mystery* have, with lesser or greater success, all argued the religious. Understandably, studies have also attended to his language, but, except for Cary Plotkin's *The Tenth Muse:*

Victorian Philology and the Genesis of the Poetic Language of Gerard Manley Hopkins and, to a lesser extent, Linda Dowling's *Language and Decadence in the Victorian Fin de Siècle*, none has really paid much attention to the historical and evolutionary context, or reaction to that context, in which Hopkins's philological speculations and praxis operate. Other than Wendell Johnson's *The Poet as Victorian* and Allison Sulloway's *Gerard Manley Hopkins and the Victorian Temper*, none of the recent works has seen fit to explore the depth of Hopkins's historicity. And even in the long anticipated biographies—Robert Martin's *Gerard Manley Hopkins: A Very Private Life* and Norman White's *Hopkins: A Literary Biography*—Hopkins's historicism (by which I mean the ways in which his discourse commented on, responded to, and revised nineteenth–century historical assumptions and anticipated modernity) has again been given superficial play. The prevailing assumption has been that if it is not known for certain that Hopkins read particular works, then the influence cannot be located anywhere in him. Such an assumption—on Darwin in particular—ignores, for example, Hopkins's familiarity with the literary organs in which Darwinism was most hotly debated. To say, furthermore, that Hopkins knew nothing of Darwin is to grossly underestimate the subtle ways in which intellectual ideas permeate a culture. For if George Levine is right, profound ideas operate surreptitiously rather than consciously and deliberately. Using Hopkins's poetry, essays, religious writings, and letters, I have sought to encode his epistemological strategies and to show how these strategies were influenced by people he knew and whose works informed the nineteenth century.

Hopkins's historicism merits further examination. What, for example, does Hopkins have to say about the environment, about society, about politics? These topics have only been broached, the most successful effort being *The Hopkins Quarterly* monograph entitled *Hopkins the Man & the City Dublin*. Also valuable are Bill Thesing's "Gerard Manley Hopkins's Response to the City," Mike Sundermeier's "Of Wet and of Wildness: Hopkins and the Environment," and Norman White's "Hopkins and County Kildare." Still lacking is a competent, though cautious, treatment of the vexed issue of Hopkins and sexuality. Norman MacKenzie's terse remarks on the subject in his facsimile of *The Early Poetic Manuscripts and Note–books of Gerard Manley Hopkins* provide some direction for such a study. More is yet to be done on Hopkins and science along the lines of what I have attempted here and what Tom Zaniello has done in his *Hopkins in the Age of Darwin*. Only recently, Gillian Beer has applied to Hopkins her concern with the effects of nineteenth–century science on narrative structures, an interest evident in her study *Darwin's Plots*. Her essay, "Helmholtz, Tyndall, Gerard Manley Hopkins: leaps of the prepared imagination," has opened up fruitful ways to consider the historical dimensions of Hopkins and science.

I trust that I have demonstrated in this study that the post–modern condition of literary and historical criticism has generated refreshing and fruitful ways of looking at Hopkins. These treatments show that not only was Hopkins a great deal more aware of his time than he is credited with but—and equally significant—that our engagement of and responses to questions on religion, science, and aesthetics raised in the nineteenth century will provide a clearer understanding of our own contemporary discourse.

Notes

Introduction

1. *Transfigured World*, 53.
2. *Renaissance*, xxiii-xxiv.
3. Ibid., 158.
4. Ibid., 137.
5. *Walter Pater*, 17.
6. *Letters* 1:290-91.
7. *Journals*, 97-98; "Is history governed by general laws?" from Unpublished Campion Hall ms. D V/9-10.

Chapter 1

1. The first study to have explored, however superficially, the significance of that relationship was Joseph Keating's early influential essay, "Impressions of Father Gerard Hopkins, S.J." Alison Sulloway's *Gerard Manley Hopkins and the Victorian Temper* (1972) is also a competent examination of that relationship.
2. "To Oxford." The word "pleasaunce" denotes not only pleasure or delight, but also a pleasure ground, a secluded area of a garden, and more often a "separate enclosure laid out with shady walks, trees and shrubs" (*OED*). Hopkins is obviously viewing Oxford in Epicurean terms. However, Oxford's religious turmoil would soon necessitate a new pleasaunce, the precise expression of which is found in "Heaven–Haven." Hopkins's love for Oxford is matched only by Newman's and Arnold's. Hopkins wrote three Oxford poems, a fourth, "Duns Scotus's Oxford," that protests destruction of the medieval architectural beauty that "country and town did / Once encounter in," and a fifth, "Binsey Poplars," that expresses disgust at man's ruinous hand in Oxford's "rural scene." For a treatment of these and the Arnoldian echoes in Hopkins's Oxford poems, see my essay "'Sweet especial rural scene': Revisiting Binsey."
3. *Letters* 3:77. In *The Mind of the Oxford Movement*, Owen Chadwick regards Liddon an "abler theological mind than anyone in the Movement except Newman and J.B. Mozley." Chadwick also notes Liddon's faithfulness to Pusey (60), which would later prompt Liddon to write the definitive biography of Pusey.

4. *The Diaries of Liddon.*

5. Ms. St. Edmund Hall 69/2.

6. For an additional treatment of Liddon's tenure at Cuddesdon, see Owen Chadwick's "The Young Liddon" in his *The Spirit of the Oxford Movement: Tractarian Essays.*

7. *The Diaries of Liddon.*

8. Liddon, *Centenary Memoir*, 2–3.

9. Johnston, *Life and Letters of Liddon*, 50.

10. *The Diaries of Liddon.*

11. Ibid.

12. *Centenary Memoir*, 30.

13. *The Diaries of Liddon.*

14. Keble College Ms.

15. *Centenary Memoir*, 5.

16. Lahey, *Gerard Manley Hopkins*, 19.

17. *Letters* 3:16–17.

18. Geldart, *A Son of Belial*, 167–70. One wonders if Geldart's fictional name for Hopkins was not his humorous yet subtle way of connecting Hopkins with Newman's Gerontius, from the poem *The Dream of Gerontius* (1865). The title of Geldart's book was taken either from Milton (*Paradise Lost* 1:501–2) or from Dryden (*Absalom and Achitophel*, 598). Newman also used the phrase "sons of Belial" to describe the orgies that took place at his college on Trinity Monday, and especially when the day before so many had "pledged . . . at His Table" (*Letters* 1:66). From Ireland on 24 April 1885, Hopkins informed Baillie of Geldart's death, which, it appears, had been suicidal. Hopkins regretted that three of his "intimate friends at Oxford have thus drowned themselves, a good many more of my acquaintances and contemporaries have died by their own hands in other ways; it may be . . . a dreadful feature of our days." Hopkins told of having been lent a copy of Geldart's *A Son of Belial*. "I wish it had another name," he added. "It is an amusing and a sad book" (*Letters* 3:254).

19. *Letters* 3:17.

20. *The Diaries of Liddon.*

21. Liddon, *Centenary Memoir*, 13–14.

22. Ibid., 25.

23. Geldart, *A Son of Belial*, 168–69

24. Ibid., 138–39.

25. Symonds developed a friendship with the Scotsman Edward Urquhart, the same Urquhart whom Hopkins himself later befriended. Symonds re-

called Urquhart's high–church zeal and especially his homosexual attraction to choristers. According to Symonds, it was the reticence on his part to be made love to by Urquhart that caused the former to sever their relationship. *The Memoirs of Symonds*, 108–21; Horatio Brown, *John Addington Symonds*, 77.

26. Like many others in Liddon's circle, he too would later convert to Roman Catholicism. *The Diaries of Liddon*.

27. Monsman, "Pater, Hopkins, and Fichte's Ideal Student," 366.

28. *The Diaries of Liddon*.

29. *Journals*, 328.

30. Johnston, *Life and Letters of Liddon*, 90–91.

31. Ibid., 62.

32. *Letters* 3:215–16, 224. For details on the origin of the Hexameron, see Monsman's "Pater, Hopkins, and Fichte's Ideal Student," 368–70, and Jerome Bump's "Hopkins, Pater, and Medievalism," 14–15.

33. Liddon, *Centenary Memoir*, 25.

34. Johnston, *Life and Letters of Liddon*, 80–81.

35. Liddon, *Centenary Memoir*, 3–4.

36. *The Diaries of Liddon*.

37. The book's lack of a general editor, a decision deliberately made, is reflected in its disorganization and absence of genuine focus. The preface, a brief two–paragraph explanation to the reader, claims that the authors are "responsible for their respective articles only." Yet the work was never seen as such. For example, Temple, as much as he wished, could not separate himself from the tenor of the volume. And even though the Anglican clergy almost without exception desired that the essays by Temple, Pattison, and Jowett be considered separately from the remaining essays, the general public regarded the volume singularly. The only unifying focus to all seven essays is the capitulation of the historicity of the Bible to advancing scientific interpretive models. The idea for *Essays and Reviews*, if one were to accept completely Frederick Temple's account, was originally Jowett's. It was he who first expressed the desire to see such a document around 1850, believing that there needs to be an open and honest inquiry in matters of religion. Jowett felt that Oxford and Balliol entertained reticence and hypocrisy, and so wanted the university to assume a free spirit of inquiry, rather than holding to a belief only because it was consistent with the received tradition. *Essays and Reviews*, Jowett was convinced, would open up the field of religion for examination. He had all along held that Anglican clerics were deliberately ignoring the

significance of historical criticism. Speaking for himself and the other essayists, Frederick Temple told his students at Rugby: "We thought it might encourage free and honest discussion of Biblical topics" (1:223). This admission from Temple comes some eight years before Jowett's letter to Stanley mentioning that the request for such a document came from Henry Bristow Wilson. However, most of the commentators on *Essays and Reviews* (apparently unaware of Temple's account, or else slighting it) maintain that the idea was originally Wilson's. Ieuan Ellis, for one, traced the idea back to Wilson and Pattison, who then left Jowett to advance it. For cogent treatments of the *Essays and Reviews* controversy, see Geoffrey Faber, *Benjamin Jowett: A Portrait with Background* (229–88), F. Warre Cornish, *A History of the English Church in the Nineteenth Century* (8.2:215–44), Basil Willey, *More Nineteenth Century Studies* (137–85), H. P. Liddon, *Life of Edward Bouverie Pusey* (4:1–78), *Life of Archibald Campbell Tait* (1:275–325), and Peter Hinchliff, *Benjamin Jowett and the Christian Religion* (69–94). For a treatment of how the volume relates to German and English higher criticism, see John Rogerson, *Old Testament Criticism in the Nineteenth Century.* Ieuan Ellis's seminal study, *Seven against Christ: A Study of "Essays and Reviews,"* to which my thoughts are greatly indebted, remains the most exhaustive treatment of this critical nineteenth–century document.

38. Newman, *Apologia*, 42–43.
39. Newman, *Letters*, 2:264.
40. Newman, *Apologia*, 200, 218.
41. Willey, *More Nineteenth Century Studies*, 139.
42. Newman, *Letters*, 19:482–83.
43. Ibid., 487–88.
44. Reardon, *Religious Thought in the Nineteenth Century*, 309.
45. Chapter 47.
46. Ellis, *Seven Against Christ*, 92.
47. *More Nineteenth Century Studies*, 137.
48. *The Guardian*, 23 May 1860, 474.
49. Ellis, *Seven Against Christ*, 303.
50. *The Poetical Works of Robert Browning.* "Gold Hair" was published with *Dramatis Personae* (1864) and is believed to have been written in 1862.
51. Temple, *Memoirs*, 220.
52. *Essays and Reviews*, 3, 44, 47.
53. In February 1870 when Temple was consecrated Bishop of Exeter, he pulled his essay from further publication.

54. During their 1833 trip to the Mediterranean, Newman and Froude borrowed from Bunsen, then the Prussian representative to the Vatican, a copy of Homer's *Iliad*. Out of it Froude chose the phrase announcing Achille's return to battle as the motto for *Lyra Apostolica*, an anthology of Tractarian poems.
55. *Essays and Reviews*, 52.
56. Ibid., 72–74.
57. Ibid., 78–79.
58. Ibid., 100.
59. Ibid., 96–97.
60. Ibid., 112.
61. Ibid., 142.
62. Ibid., 112, 142, 127.
63. Ibid., 128.
64. Ibid., 128–129.
65. *Fragments of Science*, 2:224.
66. *Essays and Reviews*, 211, 235.
67. A.O.J. Cockshut, *Religious Controversies*, 136.
68. Butler, *Ernest Pontifex; or, The Way of All Flesh*, 47.
69. Willey, *More Nineteenth Century Studies*, 151.
70. Newman was quite likely referring to Pattison when he told Malcolm MacColl that one of the authors of *Essays and Reviews* "I may still call my friend" (*Letters*, 19:487).
71. *Essays and Reviews*, 278.
72. For Hopkins's extract of Pattison's essay, see Campion Hall Ms., DVII/1.
73. *Essays and Reviews*, 278–79.
74. Ibid., 329.
75. "Learning against Religion," 318–19.
76. Jowett and Stanley were fast friends. They entered Balliol together, Jowett on a Hertford scholarship and Stanley on an Ireland. The two vacationed together and had other things in common, one of which was that Stanley's sister, Mary, who would later convert to Roman Catholicism, had joined Jowett's paramour Florence Nightingale in her work in the Crimea. Stanley valued Temple's and Jowett's contributions in *Essays and Reviews*, but felt that the work was an error in judgment.
77. Review of *Essays and Reviews*, *The Guardian*, 23 May 1860, 473.
78. In a 16 April 1865 letter, Jowett told Florence Nightingale: "This is Easter Sunday. I don't suppose that we either have, or could by any possibility

have, sufficient evidence of the resurrection to justify us in resting religion upon that. . . . I sometimes think that the death, & not the resurrection of Christ, is the really strengthening & consoling fact—that human nature could have risen to that does show that it is divine" (*Dear Miss Nightingale*, 52). Jowett's skeptical stance on the Resurrection is proof of his disbelief in miracles, those of Elisha's for instance. He believed that religion should not be based on them, and had planned to address this view in the aborted second volume of *Essays and Reviews*.

79. Geldart, *A Son of Belial*, 154.

80. *Essays and Reviews*, 377–78.

81. Ibid., 348.

82. Ibid., 375.

83. Ibid., 348, 374–75.

84. Geldart, *A Son of Belial*, 160.

85. In an undergraduate essay for Jowett, entitled "Is history governed by general laws?" Hopkins, discussing the influence of notable figures, insisted that the Elizabethan playwrights would have lost little had Shakespeare not been around: "his individual influence is, we may believe, compared with his greatness of mind, almost incredibly small." As if seeing himself in a similar light, Jowett disagreed. According to Hopkins, Jowett "thought this about Shakspere was quite untrue," that "the whole of subsequent literature [was] deeply influenced by him." Campion Hall Ms. DV/9.

86. In December 1878, when Hopkins returned to Oxford as a priest at St. Aloysius, at which time Jowett had been Master of Balliol for eight years and was preaching twice each term in the college chapel, Hopkins attended one such sermon and told Bridges that Jowett "has been preaching curiously" (*Letters* 1:74). The sermon was probably "The Permanent Element of Religion," which argues for an "ordinary" Christianity instead of an "extraordinary" or evidential one. The sermon recalled the Tractarians, that "small band of distinguished men" who "knocked at the door of a small despised chapel [Littlemore] in the suburbs of this city, and humbly asked for admission into the bosom of the universal Church." Admitting that "conventional Christianity is beginning to pass away," the permanent element of religion, says Jowett, is to be found not in political or ecclesiastical organizations, nor in religious providence, nor in historical facts ["With the advance of knowledge we have to shift our ground, and most of the old defences of Christianity, and many of the objections to it, have gone out of fashion, and are no longer convincing to the mind"];

rather, the permanent element must be foregrounded in "the perfection of the Divine nature," statements all demonstrating Jowett's familiar attraction to the *Imatatio Christi*, and the caviling of "well–ascertained facts of history, or science."

87. Johnston, *Life and Letters of Liddon*, 63. "We can no longer speak of three independent witnesses of the Gospel narrative," Jowett urges. As a result, he suggests that there was no need to reconcile inconsistent narratives; whatever harmony there is pertains to the parallelism of similar words. Jowett also finds it unnecessary to harmonize verses, for the same words will be used differently among the Gospels; nor, he adds, can we simply attribute differences in the accounts to writers freelancing on the same subject and so including or omitting at will certain passages. Thus, he concludes, facts supporting the traditional view of authorship remain groundless (*Essays and Reviews*, 371).

88. Ibid.

89. C.P.S. Clarke, *The Oxford Movement and After*, 240.

90. Bodleian Ms. Eng. Lett.d 300, fols. 3–4. Liddon's friend and fellow conservative, Max Müller, was just as shocked by the document. In a 6 May letter, he asked M. Renan if he had seen the book, and remarked, however inaccurately on the religious affiliation of all the subscribers: "It would interest you and somewhat surprise you, if you consider that all the writers are clergymen of the Church of England" (*Life of Max Müller*, 1:246), the point being that had the book been written by laymen it would not have been so unsettling.

91. Bodleian Ms. Eng. Th. L.42, 167–69.

92. Somewhat ironically, Geldart perceptively noted that because Pusey was known to "practice and encourage confession," he too was regarded by many orthodox members of the university "as on the whole a rather worse heretic than the Professor of Greek" (*A Son of Belial*, 155).

93. Pusey told Keble in a May 1858 letter: "It is the Professorship, not the Professor, which is endowed." But he does admit some difficulty in keeping the two separate: "But I cannot, in my own mind, separate them. . . . It seems to me that we should be declaring ourselves indifferent as to Professor Jowett's misbelief if we make the grant" (*Life of Pusey*, 4:12).

94. Johnston, *Life and Letters of Liddon*, 60.

95. *The Diaries of Liddon.*

96. Bodleian Library Ms. Wilberforce D.41 fol. 1.

97. Keble College Ms. A married student, Burrows entered Magdalen Hall in 1853 at age 34. At Oxford he associated with moderate church policies and

conservative politics. He founded the conservative *Church and State Review* (1861) in order to offset the views expressed by the *Guardian*, was elected the Chichele Professor of Modern History (1862) over Froude, made a fellow of All Souls (1865), and was instrumental in founding Keble College (1870). He was probably the only naval officer to occupy a professorial chair at Oxford (*Dictionary of National Biography*).

98. Geldart, *A Son of Belial*, 154–55.
99. *The Diaries of Liddon.*
100. Ibid.
101. There are some twelve or so references to bluebells in Hopkins's diary and journals, the accounts of which were at times incorporated within poems. For example, an 1864 entry, "Sheaved of bluebells with silver tails," was later used in the poem "The furl of fresh–leaved dogrose down" to describe a young boy whose appearance was "like a juicy and jostling shock / Of bluebells sheaved in May."
102. *Journals*, 199.
103. Hopkins had a related experience. Taking with him the Frenchman Br. Tournade to Combe Wood near Roehampton "to see and gather blue-bells," he and Tournade "fell in bluehanded with a gamekeeper, . . . a humbling thing to do," says Hopkins (*Journals*, 243).
104. Bodleian Library unpublished Ms Eng. Poet e. 90. For the edited notes, see my essay "Gerard Manley Hopkins and Henry Parry Liddon."
105. *Journals*, 54.
106. *The Diaries of Liddon.*
107. *Bampton Lectures*, 453.
108. *Letters* 3:207. The inscription on Plato's door, probably in the Academy at Athens, read: "Let no one enter who does not know geometry" (*Oxford Dictionary of Quotation*, 3rd ed. [Oxford: Oxford University Press, 1979]). Hopkins tailored the inscription to read: "Whoso is a non–Oxford person let him (or her, which is more likely) not enter here." Bos–phoros, really Bosporos (literally an ox–carrying person), is the Greek version of the Latin Ox–ford, the name of several straits of which the Thracian and Cimmerian are best known (*Greek–English Lexicon*, 7th ed., ed. Henry George Liddell and Robert Scott [Oxford: The Clarendon Press, 1890]). Hopkins was probably familiar with the fifth edition (1861). I was assisted in this discovery by Dr. Penelope Bulloch and Alan Tadiello, librarians at Balliol College. Apparently the term "Bosphorus" was in Hopkins's time used regularly to describe Oxford. Geldart uses it repeatedly in his book to signify not only the city of Oxford but also the university.

109. *Journals*, 71.

110. Ibid., 72.

111. *Letters* 3:434.

112. In a letter to Arthur Hopkins, Gerard's brother, C. N. Luxmoore recalled that as a fourth–former, Gerard abstained "from all drink for three weeks, the pretext being a bet of 10/ to 6d, the real reason a conversation on seamen's suffering and human powers of endurance" (*Letters* 3:395). "On another occasion Gerard discovered that everyone ate too much salt at their meals, and passed a week without taking any" (Lahey, *Gerard Manley Hopkins*, 7).

113. Bodleian Ms. Eng. Th. L. 42, 50–63.

114. *Letters* 1:270.

115. Johnston, *Life and Letters of Liddon*, 79.

116. *Journals*, 55, 59; Hopkins noted the last three in his diary. The Bampton Lectures were named after John Bampton who bequeathed the income from his property and investments to endow eight divinity lecture sermons at Oxford. They were established

> to confirm and establish the Christian faith, and to confute all heretics and schismatics—upon the divine authority of the holy Scriptures—upon the authority of the writings of the primitive Fathers, as to the faith and practice of the primitive Church—upon the Divinity of the Holy Ghost—upon the Articles of the Christian Faith, as comprehended in the Apostles' and Nicene Creeds. (Liddon, *Bampton Lectures*, v–vi)

Gerard's interest in Liddon's Bamptons, which he conveyed in letters to his family, might have prompted Manley Hopkins to purchase a copy of it, signed and dated on 9 July 1868.

117. The first was made a year earlier, on 10 November 1864.

118. *Diaries of Liddon*,

119. Liddon, *Centenary Memoir*, 20.

120. In his contribution to *Essays and Reviews*, Henry Wilson faults Strauss for carrying critical ideology to excess and for not balancing it with an exegetical approach to Scripture. This imbalance, say Wilson, causes Strauss to substitute "a mere shadow for the Jesus of the Evangelists" (200).

121. *Diaries of Liddon*.

122. Bodleian Ms. Eng. Th. e.170, fol. 132.
123. Nixon, "Gerard Manley Hopkins and Henry Parry Liddon," 106.
124. Ibid., 105.
125. Ibid., 92.
126. Liddon, *Bampton Lectures*, 16–18.
127. Ibid., 17.
128. Ibid., 18.
129. Ibid., 9, 34, 27.
130. Ibid., 44.
131. Ibid., 45.
132. Ibid., 46.
133. On 21 January 1866 while Liddon was working on the fourth Bampton, he noted thinking "much about St. Paul on the doctrine of our Saviour's Godhead."
134 6:14–15; Nixon, "Gerard Manley Hopkins and Henry Parry Liddon," 102.
135. Liddon, *Bampton Lectures*, 161.
136. Ibid., 156.
137. Ibid., 223.
138. Ibid., 303–5.
139. Ibid., 309, 314.
140. Ibid., 321.
141. Ibid., 322–26. Liddon's rhetorical abilities were well recognized. The *Theological Review* at the time claimed that as preacher Liddon "rules over the minds of his hearers as is given perhaps to one man only in each generation. . . . 'I came to hear the finest preacher in England, and I am not disappointed,'" one member of the congregation testified; and another: "'He raised his hearers . . . from earth to heaven, and kept them there for more than an hour'" (Johnston, *Life and Letters of Liddon*, 80). Darwell Stone, in his essay, "Dr. Liddon as a Preacher," says this of Liddon's sermons:

> Every sentence was clear, nothing was left merely allusive or unexplained, every thought was in order, each section had its logical sequence, there was systematic method in the sermon as a whole, the phrasing throughout was carefully chosen and delicately balanced. The preacher's sensitive temperament made every sermon a beautiful work of art (*Centenary Memoir*, 18).

142. Hopkins, *Sermons*, 98.
143. Liddon, *Bampton Lectures*, 455.
144. *Journals*, 136.
145. Geoffrey H. Hartman, *The Unmediated Vision*.
146. Liddon, *Bampton Lectures*, 365.
147. Ibid.
148. Ibid., 386.
149. James Cotter speculates that the passage Hopkins had in mind called for one's own "intellectual and active dedication to a 'higher knowledge and adoration'" (*Inscape*, 6). That passage from the seventh Bampton reads:

> The adoring soul bends thought and heart and will before the footstool of the One Self–existing, All–creating, All–upholding Being; the soul wills to be as nothing before Him, or to exist only that it may recognize His Glory as altogether surpassing its words and thoughts (*Bampton Lectures*, 369).

150. Liddon, *Bampton Lectures*, 449.
151. Ibid., 449–50.
152. In the *Apologia*, which antedates the philosophical *An Essay in Aid of a Grammar* (1870) by six years, Newman broached the argument on certitude and probability. He declares, speaking in regard to his *Oxford University Sermons*, that "absolute certitude" on matters of natural theology and revelation "was the result of an *assemblage* of concurring and converging possibilities." He calls certitude a "habit of the mind," a "quality of propositions," and believes that even "probabilities which did not reach to logical certainty, might suffice for a mental certitude." Newman maintains that such mental certitude "might equal in measure and strength the certitude which was created by the strictest scientific demonstration." But such certitude, he insists, demands "plain duty" (*Apologia*, 31). So confident is Newman about his theory that he grounds his belief in God, in Christianity, and in Catholicism in probability; and that these beliefs, though dissimilar, yet demand "one and the same in nature of proof, as being probabilities—probabilities of a special kind, a cumulative, a transcendent probability but still probability." And it is God who willed that as we arrive at certitude in mathematics "by rigid demonstrations," so in religious inquiry we arrive at certitude on the grounds of "accumulated probabilities" (*Apologia*, 180–181).
153. Liddon, *Bampton Lectures*, 499.

154. Ibid., 505.
155. Cotter, *Inscape*, 7.
156. The poet's desire here is similar to the one expressed in Keats's "Ode To a Nightingale."
157. This last line echoes the penultimate line in Milton's *Paradise Lost* that describes the departure of Adam and Eve from Eden ("They hand in hand with wand'ring steps and slow"; I owe this connection to Donald Rackin). The expression also evokes the exchange that occurs in "The Habit of Perfection": "O feet / That want the yield of plushy sward, / But you shall walk the golden street."
158. We get a sense of this in a 16 October 1866 letter to Manley Hopkins. Asked to suspend his decision for a year or so, Gerard responded: "to stand still is not possible, thus: I must either obey the [Roman Catholic] Church or disobey"; for, he went on, "the Tractarian ground I have seen broken to pieces under my feet. What end then can be served by a delay in wh. I shd. go on believing this doctrine as long as I believed in God and shd. be by the fact of my belief drawn by a lasting strain towards the Catholic Church?" (*Letters* 3:91–92). In this letter to his father, Hopkins felt that even though Pusey and Liddon were "the only two men in the world who cd. avail to detain me: the fact that they were Anglicans kept me one, for arguments for the Church of England I had long ago felt there were none that wd. hold water, and when that influence gave way everything was gone" (94).
159. *Journals*, 146.
160. *Letters* 3:397; *Journals*, 147.
161. *Letters* 3:21–27.
162. Ibid., 29.
163. Bodleian Library Ms. Eng. Lett. D. 300, fol. 38.
164. *Diaries of Liddon.*
165. *Letters* 3:400. In this letter Hopkins tells of his desire to see Pusey when he returns to Oxford. This same wish was expressed in a letter to his mother two days later (*Letters* 3:97). We do know that Hopkins had heard from Pusey six or so days earlier, and Pusey declined to see him, for to do so, in Pusey's words, would be "simply 'to satisfy relations.'" Pusey resented being used by young men who, already determined to convert, came to see him only to say that he could not dissuade them: "This is merely to waste my time, and create the impression that I have nothing to say. It has, in fact, when done, been a great abuse of the love I have for all, especial[l]y the young" (*Letters* 3:400). Apparently Pusey's reticence towards opportu-

nistic undergraduates was well known. R.W. Church said of him that though he was "accessible; he allowed his friends to bring their friends to him, and met them more than half–way." Still, "He was impatient of mere idle worldliness, of conceit and impertinence" (*The Oxford Movement*, 129). This feeling seems hinted at in Hopkins's letter to his father: "those who do apply to see him [Pusey] may get such answers as young Mr. Lane Fox did, who gave up 30,000 a year just lately to become a Catholic" (*Letters* 3:94). Why then the discrepancy between Hopkins's expressed desire to see Pusey and Pusey's already expressed rejection? I believe it was always Hopkins's desire to see Pusey, and not simply to hear from him. So even though he had heard from Pusey, Hopkins seemed still resolved to converse with Pusey—a meeting that never took place.

166. Johnston, *Life and Letters of Liddon*, 33, 38.

167. Keble College Ms.

168. Johnston, *Life and Letters of Liddon*, 43. Liddon's language here echoes Wordsworth and Newman. Wordsworth informs us in his *Preface to the Lyrical Ballads* that "I have at all times endeavoured to look steadily at my subject, consequently I hope it will be found that there is in these Poems little falsehood of description" (*The Prose Works*, 1:132); and Newman talks of steadily contemplating the object of faith ("The Glories of Mary," *Discourses to Mixed Congregations*, 364).

169. "Some Recollections," *Centenary Memoir*, 25.

170. Johnston, *Life and Letters of Liddon*, 79–80.

171. 15 October 1867 letter to the *Theological Review*, Keble College Ms.

172. Johnston, *Life and Letters of Liddon*, 259.

173. *Letters* 3:434–35.

174. Ibid., 435–36.

175. Ibid., 92, 400–1, 436. Hopkins hinted at this in a letter to his father: "Three of my friends, whose conversions were later than mine, Garrett, Addis, and Wood, have already been received." Even Bright, in a letter to Liddon, implied that Hopkins's decision to convert was prompted in part by Addis's conversion (*Letters* 3:92, 436).

176. Ibid., 401–2.

177. Ibid., 402–3.

178. Ibid., 403–4.

179. Ibid., 436.

180. Bodleian Library Ms. Eng. Lett. D.300, fol. 55. The exception Liddon most likely had in mind was G.A. Simcox. In his diary of 25 October, after

he had returned posthaste on the Hopkins affair, Liddon noted: "Walked with G. A. Simcox. I feel that he will follow Addis. He seems to think that the practical dilemma lies between Rome and infidelity" (*The Diaries of Liddon*). Simcox had obviously been reading Newman's *Apologia*.
181. Bodleian Library Ms. Wilberforce D.41, fol. 64.
182. *The Diaries of Liddon.*
183. Ibid.
184. *Letters* 3:98.
185. Keating, "Impressions of Father Gerard Hopkins, S. J.," 63.
186. *Letters* 3:31–34.
187. Ibid., 42.
188. *Journals*, 158.
189. *Letters* 3:49–50.
190. "The Half–Way House." The closing line of the poem, "He is with you in the breaking of the bread," clearly articulates the doctrine of Real Presence. In a 1 June 1864, letter to his Highgate friend, E. H. Coleridge (grandson to the poet), Hopkins wrote: "The great aid to belief and object of belief is the doctrine of the Real Presence in the Blessed Sacrament of the Altar. . . . Hold that and you will gain all Catholic truth" (*Letters* 3:17). This doctrine will prove important to the Christology in Hopkins's poetry, and will account in part for the logocentricity and the theodicy of his poetic landscape. Like "The Half–Way House," "A soliloquy of one of the spies left in the wilderness," written on or around 20 July 1864, was the beginning of Hopkins's exodus from Anglicanism.

Chapter 2

1.   "Impressions of Father Gerard Hopkins, S.J.," 68.
2.   G.F. Lahey, *Gerard Manley Hopkins*, 44; Unpublished Bodleian MS, Dep. Bridges 62, fol. 85–86; John Pick, *Gerard Manley Hopkins:* Additional biographies of Hopkins, such as Eleanor Ruggles's *Gerard Manley Hopkins*, Paddy Kitchen's *Gerard Manley Hopkins*, and Bernard Bergonzi's *Gerard Manley Hopkins* have also acknowledged the relationship. Other studies have also acknowledged the relationship: Harold Weatherby's "Hopkins, Newman, and Scotus"; Michael D. Moore's "Newman and the Motif of Intellectual Pain in Hopkins' 'Terrible Sonnets'"; Norman MacKenzie's *A Reader's Guide to Gerard Manley Hopkins*, which notes literary echoes from Newman in several of Hopkins's pieces; and Sjaak Zonneveld's "Hopkins and Newman's Oxford Oratory."

3.   Robert Martin, 44.

4.   Ian Ker, "The Poet and His God," *The Washington Post*, 23 June 1991, 4.

5.   White, *Hopkins*, 137, 155–57.

6.   "Newman and Victorian Liberalism," 206.

7.   Moore, "Newman and the Motif of Intellectual Pain," 30.

8.   Horatio Brown, *John Addington Symonds*, 77.

9.   Chapman, *Faith and Revolt*, 13.

10. *Letters* 3:30, 93. Several of Hopkins's Oxford friends converted to Roman
     Catholicism: William Addis, Alfred Garrett, Alexander Wood, V.S.S.
     Coles, and Henry Challis.

11. Katherine Brégy, "Gerard Hopkins: An Epitaph and an Appreciation,"
     433; Alison Sulloway, *Gerard Manley Hopkins and the Victorian Temper*,
     23. Sulloway's is the most historically satisfying account of Hopkins
     within the context of the Tractarian Movement.

12. Newman's 2 June 1860 letter to E.E. Estcourt (*Letters*, 19:352). The letter
     addresses the building of a new Catholic Church in Oxford.

13. Martin Geldart, *A Son of Belial*, 168. Geldart humorously called Gerard
     Gerontius, a fictional name possibly intended to link him to Newman's
     character, Gerontius.

14. *Letters* 3:32.

15. Ward, *The Life of Newman*, 1: 23. Liddon faulted Newman for this extreme
     position ("Rome or nothing"), believing that such reasoning, if followed,
     would lead to "sheer unbelief," the very plight Newman sought to avoid
     (Johnston, 94).

16. Newman, 2:312–13.

17. Ibid. 1:150.

18. White, *Hopkins*, 56.

19. *Letters* 3:74.

20. Ibid., 221.

21. Ian Ker, *The Achievement of John Henry Newman*, 153; J. Cameron, *John
     Henry Newman*, 7.

22. Gardner, *Gerard Manley Hopkins*, 2:17.

23. *Journals*, 71.

24. *Facsimile*, 190.

25. Ward, *The Life of Newman*, 1:55.

26. *Journals*, 71. Provost Fortescue, an Anglican who showed strong Roman
     Catholic leanings, chose temporarily to remain an Anglican on the
     rationale of the Branch Church theory. The theory maintains that the
     Church of England is a legitimate extension or arm of the old Catholic

Church. In *Certain Difficulties*, Newman defines "Branch Church" as one "separate from its stem; and if we ask what is meant by the stem, I suppose it means the 'Universal Church'" (1:170). See Hopkins's discussion of Branch Church in a 15 August 1867 letter to his friend Urquhart (*Letters* 3:40–41), and for more information on Provost Fortescue, who finally converted to Roman Catholicism in 1871, see *Journals*, 338–39.

27.   Newman expressed a similar idea in dealing with religious compromises that disciples of Tractarianism were forced to confront: "It will be a miserable thing for you and for me, if I have been instrumental in bringing you but half–way" (*Certain Difficulties*, 1:4). In the *Grammar* he rejects the notion of "half–assents," calling it no more an assent than a "half–truth is a kind of truth" (116). Darwin, too, felt similarly about halfway positions. Regarding his theory of natural selection, he wrote: "For a very long time I halted half way; but I do not believe that any inquiring mind will rest half–way" (*Life* 2:58), a sentiment that both Hopkins and Newman shared. One is reminded here of Mark Twain's "half–way house" (Hawaii), because of its location near the equator and its pleasant climate. Sensuality and paralysis are here connected to halfway positions.

28.   *Letters* 3:92. Newman talked similarly about the shattering of his religious ambivalence: "the theory of the *Via Media* was absolutely pulverized"; and again, "I was breaking the *Via Media* to pieces" (*Apologia*, 111, 185).

29.   In the first of two poems dedicated to Oxford, Hopkins describes the area in epicurean terms, fondly calling it "my park, my pleasaunce [literally "pleasure ground"]; this to me / As public is my great privacy, / All mine, yet common to my every peer."

30.   MacKenzie, *A Reader's Guide*, 26.

31.   Newman, *Apologia*, 29, 37.

32.   Ibid., 216–17.

33.   Lahey, *Gerard Manley Hopkins*, 21.

34.   *Gerard Manley Hopkins*, 127.

35.   Hopkins felt that Challis's conversion was not particularly influential to the Catholicward Movement for he "never had much belief in the Church of England" (*Letters* 1:3). Two years later Challis joined Hopkins to teach at the Birmingham Oratory (*Letters* 3:231; *Journals*, 159), but would remain a Catholic for only four more years. On 5 March 1872, Hopkins, now at Stonyhurst, heard from Challis that he had left the Roman Catholic Church (*Journals*, 218): "I have heard from Challis (you will hardly remember him) the sad news of his apostasy," Hopkins wrote William Garrett (*Letters* 3:57).

36. Ian Ker, *John Henry Newman*, 300.

37. *Letters*, 11:3.

38. Benjamin Jowett, *Dear Miss Nightingale*, 107.

39. We know, based on the replies from Newman's letters, that Hopkins wrote as many letters to Newman as he received from him. However, only three are extant. Why Newman, who so painstakingly preserved many of the letters written to him, kept so few of Hopkins's is puzzling.

40. *Letters* 3:404, 23; 1:5.

41. Ward, *The Life of Newman*, 1:62–63.

42. Church, *The Oxford Movement*, 129.

43. Pusey comes across bookish and cold. Despite, and probably because of, his "rare and conscientious learning and accuracy" (Chadwick, *The Mind of the Oxford Movement*, 37), he was "severe always in his moral judgment," according to Bernard Reardon; "his weakness lay in his shortness of intellectual vision, in his lack of understanding his own times," and in "his rigidity in positions adopted once for all" (*Religious Thought in the Victorian Age*, 126). "If he thought a party to be following him," writes Chadwick of Pusey, "he would have shut himself in his house, said his prayers, and continued with his studies" (*The Mind of the Oxford Movement*, 47); "he lived on the edge of the general society rather than in it," said his friend and biographer, Henry Parry Liddon (*Life of Edward Bouverie Pusey*, 1:25). In *Praeterita*, Ruskin recalled Pusey as one "not in the least a picturesque or tremendous figure, but only a sickly and rather ill put together English clerical gentleman, who never looked one in the face [a stunning portrait given Ruskin's own detached persona], or appeared aware of the state of the weather" (202). Thus, although Hopkins confessed to him for three years, read his tracts, attended his lectures and sermons, and was altogether an early devotee—even to term himself a "Puseyite" (as did so many, including Jowett)—Pusey's response to Hopkins's single request for advice during his religious crisis received a formal, compassionless, and uncompromising response. Newman (*Apologia*, 64–66) and R.W. Church (*The Oxford Movement*, 97–98) recalled a more amiable Pusey, although a year later (1865) when Pusey's *Eirenicon* was published, a work meant, Newman felt, to provoke Catholics, Newman was less sympathetic. He pointed to Pusey's "slovenly habit" of dress and beard, and not answering letters that "do not lie in the line of the direct work which he has on hand" (*Letters*, 22:158).

44. *Inscape*, 55.

45. Newman, *Letters*, 22:294.

46. Ibid., 302.

47. *Letters* 3:91-92.

48. Newman, *Apologia*, 181.

49. *Letters* 3:92.

50. *Certain Difficulties*, 1:164–196.

51. *Letters* 3:405–6.

52. Newman, *Letters,* 23:25.

53. *Letters* 3:407; see also Newman, *Letters,* 23:313–14. The eccentric Digby
Dolben, Bridges's cousin, was a minor poet and an enthusiastic Anglo–
Catholic who would later (1867) correspond with Newman about convert-
ing to Roman Catholicism. Bridges confessed that in their youth both he
and Dolben "regarded the claim of the church in the same way as Cardinal
Newman had elaborated it in his writings; and we were no doubt indirectly
influenced by his views" (Robert Bridges, *The Poems of Digby Mackworth
Dolben*, xiv). Dolben's family felt that he might "run off some day and be
irrevocably received into the Roman Communion by Cardinal Newman."
Hopkins met Dolben in February 1865 when Dolben visited Bridges at
Oxford. The two apparently spent much time together, for Bridges
recalled that "Gerard conceived a high admiration for [Dolben], and
always spoke of him afterwards with great affection" (Bridges, civ, lxxiii).
In a 30 August 1867 letter to Bridges concerning Dolben's death and
Newman's response to it, Hopkins wrote: "You know there can very
seldom have happened the loss of so much beauty (in body and mind and
life)" (*Letters* 1:16–17). Years later when Hopkins wrote "The Lantern out
of Doors," we are again reminded of Dolben in the lines: "Men go by me
whom either beauty bright / In mold or mind or what not else makes rare."
For more information on the relationship between Newman and Dolben,
including a long letter Dolben wrote to him on 20 March 1867, see
Newman, *Letters,* 23:313–14.

54. Robert Martin, *Gerard Manley Hopkins*, 159.

55. Newman, *Letters* 3:407.

56. *The Selected Letters of Robert Bridges*, 1:87–88. In describing himself in
the years from 1841 to 1845, Newman said that out of duty to the Anglican
Church he discouraged strongly all individuals inclined to Rome. Of the
reasons he gave for that action, the one that applies to Dolben was the belief
that some of those converts were "acting under excitement" (*Apologia*,
138).

57. Newman, *Letters*, 3:407.

58. Alfred Thomas, following Lahey (*Gerard Manley Hopkins*, 46), claims that Hopkins replaced Darnell (*Hopkins the Jesuit*, 8). But Hopkins took Walford's place, not Darnell's. Walford, an 1866 convert and former Eton master, had joined the Oratory staff that year to teach the Classics; his assignment seems to have been temporary, "helping us," Newman called it. In August of that year Walford decided to join the Jesuits. In a 6 September letter to a friend, Newman indicated: "Hopkins must show his worth in Walford's place" (Newman, *Letters*, 23:330). Hopkins met Walford when he, Hopkins, first visited Newman at the Oratory. Newman left him in Walford's charge, who took him to lunch then gave him a tour of the school and Oratory. Hopkins would again meet Walford in his novitiate at Roehampton. He and Walford read the Papal Bulls together and on one occasion, 30 April 1869, Hopkins substituted for him as a catechist to Isleworth (Thomas, *Hopkins the Jesuit*, 44, 49). Bellasis was the eldest son of Edward, a lawyer, convert to Tractarianism, and close friend of Newman, and the one to whom Newman dedicated the *Grammar*.

59. *Letters* 3:228.

60. Ibid., 43–44. During this time, Hopkins was entertained by a string quartet. Newman, an accomplished violinist, was one of the performers. Soon Hopkins was himself taking violin lessons (*Letters* 3:231).

61. *Journals*, 158.

62. The inclement weather did not help Hopkins's despondency. The first word he wrote in his journal the day after he arrived at the Oratory is "Dull." In addition, at least one of the following words—"dull," "cold," "shower," "frost," and "snow"—occupies almost every listing in his journal until 2 April (*Journals*, 157–63).

63. *Letters* 3:231–32.

64. Ibid., 45.

65. In a letter to Henry Coleridge on the *Grammar*, Newman wrote: "I have done my best, and given my all—and I leave it to Him to prosper or not, as He thinks fit, for whom I have done it" (*Letters*, 25:51). Although Hopkins was not privy to this letter, his and Newman's temperament were so similar that his expectation for his own poetry was couched in exactly the same language: "Also in some med. today I earnestly asked our Lord to watch over my compositions . . . ; that he should have them as his own and employ or not employ them as he should see fit" (*Sermons*, 253–54).

66. Newman, *Letters*, 3:408.

67. Ibid. 24:63.

68. *Journals*, 165.

69. *Gerard Manley Hopkins*, 206.

70. Newman, *Letters,* 3:408.

71. Ibid. 12:26.

72. *Hopkins the Jesuit*, 20.

73. *Letters* 3:51. Newman himself said that his lectures on *Certain Difficulties* were not "formally directed against the National Church." Rather, they were "addressed to the 'Children of the Movement of 1833,' to impress upon them, that, whatever the case with others, their duty at least was to become Catholics, since Catholicism was the real scope and issue of that Movement" (*Apologia*, 422).

74. *Certain Difficulties*, 1:9–10.

75. Ibid., 1:4, 25.

76. *Apologia*, 35, 50, 63, 112, 156, 214.

77. *Henry Scott Holland: Memoirs and Letters*, 29.

78. *Journals*, 188–89.

79. *Letters* 1:23.

80. *Letters* 3:105.

81. In a 7 February 1869 letter to his mother, Hopkins confessed: "I have been trying to write [for] some time and I am afraid you have been waiting to hear" (*Letters* 3:107). The same sentiment was expressed in his next letter to his mother, dated 30 April. In his journal of 18 September, two days after the "Long Retreat" (the thirty–day Ignatian part of the novitiate) started, Hopkins noted: "Henceforth I keep no regular weather–journal but only notes" (*Journals*, 189). This stipulation, whether it was to apply only to the retreat or to Hopkins's entire novitiate, was not altogether adhered to. Nevertheless, it explains the limited journal entries made during his novitiate.

82. Thomas, *Hopkins the Jesuit*, 27–29.

83. *Gerard Manley Hopkins*, 48.

84. On 21 April of that year, Hopkins's name was mentioned to Newman. Requesting from Newman the location of his rooms at Trinity College, Alfred Plummer, a friend of Hopkins and Liddon since 1864, used Hopkins's name as entrance to Newman: "We have several common acquaintances and friends e.g. Gerard Hopkins. . . . Once when on a visit to Gerard Hopkins, I was under the same roof with you [at the Oratory, 2 April 1868; see *Journals*, 163]. . . . But I never came across you, and neither he nor I ventured to intrude upon you" (Newman, *Letters*, 25:105n). Newman replied to Plummer the following day, providing him a pencil

sketch of his rooms at Trinity. He mentioned his celebrated snapdragon in the letter and included its location in the first sketch.

85. *Letters* 3:409.
86. Ibid.
87. Ibid.
88. Father Ambrose conveyed to Newman a message from Henry Norfolk requesting him to write a pamphlet in response to Gladstone's article on the purpose of the Church. On 3 December 1874 Newman wrote to Duke Norfolk, the notable Catholic layman: "Will you let my Pamphlet take the shape of a letter addressed to you?" later remarking, "I cannot write at all, except in the form of a letter" (Newman, *Letters*, 27:164, 171). Completed on 27 December 1874, the letter, in an essay form common at the time, reveals the occasional nature of so much of Newman's protean corpus and the significant role of Victorian letter writing. In fact, letters exchanged between clergymen on critical issues were often published.
89. *Letters* 1:31.
90. MacKenzie, *A Reader's Guide*, 60; Newman, *Sermons and Discourses, 1838–57*, 2:349–50. Alfred Thomas attributes the revival of the Jesuit Movement to this sermon of Newman's (*Hopkins the Jesuit*, 17). Interestingly, too, in the *Apologia* Newman talked of his final days as an Anglican using the metaphor as of someone on a death bed. In this same context, he told Henry Wilberforce on 27 April 1845: "My spring, my summer, are over." He obviously saw his conversion metaphorically, as a second spring or spiritual rebirth. Keble's poem for the Third Sunday after Easter from *The Christian Year* compares well with Hopkins's spring sonnet and also with the notion of spiritual rebirth.
91. Newman, *Sermons and Discourses*, 2:345–47.
92. Ibid. 2:356.
93. Newman, *Letters*, 3:292.
94. Both poems also show an awareness of Wordsworth's "Expostulation and Reply" and "The Tables Turned."
95. Newman, *Apologia*, 217.
96. Cotter sees in Hopkins's christology an indebtedness to Newman (*Inscape*, 56). Harold Weatherby also points out that during the period from 1873 to 1883, the decade of Hopkins's most fruitful poetic period, he was "occupied theologically and philosophically" with Newman ("Hopkins, Newman, and Scotus," 77).
97. *A Reader's Guide*, 81.
98. Newman, *Letters*, 3:410–11.

99. Bodleian Library Ms. Autog. b13 fol. 418.

100. *Letters* 3:257.

101. "The Month of Mary" expresses the natural splendor ("The blue transparent sky"), evanescence ("The flowrets, brightly as they smile, / Shall perish altogether"), and realism ("But earth's best joys have all an end") of Wordsworth's "Ode: Intimations of Immortality." In addition, Newman's "green grass" and "glittering grove" that "tell us of that Paradise / Of everlasting rest, / And that high Tree, all flowers and fruit, / The sweetest, yet the best" are reminiscent of Wordsworth's "there's a Tree, of many, one, / A single Field which I have looked upon, / Both of them speak of something that is gone."

102. Newman, *Letters,* 3:411.

103. *Andromeda's Chains,* 2.

104. Ibid., 52, 71. There is also in "Andromeda" an implicit indication that one of her pursuers is Darwinism. In their recent biography, *Darwin: The Life of a Tormented Evolutionist,* Adrian Desmond and James Moore provide a reading of sexuality consonant with Hopkins's employment of the Andromeda myth. They point out that in the Wilberforce-Huxley debate, Wilberforce's analogy of the ape to woman cleverly invoked a threat to the sanctity of the Victorian woman. "Maidens stood for the Church and the chaste against the sordid evolutionists" (497). Hopkins was no doubt cognizant of the analogy and its implications.

105. Ibid., 74–75.

106. *Sermons,* 104–5; I owe this observation to MacKenzie's *A Reader's Guide,* 131. Though without admitting it, or else not conscious of it, Newman is participating in the Andromeda tradition Munich describes.

107. A similar Orchean image occurs in *Gerontius:* "And circles round the Crucified, had seized, / And scorch'd and shrivell'd it; and now it lies / Passive and still before the awful Throne."

108. *Letters* 3:155.

109. Ibid., 411. Hopkins had recently written "Spring and Fall," a poem indebted to Eliot's *The Mill on the Floss.*

110. Newman, *Letters,* 24:389.

111. Martin, *Gerard Manley Hopkins,* 365.

112. *Letters* 3:63.

113. Newman, *Letters,* 3:413, 164. Hopkins had also told Bridges that the College is "a sort of ruin and for purposes of study very nearly empty" (*Letters* 1:190).

114. *Letters* 1: 190.

115. Brian Vickers, *Times Literary Supplement*, 3 March 1966, 178. In the 15 September 1966 issue of the *Supplement*, W.H. Gardner, answering Vickers's essay, agrees that Hopkins was, "possibly, evoking and exploiting Newman's passage." However, Gardner attributes the connection to "an unconscious 'echo,' the verbal resemblance being due to the fairly close 'association of ideas'" (868). Instead, Gardner argues for the origin in Shakespeare's *Antony and Cleopatra* (4.15.57–59). The opening of "Carrion Comfort" also seems indebted to "Thyrsis," Arnold's elegy to Clough. The speaker rediscovers the signal elm and is reassured emotionally that Thyrsis still lives, and so vows not to submit to despair: ". . . yet I will not despair. / Despair I will not . . . " (159.192–93). These sources reveal Hopkins's exceptional success in masking his precursors; the despair in "Carrion Comfort" and "The Leaden Echo and the Golden Echo" could well have been borrowed from all of these sources with which Hopkins was very familiar: Newman, Shakespeare, and Arnold. However, the *Gerontius* case seems most convincing because of the close relatedness of terms in Newman's poem to ones in Hopkins's (Newman's "negations," "collapse," and "Of all that makes me a man" compare with Hopkins's reiterated "not"; "untwist," and "these last strands of man / In me"). In addition, words such as "ruin," "pain," and "masterful" are used frequently by Hopkins.

116. Hopkins, says Michael Moore, rejects the "passive submission to death dramatized in Newman's poem" ("Newman and the Motif of Intellectual Pain in Hopkins's 'Terrible Sonnets,'" 35).

117. *Discourses addressed to Mixed Congregations*, 346, 41.

118. *Letters* 3:341–42.

119. *Discourses addressed to Mixed Congregations*, 344–48.

120. *Sermons*, 138.

121. Keats, *The Letters of John Keats*, 1:279–81, 185.

122. Virgil, *The Aeneid*, Book 4.

123. *Journals*, 76, 106. Chromatic and diatonic are musical terms and so forfeit some of their connotations when applied to poetry. Willi Apel, in the *Harvard Dictionary of Music* (1967), notes that chromaticism is more expressive than diatonic and that the former was used particularly for "programmatic and pictorial purposes to indicate grief or lament" (144). See chapter three for additional discussion of the terms.

124. In *The Victorian Sage*, John Holloway cites examples from Newman's works to show their reliance on the richness of metaphors and analogies.

These operate, says Holloway, to provide "vivid imagery in which we may see the life of the world and of the Church" (181).

125. *Grammar of Assent*, 186.

126. *Letters* 3:58.

127. Ibid., 373, 380.

128. Houghton, *The Art of Newman's 'Apologia'*, 48; Gates, "Newman as a Prose Writer," 65–66.

129. *Essays and Sketches*, 2:204.

130. *The Idea of a University*, 232.

131. "The Danger of Accomplishments," *Parochial and Plain Sermons*, 460–61; "Aristotle's Poetics," *Essays Critical and Historical*, 1:25.

132. *Journals*, 112.

133. Wordsworth, *Prose Works*, 1:131, 138.

134. *The Prelude*, 1805, 10:372.

135. Ibid., 2:353–55.

136. *Apologia*, 63, 27, 100, 8, 51.

137. *Letters* 3:380.

138. *Apologia*, 242, 2.

139. Ibid., 7.

140. *Journals*, 289.

141. *Letters* 1:46.

142. *Hopkins, the Self, and God*, 126.

143. *Journals*, 85.

144. *Victorian Devotional Poetry*, 8, 2.

145. *Romanticism and Religion: The Tradition of Coleridge and Wordsworth in the Victorian Church*.

146. *Letters* 2:98–99.

147. *Grammar of Assent*, 214. Several times in the *Apologia*, Newman confessed having been influenced by the Romantics. Treating that indebtedness, R.W. Church points out that "prominent among the newer ideas (which were more or less related to Romanticism) were readiness to respect and to learn from the 'primitive,' the unsophisticated, and the unfamiliar; reverence for the sublime, the mysterious, and the awe–ful" (*The Oxford Movement*, xv). In his brilliant study, *Victorian Devotional Poetry*, G.B. Tennyson maintains that the Oxford Movement was "a new kind of awareness made possible in large part by the European–wide phenomenon of Romanticism" (9). For further connection between the Oxford Movement and Romanticism, see chapter 9 of Hoxie Neal Fairchild's *Religious Trends in English Poetry* (vol. 4) and Michael

Bright's "English Literary Romanticism and the Oxford Movement," 385–404.

148. In fact, without referring to Wordsworth's "Ode: Intimations of Immortality" in his *Lectures on Poetry*, Keble talked about Pythagoras and the pre–existence of the soul; that our souls were born elsewhere, came into the world with "some tinge and temper of their past existence" that is often made conscious in a dim but still real way. "The finest poem of the greatest poet within our own times is mainly based on this belief: namely, that our recollections of childhood are touched with . . . dim feeling of a former existence and of a life closer to divine influence" (2:453).

149. *Lectures on Poetry*, 2:201, 466, 480–83.

150. *Victorian Devotional Poetry*, 68.

151. Vargish, *Newman*, 105.

152. Wordsworth, *Prose Works*, 3:65.

153. "John Keble," *Essays Critical and Historical*, 2:443–45.

154. Keble, *Lectures on Poetry*, 2:272.

155. Abrams, *The Mirror and the Lamp*, 147.

156. Jowett, *Life of Benjamin Jowett*, 1:69.

157. *The Oxford Movement and After*, 40.

158. *Apologia*, 29; *The Mind of the Oxford Movement*, 28.

159. *Victorian Devotional Poetry*, 23.

160. "Aristotle's Poetics," *Essays Critical and Historical*, 1:23; "John Keble," *Essays Critical and Historical*, 2:442–43.

161. Chadwick, *The Mind of the Oxford Movement*, 64.

162. Battiscombe, *John Keble*, 110.

163. Ellsberg, *Created to Praise*, 47.

164. "Halfway to a New Land," 115.

165. *Lectures on Poetry*, 1:21–22.

166. Newman, "John Keble," *Essays Critical and Historical*, 2:442.

167. Wordsworth, *Prose Works*, 62.

168. "Prospects of the Anglican Church," *Essays Critical and Historical*, 1:290–91.

169. Newman, "John Keble," *Essays Critical and Historical*, 2:441.

170. Newman, *Letters* 2:55, 69.

171. "Aristotle's Poetics," *Essays Critical and Historical* 1:10.

172. *Letters* 2:146–48.

173. Ibid., 8, 93.

174. Robert Bridges, *The Spirit of Man*, with an introduction by W.H. Auden.

175. Ibid. Paul Fussell felt that the comforts the anthology provided were "badly needed, for 1915 had been one of the most depressing years in British history. It had been a year not only of ironic mistakes but of a grossly unimaginative underestimation of the enemy and of the profound difficulties of siege warfare" (*The Great War and Modern Memory*, 11-12).

176. *The Oxford Movement*, 112.

177. Newman, *Apologia*, 41.

178. Tennyson, *Victorian Devotional Poetry*, 122–23; this work of Tennyson's offers the most significant treatment of Tractarian poetry and poetics.

179. "Aristotle's Poetics," *Essays Critical and Historical*, 1:12.

180. Newman, *Letters,* 3:121.

181. *The Autobiography of Isaac Williams*, 63; Newman, *Letters,* 5:26.

182. "John Keble," *Essays Critical and Historical*, 2:443.

183. *The Victorian Church, Part 1*, 67.

184. Ibid.

185. *The Victorian Church, Part 2*, 470.

186. I owe these discoveries to Joseph J. Reilly's "The Hymns of John Henry Newman."

187. Benson, *The English Hymn*, 498; most helpful in treating this topic are Louis Benson's chapters on "The Hymnody of the Oxford Revival" and "The Romantic Movement."

188. In a related context, Hopkins wrote to Bridges apologizing for how poorly performed was their Corpus Christi celebration at Roehampton which Bridges witnessed. A Corpus Christi procession should be "brisk and joyous," wrote Hopkins. And the hymns sung, "though they have the imperfect rhetoric and weakness in idiom of all medieval Latin verse . . . are never the less remarkable works of genius and would [had Bridges "a book to follow the words sung"] have given meaning to the whole, even to the music, much more to the rite." Hopkins could not resist reprimanding Bridges for his latent skepticism: "It is long since such things had any significance for you" (Letters 1:148).

189. Letters 3:140.

190. *Victorian Devotional Poetry*, 5.

191. *Letters* 1:246, 92; *Letters* 2:42, 149, *Letters* 3:140.

192. Nixon, "Portrait of a Friendship," 296.

193. Benson, *The English Hymn*, 514.

194. "Books Belonging to Hopkins and His Family," 27.

195. *Letters* 1:124.

196. *Sermons and Discourses*, 2:185.
197. Newman, *Letters*, 3:412.
198. *Letters* 3:58.
199. *Grammar*, 140.
200. Ibid., 123–24.
201. "Implicit Reason," *University Sermons*, 257.
202. Newman, *Letters*, 25:97.
203. *Grammar*, 316.
204. Ibid., 14, 140, 314.
205. Ibid., 63, 135.
206. *Apologia*, 31, 180–81.
207. Ibid., 29.
208. Newman, *Letters*, 24:274–75.
209. Downes, *Hopkins' Sanctifying Imagination*, 12; MacKenzie, "The Imperative Voice," 107.
210. Davidson, *Life of Archbishop Tait*, 1:275.
211. *Letters* 3:16–17.
212. Newman, *Letters*, 1:5.
213. *Certain Difficulties*, 2:312.
214. Downes, *Hopkins's Sanctifying Imagination*, 16.
215. *Letters* 3:31.
216. Ibid., 93.
217. *Letters* 1:186-87.
218. Ibid., 186–88.
219. Ibid., 149. Hopkins points to this doctrine in "The Bugler's First Communion" in the expression "Forth Christ from cupboard fetched."
220. Newman, *Letters*, 3:412.
221. *Grammar*, 67.
222. *The Achievement of John Henry Newman*, 22.
223. *Letters* 3:388. The previous sentence in the Newman passage reads: "To most men argument makes the point in hand only more doubtful, and considerably less impressive"; and the subsequent sentence: "He is influenced by what is direct and precise" (Grammar, 67). In "'The Ecstasy of Interest': Contemplation as Parallelism's Praxis," Maria R. Lichtmann shows that the *Grammar* was critical to Hopkins's poetics of inscape, contemplation, and apprehension. Although otherwise insightful, Lichtmann's essay fails to recognize Tractarian Romanticism as a link between Hopkins and Newman. In fact, Lichtmann even mistakenly

claims, as I have been arguing, that "Tractarian poetics, romantic in origin and in assumptions, could hold little appeal for Hopkins" (34).

224. *Letters* 3:413. The five or so years Hopkins spent in Dublin were talked about, says Norman White, mostly in terms of his reaction to the "political situation and the depressed state of his College; to read his letters from Dublin is to sense that he knew he was on the losing side of both matters" ("Gerard Manley Hopkins and the Irish Row," 93). In his first Dublin letter to his mother, Hopkins wrote: "We [the English] have enemies here—indeed what is Ireland but an open or secret war of fierce enemies of every sort?—and our College is really struggling for existence with difficulties within and without" (*Letters* 3:163–64). On his political views, see Franco Marucci's "Hopkins's Political Ideas."

225. *The Life of Newman*, 2:516.

226. Newman, *Letters*, 3:413. Newman was always perturbed by his physician's deceptive optimism regarding his health.

227. *Letters* 1:252.

228. Newman, *Letters*, 3:413–14.

229. *Letters* 3:281–83.

230. Newman, *Letters*, 3:414.

231. "Impressions of Father Gerard Hopkins, S.J.," 68.

Chapter 3

1. Henkin, *Darwinism in the English Novel*, 62; Stevenson, *Darwin among the Poets*, 5; Bibby, "Huxley and the Reception of the *Origin*," 76–78. Charles Kingsley, *His Letters and Memories of His Life*, 337. Darwin was himself conscious of the effect of his theory on the belief structure of the day. In a July 1871 letter to Wallace, he expressed great concern that Mivart's book was "producing a great effect against Natural Selection, and more especially against me" (*The Life and Letters of Charles Darwin*, 2:323–24). In letters following—mostly the ones to Wallace and Huxley—Darwin's anxiety with Mivart heightens.

2. Robert M. Young, *Darwin's Metaphors*, 1.

3. Alvar Ellegard, *Darwin and the General Reader*, 17.

4. *The Autobiography*, 119-20.

5. Darwin, *More Letters* 1:213.

6. Darwin, *Life* 1:445.

7. Ibid. 1:132.

8. On Baden Powell and science, and especially on Darwin, see Pietro
    Corsi's *Science and Religion: Baden Powell and the Anglican Debate,
    1800–1860.* Frederick Temple, another of the writers of *Essays and
    Reviews*, devoted his entire 1884 Bampton Lectures to *The Relations
    between Religion and Science.* The fourth and sixth Bamptons, "Apparent
    Conflict between Religion and the Doctrine of Evolution" and "Apparent
    Collisions between Religion and the Doctrine of Evolution," specifically
    addressed evolution. The lecture accepts evolution but with design,
    purpose, and foresight, subscribing thus to Paley's natural theology. "We
    cannot think," said Temple, "that this ["the world such as we see and all
    its endless beauty"] is not designed, nor that the Artist who produced it was
    blind to what was coming out of His work" (121). As his fellow essayist,
    C.W. Goodwin, did earlier in *Essays and Reviews*, so Temple, now Bishop
    of Exeter, sought to reconcile an evolutionary cosmogony with the Mosaic
    one by maintaining that the sense of the two accounts are different, that the
    creation process is not explained, that the number seven is used not
    literally but typologically, that the Garden of Eden is an allegory used only
    to convey a higher truth, and, finally, that man's real dignity comes from
    his spiritual faculty, not from the method by which he derived it. Temple's
    conclusion: "we cannot find that Science, in teaching Evolution, has yet
    asserted anything that is inconsistent with Revelation, unless we assume
    that Revelation was intended not to teach spiritual truth only, but physical
    truth also" (180–89). Jowett too was to address Darwinism in an 1871
    Balliol sermon entitled "Darwinism and Faith in God." Jowett asked for
    the suspension of judgment on natural selection because of the little
    evidence before us, pointed out that our concern is with man's moral and
    religious being, not with his past, and made the case that instinct in
    animals, like reason in man, assists in the struggle for survival. But Jowett
    had serious questions for evolution, two of which dealt with the develop-
    ment of the brain and the acquisition of language. And if indeed Darwin-
    ism is eroding the faith, what is needed, said Jowett, is a religion of deeds.
    He looked forward to a time when religion and science might be recon-
    ciled. The sermon is a remarkably moderate position for a Broad Church-
    man such as Jowett to assume, for, in effect, it calls not for outright
    acceptance of Darwinism but for tolerance of its positions. On Jowett and
    Darwinism, see Peter Hinchliff's chapter, "Darwnism and Faith" in his
    Benjamin Jowett and the Christian Religion.
9. *A Centenary Memoir*, 19.
10. *Darwin's Plots*, 4.

11. Peckham, "Darwinism and Darwinisticism," 19–21; Levine, *Darwin and the Novelists*, 2.

12. Young, "Darwinism Is Social," 610.

13. Feyerabend, *Realism, Rationalism, and Scientific Method*, 45.

14. *Darwin's Plots*, 91.

15. *Against Method*, 305.

16. *Darwin and the Novelists*, 4–13. There have been other studies exploring Darwinism in Victorian literature. Two of the earliest are Lionel Stevenson's *Darwin among the Poets* and Leo Henkin's *Darwinism in the English Novel*, both published in 1963. More recently, Tess Cosslett's *The "Scientific Movement" and Victorian Literature* locates in the works of Tennyson, Eliot, Meredith, and Hardy a direct scientific plot structure and epistemology. In Tennyson, Cosslett argues that the "centrality of gradualism"—erosive and evolutionary—in *In Memoriam* points out the work's pre–Darwinian topos. Eliot's gradualism—her use of "no sudden falls or conversions, no 'catastrophic' events"—and employment of "biological metaphors to describe unconscious psychological processes," especially in *Middlemarch*, demonstrate a like Darwinian interest. In the musical metaphors of Meredith's poetry, Cosslett finds a scientific conception of harmony in nature, and discovers in Hardy—the novels as well as the poetry—a hostile yet capricious universe along with the Darwinian notion of sexual selection. Also in Hardy, says Cosslett, one finds the dramatization either of the control on man of the primitive and destructive instincts inherited from his animal ancestry or the controlling of these forces by means of harmonious adaptations.

17. "The Position of Science at Oxford," 225.

18. Keble College Ms.

19. *Life* 1:348–53.

20. Jowett, *Dear Miss Nightingale*, 70.

21. A.J. Engle, *From Clergyman to Don*, 223–24.

22. "The Position of Science at Oxford," 227.

23. George Eliot, *The Mill on the Floss*, book 2, chap. 1, 122.

24. "The Position of Science at Oxford," 228.

25. A.J. Engle, *From Clergyman to Don*, 223.

26. Earwaker, "Natural Science at Oxford," 170.

27. Ibid., 226.

28. Pusey, Review of "The Position of Science at Oxford," *Nature* 1393 no. 54:342.

29. Sarolea, *Cardinal Newman*, 155.

30. Newman, *Letters*, 18:322.

31. *Idea of a University*, 189.

32. Ibid., 348–51.

33. Ibid., 375–86.

34. Ward, *The Life*, 1:637.

35. *Apologia*, 91, 12, 226.

36. Martin, *John Henry Newman*, 76, 144; Harrold, *John Henry Newman*, 73; Sarolea, *Cardinal Newman*, 155–56; more guarded, Sarolea further adds that although Newman repeatedly uses the analogy of organic development, "*his conception reminds us rather of a logical process than of an organic growth.*"

37. *Appreciations*, 16.

38. N. Katherine Hayles, "Information or Noise? Economy of Explanation in Barthes's S/Z and Shannon's Information Theory," 120. Like Hayles, George Levine, in *Darwin and the Novelists*, reminds us that science is "an unprivileged form of cultural discourse" (5).

39. *The Essential Tension*, 340.

40. Feyerabend, "Problems of Empiricism, Part II," 278; *Against Method*, 295.

41. Levine, *One Culture*, 4–5.

42. "Oxford and Science," 209.

43. Stevenson, *Darwin among the Poets*, 54.

44. The single citation is in Eleanor Ruggles's *Gerard Manley Hopkins: A Life*, where she contrasts Darwinism to Jowett's liberal theology (38). The other biographies, G.F. Lahey, *Gerard Manley Hopkins* (1930), John Pick, *Gerard Manley Hopkins: Priest and Poet* (1942), Bernard Bergonzi, *Gerard Manley Hopkins* (1977), and Paddy Kitchen, *Gerard Manley Hopkins* (1979), all ignore Darwin. Even Alison Sulloway's *Gerard Manley Hopkins and the Victorian Temper* (1972), though keenly sensitive to movements in Victorian society, incorrectly assumes that Hopkins was "apparently unconscious of the national upheaval" brought on by the *Origin* (12). The neglect reminds us of George Mivart's observation that "Few things are more remarkable than the way in which [Darwinism] has been misunderstood" (*On the Genesis of Species*, 23).

45. W.H. Gardner, *Gerard Manley Hopkins* 2:21; Walter J. Ong, *Hopkins, the Self, and God*, 158.

46. Even though Zaniello engages the very Hopkins–Darwin connection I seek to explore, I find myself relying very little on his arguments. Although Hopkins is a part of the book's title, "the Age of Darwin" is

Zaniello's primary focus. Hopkins provides intervals of stability within the book's evolutionary development. While Zaniello does not explore the Darwinian connection in Hopkins's ontology, poetics, and poetry, his treatise remains a significant contribution to Hopkins scholarship.

47. Culler, "The Darwinian Evolution and Literary Form," 224; Gillian Beer, *Darwin's Plots*, 10.

48. *Hopkins in the Age of Darwin*, 2.

49. J. Herschel's *Introduction to the Study of Natural Philosophy* (1830) and William Whewell's *History of the Inductive Sciences* (1831) gave rise to the British Association, the first successful British body formally committed to scientific research.

50. 209–17.

51. At the time of Tennyson's death on 6 October 1892, Huxley, in a letter to Sir R. Foster, called Tennyson "the only poet since the time of Lucretius, who has taken the trouble to understand the work and tendency of the men of science" (*Life and Letters*, 2:359). Lucretius's greatness was also heralded by Dixon in a 10 January 1879 letter to Hopkins. Dixon called Lucretius and Milton "the greatest writers of their kind in their language" for having given "a cosmogony in poetry: the one has perfectly expressed *Creation*, the other the *Eternity of Matter*, thus exhibiting the opposite theories" (*Letters* 2:18).

52. Tyndall, *Fragments of Science*, 2:164, 212. Hopkins was personally acquainted with Tyndall. On Sunday, 26 July 1868, he accompanied Tyndall on the ascent of the Matterhorn. Hopkins's friend Edward Bond had taken ill the day before, and Tyndall had prescribed some medicine for his recovery. Some years later Hopkins told his mother regarding Tyndall: "I fear he must be called an atheist but he is not a shameless one: I wish he might come round" (*Letters* 3:128).

53. Ibid., 151.

54. Ibid., 210–11.

55. Tennyson had complained to Tyndall of precisely this problem: "No evolutionist is able to explain the mind of Man or how any possible physiological change of tissue can produce conscious thought" (*A Memoir*, 1:323).

56. *Fragments of Science*, 2:165–204; note how materialistic the illustration is and the change in preposition: "by" in place of "over." But while Matter accounts for terrestrial life, it cannot quite explain the origin of the universe. In a lecture given seven years earlier, "Matter and Force," Tyndall pointed out then that in spite of the accomplishments of science,

it never will be able to explain the origin of the universe, a problem that "entirely transcends us," for "behind, and above, and around all, the real mystery of this universe lies unsolved, and, as far as we are concerned, is incapable of solution" (*Fragments of Science*, 2:79–80.)

57. Ibid., 2:214.

58. *Letters* 3:127–28.

59. Desmond and Moore, *Darwin*, 671. While a bit weak on the scientific aspects of Darwin's life, this prodigious biography of Darwin is well worth reading. It attempts to cover both the private and literary or scientific life and tries to do what is typically done in two separate biographies. While this makes for more interesting reading, it is the work's inherent flaw, albeit unavoidable.

60. *Darwin*, 671.

61. Bodleian Library Ms., 100 i 86, 3–15.

62. Ibid., 22–26.

63. Ibid., 27.

64. Ibid.

65. Ibid., 28–29.

66. *Sermons at St. Paul's*, 2–3.

67. Ibid., 6–7.

68. Pusey, *Un–Science, Not Science*, 6–13, 55. Darwin in fact read Pusey's sermon in late November 1978 in the *Guardian*. He did not consider it "worthy of attention," and held to the position never to answer criticism "excepting those made by scientific men." Yet Darwin remarked that while he did not seek to connect theology to the *Origin*, his belief then "in what is called a personal God was as firm as that of Dr. Pusey himself"; as to the eternity of matter, Darwin insisted that he has never troubled himself about such "insoluble questions." Darwin saw Pusey's attempt "powerless to retard by a day the belief in Evolution, as were virulent attacks made by divines fifty years ago against Geology." Additionally, he felt that the public was "wise enough always to follow Scientific men when they agree on any subject" (*Life*, 2:412).

69. *Letters* 3:128.

70. *On the Genesis of Species*, Mivart, 16. In his closing chapter, "Theology and Evolution," Mivart attempts to harmonize the two positions: "As the earth has gone through its grand cycles of geological, climatal, and organic progress, every form of life has been subject to its irresistible action and has been continually but imperceptibly molded into such new shapes as would preserve their harmony with the ever–changing universe" (301–2).

71. *More Letters* 1:333.

72. Peter J. Bowler, "Darwinism and the Argument from Design," 39.

73. *Letters* 1:84.

74. *Essays Scientific, Political, and Speculative,* 2:404.

75. Ibid., 411–13.

76. *Life,* 1:497.

77. *The Autobiography,* 109.

78. *The Descent of Man,* 561–68.

79. "On Some disputed Points in Music," 113; *The Power of Sound,* 59.

80. When Spencer's "The Origin and Function of Music" was published in book form as part of *Essays Scientific, Political, And Speculative* (1892), he added a postscript. Acknowledging its lateness, for Darwin and Gurney had since died (Darwin in 1882 and Gurney in 1888), Spencer offered rebuttals to the two men. The gist of his argument against Darwin is that animal sounds are unrelated to mating and thus procreation; animals make sounds whether or not it is the mating season, and females are just as prone to do so as are males. The relationship, he insisted, is "not a relation of cause and effect, but a relation of concomitance: the two are simultaneous results of the same cause" (2:431). Spencer saw in Gurney a basic lack of knowledge of the principle of evolution: evolution proceeds from the general to the special or from the indefinite to the definite. Gurney's idea that, for example, "Vocal expressions of a particular emotion came first, and from this proceeded vocal expressions of emotions in general" (2:438) contradicts this basic principle and in fact reverses evolution.

81. Lee, 858.

82. Ibid., 848, 851–56.

83. *Letters* 1:171n.2, 172.

84. *Life,* 2:363–64.

85. Darwin, *The Origin,* 242–50.

86. *Letters* 1:281; *Journals,* 252.

87. Zaniello, 116.

88. *Journals,* 137, 191; Fragments III, q.

89. Hopkins's ornithological interests are here most noticeable. He was able to capture the welcoming notes of the cuckoos on their arrival in early to mid May. Not being able to discover these shy and solitary birds that love concealment, Hopkins was able to capture their apparent mating calls. One wonders, too, if he was drawn to nature through the poetry of Shakespeare's *Henry IV,* Part I, where in correcting the prodigal prince Hal, the King warns him of a fate similar to Richard's, who when, "he had occasion to

be seen, / He was but as the cuckoo is in June, / Heard, not regarded"
(3.2.74–76).

90.   This was in fact a Romantic penchant for the particular. Wordsworth, in
the *Preface to the Lyrical Ballads*, talks about the poet as one who looks
closely at his subject. Later, Arnold would talk about seeing the object as
it really is, Newman about contemplating steadily the object of faith, and
Pater about getting to know one's impression as it really is. These
reactions, like Darwin's, were adjustments to the new science of the
particular. Hopkins made similar claims for the exchange between the
subject and object in the process of observation: "What you look hard at
seems to look hard at you"; this he felt determines between the "true and
the false instress of nature" (*Journals*, 204).

91.   *Journals*, 153.

92.   Lahey, *Gerard Manley Hopkins*, 3.

93.   *Journals*, 421, 408.

94.   Ibid., 250, 134, 176.

95.   Ibid., 364, 143.

96.   Ibid., 200, 199, 254.

97.   *The Language of Gerard Manley Hopkins*, 52. Hopkins's science of
aspects, his scrupulous attention to nature and language, is also revealed
in his approach to texts. Bridges recorded that in August 1866, when he
and Hopkins spent some weeks together in Rochdale reading Herodotus,
Hopkins was "so punctilious about the text, and so enjoyed loitering over
the difficulties, that I foresaw we should never get through, and broke off
from him to go my own way" (Dolben, *The Poems of Digby Mackworth
Dolben*, ci). Hopkins demanded repeatedly that poetry be scientifically
precise; he vowed to avoid obscurity in his own poetry and challenged
Bridges's response to "Henry Purcell": "'Purcell's music is none of your
d—d subjective rot'" (*Letters* 1:54, 84); he insisted that Dixon's "Falling
Rain" and "To Fancy" renounce the "imagination of the 'prescientific'
child" for a greater "precision of imagery," and called the "false perspective" in Browning's images "monstrous."

98.   Hans Aarsleff, *From Locke to Saussure*, 38.

99.   Milroy, 45.

100. John MacLeod, "The Diary of a Devoted Student of Nature," 65.

101. *Journals*, 125, 5.

102. *The Origin*, 401-403.

103. For example, "*fleck* is the next tone above flick," Hopkins pointed out
(*Journals*, 11).

104. *Poems, The Wreck*, 11, 25.

105. *The Tenth Muse*, 103.

106. J. Hillis Miller, "Hopkins," in *The Linguistic Moment*, 250.

107. *Sermons*, 129.

108. *The World, the Text, and the Critic*, 41.

109. Miller, "Hopkins," 248–249.

110. Gillian Beer, *Darwin's Plots*, 53.

111. In a letter to Bridges concerning his (Hopkins's) proposed book on Dorian Measure, Hopkins connected the two concepts of language and science: "It is full of new words, without which there can be no new science" (*Letters*, 1:254). Believing that "all true classification" is "genealogical," Darwin looks to language to illustrate his theory of classification of species: "The various degrees of difference between the languages of the same stock would have to be expressed by groups subordinate to groups; but the proper or even the only possible arrangement would still be genealogical; and this would be strictly natural, as it would connect together all languages, extinct and recent, by the closest affinities, and would give the filiation and origin of each tongue" (*The Origin*, 393); Tyndall, *Method and Results*, 142.

112. Although Darwin was astonished that Kingsley spoke of Carlyle as one "well fitted to advance science," and confessed never having met a man "with a mind so ill adapted for scientific research" (*The Autobiography*, 113–14), there is no doubt that his tree metaphor was reinforced by Carlyle's organic philosophy espoused often in that same metaphor: "the Present is not needlessly tramelled with the Past; and only grows out of it, like a Tree, whose roots are not intertangled with its branches"; or, "when the whole soul is yet infantine, soft, and the invisible seed–grain will grow to be an all overshadowing tree"; and in a more familiar analogy on the virtue of books: "Not like a dead City of stones," but "more like a tilled Field, but then a spiritual Field: like a spiritual Tree" (Carlyle, *Sartor Resartus*, 37, 67–68, 132); *Life* 2:42.

113. "John Herschel and Charles Darwin," 51. For a more thorough discussion of Darwin's metaphor of the irregularly branching tree, see Howard E. Gruber, "Darwin's 'Tree of Nature' and Other Images of Wide Scope."

114. George John Romanes, *Darwin, and after Darwin*, 1:32. The Victorians were quite interested in origins, more particularly in the form of genealogy. Evidence for this can be found in the orphan theme prevalent in Victorian novels. *Great Expectations*, for example, opens in a cemetery with Pip deciphering the epitaphs for the genealogical keys with which to

unlock his own life; and all of *Wuthering Heights* is concerned with matters of origins. The Darwinian metaphor plays out even more intriguingly in the symmetrical pedigree of the Earnshaws and Lintons in this latter novel.

115. "Studies in Animal Life," 445.

116. Friedrich Max Müller, *The Science of Language*, 2:254; 1:28.

117. In his 29 March 1873 "Lectures on Mr. Darwin's Philosophy of Language," Müller made this claim: "in the Science of Language, I was a Darwinian before Darwin, simply because I had protested against scientific as strongly as against theological dogmatism; simply because I wished to see the question of the possibility of a common origin of language treated, at least, as an open question" (662). While in calling himself "Darwinian" Müller meant that he was an evolutionist, he did not subscribe to Darwin's brand of evolution.

118. For significant treatments of the philological controversy between Müller and the Darwinians, see Hans Aarsleff, *The Study of Language in England, 1780–1860*, Linda Dowling, *Language and Decadence in the Victorian Fin de Siècle*, and Michael Sprinker, *"A Counterpoint of Dissonance."* Particularly significant is Sprinker's chapter "Hopkins and the Theory of Language" (46–76).

119. Elizabeth Knoll, "The Science of Language and the Evolution of Mind," 6.

120. *The Science of Language*, 2:323.

121. Ibid., 257.

122. *The Science of Language*, 1:354.

123. Aarsleff, 32.

124. *Life*, 2:182.

125. *The Descent of Man*, 82-85.

126. Ibid., 87–89.

127. Müller, "Lectures on Mr. Darwin's Philosophy of Language," 666.

128. Roman Jakobson, "Closing Statement," 358.

129. Müller, "Lectures on Mr. Darwin's Philosophy of Language," 671.

130. *The Science of Language*, 2:274–75.

131. Ibid., 371–72.

132. *Gerard Manley Hopkins*, 80.

133. See Joseph A. Jungmann, *The Early Liturgy*, 35, 139.

134. *Sermons*, 38.

135. *Poems, The Wreck*, 26.

136. *Letters* 2:73. For another reference to dugs, see the first canto of Book I of Spencer's *The Faerie Queene*, where, also in a religious context, the woman–serpent Errours has her offspring "Sucking upon her poisonous dugs."

137. *The Science of Language*, 1:383; "Lectures on Mr. Darwin's Philosophy of Language," 677.

138. *The Science of Language*, 1:384–85; I owe this connection to Milroy (65–66).

139. "Lectures on Mr. Darwin's Philosophy of Language," 677.

140. *The Science of Language*, 1:342.

141. "The Science of Language," 258.

142. *Journals*, 267, 289.

143. For a discussion of the Müller–Romanes philological debate, see Elizabeth Knoll's "The Science of Language and the Evolution of Mind," 12–18, and Paul Carus's "The Continuity of Evolution."

144. *The "Scientific Movement" and Victorian Literature*, 120.

145. The cyclical rhythm of nature in the image of Hopkins's "weeds in wheels" from the sonnet ("Spring," 1877) might have been taken from Tyndall's "The Constitution of Nature" (1865). Both writers were dealing with nature's renewal. The atomistic doctrine of the Tyndall passage reads: "Thus, what is true of the earth, as she swings to and fro in her yearly journey round the sun, is also true of her minutest atom. We have wheels within wheels, and rhythm within rhythm" (*Fragments of Science*, 1:28). Earlier in the Newman chapter, I traced the natural and spiritual cycles not to Tyndall but to Newman's sermon "The Second Spring," where he calls for England's rebirth to Roman Catholicism. Tennyson too entertained this atomistic idea in "Tithonus" (1860). Hopkins could have arrived at the idea through Tennyson (Eos returning on her "silver wheels"), although Tyndall's wording seems the more likely source.

146. Hopkins's natural supernaturalism here shares something of Wordsworth's "speaking face of earth and heaven" (*The Prelude*, 5.12), though Wordsworth's nature assumes pantheistic associations.

147. *Sermons*, 195.

148. *Journals*, 76, 84.

149. Ibid., 118–21. Arguing that the diatonic view, rather than the chromatic, is more prevalent in our culture and thus becomes a fulfillment of Hopkins's prediction, Walter Ong suggests that the invention of the digital computer and the discovery of quantum physics imply that "at root diatonicity governs the physical world" (*Hopkins, the Self, and God*, 16).

150. *Darwin's Plots*, 63.

151. *The Disappearance of God*, 278. "Nature, steel–bound or stone–built in the nineteenth century," wrote W.B. Yeats, "became a flux where man drowned or swam; the moment had come for some poet to cry, 'the flux is my own mind,'" quoting the poet Walter James Turner: "it moved only in my mind" (Yeats, *The Oxford Book of Modern Verse*, 28; Turner, "From 'The Seven Days of the Sun,'" in Yeats).

152. *Sermons*, 129, 193.

153. *Disappearance*, 294.

154. *Sermons*, 122–23.

155. *The World*, 40.

156. *Letters* 2:150. Hopkins more often than not associated the paternalistic metaphor of male sexuality to literary creativity, as in "To R.B." and also in "Pied Beauty," where God is perceived as male who "fathers–forth" his unchangeable beauty to a dappled creation. In "To R.B.," inspiration is described as a male orgasm that "Breathes once and, quenched faster than it came," and leaves the now widowed mind a "mother of immortal song." Although the concept of the mothering mind is still retained, it is the masculine act, the "insight," that initiates gestation. The birthing or creative process is to Hopkins not a parthenogenic activity. The familiar example of this male association was instanced in Hopkins's 30 June 1886 letter to Dixon. Faulting the paintings of the Pre–Raphaelite Burne–Jones for demonstrating an "unmasterly" quality, Hopkins notioned that the "artist's most essential quality" is "masterly execution," a "kind of male gift," he called it, that "especially marks off men from women." For the "male quality is the creative gift." The "begetting one's thoughts" would then be the male phallus, the writing implement, the "paper," the female body (*Letters* 2:133), analogous, say, to Othello's jointly erroneous and erotic indictment of Desdemona's alleged infidelity: "Was this fair paper [her body], this most goodly book, / Made to write 'whore' upon?" (4.2.70–71). The sonnet "Thou art indeed just" offers yet another example of creativity as male execution. Intoxication and slavery to lust accomplish more in a shorter time than the poets who "spend," unable to "breed one work that wakes." I suspect too that the homoeroticism critics find in Hopkins's admiration for the robust physical body of men should best be read as Hopkins's own masculine inadequacies (possibly made more intense by his middle name) that find a necessary attraction to male models. For studies on Hopkins and sexuality, see Sandra Gilbert and

Susan Gubar, *The Madwoman in the Attic*, Allison Sulloway, "Hopkins and 'Women and Men,'" and Richard Dellamora, *Masculine Desire.*

157. *David Copperfield*, 581.

158. *Journals*, 230.

159. *Sermons, 123–25.*

160. Ibid., 128.

161. *The Autobiography*, 87.

162. Leo J. Henkin, *Darwinism in the English Novel*, 64. Peter J. Bowler, "Darwinism and the Argument from Design," 29. Darwin, however, remains equivocal—maybe even contradictory—on the question of chance. While his theory obviously rejects design, it does not part with laws. Darwin seems more comfortable with the accidental or catastrophic, which does not result necessarily from chance. When in his *Autobiography* he dispenses with Paley's design argument, he ends with this remark, which, on the surface, might seem to support the very position he rejected: "Everything in nature is the result of fixed laws" (87). But, as George Levine observes, "Chance and the random become great creative forces in Darwin's theory," and his argument was founded on an apparent "strange combination of the random and the orderly" (*Darwin and the Novelists*, 93). For another essay on the complex relations between design and natural selection in Darwin, see Dov Ospovat's "God and Natural Selection."

163. Don Cupitt, "Darwinism and English Religious Thought," 127.

164. *Life*, 2:105,146; the letter to Herschel is quoted in S.S. Schweber, "John Herschel and Charles Darwin," 66.

165. *More Letters*, 2:190–91.

166. *Life*, 1:282–83.

167. *More Letters*, 1:321.

168. *Life*, 1:276.

169. Darwin's "Essay on Theology and Natural Selection" is not dated, but was apparently composed as early as 1838 when he began work on the *Origin*. The essay was assembled from Darwin's marginalia in Macculloch's *Proofs and Illustrations of the Attributes of God*, a book Darwin first read in the fall of 1838.

170. James Collins, "Philosophical Themes in G.M. Hopkins," 96.

171. *Letters* 3:227.

172. Harrold, *John Henry Newman*, 76. Writing to Pusey on 5 June 1870 regarding *The Origin of Species* and whether Darwin should be awarded an honorary degree at Oxford, Newman admitted not having "fallen in

with Darwin's book" but still felt that it does not advocate an "antichristian theory," that it is not "against Theism" ("I don't know why Adam needs be immediately out of dust . . . i.e. out of what really was dust and mud in its nature, before He made it what it was, living"), and that "Darwin does not 'profess' to oppose Religion" (Newman, *Letters* 25:137–38). A year later Newman congratulated the Catholic Mivart on providing the first "real exposition of the logical insufficiency of Mr. Darwin's theory" but hastily added: "In saying this, you must not suppose I have personally any great dislike or dread of his theory" (25:446). One corrective must be added to Harrold's optimistic confidence in Newman's belief. When the Metaphysical Society was being formed by Tennyson and James Knowles, Newman was invited to join; but declined. It was felt by several members that his refusal was on the grounds that the society was too controversial and combative.

173. Newman, *Callista*, 174–75. Newman's faith in God comes ultimately from within himself. Tennyson too rejects natural theology in favor of personal experience and feelings: "I found Him not in world or sun, / Or eagle's wing, or insect's eye; / Nor thro' the questions men may try, / The petty cobwebs we have spun. . . . A warmth within the breast would melt / The freezing reason's colder part . . . Stood up and answer'd 'I have felt'" (*In Memoriam*, 124.5–16).

174. *Apologia*, 216-17.

175. *The Idea of a University*, 192–93.

176. Newman, *The Philosophical Notebook*, 125.

177. *The "Scientific Movement" and Victorian Literature*, 101.

178. *Counterpoint of Dissonance*, 52.

179. Walter Pater, *Renaissance*, 186.

180. *Plato and Platonism*, 19–20.

181. *Journals*, 120.

182. James Finn Cotter, *Inscape*, 309.

183. Hopkins's interest in natural events is disclosed in the inception of the poem supplied to Dixon on 29 July 1888: "What a preposterous summer! It is raining now: when is it not? However there was one windy bright day between floods last week. . . . I put work aside and went out for the day, and conceived a sonnet" (Letters 2:157).

184. The refining of base properties is also treated in three other poems of Hopkins. In the semi–autobiographical "The Alchemist in the City," the poet bemoans his literary unproductivity ("not to be discover'd gold"). In "The Windhover," the poet tells us "sheer plod makes plough down sillion

/ Shine," and the base "embers," when agitated, transform into "gold vermillion." In "Carrion Comfort," the spiritual struggle with God constitutes a winnowing: "That my chaff might fly; my grain lie, sheer and clear." Fire motif pervades Hopkins's poetry: "The Wreck of the Deutschland," "God's Grandeur," "The Starlight Night," "The Windhover," "The Lantern out of Doors," "The Candle Indoors," "As kingfishers catch fire, dragonflies draw flame," "The shepherd's brow," and "To R. B." Fire in these poems is polysemous: it can be punitive, destructive, aesthetic, reassuring, folklorish, messianic, proselytic, and self–correcting. It can also be sexual and creative, as in "To R. B.," or as in this 19 October 1888 letter to Bridges: "I am warming myself at the flame of a little exploit of my own done last night" (Letters 1:297).

185. *Darwin's Plots*, 23.

186. *The Autobiography*, 92.

187. "Lectures on Mr. Darwin's Philosophy of Language," 668–69; modern atomism plays out most fully in the novels of Virginia Woolf. The instability of their world, and the suggestion that only art organizes and contains it, espouses a Paterean, Darwinian, and hence modern atomistic notion. For example, everywhere in *Mrs. Dalloway* this creative heroine, in her myth of immortality, sees herself connected to the elements and seeks to assemble the meaningless aggregations of life. Thus crossing Victoria Street, she rejoices in her love of life: "how one sees it so, making it up, building it round one, tumbling it, creating it every moment afresh"; and later as she headed towards Bond Street, she felt that "somehow in the streets of London, on the ebb and flow of things, here, there, she survived ... she being a part, she was positive, of the trees at home; of the house there ... part of people she had never met" (4–9). D.H. Lawrence, too, espouses a similar atomism position, when, early in *Women in Love*, he describes Birkin's restless life as one "without any definite rhythm" (104). Here Lawrence links atomism with the typical associated musical metaphor evident in Tyndall and Darwin.

188. In his closing remarks in the *Origin*, Darwin posits: "Hence we may look with some confidence to a secure future of great length. And as natural selection works solely by and for the good of each being, all corporeal and mental endowments will tend to progress towards perfection" (450). Adam Sedgwick, Professor of Geology at Cambridge and friend of Darwin, cringed at this overly optimistic conclusion, charging it with brazen and atheistic materialism.

189. *Sermons*, 124.

190. *Renaissance*, 189–90.

191. *Darwinism and Darwinisticism*, 39.

192. *Letters* 1:291.

193. Lucretius, *The Nature of the Universe*, 122.

194. The phrase "spill nor spend" might be taken as sublimated sexual metaphors, as in "Since country is so tender / To touch her being so slender" ("Binsey Poplars"), or as the kind frequently employed in *The Wreck* ("swoon," "stroke," "deliver," "driven Passion," "frightful sweat," "discharge," "swelling," "high flood"). Clearly, while renouncing sexuality, Hopkins still saw it as the "one rapture of an inspiration," which, "like the blowpipe flame, / Breathes once and, quenched faster than it came" ("To R.B.").

195. *Reader's Guide*, 73.

196. Ibid., 75.

197. *Journals*, 130.

198. Ibid., 67.

199. Alfred Thomas, *Hopkins the Jesuit*, 173n. Norman MacKenzie tells me that none of the papers listed on page 173 of Thomas's work survived. Thus what precisely was addressed on evolution that evening remains unknown (Letter of 27 November 1989).

200. *Journals*, 17.

201. *Darwin's Plots*, 48.

202. *Preliminary Discourse*, 137.

203. *Letters* 3:202.

204. Carol T. Christ, *The Finer Optic*, 31.

205. *Letters* 2:98.

206. *The Finer Optic*, 101.

207. This individualizing aspect of Hopkins's poetry also attracted him to the music of Henry Purcell, which captures "the very make and species of man." Hopkins also noted to Bridges that, like a seabird "opening his wings" but unaware of emitting "a whiff of knowledge about his plumage, the marking of which stamps his species," so Purcell's music selfidentificates: it "lets you remark the individualising marks of his own genius" (*Letters* 1:83).

208. *Origin*, 382.

209. I am using here the three existing copies of "St. Alphonsus Rodriguez." In his Oxford English Texts edition of the poems, Norman Mackenzie gives all three drafts. Readers of Hopkins are more familiar with the third poem, the one that begins "Honour is flashed." Catherine Phillips is convinced

that the draft that begins "Glory should a flame" is the most finished draft. The one Hopkins supplied Bridges in the 1888 Dublin letter is the first and yet another draft of the poem.

210. *Letters* 1:296.

Chapter 4

1. Charles Darwin, *The Autobiography*, 138–39. A similar regret over the loss of aesthetic passion by a scientist was expressed by the physician Lydgate in George Eliot's *Middlemarch*.

2. Ibid., 94.

3. Wordsworth, *The Prose Works*, 1:140–41.

4. *Journals*, 133.

5. *Life of Benjamin Jowett*, 1:329–30. Jowett later broke ties with Pater over, it seems, aesthetic issues, and developed an animus for him. Writing to Florence Nightingale on 4 July 1871, and after raising the question of how much we can learn from art and nature, Jowett remarked that "One of the phenomena of Sceptical times is the love of art, in which men fancy that they have a kind of rest." That Jowett had Pater in mind, both because of Pater's early essays ("Botticelli," "Mirandola," and "Michelangelo"), later anthologized in *The Renaissance*, and because of Pater's cult status among Oxford undergraduates, is quite clear, as the rest of the letter indicates: "I see this . . . in a small knot of people at Oxford who preach art & necessity, & believe in a man named Pater, of Brasenose. Goethe did a great deal of harm to the world by turning all things, including human characters, into forms of art, & he [Pater] is the great Apostle of the Sect" (*Dear Miss Nightingale*, 210). Jowett apparently felt it his duty to squelch that influence. Calling Jowett's lecture a "book of loose notes" recalls Pater's criticism of Wordsworth's "work of almost no character at all" that would "gain most by a skilfully made anthology." Such would have "purged away" all "alien element," leaving a "little treasury, shut between the covers of how thin a book" (*Appreciations*, 40, 42).

6. Ward, "Reminiscences," 74; Buchan, "Nine Brasenose Worthies," 23.

7. In "Hopkins, Pater, and Fichte's Ideal Student," Gerald Monsman argues that "Diaphaneitè" is actually the published version of the paper on Fichte Pater delivered to the Old Mortality.

8. Levey, *The Case of Walter Pater*, 102; Buchan, "Nine Brasenose Worthies," 24.

9. Pater, *Marius*, 1:93, 97.

10. John Buchan, "Nine Brasenose Worthies," 25.

11. Ibid.

12. *Renaissance,* 137. For example, Pater finds that Dante's subject is "like the course of his own life" (*Uncollected Essays*, 148). The work of fiction and the personality are again one.

13. Paul de Man, "Autobiography as De–facement," 926.

14. *Letters of Pater*, 59.

15. Pater, *Appreciations*, 111, 117.

16. *Art of Biography*, 7.

17. Ibid., 25–26.

18. *Memoir of John Nichol*, 151. Much of the information on the Old Mortality is supplied by Nichol.

19. Ibid., 146.

20. *The Diaries of Liddon*; Johnston, *Life of Liddon*, 90–92.

21. Quoted in Monsman, "Pater, Hopkins, and Fichte's Ideal Student," 366, 370. See this study of Monsman's for Fichte's statements on "the Divine Idea," "spiritual culture," "Learned culture," and a rebuttal of Brooke's charges; the essay also provides additional information on the Hexameron and the Old Mortality.

22. Quoted in Monsman, "Pater, Hopkins, and Fichte's Ideal Student," 371.

23. *Miscellaneous Studies*, 247–50.

24. Ibid., 247–48. One of Pater's models of that exceptional artist is Charles Lamb, who saw things "always by the light of an understanding more entire than is possible for ordinary minds," and saw them "always in strict connexion with the spiritual condition which determined it" (*Appreciations*, 115).

25. *Journals*, 138.

26. *Memoir of John Nichol*, 150.

27. In 1860 at the age of twenty one, Pater, according to Levey, burned his poems and sold his copy of Keble's *The Christian Year.*

28. *The Life of Walter Pater*, 1:169, 201, 207.

29. Pater, *Miscellaneous Studies*, 193.

30. *Marius*, 2:17.

31. *Walter Pater*, 212.

32. Humphry Ward, "Reminiscences," 75.

33. Three weeks earlier when he made a two–day visit to Oxford to pick up his degree, Hopkins met with Swinburne and Solomon, but apparently not with Pater.

34. *Victorian Portraits: Hopkins and Pater*, 31. Downes's is the most exhaus-
     tive study of the personal and temperamental relationship between Hopkins
     and Pater. The one major flaw is Downes's excessive reliance on Wright's
     questionable accounts, whereby, for example, Pater is treated more
     orthodox than he in fact was. The point obviously is to argue more
     compellingly for Hopkins's relatedness to Pater. This misreading is most
     noticeable, for example, when Downes sees Pater in harmony with
     Ruskin, and concludes that for Pater "art always encompasses religious
     experience and religion is made remarkable by aesthetics" (19). The
     statement is entirely true to Ruskin's and Hopkins's aesthetics; it is,
     however, inconsistent with Pater's, whose aesthetics, though retaining
     some of the vision of its medieval origins, becomes a substitute for
     religion.
35. Evans, *Letters of Walter Pater*, 36.
36. *Letters* 3:242–46.
37. *Victorian Portraits*, 45.
38. *Renaissance*, xix.
39. *Appreciations*, 68; *Marius*, 1:243.
40. *Transfigured World*, 33.
41. *Renaissance*, xx–xxi.
42. Ibid., 102.
43. Ibid., xxi–xxii.
44. *Uncollected Essays*, 160, 155–56.
45. *Renaissance*, 23, 25, 26, 36.
46. Ibid., 145.
47. Ibid., 163.
48. Ibid., 164, 177.
49. Ibid., 18–19, 146.
50. Ibid., 102, 104. Here, as elsewhere, the sensuous dimension of Pater's
     aesthetic and his images reveal an indebtedness to Hegel. Hegel makes a
     similar claim for art supplanting nature: "What in nature slips past, art ties
     down to permanence: a quickly vanishing smile, a sudden roguish expres-
     sion in the mouth, a glance, a fleeting ray of light . . . incidents and events
     that come and go . . . art wrests from momentary existence, and in this
     respect too conquers nature" (Hegel, *Aesthetics* 1:163). For further treat-
     ment of Pater and Hegel, see William Shuter, "History as Palingenesis in
     Pater and Hegel." On Pater's reading of Hegel, see Billie Inman's *Walter
     Pater and His Reading*, 49–50, 143.

51. *Appreciations*, 17. Pater was here lauding the economy of words, the "frugal closeness of style which makes the most of a word, in the exaction from every sentence of a precise thought, in the logically filled space connected always with the delightful sense of difficulty overcome." Hopkins's pruned poetry resonates well with this description of a style marked by ascesis. This quality in part accounts for the difficulty of his poetry. In this regard, see Newman's sermon, "Unreal Words."

52. *Plato and Platonism*, 58.

53. *Renaissance*, xxiii; Wright,*The Life of Walter Pater*, 1:98–99. Denouncing Roman Catholic atrocities, Lucy Snow, in Charlotte Bronte's *Villette*, recalls the martyrdom of Elizabeth of Hungary.

54. *Miscellaneous Studies*, 210–11.

55. Ibid., 181, 189–90. The connection here between beauty and death echoes Keats.

56. *Marius*, 2:121.

57. *Renaissance*, 140, 118.

58. *Transfigured World*, 31.

59. *Journals*, 126.

60. Ibid., 126.

61. *Letters* 3:373; Fraser, *Beauty and Belief*, 67.

62. Eliot, *Essays of George Eliot*, 432–33. I owe this discovery to Michael Sprinker. Hopkins, we know, had always read and liked Eliot. Several lines from his poem "Spring and Fall," including the name of his little girl and even the theme, were all taken from Eliot's *The Mill on the Floss*. Once desiring Newman's approval of Eliot, Hopkins asked him what he thought of her. Newman expressed candidly that he did not care much for her, and felt that one page of Carlyle would equal several pages of Eliot.

63. *Journals*, 104, 105, 120.

64. Ibid., 84–85.

65. Ibid., 171, 209, 202, 163, 199.

66. Devlin, "The Image and the Word—II," 195. Devlin's two–part essay provides valuable insights into how inscape and the senses cooperate in the act of contemplation in Hopkins.

67. *Marius*, 1:24, 124.

68. Ibid. 1:146; *Renaissance*, 188.

69. *Marius*, 1:24–25.

70. *Appreciations*, 60–62.

71. Ibid., 59.

72. *Marius*, 2:183–84.

73. *Appreciations*, 59–63. For epistemological parallels, compare this to the conclusion of Wordsworth's "Ode: Intimations of Immortality."

74. *Walter Pater*, 68.

75. *Renaissance*, 170.

76. Ibid., 42, 51, 54.

77. Ibid., 87, 170, 172. For treatment of the type in Pater, see Wolfgang Iser's *Walter Pater*.

78. Pater's argument was influenced by Darwin's and that of other materialists. It is, for example, similar to T.H. Huxley's 1869 essay, "On the Physical Basis of Life," which, Billie Inman believes, Pater read in 1875, much too late, however, to have influenced his "Conclusion" to *The Renaissance*. Huxley theorizes that "Protoplasm, simple or nucleated, is the formal basis of all life," and that all animals undergo "transitory changes of form" (Huxley, "On the Physical Basis of Life," 142, 134; Inman, *Walter Pater and His Reading*, 180). Pater's access to the protoplasmic idea of human life could have come, Inman believes, by way of George Henry Lewes's July 1868 four–part essay in the *Fortnightly Review*, entitled "Mr. Darwin's Hypothesis," or from Herbert Spencer's *The Principles of Biology* (1864–67). See Inman's "The Intellectual Context of Walter Pater's 'Conclusion.'"

79. *Miscellaneous Studies*, 252.

80. *Renaissance*, 186–87.

81. Ibid., 187–90; *Appreciations*, 67. Pater's image of the weaving and unweaving of ourselves might be compared to the images of slack in Hopkins's poems, especially *The Wreck*, "Spelt from Sibyl's Leaves," and "Not, I'll not." Carolyn Williams argues that Pater's was an attempt to preserve the centrality and wholeness of the self within the continuity of history (Hopkins's would be the continuity of Christian or providential history). "In an effort to preserve its wholeness, this aesthetically or critically divided self," says Willimas, "is continually in the process of projecting a transcendent identity to oversee its own passages of experience" (*Transfigured World*, 36). Regarding true self–education and not succumbing to religious orthodoxy, Pater remains convinced that it is "Not the conveyance of an abstract body of truths or principles" but of any art "in some degree peculiar to each individual" (*Marius*, 1:143).

82. Philip Toynbee, "Rebel into Pussycat," 21.

83. *Letters of Pater*, 13–14. Pater did not deceive himself into thinking that his was an age of faith. In his introduction for Shadwell's *Dante*, Pater states unequivocally that if there is any such thing as an age of faith, "our age

certainly is not"; however, it might be an age of hope, "of a development of religious hope or hopefulness" (*Uncollected Essays*, 153). This might indicate the muscular Christianity Pater was in part pursuing.

84. *Appreciations*, 66–74
85. *In Extremity*, 27.
86. *Appreciations*, 69–70.
87. *Journals*, 120; Pater, *Appreciations*, 66.
88. *Renaissance*, 189–90.
89. *Marius*, 1:97; *Gaston*, 55.
90. *Renaissance*, 190. Art to Pater, says Wolfgang Iser, is "conceived as the countervailing power to the temporality of human existence" (*Walter Pater*, 31).
91. Ibid., 5, 15, 43, 170.
92. Ibid., 93, 155, 190.
93. *Marius*, 1:142–52.
94. *Renaissance*, 149–50.
95. *Victorian Portraits*, 52.
96. T.S. Eliot, "The Place of Pater," 99, 93. The most profound study of the Classical and Christian impulse in Arnold, Pater, and Newman remains David DeLaura's *Hebrew and Hellene in Victorian England*.
97. *Appreciations*, 18. Pater is here espousing a Tractarian understanding of art and poetry, which he got through Wordsworth, Keble, and Newman, a religious claim for literature that will, in the modern period, dislodge it from the religious, making literature a substitute for religion. "The cult of art," says Wolfgang Iser, "not only arose from the ruins of beliefs, creeds and thought systems of yore, but it also had to assume some of the functions once fulfilled by them. The aesthetic attitude as an answer to the existing challenge was promulgated as the new horizon encompassing all the remnants of former conceptualisations of life" (*Walter Pater*, 37).
98. *Walter Pater*, 32. This post–Romantic attitude to art finds expression in Yeats (especially the Yeats of the Byzantium poems) through Tennyson.
99. *Appreciations*, 44, 46, 62.
100. *Miscellaneous Studies*, 249, 253.
101. Jenkyns, *The Victorians and Ancient Greece*, 150. Despite these assertions, says Robert Crawford, Pater's "Winckelmann" is not exempt from a "powerfully homoerotic tone" ("Pater's *Renaissance*," 850).
102. *Renaissance*, 145, 147, 176–77, 152.
103. Ibid., 149–50. Pater's artistic claims are consistent with Arnold's, and the Winckelmann chapter in particular contains not so subtle echoes of

Arnold. For example, Pater also talks of "self–culture," stating that an important function of modern art in "the service of culture is so to rearrange the details of modern life, so to reflect it, that it may satisfy the spirit." Pater's language is also that of Arnold's "The Scholar–Gipsy" (1853) when he, Pater, describes the modern world with its "conflicting claims, its entangled interests, distracted by so many sorrows, with many preoccupations, so bewildering an experience, the problem of unity with ourselves, in blitheness and repose" (*Renaissance*, 182–84). This is the exact language of Arnold's scholar–gipsy.

104. *Marius*, 1:41, 92, 109. Marius feels, however, that his sexual attraction to Flavian is not entirely wholesome. A disease of some sort, whether actual or symbolic ("under many disguises") soon becomes associated with that love: "There had been something feverish, perhaps," he detected, "like the beginning of sickness, about his almost forced gaiety, in this sudden spasm of spring [note the language of sexual orgasm]; and by the evening of the next day he was lying with a burning spot on his forehead, stricken, as was thought from the first, by the terrible new disease" (1:110).

105. Sedgwick, *Between Men*, 4; Dellamora, *Masculine Desire*, 47.

106. "One Hundred Years of Homosexuality," 37.

107. *Greek Homosexuality*, 1.

108. "Pater's *Renaissance*," 854.

109. Linda Dowling, "Ruskin's Pied Beauty," 1.

110. See Eve Sedgwick's *Between Men* and David Halperin's "One Hundred Years of Homosexuality" on the line of continuum that exists between homosocial desire and power relations in a patriarchal culture.

111. *Greek Homosexuality*, 81.

112. *Masculine Desire*, 46.

113. Robert Crawford, "Pater's *Renaissance*," 852.

114. The expression "heavenfallen freshness" points to the innocence and the Edenic nature of the scene. In fact, the language has an imagistic relationship to the "juice" and "joy" of natural innocence (the sky as "descending blue" and the eggs as "little low heavens") in the sonnet "Spring."

115. *Masculine Desire*, 43. See also for further treatment of the homosocial desire in Hopkins.

116. Rampant homosocial, sometimes homosexual, activities at Oxford in the nineteenth century should not appear surprising, given the exclusively classical education at Oxford in which male homo–social/sexual desire appear prominent in the texts studied and the culture from which those texts evolved. The just–as–exclusive patriarchal culture at Oxford, with its

ties to class, economy, and dominance (male "passives," for example, were assigned female pseudonyms) also lends itself to the desire of males for other males. This "love relationship," Eve Sedgwick detects, "had a strongly educational function." The young boy as object was expected to grow into manhood, terminating the temporary homosexual engagement (*Between Men*, 4). That a friend of Hopkins, like Edward Urquhart, could set aside his homosexual desire and move on to what appears to have been a happy and stable heterosexual marriage proves the loose contractural ties that existed between males. Boys loving boys at Oxford fits precisely the type of Classical Greek pederasty Harald Patzer describes. (See his categorization of this in David Halperin's "One Hundred Years of Homosexuality," 41). For additional studies on male homosocial desire in Victorian literature, see Linda Dowling's "Ruskin's Pied Beauty and the Constitution of a 'Homosexual' Code," Robert Crawford's "Pater's *Renaissance*, Andrew Lang, and Anthropological Romanticism," and Martha Nussbaum's "Steerforth's Arm: Love and the Moral Point of View."

117. *Renaissance*, 177.
118. *Appreciations*, 38. Like Iser, I take Pater's moralizing here quite seriously, reading his subversion as a "fusion of form and content," the "transformation of the world through the imagination," especially in a world with "fundamental beliefs gone" (*Walter Pater*, 55, 56). This position, however, is not quite the same as Downes's: "Pater does not contradict himself nor does he abruptly dismiss aesthetic criticism as effete." At the last moment, says Downes, Pater "provides a corrective on the aesthetic phase of criticism," affirming "the proposition that the judgment of literary art is not solely aesthetic because the completeness of the critical act demands philosophical judgment" (*Victorian Portraits*, 139–41). A skeptic might be prone to read the conclusion of "Style" as Pater's gesture to the Victorians, the kind of gesture popular in the conclusion of much of Victorian fiction.
119. Eliot, *Middlemarch*, 131–32, 153, 271.
120. *The George Eliot Letters*, 1:118.
121. *Letters* 2:135.
122. *Renaissance*, 169, 173.
123. Ibid., 52–53; *Appreciations*, 30.
124. *Renaissance*, 106–9.; *Appreciations*, 26; *Renaissance*, 184.
125. Ibid., 105–9, 117. Pater makes the same claim for prose, seeing in Newman's, for example, a certain "musical value" (*Appreciations*, 12). In

The Power of Sound (1880), Edmund Gurney takes issue with Pater's promotion of music and with his assertion in "The School of Giorgione" that music, rather than painting, most touches us because it most success-fully weds matter and form. Regarding Pater's privileging of music because of the interpenetration of matter and form, Gurney finds that Pater's use of form (as "mode of handling, mood, emotional and informing expression") departs radically from the more normal conception of form as relating to the "abstract shapes of sound presented to the ear by Music." Gurney also rejects Pater's stance on painting, which Pater dismissed as having "no more definite message for us than an accidental play of sunlight and shadow for a moment, on one's wall or floor." However, painting, the "visible representation," says Gurney, touches us most, while poetry speaks to the educated, the intellectual (396–97). Following Pater, Gurney seeks also to codify the arts. He calls poetry, sculpture, and painting "Arts of Representation," and architecture and music "Arts of Presentation"; painting, architecture, and music fall under "Arts of Colour." Gurney uses the categories of subject matter, material, and form to categorize the five branches of art, and unlike Pater, interprets form as either conveying or constituting subject matter.

126. Carl Schmidt, "Classical Studies at Balliol in the 1860's," 169.

127. Ibid., 166.

128. See Henry Sidwick's chapter "Ethical Principles and Methods" in his *The Methods of Ethics*. On William Paley, Francis Hutcheson, and Richard Price, see J.B. Schneewind's *Moral Philosophy from Montaigne to Kant*, vol. 2.

129. In one of his other undergraduate essays, "The Probable Future of Metaphysics," Hopkins finds that opposition to the two schools of thought, idealism and materialism, will continue to be more intellectually pro-found, but Hume's emphasis upon the concrete and the particular, with gestures toward atomism "in some shape or other," and his attempt to reassert "transcendent idealism" will have either victory or at least some say in the argument: an apparent return to Platonic Ideas but with a consciousness of "atomism of personality" (*Journals*, 119–21).

130. *Miscellaneous Studies*, 175–77. In Florian, the birth of suffering is tied with a fascination with bright colors: "earlier, in some degree, we see inwardly; and the child finds for itself, and with unstinted delight, a difference for the sense, in those whites and reds . . . in the lack of better ministries to its desire for beauty"; and, "From this point he [Florian] could trace two predominant processes of mental change in him—the growth of

an almost diseased sensibility to the spectacle of suffering, and, parallel with this, the rapid growth of a certain capacity of fascination by bright colours" (*Miscellaneous Studies*, 175, 181). Hopkins, following Wordsworth, Keats, and Pater, makes a similar association with the concepts of suffering, bright colors, and intuition. In a 22 December 1880, he told Dixon: "insight is more sensitive, in fact is more perfect, earlier in life than later and especially towards elementary impressions: I remember that crimson and pure blues seemed to me spiritual and heavenly sights fit to draw tears once; now I can just see what I once saw, but can hardly dwell on it and should not care to do so" (*Letters* 2:38). This entire experience is the same as Margaret's in Hopkins's "Spring and Fall" and Florian's in Pater's "The Child in the House."

131. *Journals*, 80–83.
132. Ibid., 99.
133. To Pater, says Iser, "Beauty and truth are mutually exclusive." Emptied of all "abstract values," beauty exists only as a "particular form of appearance." The "aesthetic experience of beauty is now possible only by way of an ever–changing pageant of extraordinary appearances. . . . Beauty will vary from one observer to the next." For "instead of comforting the beholder with the illusion of permanence, as did the classical concept, beauty confronts the beholder with its and therefore his own temporality, and ultimately death." All that remain, then, are only "aesthetic potentials in the empirical world which must each be realised individually" (*Walter Pater*, 63–65).
134. *Journals*, 74–75, 113.
135. *Letters* 2:85, 113.
136. *Journals*, 75–79.
137. Ibid., 78–79.
138. *The Victorians and Ancient Greece*, 72.
139. *Letters* 2:157.
140. *The Victorians and Ancient Greece*, 90. The bleak images in Hopkins's Dublin sonnets reminds one also of Pindar's images; so too does Hopkins's difficult and contrived metrical vocabulary.
141. Ibid., 64.
142. *Letters* 1:254–56, 270.
143. *Letters* 2:141.
144. Ibid., 17.
145. *Letters* 1:150.
146. Jenkyns, *The Victorians and Ancient Greece*, 70.

147. *Letters* 1:217.

148. *Letters* 3:360.

149. *Letters* 2:146.

150. *Renaissance*, 162.

151. This stance is similar to that of Newman's Callista, who resigned her profession of sculpting Greek art after she converted to Christianity. She was later martyred for that conviction.

152. *Letters* 2:145–47

153. Newman, *Verses on Various Occasions*. I owe this discovery to Richard Jenkyns.

154. Newman, *Apologia*, 36.

155. *Transfigured World*, 4.

156. *Journals*, 86–90, 92.

157. Ibid., 230, 211, 175, 153, 139, 146.

158. Ibid., 90. It is contrast and disparities, Hopkins would say, that give "complexity and interest to the lives or writings of great thinkers so clearly beyond what they would otherwise have had" (*Journals*, 115).

159. Ibid., 90–95

160. Ibid., 101–2.

161. Ibid., 118–21.

162. Ibid., 115.

163. Unpublished Campion Hall Ms., DIII/6–8.

164. Ibid., 10–13.

165. Ibid., 13.

166. Ibid.

167. Ibid., 14.

168. *Journals*, 127, 130. For a discussion of Hopkins's understanding of being, inscape, and their epistemological bases, see Tom Zaniello's "The Source of Hopkins' Inscape."

169. Unpublished Campion Hall ms. D III/15.

170. Ibid., 9.

171. Benson, *Walter Pater*, 111.

172. *Marius*, 2:123; Benson, *Walter Pater*, 111.

173. *Letters* 3:434, 93.

174. *Discourses addressed to Mixed Congregations*, 185, 219.

175. Unpublished Campion Hall ms. D V/1–2.

176. Ibid., 2.

177. Ibid., 3–5.

178. *Marius*, 1:53.

179. *Letters* 1:17, 95. The reference to "handsome heart" is to Hopkins's poem of the same name. Subscribing to the Keatsean idea of beauty, Pater, in his essay on "Style," believes that "the one indispensable beauty is, after all, truth," as it pertains to accuracy and expression (*Appreciations*, 34.)

180. *Letters* 3:231.

181. Loomis, "A Defense of Hopkins' 'Brothers,'" 38. In a 14 August 1879 letter to Bridges, Hopkins, relating his poem to Wordsworth's version, called "Brothers" "inimitable and unapproachable," and felt that the poem shows that "pathos has a point as precise as jest has and its happiness 'lies ever in the ear of him that hears, not in the mouth of him that makes'" (*Letters* 1:86.)

182. Ibid., 40.

183. This poem, as Hopkins told Bridges, evolved from an actual experience he had: "The Story was that last Lent, when Fr. Parkinson was laid up in the country, two boys of our congregation gave me much help in the sacristy in Holy Week. I offered them money for their services, which the elder refused, but being pressed consented to take it laid out in a book. The younger followed suit; then when some days after I asked him what I shd. buy answered as in the sonnet. His father is Italian and therefore sells ices. I find within my professional experience now a good deal of matter to write on." I quote this account in full to show that the innocence of Hopkins's love for the younger boy must be read in the same context as "The Brothers," which Hopkins alluded to following the above history of the inception of "The Handsome Heart": "I hope to enclose a little scene ["The Brothers"] that touched me at Mount St. Mary's" (*Letters* 1:86).

184. MacKenzie, *Reader's Guide*, 121; Letters 1:92.

185. *Marius*, 2:214–221.

186. *Letters* 2:97. Hopkins's sister Kate recalled a similar account of the "prevailing wind" of Hopkins's disgust with ugliness in all forms: when a "little fellow of four," Gerard was discovered crying because "'Cyril [during an attack of whooping cough] looked so ugly.' Just as in later life his friends in Ireland said he was made miserable by the untidiness, disorder & dirt of Irish ways, the ugliness of it all" (Nixon, "Portrait of a Friendship," 296).

187. *Selected Writings of Walter Pater*, 264.

188. *Letters* 1:27.

189. The line "His sweetest nectar hides behind" might be an allusion to the miracle Christ performed at the wedding feast where he turned water into

wine. The wedding host was subsequently accused of saving the best wine for last.

190. The first two metaphors echo Shakespeare's *Othello* and the third Wordsworth's "Ode: Intimations of Immortality."

191. *Letters* 1:47.

192. The opening of *The Wreck* alludes to an historical unfastening, akin to atomism, that took place in Christian history. The first line alludes to the creation of man and the second to a near uncreation, presumably the fall of man: "Thou hast bound bones and veins in me, fastened me flesh, / And after it almost unmade."

193. *Transfigured World*, 38. This in fact is one significant way in which Pater's notion of the self is different from Darwin's and Tyndall's. In Pater, nothing of the self is lost in the infinite azure. Rather, the properties of the self are merely reorganized.

194. Germain d'Hangest, *Walter Pater*, 343.

195. William Shuter, "History as Palingenesis," 416.

196. Hopkins, *Journals*, 127. Recalling Heraclitus, Pater felt that in Darwin, in whom the Heraclitean philosophy, "the entire modern theory of 'development,'" experienced a rebirth, "'type' itself properly *is* not but is only always *becoming*" (*Plato and Platonism*, 19).

197. *Sermons*, 158.

198. Ibid., 147, 153.

199. Ibid., 146–54.

200. Ibid., 123.

201. Ibid., 125–26.

202. *Gerard Manley Hopkins*, 23.

203. For Hopkins's very interesting treatment of the nature of the self and how it relates to freedom, the will, grace, and pitch, see his essays "First Principle and Foundation" and "On Personality, Grace and Free Will" (*Sermons*, 122–30, 146–59).

204. Extracted from Max Müller's *Chips from a German Workshop*. Unpublished Campion Hall ms. D VII/2.

205. *Letters* 3:306–7.

206. How the natural (the sensible) evokes the supernatural (the super–sensible) is made explicit in Hopkins's note on the well: "The strong unfailing flow of the water and the chain of cures from year to year all these centuries took hold of my mind with wonder at the bounty of God in one of His saints, the sensible thing so naturally and gracefully uttering the spiritual reason of its being (which is all in true keeping with the story of

St. Winefred's death and recovery) and the spring in place leading back the thoughts by its spring in time to its springs in eternity: even now the stress and buoyancy and abundance of the water is before my eyes" (*Journals*, 261).

207. *Marius*, 2:214.
208. *Letters* 1:25.
209. *Marius*, 2:223.
210. *Letters* 1:264.
211. Robert Bridges, in a 14 December 1918 letter to Hopkins's sister Grace, used the expression "natural heart's ivy" to describe the difficulty involved in getting out the first edition of Hopkins's poems. See Bridges, *The Selected Letters*, 2:747–48, and Nixon, "Portrait of a Friendship," 293.
212. *In Extremity*, 17.
213. *Appreciations*, 65. Following Hegel, says William Shuter, Pater "conceived all historical change as part of the continuous evolutionary growth of the human spirit" ("History as Palingenesis," 414).
214. *In Extremity*, 18–19.
215. *Letters* 1:231.
216. *Walter Pater*, 33–34.
217. *"A Counterpoint of Dissonance": The Aesthetics and Poetry of Gerard Manley Hopkins*, 24.
218. *Letters* 2:7; *Poems*, "It was a hard thing to undo this knot."
219. *"A Counterpoint of Dissonance,"* 47.
220. *Poems*, "Henry Purcell"; *Letters* 2:13.
221. *Letters* 1:95.
222. *Greek Homosexuality*, 12.
223. *A Reader's Guide*, 164.
224. *Letters* 1:231.
225. Robinson, *In Extremity*, 13–14.
226. See *Journals*, 71, 138.
227. *Letters* 1:24. Hopkins's was a self–imposed prohibition against writing poetry, and even then his vows seem at times only temporary ones, as when, for example, he told Urquhart in 1867 that during reading for the schools he "made a rule . . . to have nothing to do with versemaking" (*Letters* 3:38).
228. *Letters* 1:270–71.
229. *Letters* 2:14, 88.
230. *Letters* 1:66.

231. *Letters* 3:385.
232. *Letters* 1:197.
233. *Letters* 2:88; *Letters* 1:231.
234. *Letters* 1:222.
235. *Letters* 2:8; *Letters* 1:46.
236. *Letters* 3:139; *Letters* 2:30–31.
237. *Letters* 2: 88, 93.
238. *Sermons*, 253–54.
239. *Letters* 2:88.
240. Philip Toynbee, "Rebel in Pussycat," 21.

Conclusion

1.   Hopkins, *Letters* 1:xxi.

Bibliography

Aarsleff, Hans. *From Locke to Saussure: Essays on the Study of Language and Intellectual History*. Minneapolis: University of Minnesota Press, 1982.

———. *The Study of Language in England, 1780-1860*. New Jersey: Princeton University Press, 1967.

Abrams, M.H. *The Mirror and the Lamp: Romantic Theory and the Cultural Tradition*. London: Oxford University Press, 1953.

Apel, Willi. In *Harvard Dictionary of Music*. Cambridge: Harvard University Press, 1967.

Arnold, Matthew. *Poetry and Criticism of Matthew Arnold*. Edited with an introduction and notes by A. Dwight Culler. Boston: Houghton Mifflin Co. (The Riverside Press Cambridge), 1961.

Battiscombe, Georgina. *John Keble: A Study in Limitations*. London: Constable, 1963.

Beer, Gillian. *Darwin's Plots*. London: Routledge & Kegan Paul, 1983.

———. "Helmholtz, Tyndall, Gerard Manley Hopkins: leaps of the prepared imagination." *Comparative Criticism* 13 (1992): 117-45.

Beer, John. "Newman and the Romantic Sensibility." In *The English Mind*, edited by Hugh Sykes Davies, 193-218. London: Cambridge University Press, 1964.

Bender, Todd K. *Gerard Manley Hopkins: The Classical Background and Critical Reception of His Work*. Baltimore: Johns Hopkins University Press, 1966.

Benson, A.C. *Walter Pater*. London: Macmillan and Co., 1906, republished by Gale Research Co., 1968.

Benson, Louis F. *The English Hymn: Its Development and Use in Worship*. Virginia: John Knox Press, 1962.

Bergonzi, Bernard. *Gerard Manley Hopkins*. New York: Collier Books, 1977.

Bibby, Cyril. "Huxley and the Reception of the Origin." *Victorian Studies* 3, no. 1 (1959): 76-86.

Binyon, Laurence. "Gerard Hopkins and His Influence." *University of Toronto Quarterly* 8, no. 3 (1939): 264-70.

Bloom, Harold, ed. *Selected Writings of Walter Pater*. New York: Signet, 1974.

———. *Walter Pater*. New York: Chelsea House Publishers, 1985.

Bowler, Peter J. "Darwinism and the Argument from Design." *Journal of the History of Biology* 10, no. 1 (1977): 29-43.

Bregy, Katherine. "Gerard Hopkins: An Epitaph and an Appreciation." *Catholic World* 88, no. 526 (1909): 433.

Bridges, Robert. *The Selected Letters of Robert Bridges.* Edited by Donald E. Stanford. 2 vols. Newark: University of Delaware Press, 1983, 1984.

———. *The Spirit of Man: An Anthology in English and French from the Philosophers and Poets.* Introduction by W.H. Auden. London: Longman, 1973.

Bright, Michael. "English Literary Romanticism and the Oxford Movement." *Journal of the History of Ideas* 40, no. 2 (1977): 385-404.

Brown, Horatio F. *John Addington Symonds: A Biography.* 2d ed. London: Smith, Elder, 1903.

Buchan, John. "Nine Brasenose Worthies." *Brasenose Quatercentenary Monographs.* (Oxford: Clarendon Press), 14, no. 2 (1909): 3-30.

Bump, Jerome. "Hopkins, Pater, and Medievalism." *Victorian Newsletter* 50 (1976): 10-15.

———. "The Month's amends to Gerard Manley Hopkins." *The Month* 22, no. 12 (1989): 482-6.

Butler, Samuel. *Ernest Pontifex; or The Way of All Flesh.* Riverside Edition. Ed. with an intro. and notes by Daniel F. Howard. Boston: Houghton-Mifflin, 1964.

Cameron, J. *John Henry Newman.* London: Longmans, Green, 1956.

Carlyle, Thomas. *Sartor Resartus.* Edited by Kerry McSweeney and Peter Sabor. Oxford: Oxford University Press, 1987.

Carus, Paul. "The Continuity of Evolution: The Science of Language versus the Science of Life as Represented by Prof. F. Max Müller and Prof. George John Romanes." *The Monist: A Quarterly Magazine* 2 (1892): 70-94.

Castle, W. R. "Newman and Coleridge." *The Sewanee Review* 17 (1909): 139-52.

Chadwick, Owen. *The Mind of the Oxford Movement.* Stanford: Stanford University Press, 1960.

———. *The Spirit of the Oxford Movement: Tractarian Essays.* Cambridge: Cambridge Unversity Press, 1990.

———. *The Victorian Church.* 2 vols. 3d ed. London: SCM Press, 1987.

Chapman, Raymond. *Faith and Revolt: Studies in the Literary Influence of the Oxford Movement.* London: Weidenfield & Nicolson, 1970.

Christ, Carol T. *The Finer Optic: The Aesthetics of Particularity in Victorian Poetry.* New Haven: Yale University Press, 1975.

Church, R. W. *The Oxford Movement*. California: Stanford University Press, 1960.

Clarke, C.P.S. *The Oxford Movement and After*. London: A.R. Mowbray, 1932.

Cockshut, A.O.J. *Religious Controversies of the Nineteenth Century: Selected Documents*. London: Methuen, 1966.

Coleridge, Samuel Taylor. *Biographia Literaria*. Edited by J. Shawcross. 2 vols. Oxford: Oxford University Press, 1968.

———. *Lay Sermons*. Edited by R. J. White. New Jersey: Princeton University Press, 1972.

Collins, James. "Philosophical Themes in G. M. Hopkins." *Thought* 22, no. 84 (1947): 96.

Cornish, Francis Warre. *A History of the English Church in the Nineteenth Century, parts 1 & 2*. Vols. 8-9. London: Macmillan and Co., 1910.

Corsi, Pietro. *Science and Religion: Baden Powell and the Anglican Debate, 1800-1860*. Cambridge: Cambridge University Press, 1988.

Cosslett, Tess, ed. *Science and Religion in the Nineteenth Century*. Cambridge: Cambridge University Press, 1984.

———. *The "Scientific Movement" and Victorian Literature*. Sussex: Harvester Press, 1982.

Cotter, James Finn. *Inscape: The Christology and Poetry of Gerard Manley Hopkins*. Pennsylvania: University of Pittsburgh Press, 1972.

Coulson, John. *Newman and Common Tradition: A Study in the Language of Church and Society*. Oxford: Clarendon Press, 1970.

———. *Religion and Imagination*. Oxford: Clarendon Press, 1981.

Crawford, Robert. "Pater's *Renaissance*, Andrew Lang, and Anthropological Romanticism." *ELH* 53 (1986): 849-79.

Culler, A. Dwight. "The Darwinian Evolution and Literary Form." In *The Art of Victorian Prose*, edited by George Levine and William Madden, 224-46. New York: Oxford University Press, 1968.

Cupitt, Don. "Darwinism and English Religious Thought." *Theology* 78, no. 657 (1975): 125-31.

D'Hangest, Germain. *Walter Pater: L'Homme et L'Oeuvre*. Vol. 1. Paris: Didier, 1961.

Darwin, Charles. *The Autobiography of Charles Darwin 1809-1882*. Edited by Nora Barlow. New York: W. W. Norton & Company, 1969.

———. *The Correspondence of Charles Darwin, Vol 1: 1821-1836*. Edited by Frederick Burkhardt, Sydney Smith, et al. Cambridge: Cambridge University Press, 1985.

————. *The Descent of Man and Selection in Relation to Sex.* 2d ed. New York: Merill and Baker, 1874.

————. "Essay on Theology and Natural Selection." In *Darwin on Man: A Psychological Study of Scientific Creativity Together with Darwin's Early and Unpublished Notebooks*, by Howard E. Gruber and Paul H. Barrett, 414-22. New York: E. P. Dutton, 1974.

————. *The Life and Letters of Charles Darwin.*. Edited by Francis Darwin. 2 vols. New York: D. Appleton, 1888-97.

————. *More Letters of Charles Darwin.* Edited by Francis Darwin. 2 vols. New York: D. Appleton, 1903.

————. *The Origin of Species.* New York: Penguin, 1958.

Davis, H. W. Carless. *A History of Balliol College.* Oxford: Basil Blackwell, 1963.

Davidson, Randall T. and William Benham. *The Life of Archbishop Campbell Tait.* 3d ed. 2 vols. London: Macmillan, 1891.

DeLaura, David J. *Hebrew and Hellene in Victorian England.* Austin: University of Texas Press, 1969.

De Man, Paul. "Autobiography as De-facement." *Modern Language Notes* 94, no. 5 (1979): 919-30.

Dellamora, Richard. *Masculine Desire: The Sexual Politics of Victorian Aestheticism.* Chapel Hill: University of North Carolina Press, 1990.

Desmond, Adrian and James Moore. *Darwin: The Life of a Tormented Evolutionist.* New York: Warner Books, 1991.

Devane, William Clyde. *A Browning Handbook.* 2d. ed. New York: Appleton–Century–Crofts, 1955.

Devlin, Christopher. "The Image and the Word—I." *The Month* 3 (February 1950): 114-27.

————. "The Image and the Word—II." *The Month* 3 (March 1950): 191-202.

Dickens, Charles. *David Copperfield.* Edited by Jerome H. Buckley. New York: W.W. Norton & Company, 1990.

Dilligan, Robert J, and Todd K. Bender, comps. *A Concordance to the English Poetry of Gerard Manley Hopkins.* Madison: The University of Wisconsin Press, 1970.

Dolben, Digby M. *The Poems of Digby Mackworth Dolben.* London: Oxford University Press, 1915.

Dover, K.J. *Greek Homosexuality.* London: Duckworth, 1978.

Dowling, Linda. *Language and Decadence in the Victorian Fin de Siècle.* New Jersey: Princeton University Press, 1986.

————. "Ruskin's Pied Beauty and the Constitution of a 'Homosexual' Code." *Victorian Newsletter* 75 (1989): 1-8.

Downes, David A. *Hopkins' Sanctifying Imagination*. New York: University Press of America, 1985.

————. *Victorian Portraits: Hopkins and Pater*. New York: Bookman Associates, 1965.

Durant, John, ed. *Darwinism and Divinity: Essays on Evolution and Religious Belief*. Oxford: Basil Blackwell, 1985.

Earwaker, J.P. "Natural Science at Oxford." *Nature* 29 December1870, 170-71.

Eliot, George. *Middlemarch*. Edited by Bert G. Hornback. New York: W. W. Norton & Co., 1977.

————. *The Mill on the Floss*. Edited by Gordon S. Haight. Oxford: Clarendon Press, 1980.

Eliot, T. S. "Philip Massinger." In *Selected Essays*, new edition, 181-95. New York: Harcourt, Brace & World, Inc., 1964.

————. "The Place of Pater." In *The Eighteen-Eighties*, edited by Walter De la Mare, 93-106. Cambridge: Cambridge University Press, 1930.

Ellegard, Alvar. *Darwin and the General Reader: The Reception of Darwin's Theory of Evolution in the British Press, 1859-1872*. Stockholm: Goteborg, 1958.

Ellis, Ieuan. *Seven Against Christ: A Study of 'Essays and Reviews'*. Leiden: E.J. Brill, 1980.

Ellsberg, Margaret R. *Created to Praise: The Language of Gerard Manley Hopkins*. New York: Oxford University Press, 1987.

Emden, Alfred. "Liddon at S. Edmund Hall." In *Henry Parry Liddon 1829-1929: A Centenary Memoir*, Edited by W. M. Whitley, 29-33. London: A. R. Mowbray & Co., 1927.

Engle, A. J. *From Clergyman to Don: The Rise of the Academic Profession in Nineteenth-Century Oxford*. New York: Clarendon Press, 1984.

Essays and Reviews. London: John W. Parker, 1860.

Faber, Geoffrey. *Benjamin Jowett: A Portrait with Background*. London: Faber & Faber, 1957.

Fairchild, Hoxie Neal. *Religious Trends in English Poetry*. Vol. 4. New York: Columbia University Press, 1976.

Feeney, Jospeh J. "The Highgate Hopkins Obituary, With Introduction and Commentary." *Renascence* 42, no. 1 (1989-90):4-5.

Feyerabend, Paul K. *Against Method: Outline of an anarchist theory of knowledge*. London: Verso, 1978.

————. "Problems of Empiricism, Part II." In *The Nature & Function of Scientic Theories: Essays in Contemporary Science and Philosophy*, edited by Robert G. Colodny, 275-353. Pennsylvania: University of Pittsburgh Press, 1970.

————. *Realism, Rationalism, and Scientific Method.* Vol. 1. Cambridge: Cambridge University Press, 1981.

Fussell, Paul. *The Great War and Modern Memory.* New York: Oxford University Press, 1975.

Gardner, W. H. *Gerard Manley Hopkins (1844-1889): A Study of Poetic Idiosyncrasy in Relation to Poetic Tradition.* 2 vols. London: Oxford University Press, 1969.

————. "Hopkins and Newman." *Times Literary Supplement* 15 Sept 1966, 868.

Gates, Lewis E. "Newman as a Prose Writer." In *Three Studies in Literature*, 64-123. New York: Macmillan, 1899.

Geldart, Martin (Nitram Tradleg). *A Son of Belial: Autobiographical Sketches.* London: Trubner & Co., 1882.

Gilbert, Sandra M. and Susan Gubar. *The Madwoman in the Attic: The Woman Writer and the Nineteenth-Century Literary Imagination.* New Haven: Yale University Press, 1979.

Giles, Richard F., ed. *Hopkins and Dublin: The Man and the City. The Hopkins Quarterly Special Issue*, 1987.

Gordon, George. "Gerard Manley Hopkins and Robert Bridges." In *The Discipline of Letters*, 168-84. Oxford: Clarendon, 1946.

Guiney, Louis. "Gerard Hopkins: a Rediscovered Poet." *Month* 133, no. 657 (1919): 205-14.

Gurney, Edmund. "On Music and Musical Criticism." *Nineteenth Century* (June 1879): 1060-78.

————. "On Some Disputed Points in Music." *Fortnightly Review* (1 July 1876): 106-30.

————. *The Power of Sound.* London: Smith, Elder, 1880.

Haight, Gordon S. *The George Eliot Letters.* Vol. 1, 1836-1851. London: Oxford University Press, 1954.

Halperin, David M. "One Hundred Years of Homosexuality." *Diacritics* 16, no. 2 (1986): 34-45.

Hardy, Thomas. *Far from the Madding Crowd.* Edited by Robert C. Schweik. New York: W. W. Norton & Co., 1986.

Harrold, Charles Frederick. *John Henry Newman: An Expository and Critical Study of His Mind, Thought and Art.* London: Longmans, Green & Co., Inc.,

1948.

Harrold, Charles F. and William D. Templeman. *English Prose of the Victorian Period*. New York: Oxford University Press, 1938.

Hartman, Geoffrey H. *The Unmediated Vision: An Interpretation of Wordsworth, Hopkins, Rilke, and Valéry*. New York: Harcourt, Brace, & World, Inc., 1966.

Hayles, N. Katherine. "Information or Noise? Economy of Explanation in Barthes's S/Z and Shannon's Information Theory." In *One Culture: Essays in Science and Literature*, edited by George Levine, 119-42. Madison: The Univeristy of Wisconsin Press, 1987.

Hegel, G.W.F. *Aesthetics: Lectures on Fine Art*. Vol.1. Translated by T.M.Knox. Oxford: Clarendon Press, 1975.

Henkin, Leo J. *Darwinism in the English Novel, 1860-1910: The Impact of Evolution on Victorian Fiction*. New York: Russell & Russell, 1963.

Henry Scott Holland: Memoir and Letters. 2d ed. Edited by Stephen Paget. London: John Murray, 1921.

Herschel, John. *A Preliminary Discourse on the Study of Natural Philosophy*. Rpt. London: Longman, 1830. Chicago: University of Chicago Press, 1987.

Hinchcliff, Peter. *Benjamin Jowett and the Christian Religion*. Oxford: Clarendon Press, 1987.

Hollis, Christopher. *Newman and the Modern World*. New York: Doubleday & Co., 1968.

Holloway, John. *The Victorian Sage: Studies in Argument*. London: Archon, 1962.

Hopkins, Gerald Manley. *The Correspondence of Gerard Manley Hopkins and Richard Watson Dixon*. Edited by Claude Colleer Abbott. 2nd ed. London: Oxford University Press, 1970.

―――. *Further Letters of Gerard Manley Hopkins*. 2d ed. Edited by Claude Colleer Abbott. London: Oxford University Press, 1970.

―――. *Gerard Manley Hopkins*. Edited by Catherine Phillips. Oxford: Oxford University Press, 1986.

―――. *The Letters of Gerard Manley Hopkins to Robert Bridges*. 2d ed. Edited by Claude Colleer Abbott. London: Oxford University Press, 1970.

―――. *The Journals and Papers of Gerard Manley Hopkins*. 2d ed. Edited by Humphry House and Graham Storey. London: Oxford University Press, 1966.

―――. *The Poetical Works of Gerald Manley Hopkins*. Edited by Norman MacKenzie. Oxford: Clarendon Press, 1990.

————. *The Sermons and Devotional Writings of Gerard Manley Hopkins.* Edited by Christopher Devlin. London: Oxford University Press, 1959.

Houghton, Walter E. *The Art of Newman's Apologia.* New Haven: Yale University Press, 1945.

House, Madeline. "Books Belonging to Hopkins and His Family." *The Hopkins Research Bulletin,* no. 5 (1974): 26-41.

Hulme, T. E. "Romanticism and Classicism." In *Speculations: Essays on Humanism and the Philosophy of Art,* edited by Herbert Read, 113-40. 1924. Reprint. London: Routledge & Kegan Paul, 1971.

Huxley, Thomas Henry. *Life and Letters of Thomas Henry Huxley.* Edited by Leonard Huxley. 2 vols. New York: D. Appleton and Company, 1901.

————. *Methods and Results.* Vol. 1. London: Macmillan, 1893.

Inman, Billie Andrew. *Walter Pater and His Reading, 1874-1877: With a Bibliography of His Library Borrowings, 1878-1894.* New York: Garland Publishing, 1990.

Irvine, William. *Apes, Angels, and Victorians.* New York: McGraw-Hill Book Co., 1955.

Iser, Wolfgang. *Walter Pater: The aesthetic moment.* Translated by David Henry Wilson. Cambridge: Cambridge University Press, 1987.

Jakobson, Roman. "Closing Statement: Linguistics and Poetics." In *Style in Language,* edited by Thomas A. Sebeok, 350-377. Massachusetts: MIT Press, 1960.

James, D.G. *The Romantic Comedy: An Essay on English Romanticism.* London: Oxford University Press, 1963.

Jenkyns, Richard. *The Victorians and Ancient Greece.* Cambridge: Harvard University Press, 1980.

Johnson, Wendell Stacy. *Gerard Manley Hopkins: The Poet as Victorian.* Ithaca: Cornell University Press, 1968.

————. "Halfway to a New Land: Herbert, Tennyson and the Early Hopkins." *The Hopkins Quarterly* 10, no. 3 (1983): 115-23.

Johnston, John O. *Life and Letters of Henry Parry Liddon.* New York: Longmans, Green, & Co., 1904.

Jowett, Benjamin. *Dear Miss Nightingale: A Selection of Benjamin Jowett's Letters to Florence Nightingale, 1860-1893.* Edited by Vincent Quinn and John Prest. Oxford: Clarendon Press, 1987.

————. "Darwinism and Faith in God." In *Sermons on Faith and Doctrine,* edited by W. H. Fremantle, 1-22. London: John Murray, 1901.

————. *The Life and Letters of Benjamin Jowett, M.A.* Edited by Evelyn Abbott and Lewis Campbell. 3d ed. 2 vols. New York: E. P. Dutton, 1897.

————. "The Permanent Element of Religion." *Sermons on Faith and Doctrine*. Edited by W. H. Fremantle, 380-400. London: John Murray, 1901.

Jungmann, Joseph A. *The Early Liturgy to the Time of Gregory the Great*. Translated by Francis A. Brunner. Indiana: University of Notre Dame Press, 1959.

Keating, Joseph. "Impressions of Father Gerard Hopkins, S. J." *Month* 114, no. 541 (1909): 59-68.

Keats, John. *The Letters of John Keats*. Vol. 1. Edited by Hyder Edward Rollins. Cambridge: Harvard University Press, 1958.

Keble, John. *The Christian Year: Thoughts in Verse for Sundays and Holidays*. London: James Parker, 1880.

————. *Lectures on Poetry, 1832-1841*. Translated by Edward Kershaw Francis. 2 vols. Oxford: Clarendon Press, 1912.

Ker, Ian. *The Achievement of John Henry Newman*. Notre Dame, Indiana: University of Notre Dame Press, 1990.

————. *John Henry Newman: A Biography*. New York: Oxford University Press, 1988.

Kingsley, Charles. *His Letters and Memories of His Life*. Edited by Frances E. G. Kingsley. New York: Scribner, Armstrong, 1877.

Kitchen, Paddy. *Gerard Manley Hopkins*. New York: Atheneum, 1979.

Knight, W. *Memoir of John Nichol Professor of English Literature in the University of Glasgow*. Glasgow: James MacLehose & Sons, 1896.

Knoll, Elizabeth. "The Science of Language and the Evolution of Mind: Max Muller's Quarrel with Darwinism." *Journal of the History of the Behavioral Sciences* 22 (1986): 3-22.

Kranz, Gisbert. "Gerard Manley Hopkins." In *Three Centuries of Christian Literature*, 118-26. London: Burns & Oates, 1961.

Kuhn, Thomas S. *The Essential Tension: Selected Studies in Scientific Tradition and Change*. Chicago: The University of Chicago Press, 1977.

Lahey, G. F. *Gerard Manley Hopkins*. London: Oxford University Press, 1930.

Landow, George P. *Victorian Types, Victorian Shadows: Biblical Typology in Victorian Literature, Art, and Thought*. Boston: Routledge & Kegan Paul, 1980.

Lappin, Henry A. "Gerard Hopkins and His Poetry." *Catholic World* 109 no. 652 (1919): 501-12.

Lawrence, D. H. *Women in Love*. New York: Penguin, 1989.

Lee, Vernon. "Impersonality and Evolution in Music." *Contemporary Review* (December 1882): 840-58.

Letters of Walter Pater. Edited by Lawrence Evans. Oxford: Clarendon Press, 1970.

Levey, Michael. *The Case of Walter Pater.* Plymouth: Thames and Hudson, 1978.

Levine, George. *Darwin and the Novelists: Patterns of Science in Victorian Fiction.* Cambridge: Harvard University Press, 1988.

———. ed. *One Culture: Essays in Science and Literature.* Madison: The University of Wisconsin Press, 1987.

Lichtmann, Maria R. "'The Ecstacy of Interest': Contemplation as Parallelism's Praxis." *The Hopkins Quarterly* 13, no. 1 (1986): 21-45.

Liddon, Henry Parry. "The Creation." In *Sermons at St. Paul's and Elsewhere*, edited by Francis Paget, 1-25. London: Longmans, Green, 1907.

———. *The Divinity of Our Lord and Saviour Jesus Christ: Eight Lectures Preached before the University of Oxford in the Year 1866.* 14th ed. London: Longmans, Green, and Co., 1890.

———. *1829-1929: A Centenary Memoir*, edited by W.M. Whitley. London: A. R. Mowbray, 1929.

———. "The Recovery of St. Thomas, with a Prefatory Note on the Late Mr. Darwin." Bodleian MS. 100 i 86 (27): 3-36.

Loomis, Jeffrey B. "A Defense of Hopkins' 'Brothers.'" *The Hopkins Quarterly.* 11, nos. 1 and 2 (1984): 35-42.

Lucretius. *The Nature of the Universe.* Translated by Ronald Latham. Baltimore: Penguin, 1965.

MacKenzie, Norman. *The Early Poetic Manuscripts and Note-Books of Gerard Manley Hopkins in Facsimile.* New York: Garland, 1989.

———. "Hopkins and Science." *Studies in the Literary Imagination* 21, no. 1 (1988): 41-56.

———. "The Imperative Voice—An Unpublished Lecture by Hopkins." *The Hopkins Quarterly* 2 (1975): 101-16.

———. *A Reader's Guide to Gerard Manley Hopkins.* Ithaca, New York: Cornell University Press, 1981.

MacLeod, John. "The Diary of a Devoted Student of Nature." In *Gerard Manley Hopkins: The Critical Heritage*, edited by Gerald Roberts, 64-68. London: Routledge & Kegan Paul, 1987.

Mariani, Paul. *A Commentary on the Complete Poems of Gerard Manley Hopkins.* Ithaca: Cornell University Press, 1970.

Martin, Brian. *John Henry Newman: His Life and Work.* New York: Oxford University Press, 1982.

Martin, Robert Bernard. *Gerard Manley Hopkins: A Very Private Life.* New York: G.P. Putnam's Sons, 1991.

Marucci, Franco. "Hopkins' Political Ideas." *The Hopkins Quarterly* 4, nos. 1-4 (1987-1988): 127-143.

McNeese, Eleanor. "Beyond 'The Half-way House': Hopkins and Real Presence." *Texas Studies in Literature and Language* 31, no. 1 (1989): 85-104.

Mellown, Elgin W. "Gerard Manley Hopkins and His Public, 1889-1918." *Modern Philology* 57, no. 2 (1959): 94-99.

———. "The Reception of Gerard Manley Hopkins's Poems, 1918-30." *Modern Philology* 63, no. 1 (1965): 38-51.

Memoirs of Archbishop Temple by Seven Friends. Edited by E.G. Sanford. 2 vols. London: Macmillan and Co., Limited, 1906.

The Memoirs of John Addington Symonds. Edited by Phyllis Grosskurth. New York: Random House, 1984.

Metaphysics, Materialism, and the Evolution of the Mind: Early Writings of Charles Darwin. Transcribed by Paul H. Barrett. Chicago: University of Chicago Press, 1974.

Miller, J. Hillis. *The Disappearance of God: Five Nineteenth Century Writers.* Cambridge: Harvard University Press, 1963.

———. "Hopkins." In *The Linguistic Moment: From Wordsworth to Stevens,* 229-66. New Jersey: Princeton University Press, 1985.

Milroy, James. *The Language of Gerard Manley Hopkins.* London: Andre Deutsch, 1977.

Mivart, St. George. *On the Genesis of Species.* New York: D. Appleton & Co., 1871.

Monsman, Gerald. "Pater, Hopkins, and Fichte's Ideal Student." *The South Atlantic Quarterly* 70, no. 3 (1971): 365-76.

———. *Pater's Portraits: Mythic Patter in the Fiction of Walter Pater.* Maryland: Johns Hopkins University Press, 1967.

———. *Walter Pater's Art of Biography.* New Haven: Yale University Press, 1980.

Moore, Michael D. "Newman and the Motif of Intellectual Pain in Hopkins' 'Terrible Sonnets.'" *Mosaic* 12, no. 4 (1979): 29-46.

Moorman, Mary. *William Wordsworth: A Biography, The Later Years, 1803-1850.* Oxford: Clarendon Press, 1965.

Müller, Friedrich Max. "Lectures on Mr. Darwin's Philosophy of Language." *Fraser's Magazine* (June 1873): 659-78.

———. *The Life and Letters.* Vol. 1. New York: Longmans, 1902.

———. *The Science of Language.* 2d ed. New York: Charles Scribner, 1868.

————. "The Science of Language." *Nature.* January 6, 1870, 256-9.

Murray, John Middleton. "Gerard Manley Hopkins." *Athenaeum* 4649 (1919): 425-26.

Munich, Adrienne Auslander. *Andromeda's Chains: Gender and Interpretation in Victorian Literature and Art.* New York: Columbia University Press, 1989.

Newman, John Henry Cardinal. *Apologia Pro Vita Sua.* Edited by Martin J. Svaglic. Oxford: Clarendon Press, 1967.

————. *Callista: A Sketch of the Third Century.* London: Burns & Oates, 1962.

————. *Certain Difficulties Felt by Anglicans in Catholic Teaching.* 2 vols. London: Longmans, Green, 1918.

————. *Ibid.* vol. 1. Westminster, Md.: Christian Classics, 1969.

————. *Discourses Addressed to Mixed Congregations.* London: Longman, Brown, Green, and Longmans, 1849.

————. *An Essay in Aid of a Grammar of Assent.* Edited by I. T. Ker. London: Oxford University Press, 1985.

————. *An Essay on the Development of Christian Doctrine.* New York: Longmans, Green, and Co., 1903.

————. *Essays and Sketches.* Edited by Charles Frederick Harrold. 2 vols. New York: Longmans, Green, 1948.

————. *Essays Critical and Historical.* 2 vols. London: Longmans, Green, 1919.

————. *Historical Sketches.* 2 vols. London: Longman, 1894.

————. *The Idea of a University.* Edited by I. T. Ker. Oxford: Clarendon Press, 1976.

————. *The Letters and Diaries of John Henry Newman.* Edited by Charles Stephen Dessain. 31 vols. Oxford: Clarendon Press, 1973.

————. *Parochial and Plain Sermons.* San Francisco: Ignatius Press, 1987.

————. *The Philosophical Notebook.* Vol. 2. Edited by J. Sillem. New York: Humanities Press, 1970.

————. *Sermons and Discourses.* 2 vols. London: Longmans, 1949.

————. *University Sermons.* Eds. D.M. MacKinnon and J.D. Holmes. Westminster, Maryland: Christian Classics, 1970.

————. *Verses on Various Occasions.* London: Longmans, Green, 1890.

Nimmo, Duncan. "Learning Against Religion; Learning As Religion: Mark Pattison and the 'Victorian Crisis of Faith.'" In *Religion and Humanism.* Vol. 17. Edited by Keith Robbins, 311-24. Oxford: Basil Blackwell, 1981.

Nixon, Jude V. "Gerard Manley Hopkins and Henry Parry Liddon: An Unacknowledged Influence." *Renascence* 42, no. 1-2 (1989-90):87-110.

————. "Portrait of a Friendship: The Unpublished Letters of the Hopkins Family to Robert Bridges." *Renascence* 44, no. 4 (1992): 265-302.

————. "'Steadily Contemplating the Object of Faith': Newman, the *Apologia*, and Romantic Aesthetics." *Nineteenth Century Prose* 18, no. 2 (1991): 59-82.

————. "'Sweet especial rural scene': Revisting Binsey." *The Hopkins Quarterly* 26, no. 1-2 (1989): 39-60.

Nussbaum, Martha C. *Love's Knowledge: Essays on Philosophy and Literature*. Oxford: Oxford University Press, 1990.

Ong, Walter J. *Hopkins, the Self, and God*. Toronto: University of Toronto Press, 1986.

Ospovat, Dov. "God and Natural Selection: The Darwinian Idea of Design." *Journal of the History of Biology* 13, no.2 (1980): 169-94.

Page, Frederick. "Father Gerard Hopkins: I—his Poetry." *Dublin Review* 167, no. 334 (1920): 40-5.

Pater, Walter. *Appreciations with an Essay on Style*. London: Macmillan and Co., 1915.

————. *Gaston de Latour: an Unfinished Romance*. Prepared for the press by Charles L. Shadwell. London: Macmillan and Co., 1910.

————. *Imaginary Portraits*. Edited and with an introduction by Eugene J. Brzenk. New York: Harper and Row, 1964.

————. *Marius the Epicurean: His Sensations and Ideas*. 2 vols. London: Macmillan and Co., 1914.

————. *Miscellaneous Studies: A Series of Essays*. London: Macmillan and Co., 1913.

————. *Plato and Platonism: A Series of Lectures*. London: Macmillan and Co., 1912.

————. *The Renaissance: Studies in Art and Poetry*. Edited by Donald Hill. Berkeley: University of California Press, 1980.

————. *Uncollected Essays*. New York: AMS Press, 1978.

Peckham, Morse. "Darwinism and Darwinisticism." *Victorian Studies* 3, no. 1 (1959), 19-40.

Perry, John. "Oxford and Science." *Nature* 69 (1903): 207-14.

Peterfreund, Stuart, ed. *Literature and Science*. Boston: Northeastern University Press, 1990.

Phillips, Catherine. "Robert Bridges and the First Edition of Gerard Manley Hopkins's Poems." *Studies in the Literary Imagination* 21, no. 1 (1988): 7-21.

Pick, John. *Gerard Manley Hopkins: Priest and Poet.* London: Oxford University Press, 1942.

Pinney, Thomas, ed. *Essays of George Eliot.* New York: Columbia University Press, 1963.

Plotkin, Cary H. *The Tenth Muse: Victorian Philology and the Genesis of the Poetic Language of Gerard Manley Hopkins.* Carbondale: Southern Illinois University Press, 1989.

"The Position of Science at Oxford." *Nature* 9 July 1896, 225-28.

Prickett, Stephen. *Romanticism and Religion: The Tradition of Coleridge and Wordsworth in the Victorian Church.* Cambridge: Cambridge University Press, 1976.

————. *Words and The Word: Language, Poetics and Biblical Interpretation.* Cambridge: Cambridge University Press, 1986.

Pusey, Edward Bouverie. *Life of Edward Bouverie Pusey.* Edited by Henry Parry Liddon. 4 vols. London: Longmans, Green, and Co., 1897.

————. *Un-Science, Not Science, Adverse to Faith.* Oxford: James Parker, 1878.

Pusey, W.E. Review of "The Position of Science at Oxford." *Nature* 13 August 1896, 342-43.

Rackin, Donald. "'God's Grandeur': Hopkins' Sermon to Wordsworth." *Wordsworth Circle* 11, no. 2 (1980): 66-73.

Read, Herbert. "Gerard Manley Hopkins." In *In Defence of Shelley & Other Essays,* 111-144. London: William Heinemann, 1936.

Reardon, Bernard M. *Religious Thought in the Nineteenth Century.* Cambridge: The University Press, 1966.

————. *Religious Thought in the Victorian Age: A Survey from Coleridge to Gore.* New York: Longman, 1980.

Reilly, Joseph J. "The Hymns of John Henry Newman." *The Hymn* 2, no. 1 (1951): 5-10, 20.

Review of "The Origin of Species." *The Guardian* 23 May 1860.

Ritz, Jean-Georges. *Robert Bridges and Gerard Manley Hopkins 1863-1889: A Literary Friendship.* London: Oxford University Press, 1960.

Robbins, Keith, ed. *Religion and Humanism.* Vol. 17 of *Studies in Church History.* Oxford: Basil Blackwell, 1981.

Robinson, John. *In Extremity: A Study of Gerard Manley Hopkins.* Cambridge: Cambridge University Press, 1978.

Rogerson, J.W. *Old Testament Criticism in the Nineteenth Century.* London: Fortress Press, 1985.

Romanes, George John. *Darwin, and After Darwin*. Chicago: The Open House, 1892.

Ross, Malcom M. *Poetry and Dogma: The Transfiguration of Uncharacteristic Symbols in Seventeenth Century English Poetry*. New Brunswick, New Jersey: Rutgers University Press, 1954.

Ruggles, Eleanor. *Gerard Manley Hopkins: A Life*. New York: Norton, 1944.

Ruskin, John. *Praeterita*. Vol. 35 of *The Works of John Ruskin*. Edited by E.T. Cook and Alexander Wedderburn. London: George Allen, 1908.

Ryan, Alvan S. "Newman's Conception of Literature." In *Critical Studies in Arnold, Emerson, and Newman*, edited by John Hicks et al, 123-72. Iowa City: University of Iowa Press, 1942.

Said, Edward. *The World, the Text, and the Critic*. Cambridge: Harvard University Press, 1983.

Sarolea, Charles. *Cardinal Newman and His Influence on Religious Life and Thought*. Edinburgh: T. & T. Clark, 1908.

Sedgwick, Eve Kosofsky. *Between Men: English Literature and Male Homosocial Desire*. New York: Columbia University Press, 1985.

Schmidt, Carl. "Classical Studies at Balliol in the 1860's: The Undergraduate Essays of Gerard Manley Hopkins." In *Balliol Studies*, edited by John Prest. London: Leopard's Head Press, 1982.

Schneewind, J.B., ed. *Moral philosophy from Montaigne to Kant: An Anthology*. Vol. 2. Cambridge: Cambridge University Press, 1990.

Selected Writings of Walter Pater. Edited by Harold Bloom. New York: Signet Classic, 1974.

Shuter, William. "History as Palingenesis in Pater and Hegel." *PMLA* 86 (1971): 411-21.

Schweber, S.S. "John Herschel and Charles Darwin: A Study in Parallel Lives." *Journal of the History of Biology* 22, no. 1 (1989): 1-71.

Sidgwick, Henry. *The Methods of Ethics*. New York: Dover Publications, 1966.

Southey, Robert. *Poems of Robert Southey*. Edited by Maurice H. Fitzgerald. London: Oxford University Press, 1909.

Spenser, Herbert. *Essays Scientific, Political, and Speculative*. 3 vols. New York: D. Appleton & Co., 1892.

Sprinker, Michael. *"A Counterpoint of Dissonance": The Aesthetics and Poetry of Gerard Manley Hopkins*. Baltimore, Maryland: The Johns Hopkins University Press, 1980.

Stevenson, Lionel. *Darwin Among the Poets*. New York: Russell & Russell, 1963.

Stone, Darwell. "Dr. Liddon as a Preacher." In *Henry Parry Liddon 1829-1929: A Centenary Memoir*, edited by W.M. Whitley, 17-23. London: A.R. Mowbray & Co., 1927.

Sulloway, Alison. *Gerard Manley Hopkins and the Victorian Temper*. New York: Columbia University Press, 1972.

———. "Gerard Manley Hopkins and 'Women and Men' as 'Partners in the Mystery of Redemption.'" *Texas Studies in Literature and Language* 31, no. 1 (1989): 31-51.

Svaglic, Martin J., ed. *Apologia Pro Vita Sua*. Oxford: Clarendon Press, 1967.

Talbot, Bishop. "Some Recollections." In *Henry Parry Liddon 1829-1929: A Centenary Memoir*, edited by W.M. Whitley, 24-28. London: A.R. Mowbray & Co., 1927.

Temple, Frederick. *The Relations between Religion and Science: Eight Lectures Preached Before The University of Oxford in the Year 1884*. New York: Macmillan & Co., 1884.

Tennyson, Alfred Lord. *The Poems of Tennyson*. 2d ed. Edited by Christopher Ricks. 3 vols. Berkeley: University of California Press, 1987.

———. *A Memoir*. Edited by Hallam Tennyson. 2 vols. London: Macmillan and Co., Inc., 1898.

Tennyson, G.B. *Victorian Devotional Poetry: The Tractarian Mode*. Cambridge: Harvard University Press, 1981.

———. "Tractarian Aesthetics: Analogy and Reserve in Keble and Newman." *Victorian Newsletter* 55 (1979): 8-10.

Thesing, William B. "Gerard Manley Hopkins's Responses to the City: The 'Composition of the Crowd.'" *Victorian Studies* 30, no. 3 (1987): 385-408.

Thomas, Alfred. *Hopkins the Jesuit: The Years of Training*. London: Oxford University Press, 1969.

Thompson, Edward. *Robert Bridges: 1844-1930*. London: Oxford University Press, 1944.

Thornton, R.K.R. *All My Eyes See: The Visual World of Gerard Manley Hopkins*. Sunderland: Ceolfrith Press, 1975.

Toynbee, Arnold. "Rebel in Pussycat." *The Observer* 16 August 1970, 21.

Tyndall, John. *Fragments of Science*. 2 vols. New York: P.F. Collier, 1900.

———. *Hours of Exercise in the Alps*. Rev. ed. New York: D. Appleton and Company, 1899.

Vargish, Thomas. *Newman: The Contemplation of Mind*. Oxford: Clarendon Press, 1970.

Vickers, Brian. "Hopkins and Newman." *Times Literary Supplement* 3 March 1966, 178.

Virgil. *The Aeneid*. Translated by Robert Fitzgerald. New York: Random House, 1983.

Ward, Humphry. "Reminiscences." *Brasenose Quatercentenary Monographs.* 14, no. 2 (Oxford: Clarendon Press) (1909): 71-78.

Ward, Wilfrid. *The Life of John Henry Cardinal Newman* 2 vols. London: Longmans, Green, 1912.

Weatherby, Harold. "Hopkins, Newman, and Scotus." In *The Keen Delight: The Christian Poet in the Modern World*, 74-98. Athens: University of Georgia Press, 1975.

———. "Newman and Victorian Liberalism: A Study in the Failure of Influence." *Critical Quarterly* 13 (1971): 205-13.

Wechsler, Judith, ed. *On Aesthetics in Science*. Cambridge, MA: MIT Press, 1978.

White, Norman. "Gerard Manley Hopkins and the Irish Row." *The Hopkins Quarterly* 2, no. 3 (1982): 91-107.

———. *Hopkins: A Literary Biography*. Oxford: Clarendon Press, 1992.

———. "Hopkins and the County Kildare." *Gerard Manley Hopkins Annual* (1992):19-36.

Whitley, W. M. "Henry Parry Liddon: An Appreciation." In *Henry Parry Liddon 1829-1929: A Centenary Memoir*. London: A. R. Mowbray & Co., 1927.

Willey, Basil. *More Nineteenth Century Studies, A Group of Honest Doubters*. New York: Columbia University Press, 1956.

Williams, Carolyn. *Transfigured World: Walter Pater's Aesthetic Historicism*. Ithaca: Cornell University Press, 1989.

Williams, Isaac. *The Autobiography of Isaac Williams*. Edited by Sir. George Prevost. London: Longmans, Green, 1892.

Wright, Thomas. *The Life of Walter Pater*. 2 vols. London: Everett and Co., 1907.

Woolf, Virginia. *Mrs. Dalloway*. New York: Harcourt Brace Jovanovich, 1981.

Wordsworth, Willliam. *The Poetical Works of William Wordsworth*. Edited by E. DeSelincourt. 5 vols. Oxford: Clarendon Press, 1940-49.

———. *The Prelude 1799, 1805, 1850*. Edited by Jonathan Wordsworth, M. H. Abrams, and Stephen Gill. New York: W.W. Norton & Co., 1979.

———. *The Prose Works of William Wordsworth*. Vol. 1. Edited by W.J.B. Owen and Jane Worthington Smyser. Oxford: Clarendon Press, 1974.

Young, Francis Brett. *Robert Bridges: A Critical Study*. London: Secker, 1914.

Young, Robert M. "Darwinism is Social." In *The Darwinian Heritage*, edited by David Kohn, 609-38. New Jersey: Princeton University Press, 1985.

————. *Darwin's Metaphors: Nature's Place in Victorian Culture.* New York: Cambridge University Press, 1985.

Zaniello, Tom. *Hopkins in the Age of Darwin.* Iowa City, Iowa: University of Iowa Press, 1988.

————. "The Sources of Hopkins' Inscape: Epistemology at Oxford, 1864-1868." *The Victorian Newsletter* 52 (1977): 18-24.

Zonneveld, Sjaak. "Hopkins and Newman's Oxford Oratory." *Hopkins Quarterly* 11, no. 4 (1985): 119-23.

Index